KING'S
BOUNTY

William, second Earl of Shelburne, Marquis of Landsdowne, born May 2, 1737, died May 7, 1805.

KING'S BOUNTY

A HISTORY OF EARLY
SHELBURNE
NOVA SCOTIA

*Founded in 1783
by the Port Roseway Associates
Loyalists of the American Revolution*

MARION ROBERTSON

NOVA SCOTIA MUSEUM
Halifax
1983

© Marion Robertson 1978
Published by the
Nova Scotia Museum
as a part of the
Education Resource Services Program
of the Department of Education
Province of Nova Scotia

Hon. Terence R.B. Donahoe
Minister
Gerald J. McCarthy
Deputy Minister

Canadian Cataloguing in Publication Data

Robertson, Marion, 1910-
King's bounty

Includes bibliographical references and index.
ISBN 0-919680-24-0 (bound). - ISBN 0-919680-21-6 (pbk.)

I. Shelburne (N.S.) - History. 2. United Empire Loyalists. I. Nova Scotia Museum. II. Title

FC2349.S5.R62   971.6'25   C83-096002-3
F1039.5.S5. R62

Produced by the
Department of Government Services
Information Division

Printed in Canada
1983

This book is for
DONALD MACKENZIE ROBERTSON

ACKNOWLEDGEMENTS

To write a history of early Shelburne required many years of searching in archives and libraries for the hundreds of documents pertaining to the town and district. During the twenty or more years of research, many who had valuable papers gave or loaned me material which I used in this study. For their gifts and for the loan of documents I wish to thank Miss Marjorie M. Bruce, Mrs. Clifford Coutanche, Dr. Phyllis Blakeley, Mrs. Mary Harvey, Dr. Esther Clark Wright, Mr. Herbert Banks, Dr. Wilfred Smith, Mr. Donald Bird, Mrs. Dorothy Freeman, Mr. John Langdon, Mr. John Grant, Mr. Ian Campbell, Miss Eleanor Berry and Mr. Wayne Butler.

Others who are no longer living gave me valuable papers which I used in the writing of this history: Mrs. Hazel C. Mathews, Mr. J.J. Cox, Mr. Grandy Irwin, Miss Bella Williams, Mrs. Mary Muir, Mr. J.K. McKay, Miss Annie McKay, Mrs. Lewis Cook, Mrs. Lois Doane, Mr. William Moore, Mr. H.F. Williams, Dr. Winthrop Bell.

To Miss Marjorie Bruce for permission to use watercolour sketches by her mother, Mrs. A.P. Bruce; to Mr. Eldon Whynot for permission to use his photo of the Charles Mason-James Humphrey house; and to Miss Nancy Hart for photos of the Joseph Bell and the Samuel Marshall houses, my grateful thanks. I also wish to acknowledge the gracious permission given to use paintings, photographs and maps from the Special Collections of the Killam Library, Dalhousie University; the Public Archives of Canada; the Public Archives of Nova Scotia; Land Registry Office (Crown Grants), Department of Lands and Forests, Halifax; and the Nova Scotia Museum.

Others have also helped and to them I am indebted for their assistance: Miss Catherine Servant, for her assistance in translating an early French document; Miss Shirley Elliott, Legislative Librarian, for arranging interlibrary loans; Mr. Hervey Jones, for aid in locating valuable information among the records in the Shelburne Court House; Mr. Arthur E. Barker, Archivist and Librarian, Society for Promoting Christian Knowledge, London, England, for permission to use material relative to the Bray schools; and to the late Dr. C. Bruce Fergusson, Archivist, and members of the staff of the Public Archives of Nova Scotia for their help in locating many documents. I am grateful to Miss Mamie Harmon and Miss Theresa Brakeley for their editorial suggestions; Dr. Phyllis Blakeley, Associate Archivist, Public Archives of Nova Scotia, for her invaluable assistance during the writing of this book, and Dr. Malcolm Ross of Dalhousie University, for his encouragement and interest in my work. To Mr. J. Lynton Martin, Director, and the Board of Governors of the Nova Scotia Museum, for their support in the publication of this segment of Nova Scotia history and to Mrs. Barbara Shaw for valuable assistance in editing and preparation of the manuscript for publication, I am deeply indebted.

To all who helped, may this history of early days in Shelburne be deemed worthy of their interest and assistance.

MARION ROBERTSON
Shelburne, Nova Scotia

CONTENTS

Acknowledgements vii

1
Prologue to 1783   *1*

2
The Port Roseway Associates, the Provincial Regiments and the Freed Blacks   *29*

3
Arrival and Early Days in Shelburne   *51*

4
The Freed Blacks   *83*

5
The Army, the Navy and Fort Elliott   *107*

6
Building the Town   *117*

7
Distribution of the Land   *123*

8
The Courts of Sessions and the Courts of Justice; the first Members of the House of Assembly   *138*

9
Churches, Schools and Social Life   *171*

10
Taverns and Inns, Post Offices, and the Cape Roseway Lighthouse   *186*

11
Early Industries, Trades and Professions   *193*

12
Use of the Land and Sea   *213*

13
Ships and Shipbuilding   *223*

14
Trade and Commerce   *230*

15
The Deline of Shelburne   *240*

16
Epilogue   *246*

Notes   *261*

Appendix   *285*

References   *307*

Index   *315*

ILLUSTRATIONS

William, second Earl of Shelburne, Marquis of Lansdowne, born May 2, 1737, died May 7, 1805. *ii*

Silhouette of Governor John Parr. (Courtesy Public Archives of Nova Scotia) *36*

Photograph of "A Plan of a Town Plott projected for a Town at Port Roseway," approved and signed by Governor Parr, April·21, 1783. (Courtesy Land Registry and Research, Nova Scotia Department of Lands and Forests) *46*

Enlargement of Governor Parr's signature approving the 'Plan of a Town Plott', April 3, 1783. (Land Registry and Research, Nova Scotia Department of Lands and Forests) *48*

The divisions of the town as laid out by the surveyors Marston and Morris. *54*

Map of Shelburne compiled from early plans of the town. *58*

Stephen Shakespear house at the southwest corner of George (formerly St. George's) and Water Streets, built of logs in

1783 and later clapboarded. Watercolour by Mrs. Annie Bruce. (Courtesy Miss Marjorie Bruce) *74*

Black woodcutter at Shelburne, 1788. Watercolour by William Booth. (Courtesy Public Archives of Canada, C-40162) *90*

Shelburne Harbour, showing the Barracks. Watercolour by H. Pooley, approximately 1818. (Courtesy Special Collections, Killam Library, Dalhousie University) *109*

Part of the Town of Shelburne in Nova Scotia, with the Barracks opposite, 1789. Wash drawing by William Booth. (Courtesy Public Archives of Canada, C-10548) *119*

Town of Shelburne from the Barracks. Watercolour by H. Pooley, approximately 1818. (Courtesy Special Collections, Killam Library, Dalhousie University) *121*

The Minshull house, northeast corner of Ann and Water Streets, sketched by the owner, John Minshull, approximately 1784. Farther down Ann Street was the Minshull stable and the home of Rev. William Walter, an Anglican clergyman. Next to the dwelling on Water Street was Mr. Minshull's warehouse. In the 1920s the house was moved to a new site and remodelled by Mr. John J. Cox. *122*

House built by Robert Wilkins on the northwest corner of St. John's and Water Streets. It was later the house of Alexander Houston, an early Shelburne schoolmaster. Watercolour by Mrs. Annie Bruce, painted approximately 1906. (Courtesy Miss Marjorie Bruce) *132*

Charles Mason-James Humphrey house, built 1783-1785, as it appeared in the 1930s. (Photography courtesy Eldon Whynot) *145*

Fire engine purchased by the town of Shelburne in 1786. *156*

The Joseph Bell house, built 1783-1784. (Photo by Nancy Hart) *165*

St. John's Kirk, opened July 4, 1805, during the ministry of the Rev. Matthew Dripps. *176*

Shelburne Harbour, sketched from the town, showing Christ Church, by John Elliott Woolford, July 1817. (Nova Scotia Museum Collection) *180*

House and store of George and Robert Ross, Shelburne merchants and ship owners, built circa 1785, photographed approximately 1958. The building is now operated as a branch of the Nova Scotia Museum. *183*

The original Roseway Lighthouse, first operated in 1792, as it appeared in the 1930s. It has since been replaced by a modern structure. (Photograph by Eldon Whynot) *190*

Mill on the Roseway River, by John Elliot Woolford, July 1817. (Nova Scotia Museum Collection) *196*

House built for Edward Brindley, Commissary, in the summer of 1783. Later known as the Firth house, it was demolished in the 1920s. It is shown as it appeared in the latter nineteenth century. *221*

Mediterranean Sea Pass issued by the Commissioners for Executing the Office of Lord High Admiral of Great Britain to Captain Douglas of the brigantine *Robert* in 1789. Note that the top edge of the document is scalloped or "indented", so that it would exactly match the second copy, thus guaranteeing its authenticity.
(Courtesy Public Archives of Nova Scotia) *232*

The home of Samuel Marshall, potter and brickmaker, built 1783-1784. In more recent years it was the home of the Hon. Robert Irwin, Lieutenant Governor of Nova Scotia from 1938-1940. (Photograph by Nancy Hart) *249*

1
Prologue to 1783

THE EARLY YEARS: NATIVE PEOPLES, ADVENTURERS AND FISHERMEN

When a number of Loyalist refugees of the American Revolution chose Port Roseway (Shelburne) on the southwestern shores of Nova Scotia as their haven of refuge, the area was well known to seafarers from across the Atlantic and to the people of New England. Basque and Portuguese fishermen, French adventurers and settlers, fur traders and a scattering of English-speaking fishermen and colonists had pushed their way along the shores and into the bays and inlets for two centuries and more – leaving in scant records and in their place-names the evidence of their presence. And long before they came, the land belonged to the Indians, whom archaeologists tell us were here perhaps four to six thousand years ago.

The Indians who greeted the first white men, when they came to the coast of Nova Scotia, were of Algonkian stock and of northeastern woodland culture. They hunted and fished for a livelihood with little cultivation of the soil. They called themselves *Megumawaach* from the name of their land, *Megumaagee*, which the white man twisted to 'Micmac.' Those who lived on the southwestern shores and on the land later known as Shelburne County referred to themselves as the *Kespoogwitunak*, the inhabitants of *Kespoogwit* ('land's end'). Shelburne they knew as *Sogumkeagun* ('canal cut through a sandbank' or 'a short cut through a sandbar'). To a Micmac of this century the word was *Sawgumgeegum* ('the bend of the water'), conveying to the Indians the meaning of the ocean bending far into the land.[1]

All the land given to the Loyalists and disbanded soldiers was known to the Micmacs and was used in their endless quest for food and shelter: the land of the Sable known for its river, the *Pijeboogawek* ('long river'), *Neseamk* ('flowing down over sand'); the land of the Jordan where its river, the *Sesiktaweak*, went 'whimpering and whining as it goes out'; and to the westward was the land of the Clyde, *Oonigunsuk* ('a portage'), a good way through the wilderness, before reaching the 'bad, rough water,' *Cobscooch*.[2] The Micmac name for the Roseway River flowing into Shelburne Harbour has been lost. Evidence of their living along the banks of the river and fishing its waters is found in numerous places – in rocks placed across narrows of the river for hurdles to catch fish; in camp grounds where they left the ashes of their fires, arrowheads, gouges, hammerheads and pieces of pottery. The importance of the Roseway River and Shelburne Harbour to the Micmacs is suggested on Durell's Chart of 1734, with the stretch of water at the head of the harbour marked 'Sagamore Reach' and the river, 'Sagamore River.' Long Island, in the Roseway River, was traversed by the Micmacs along a path running the length of the island. At its northern end they had small plots of land under cultivation in 1818, when they protested the giving of the land they had laboured to clear and cultivate to Welsh settlers.[3] Until fairly recent years an island near the foot of Lake Deception was cared for by the Micmacs as one of their burial grounds, the Indians coming each year from Bear River, on the other side of the province, to tend the graves. The grounds marked with a cross until recent years indicated a cemetery from the Christian era or, if an older burial ground, one which they continued to use into the post-Christian era. An indication that the island was a haunt of the Micmacs in earlier years is a small stone doll found on the shores of the island. The Roseway River, like other rivers in the nearby area, was a good waterway inland. With portages to brooks and lakes, the Micmacs crossed the land from the southern shores of *Kespoogwit* to the Bay of Fundy and to the farther shores across the Bay.

Just when the Micmacs of *Kespoogwit* first spotted the white sails of Basque and Portuguese fishing vessels working their way along the shores is uncertain, for with their tarry fingers, sailors and fishermen write few records of their adventures. The earliest map of 'the new fonde lande quhar men goeth a fisching,' the Jean Rotz map of 1535 (completed in 1542), has the southern shores of Nova Scotia roughly traced, but no place names. The first map of northeastern North America to show place names on the coast of Shelburne County was Diego Homem's of 1558. Marking the places frequented by the early French, Basque and Portuguese fishermen, they indicate the importance of the fisheries along the southwestern coast of Nova Scotia. Beginning at the eastern side of the county was C. de S. Jaque (names are given as they appear on the map) near the estuary and on the eastern shores of the Ribera de Jardins, the Jordan River. A little west of the Jordan was the Ribera de Montanas, evidently the Roseway River. The water west of McNutt's Island was Golfe de Petis. West of Golfe de Petis was La Beaubai, roughly the location of Port La Tour Harbour. Beusablom and Les Jardines marked Barrington Bay and Barrington River. Five years later the map of Lazaro Luis (1563) had only one place name along the Shelburne County coast, that of Bacalhaos (Baccaro), from *bacalhao* (cod), the name given in Portugal to dried codfish, the stockfish of the north, split and dried hard in the open air without salt.

With the coming of Champlain along the shores of 'land's end' in 1604, the first records were written describing its shoals and bird-filled islands, its bays and rocky reefs. Setting out from Port Mouton[4] on May 19 in a pinnace of eight tons to search for a suitable site for settlement, Sieur de Monts skirted the coast until he and his men 'reached a very good port for vessels, at the head of which is a little river extending a good way inland. I named this the harbor of Cape Negro, on account of a rock which from a distance looks like one. This cape is very dangerous because of the rocks which extend out to sea.' The coast thus far was low and covered with the same wood he had seen at Cape La Heve, 'while the islands are all full of water fowl.' Continuing on their way they passed the night in Sable Bay[5] 'where vessels can anchor without the least fear of danger.' Sailing on, they rounded Cape Sable, 'very dangerous on account of certain rocks and shoals which project almost a league out to sea... thence we went to the Isle of Cormorants,[6] a league beyond, and so named because of the infinite number of these birds, of whose eggs we took a barrel full.' Holding to the westward six leagues, they crossed a bay running to the north[7] and came to several islands.[8] 'They are for the most part very dangerous of approach for large ships because of the strong tides, and for the rocks which lie on a level with the surface of the water.' They were tree-covered islands, with pines, firs, birches and poplars. Further on they came to four other islands,[9] one with numberless gannets, 'so great a number we killed them easily with a stick.' On another they found the shores covered with seals 'whereof we took as many as we wished.' On the other two, in great abundance, were 'cormorants, ducks of three kinds, snow geese, murres, wild geese, puffins, snipe, fish-hawks and other birds of prey, sea gulls, plover of two or three kinds, herons, herring gulls, curlews, turnstones, divers, loons, eiders, ravens, cranes and other kinds unknown to me which make their nests there.'

Unfortunately Champlain did not enter Shelburne Harbour. Searching for a site for the proposed settlement of the Sieur de Monts, close to good fishing and hunting and good land for farming, he was told (perhaps by fishermen who knew the harbour) that it was not suitable, and he passed by, marking for future voyagers the rocks and shoals and tugging currents along the shores.

It would seem that Jean Baptiste Louis Franquelin, the King's hydrographer, in 1686 was the first to record the early French name for Shelburne Harbour, Port Rasoir, variously spelled 'Port Rasair' and 'Port Razoir.'[10] *Rasair*, the razor clam, breeds in the sand bar jutting out into the bay midway on the eastern shore of the harbour. The early French and Portuguese place names were mostly descriptive of the area. As fishermen stepped ashore on the sand bar, perhaps a razor clam, not found on all sand flats, was the first thing they noticed to distinguish the harbour from others along the shores. The word *rasair*, twisted by the English, became 'rasway,' 'rosaway' and finally, 'roseway.'

Franquelin recorded a number of other place names, several for the first time. Following along the shores from the east: Port à Ours (on other maps Port aux Ours, now Port L'Hebert) evidently so named because of bears seen along the wooded shores of the harbour; R. des Sables (Sable River); Port Jolly;[11] I. aux Cannes (islands off the Roseway-Round Bay shore, named for the rock duck, *la cane de roche*, which feeds in sheltered waters near rocky shores, or for canes (reeds) growing in the area); Point Blanche, for its white sand beaches marking the point from a distance as a white point of land; C. Neigre (Cape Negro); Pointe de Baccare (Baccaro); C. de cap de Sable; I. aux Loups Marins (Seal Islands).

THE EARLY FRENCH SETTLERS

By 1686, when Franquelin drew his map of the Terres de l'Accadie there were then a few records of the early French fishermen and settlers along the Shelburne County shores. Some of these people were living on the land later occupied by the Scots-Irish and the New England settlers and still later by Loyalists and disbanded soldiers. In the census of 1671[12] prepared by Laurent Molin, *religieux cordelier*, there were living at Cape Negro: Amand Lalloue, Sieur de Rivedu,[13] aged 58: his wife, Ellisabet Nicollas, aged 40; their eldest son, age 24; their sons, Ammant Lalloue, 14, and Amand, aged 12; their two daughters, Janne, 20, and Ellisabet, 12. They had two arpents of land under cultivation, 20 goats and 29 pigs. A few miles eastward of Amand Lalloue and his family, on the Rivière au Rocheloy,[14] lived Guillaume Poulet, his wife and their one child. They had an arpent of cleared land and a dozen pigs. In 1687 at Port Rochelois lived five men, three boys over fifteen, four boys under fifteen, five women and three girls under twelve. They had four houses, an acre of upland cultivated, and the men had in their possession six guns. In three wigwams near the French settlers lived 21 Indians: six men, six women and nine children. Along with his report of those living at Port Rochelois, de Gargas remarked that the two ports, Port Rochelois and Port Razoir, 'are contiguous and actually rather beautiful. They abound in fish, and the soil is good. Thirty or forty colonists could be settled here.' An advantage of the ports was their convenient situation for communication by land with Port Royal, Mines, La Heve and other places.[15]

When the first French settlers came to Port Razoir is uncertain. In 1693 there were two families – those of Claude Bertrand, 44, his wife Caterine Petri, 28, and their four children and Francis Nouranjean, 38, his wife Marie Petri, 26, and their four children. The port was described as a beautiful river with an island to the southwest of the entrance, which must be passed on the northeast to enter the port – a long arm of nine miles of water.[16] Six years later, in 1699, Governor de Villebon reported the son of Sieur Phillippe Mins d'Entremont of Pubnico, his wife and four children, an unnamed settler with his wife and two children, and three Irishmen (fishermen who had left their fishing post at Chebucto) living at Port Razoir. The d'Entremonts had horned cattle and sheep grazing in their fields and were prosperous; the unnamed settler was a capable fisherman but no farmer. By 1699 Port Razoir was considered by the French to be one of the finest harbours along the coast of Nova Scotia, with an entrance suitable for all vessels, and where fish were abundant. The soil was good for cultivation and there were many red oaks.[17]

Fishing and farming, furs and timber, some shipbuilding and mast-making sustained the economy of the French in Acadia. Fishing was at first a summer occupation. Their vessels laden, the fishermen returned to their home ports for the winter. The first to establish a sedentary fishery on the shores of Shelburne County was a man named Rivedon.[18] He came from La Rochelle to Cap de Sable with his wife and a number of fishermen under a commission from the Governor of New England. He set his men fishing, but their labour did not turn out well partly because of their late arrival on the fishing grounds. His ship returned to France with what few fish had been caught, to come back the following spring to recoup his losses. During the winter the fishermen who remained were sent to the islands to hunt seals. Again he met with poor success, the English having ruined the seal fishery on the Isles of Tousquet. In the spring his ship returned laden with provisions and with men to fish. They did so well that he loaded his vessel and sent it back to France. When his fish were sold, he was without a profit and no reimbursement for half his expenses, so he did not return the following spring. His fishing establishment shortly afterward caught fire and he lost what little he had left.[19]

Governor Villebon reported in 1699 to Pontchartrain, the minister of state,[20] that cod, the mainstay of the French fisheries in Acadia, first appear along the Cape Sable shores in the month of March and in May distribute themselves along the coast to the eastward. 'At the beginning of July a change takes place,' he told Ponchartrain, 'and the fish seldom bite after eight or nine in the morning. The fishermen take up their lines at that time and rest till four or five in the evening when they resume work till the next morning at the same hour, and there are fish on every line. As the fishing is not done at great depth, there are two hooks to each line and often two cod are caught at once. The fish caught within sight of land are of medium size and good for salting; those taken on the banks out at sea are large, and are good green.' The fishing boats used by the French settlers were *biscaynes*, fishing craft pointed at both ends, and *charrois*, fishing shallops. They were too small to be exposed at night to the open sea on the offshore fishing grounds and could not go out at all if the wind was against them. Confined mainly to the inshore fishing, the French caught mostly smaller cod lurking near the shores. These they split and salted and dried on the beaches or spread on wooden frames to dry in the summer sun.[21]

Many of the French settlers were good farmers, growing wheat, rye, oats and many kinds of vegetables: peas, corn, cabbage, beets, onions, carrots, chives, shallots, turnips, parsnips and salad greens. Apple trees from Normandy and russet pears and cherries in their flowering made the clearings in the wilderness a bit of their old homeland. Geese and hens were in the yards; horned cattle, sheep, pigs and goats in the pastures. From salt and fresh meadows they cut hay for their livestock; and they ground their grain in a water mill operated by a son of the Sieur d'Entremont on the Rivière de Pomon'coup (Pubnico). From flax and hemp grown on their land and wool from their sheep the women wove linen and woolen cloth to make garments. Furs provided them with added income; and, in the early years of their coming, a trading post was established at Port La Tour, not only for the French furs but for trade with the Indians.[22]

Pirates and freebooters harassed the French settlements. Freebooters, Villebon believed, came from New England. All of New England 'is concerned in the fishing industry,' he wrote Pontchartrain in 1699, 'and there is danger that they might secretly instigate some freebooter, as they have done in the past, to harry our young settlements without appearing to have anything to do with the matter.'[23] Whether pirates or freebooters were encouraged by the New Englanders, the French settlers on a number of occasions were the victims of unscrupulous attacks. On three occasions the French at Port Razoir were molested. In August 1699, a pirate off the coast near Cape Sable captured a ship from New York, London bound. In passing Port Razoir, they swung into the harbour, killed some cattle (for which they later paid), but committed no other depredations.[24] Some six years later, in 1705, a small privateer from Boston came into the harbour, burned the dwellings and 'almost the inhabitants who had begun to settle at Port Razoir.'[25] Three years later, in 1708, an English vessel gathering wood along the eastern coast of Nova Scotia put into Port Razoir, burned a man's house, and carried him off and sent him to Subercase, the governor of Acadia, with letters from the governor of Boston.[26]

If these were freebooters raiding the French to discourage their fishing, pirates indiscriminately robbed and captured ships of any nationality so unfortunate as to sail within their grasp. In 1688, not far off the coast, a Portuguese vessel was taken by pirates, who robbed her of 3,700 Spanish hides, threw her men and £2,000 worth of goods overboard, sent the hides in a ketch to Boston, and went into the harbour of Port à Bear (Port L'Hebert) to the east of Port Razoir.[27] In 1722 pirates came boldly into Port Razoir when the notorious Ned Low and his crew pressed men from the New England fishing shallops to man their pirate ships. Among those forced from one of the shallops was Philip Ashton, a Marblehead fisherman. Despite lash and starvation he stoutly refused to do the will of Ned Low or to serve his crew. Watching for a way to escape, he saw his chance when the pirates put into a remote harbour on Roatan Island in the Bay of Honduras to fill their water casks. When they were ready to return to the ship, Ashton had disappeared into the jungle. Months later he was found by refugees fleeing from the Spaniards and was taken to Bonacco Island. Shortly afterwards a Salem brigantine caught in a tropical gale put into Bonacco. On her, Philip Ashton returned to Salem and to his home in Marblehead, two years and two months from the day of his escape into the jungle of Roatan.[28]

Beyond the records of Governor Villebon, the early census rolls and the reports of the harassment of the French settlers, there are few references to the French at Port Razoir. The continuing and growing interest of the French settlers and the French authorities in the area along the southwestern shores of Nova Scotia is evident from the maps and sea charts which appeared from time to time, marking Port Razoir and other early settlements and adding new place names. In 1703 on the 'Carte de l'Acadie,' the following were recorded: I. Moillée off the shore of Shag Harbour, I. aux Herons (Ragged Islands), Havre Vert (Green Harbour) and the water between Cap Nègre (Cape Negro) and the mainland marked *passage pour les moiens navires*. In 1703, well to the west of C. Nègre was the I. du Bon Portage; in 1744 was added I. aux Cannes (Duck Island) off Cap de Sable. Chabert de Cogelin, sent to America by the King to rectify the earlier charts of the coast of Acadia, reported in 1750 that, in the unanimous opinion of the inhabitants, the harbour of Port Razoir was large and very beautiful and excellent for all kinds of vessels. At the mouth of the harbour was an island, half a league long, separated from the mainland on the west by a false passage. On the eastern end of the island, a cape, with the eastern coast of the mainland, formed the true passage, four or five cables wide.[29]

With the reduction of Port Royal by General Nicholson in 1710 followed by the Treaty of Utrecht three years later, Acadia became British. Port Roseway (the anglicized version of the name Port Razoir) was first noted by Paul Mascarene, the provincial engineer, as a suitable site for a future British settlement and a convenient situation for the chief seat of government in 1720.[30]

Governor Philipps and the Council of Nova Scotia agreed with Mascarene and recommended Port Roseway to the secretary of state as a suitable harbour for a British settlement.[31] The fact that English-speaking fishermen from New England and perhaps some from England had for years used the shores of Port Roseway as a base for summer fishing, (some possibly making their homes on the shores of the harbour) is evident from Captain Thomas Durell's Draught of Port Wager, 1734.[32] On it he marked the depth of water, rocky and sandy shoals, good places to anchor, and the good watering sites for fishermen to fill their water casks. For the first time the early English place names appeared in print. On McNûtt's Island, which Durell called Port Roseway Island, Cape Roseway was Harbour Point; the northwest point dipping into False Passage was Mistaken Point; the crescent cove sheltering behind the long bending arm of sand and rock at the northeast tip of the island was Black Strap Cove, and was marked 'Fitt for small fishing vessels.' Opposite Harbour Point on the eastern shores of the harbour was Porpus Point (Government Point). Following along the shores northward the points like stubby thumbs thrust out into the harbour were Maple Point, Indian Leap (marking the rectangular rock now known as the Tea Chest), and Willock Point, swinging into the bay below Lobster Shoal, the sandy spit where the Sandy Point Light guards the harbour. The eastern arm of the upper harbour lying between Hart's Point (called Loon's Point by Durell) and the eastern shores of the bay, noted for good anchorage, was Sagamore Reach, and the river rushing into Sagamore Reach was Sagamore River (Roseway River). The western arm of the harbour (Birchtown Bay) was 'Shoale water and Rocky'. A sharp point of land extending into the bay was known as Fox Point, and the two brooks were Squaw, and to the west of it, Papoose. Following south along the western shores of the harbour were Yallow River and Anna's River (north of Churchover), both noted for good water, with Anna's River flowing into a small inlet known as Tom's Hole. Further south was Charles Point with Crab Rocks south of the point. Hawkes River, near Gunning Cove, was a good watering place. Fort Point, like a blunt, broad shoulder curving north into the harbour, was designated Scarborough Point, 'with Good wooding with white oak.' A little below Scarborough Point was Apel Creek flowing into Broad Bay, the body of water east of False Passage.

With the decision to expel the French settlers from their holdings in Nova Scotia, those living in the Cape Sable area were driven from their homes in the spring of 1756. If there were still French families living at Port Roseway there was no mention of them in Governor Lawrence's instructions to Major Prebble, unless his order to remove the French 'at Cape Sable and the places round about' included Port Roseway.[33] The final dispersal of the French who had lived in the Cape Sable area and had escaped their captors on the night of April 21, when Major Prebble's men raided their homes, and those from other parts of the province who had taken refuge with their kinsmen, was not accomplished until the fall of 1758. Word of the final successful routing of the French from the Cape Sable area reached Annapolis Royal on October 27 when it was reported that 100 men, women and children had been captured, their settlements burned and destroyed, and the captives sent to Halifax 'to be transmitted from thence to Europe.' The destruction of French property in the Cape Sable area continued for weeks. Captain Knox, looking south over the land from Annapolis on November 17, saw large fires at a very great distance which he supposed 'to be occasioned by parties from the Cape Sable detachment, who are burning settlements, and clearing the country.'[34]

With the last of the French inhabitants deported to Europe, Governor Lawrence issued a proclamation 'for the immediate settlement of this Province.'[35] In it he offered for 'peopling and cultivation... the lands vacated by the French as every other part of this valuable Province' and declared himself 'ready to receive any proposals... for effectually settling the said vacated or any other Lands within the Province.'[36]

Prospective settlers were interested, and there were many inquiries, but there were no proposals for settlements. First, they wanted to know what form of government prevailed, what freedom in religion, what terms of encouragement would be offered settlers, how much land each person would receive, what quit rent and taxes they would be required to pay.[37]

With these inquiries before him, Governor Lawrence, with the advice of His Majesty's Council of Nova Scotia, on January 11, 1759, prepared a second proclamation.[38] He was empowered, he assured prospective settlers, to create townships of 100,000 acres of 'the best and most profitable land,' including rivers at or near settlements as well as the sea coast. Land would be granted 'in proportion to the abilities of the planter to settle, cultivate and enclose.' One hundred acres of wildwood would be allowed to every person being master or mistress of a family, and fifty acres for every white or black man, woman, or child included in a family at the actual time of making the grant. No person's grant was to exceed more than one thousand acres. Grants would be 'subject to a quit rent of one shilling sterling per annum for every fifty acres – such rents to commence at the end of ten years from the date of the grant.' Grantees were to plant, cultivate, improve or enclose their land within thirty years, one-third of the land to be improved each ten years. Grantees who fulfilled the terms and conditions of their grants would 'be entitled to another grant, in the proportion and upon the conditions' of the first. No taxes had so far been laid upon His Majesty's subjects within the province and there were no fees of office for issuing grants of land. The Government of Nova Scotia was 'constituted like those of the neighbouring Colonies; the Legislature consisting of a Governor, Council and House of Assembly, and every township, as soon as it shall consist of fifty families will be entitled to send two Representatives to the General Assembly.' Respecting religion, there was 'full liberty of conscience' secured by His Majesty's instructions and by a late act of the General Assembly of Nova Scotia 'to all persuasions, Papists excepted.' Dissenters could erect and build meeting houses for public worship, could choose their ministers, and were excused 'from any rates or taxes for the support of the Established Church of England.' He was not authorized to offer any bounty of provisions, but he was 'ready to lay out the land and make the grants immediately.' In the neighbourhood 'of the lands proposed to be settled' he assured the New Englanders, there were forts garrisoned by His Majesty's troops 'with the view to giving all manner of aid and protection to the settlers, if hereafter there should be need.'

ALEXANDER MCNUTT AND HIS SCOTS-IRISH SETTLERS

In land-thirsty and adventurous New Englanders the proclamation evoked an immediate response. At the same time it sparked a flurry of land promotion, notably the efforts of Alexander McNutt, who dazzled with his schemes not only His Majesty's Council but the Lords of Trade and Plantations. He first appeared before the Council in early November, 1760, shortly after the death of Governor Lawrence.[39] He assured the Council that he had a promise from the late governor of several tracts of land on the rivers Cobequid and Shubenacadie and at Port Roseway on the Cape Sable shore on condition that he procure settlers. This he would 'have effected this year ... had not a great number of said settlers enlisted into the service for the present year.' He had, at considerable expense to himself, obtained about 850 subscribers to settle the lands promised him as early in 1761 'as they possibly can set out.' He had agents in the neighbouring provinces and in the Kingdom of Ireland, to which he himself was about to sail and had sent a vessel to bring settlers to Nova Scotia. He was promised all reasonable encouragement in his 'difficult undertaking' by the late governor; he now asked His Majesty's Council for aid and some of the province's vessels to transport settlers and their effects from the neighbouring provinces to Nova Scotia. At the same time he asked to be recommended to the Board of Trade and Plantations for assistance in bringing settlers from Ireland. With the assurance 'that he should have all the Encouragement that the Council could give him and that he should be accordingly assisted and recommended,' Alexander McNutt set sail for Ireland.

Little is known of McNutt prior to his appeal to the Council. An Ulsterman by birth or by inheritance, he was living in Stanton, Augusta County, Virginia, in 1756. Two years later he was a freeholder and inhabitant among the Scots-Irish settlers of Londonderry, New Hampshire. About this time he was employed by the Governor of Massachusetts in various military services, and in 1760 he was the captain[40] of a company of provincials, with officers and privates mainly from the Scots-Irish of Londonderry, in the regiment of Colonel Osgood raised 'for the total reduction of Canada.'[41] He probably saw the possibilities of large-scale land settlement in Nova Scotia during his military service. A letter from General Amherst to Governor Lawrence in April 1760 indicates that he had already discussed with Lawrence the settlement of the Province and had suggested 'that those persons engaged as settlers might act as those troops' (the Massachusetts forces in Nova Scotia which Governor Lawrence expected would be withdrawn) and 'desired him to give to McNutt Beating orders for that purpose.'[42] A zealous Presbyterian with sharp republican principles, Alexander McNutt's sympathies were with his Scots-Irish people, in particular the Scots-Irish Presbyterians in Ireland who struggled against the stings of political repression and the religious persecution of the English bishops of the Church of England. In Nova Scotia he saw a land waiting for settlement, where religious toleration was secured by proclamation and its governing body was a legislative assembly to which all townships would send their own representatives. By late February of 1761 he was in London, and with the recommendation from the Council of Nova Scotia he approached the Lords of Trade and Plantations with his proposals for the settlement of Nova Scotia.[43]

Seasoned with his own observations of the physical structure of the land of Nova Scotia, McNutt's proposals were more realistic in their terms than those offered by Governor Lawrence. Stony, rocky ground, barren acres, land unfit for immediate cultivation should be granted on terms different from those for land 'accounted plantable.' He proposed to the Lords of Trade that every family he introduced into Nova Scotia should, upon arrival, receive a share of land in the same proportions as offered under the governor's proclamation of January 11, 1759, and that he himself should receive a grant of one hundred acres for every five hundred acres so granted for his benefit 'as a reward for his Merit in this Service.' Townships of one hundred thousand acres of land were to be laid out in such parts of the province as he chose where the land was not 'under actual settlement or surveyed and allotted to other Persons.' For every fifty acres of land granted there should be a quit rent of one shilling sterling per annum to be paid to His Majesty, to commence at the expiration of ten years from the date of the grant.

For a grantee to hold his land, at least three of every fifty plantable acres must be cleared within three years or three acres of swampy or sunken ground or marshland cleared or drained; on barren land, within three years must be placed three neat cattle or six hogs for every fifty acres. On land unfit for immediate cultivation, a good dwelling house, at least twenty by sixteen feet, must be erected 'after the manner of Nova Scotia Building,' and three neat cattle or six hogs on every fifty acres of land. For stony land unfit for planting or for pasture, 'one good and able hand employed in digging any Stone Quarry, or Coal, or other Mine' for every hundred acres should be considered a sufficient labour to hold the land. As if mindful of the rocky land, the swamps, and the marshes of Port Roseway, he suggested that in all surveys of land to be granted, particular attention should be given to the numbers of acres plantable, to the number barren, and that the report be returned to the register's office. His proposals were considered 'just and reasonable' by the Lords of Trade and a draught was ordered to be sent to His Majesty, suggesting that the governor of Nova Scotia be instructed to make grants of land to McNutt and his associates on the terms and conditions of the proposals.

A year later, in March 1762, Alexander McNutt was back in London addressing the Lords of Trade and Plantations.[44] His terms had shifted from grants of land to assistance for his settlers and for privileges for them and for himself. At great expense he had contracted with several thousand Irish families to transport them to Nova Scotia. He asked to be recommended for aid in carrying out this agreement and for a 100 ton vessel in Nova Scotia to carry them to the various locations of their grants after they reached the province, and in return he would compensate the expense of the vessel in wood for the garrison or in work wherever required in the province. He wished to be allowed to assure 'all Denominations of Protestants that they shall bear Offices and enjoy equal Privileges' and requested appointments of clergymen to attend the settlers, 'it being impossible for them to support their Pasters for sometime.' He wished to recommend proper persons among the settlers for commissions in the militia, and to earmark the making and clearing of roads and such other public works 'as the Governor shall direct' from Halifax to the new townships as employment for the many settlers who would not reach their land in time to crop it the first summer. As security for the '26,000 Ster: and upwards' for which he was accountable as prepayment for their passage and subsistence, he asked that the grants of land allotted for the settlers should be made to him for 'parcelling it out to them' when 'they have worked out that Sum.' Special privileges he requested for himself: two thousands acres of woodland in every township to manufacture potash and 'a charter to erect a City by the Name of Jerusalem at Port Rosea on the Cape Sable shore, That being the best Harbour for carrying on the Fishing in all its Branches and most aptly situated for Extending the Settlement of the Province.'

The Committee of Council for Plantations viewed McNutt's proposals with alarm. However desirable the settling in Nova Scotia of the numbers of persons he had already taken from the north of Ireland – some three hundred in 1761 – and the seven to eight thousand for whom he had engaged ships for transportation in 1762, this depopulation was a serious threat to the stability of North Ireland. They ordered the Lords of Trade and Plantations to forbid the governor of Nova Scotia 'to grant Lands to, or permit any of His Majesty's Subjects from Ireland to become Settlers in that Province, except such as have been resident in Nova Scotia or some other of His Majesty's Colonys in America for the space of five years.'[45]

Undaunted, Alexander McNutt pressed on with his plans to colonize Nova Scotia. By late April 1765 he applied to the governor of Nova Scotia for grants of land to be settled by persons 'to be introduced by several associations of merchants in Ireland and America.' In consequence of the approval given his proposals of February 1761 by the Lords of Trade and Plantations, he had agreed with several persons in Ireland and in America to provide land in Nova Scotia for settlement on the terms of his proposals for 'as many families as they could furnish.' There were many families now 'waiting with anxiety and impatience to transport themselves' to Nova Scotia, and 'unless he was enabled to fulfill his several contracts and engagements,' he would be liable to severe penalties. The governor passed his plea to the Council. They were of the opinion that McNutt and his associates deserved 'all possible encouragement' and that it should be recommended to the Lords of Trade and Plantations to obtain such conditions of settlement as would be most likely to induce such desirable settlers to Nova Scotia and 'put the country into a condition of yielding the many advantages it would peculiarly afford from being well peopled, particularly the cultivation of hemp and the curing of Fish,' which exports were the principal objectives of McNutt's settlers. They recommended that the surveyor should be directed to make a reserve of lands suitable to the several applications, on condition that McNutt and his associates send a quarter of their settlers within one year from the date of the reservation and an equal number every year until the entire number 'shall be completed.' Along with the reservation of land for settlers, they recommended that McNutt should be granted a tract of land for a township at Port Roseway and a charter to erect a city to be named Jerusalem.[46]

By October 1765 the surveyors had the boundaries of the land established in the Port Roseway area. In four reserves, 420,000 acres were made available to Alexander McNutt and his associates. From the first falls on the Cape Negro River (Clyde River) to ten miles up the river, from thence across the land to the western boundary of Liverpool township, thence to the sea and, including the islands, along the shores westward to the falls on the Cape Negro River. The 420,000 acres included the 100,000 acres to Alexander McNutt, his heirs and assigns as a township to be called Jerusalem:

"Beginning at the first falls on Cape Negro River and Running from thence north 33°15' west and measuring ten miles, thence north 66°15' easterly till it meet with the line Beginning at the Falls of Green River[47] and Running north 33°15' west and is Bounded South Easterly By the Ocean, westerly by the Harbour and River of Cape Negro together with all the Islands South of Lands containing in the whole 100,000 acres."[48]

To the east of Alexander McNutt's Jerusalem were two tracts of land, one of 100,000 acres, the other of 200,000 acres, extending from the west boundary of Liverpool township to the east boundary of Jerusalem. The northern tract of land of 200,000 acres was granted to Alexander McNutt, William Caldwell, Arthur Vance, Joseph McNutt, Samuel Henderson, and Richard Caldwell. The southern acreage of shore land of 100,000 acres butted the northern tract of 200,000 acres and cut across the land at an angle of 33°45' to a cove near Ragged Islands and along the shores eastward to Liverpool Township and included the harbours of Port Mutton (Port Mouton) and Port Habere (Port L'Hebert). It was granted to Alexander McNutt, William Caldwell, Arthur Vance, Joseph McNutt, Samuel Henderson and Richard Caldwell. The 20,000 acres of land butting the southwest boundary of the 100,000 acres of the shore grant, from the cove near Ragged Islands to the falls of the Green River, followed the banks of the river and around the shores of Ragged Islands to the above mentioned cove, were given to Alexander McNutt, Reverend James Lyon, Arthur Vance, Jr., Anthony Henderson and Joseph Wilson.[49]

The grants were made to the landholders on terms quite impossible to fulfill, considering the hundreds of acres of barren waste land, of bogs and rocks, and the fact that many who would be interested, who would be excellent inhabitants and develop the economic possibilities of the sea, would be fishermen and mariners rather than farmers. On their 420,000 acres of land they were to pay one farthing quit rent per acre for one-half the granted premises within five years from the date of the grant; the remaining half to be paid in ten years from the date of the grant, payments to continue yearly 'thereafter forever.' If three years quit rent was unpaid 'and no distress found on the premises,' the grant would be null and void. They were to plant, cultivate, improve and enclose one-third of their premises within ten years; another third within twenty years; the remaining third within thirty years, or forfeit all unimproved acres. They were to plant, within ten years, one rood (a quarter of an acre) of hemp for every thousand acres granted and 'to keep a like quantity planted during successive years.' Within one year from November 1, 1765, they were to settle one quarter of the land with one Protestant person to every two hundred acres and to continue in like manner until in four years the land was settled, all unsettled acres to revert to the Crown.[50]

With the terms for the grants well established, the land waited for people. Of the landholders, it would seem that only Alexander and Joseph McNutt became permanent settlers. The others were either land promoters, interested as much in other areas in the province as in the district of Port Roseway, or McNutt's agents in Ireland or America. Arthur Vance and William Caldwell were merchants and shipowners of Londonderry, Ireland, and were agents for McNutt in Ulster. They came to Nova Scotia in their ship, the *Hopewell,* in October 1761, and were among the grantees of Londonderry, Nova Scotia. Samuel Henderson, of Samuel Henderson and Company, Bristol, England, was among the applicants for land in April 1765, when his company requested of the Council of Nova Scotia a grant of 200,000 acres. The Reverend James Lyon, of the Ragged Islands grant, was from Trenton, New Jersey, and was ordained in May 1765. He was the first resident Presbyterian minister in Canada. He had land grants in Onslow and in the Pictou area, where he is believed to have lived until about 1772, when he went to Machias, Maine, and was an ardent supporter of the American Revolution.[51]

The first Scots-Irish settlers brought by Alexander McNutt and his associates to their grants of land along the southwestern shores arrived with Arthur Vance, agent for Caldwell, Vance and Caldwell of Londonderry,

Ireland, in October 1766, and were landed at Port Mouton. The captain of their ship was in Liverpool on October 23 buying boards to build winter huts and arranging for timber to be cut for them at Port Mouton. 'There are 62 souls in the ship,' Simeon Perkins noted in his diary 'to settle at Port Mutton,' and four more ships were expected in the spring with settlers for different parts of the province. Of these settlers from North Ireland, some perhaps came later to McNutt's New Jerusalem, for in the early 1770s Isaac Deschamp reported: 'Port Rasoir (so called by the French) is a settlement begun by North Irish.'[52] Scots-Irish settlers known to be at Port Roseway were: the McNutts (Arthur, Benjamin, Bernard, John, Francis, Martin, Joseph and Alexander); James Colville; the widow Caldwell, her daughters and her son John; and the widow Ann Gilfillan. Of these, how many came directly from Ireland and how many from Scots-Irish settlements in America is uncertain.

All the McNutts probably came to Port Roseway from these Scots-Irish settlements. Bernard and Agnes McNutt left Ireland for America in 1760. Ten years later they came to Nova Scotia and settled in Roseway on land east of Dexter's Lake in what is now Carleton Village. They had a large family of children, eight of whom were living when Bernard McNutt died in 1780. Agnes McNutt, as a widow, continued to farm her land with her children's help, cultivating and improving her acreage, labouring to reap the produce of her fields with her own hands. In 1789 she was given a grant of 500 acres 'securing to her children that property which she has earned by her toil.'[53] Two of Bernard and Agnes McNutt's children, Martin and Joseph, received grants of land in their own right. Joseph, born in Ireland in 1753, was a pilot and had land granted to him in Shelburne in Patterson's Division (Block 2nd A, lot no. 1), where he was living prior to the coming of the Loyalists. He also did some farming and shared with his brother Martin land east of Hayden Lake near the Jordan River. He died on His Majesty's ship *Spartan* in Quebec on June 9, 1812. Martin McNutt was a farmer and a cooper. He lived on a large tract of land a mile below the falls on the east side of the Jordan, where he had a house, barn and stables and other buildings, orchards and gardens, extensive meadows, woodland, fishways and a boat. He married Rebecca Stewart and had a large family of seven sons and three daughters. Four of his sons were seafarers and lost their lives at sea or in foreign ports. In 1789 Martin McNutt sold his land on the Jordan to Stephen Skinner and established himself as a cooper in Shelburne on Brew House Lane. He later moved to Halifax, where he died in 1820.[54] John, Arthur and Francis McNutt also may have been sons of Bernard and Agnes McNutt. They had land in Shelburne in Patterson's Division near Joseph McNutt's town lot. Francis McNutt was a mariner and also a farmer, with land in Roseway and on the west side of the Jordan River. He later lived in Londonderry, Nova Scotia. John McNutt disappears from Shelburne records before 1786, when the first assessment roll was prepared for the town and the surrounding area. Arthur McNutt was a farmer and lived near and to the east of Round Bay. He was a fence viewer for Point Carleton in 1788 and served on the petit jury in Shelburne in 1797.[55] (Fence viewers checked fences on a regular basis to be sure that they were secure against wandering cows and pigs.)

Benjamin and Alexander McNutt made their home on McNutt's Island, which, until they lived there, had been variously known as Port Rasoir Island, Port Roseway Island, Rosaway, Roseway and Roseneath. Benjamin was among those associates of land agents who applied to the Council of Nova Scotia in 1765 for a grant of 100,000 acres of land for settlement. He was a farmer and, with his brother Alexander, had a considerable acreage of land cleared by 1785, when he was granted 250 acres on the north of McNutt's Island facing into False Passage and bounded on the east by the water of Shelburne Harbour. Alexander McNutt did not receive a grant. In 1768 he lost his Jerusalem for a debt he owed Henry Ferguson, a Halifax merchant.[56] The 'severe penalties' he feared for debts incurred for the 'several contracts and engagements' he had made to bring settlers to Nova Scotia were enacted, and, besides his New Jerusalem, he lost land in Cumberland County to Joshua Mauger. Undeterred by debts and the loss of his land, Alexander McNutt continued to labour for the settlement of Nova Scotia and continued to live on McNutt's Island. In 1786 and 1787, listed as a farmer on McNutt's Island, he was assessed 20 shillings county and 10 shillings poor tax and was among the few affluent taxpayers, so that he must have acquired considerable personal property. During the years of the American Revolution his house was plundered by American privateersmen, and he himself was insulted by both the Americans and the British. His sympathies were with the Americans in their struggle for political independence, and he eventually returned to America. The last record of his residing on McNutt's Island is an account addressed to him in September 1791, by the Shelburne merchant William Hale, who was himself on the point of departing from Shelburne. In 1779 Alexander McNutt had bought 200 acres of farmland in Rockbridge County at the Forks of the James River near Lexington, Virginia. There he settled when he left Nova Scotia. He died in 1811 and was buried in the Presbyterian burial ground in Falling Spring, Virginia.[57]

Of the other Scots-Irish settlers of Port Roseway, the widow Ann Gilfillan lived to the east of Agnes and Bernard McNutt and had land on the southwest side of Round Bay which she sold in 1799 to William Sutherland.

James Colville, a farmer, lived near Ann Gilfillan. Somewhere along the shore, perhaps near the Bernard McNutts, the widow Elizabeth Caldwell lived with her daughters and son, John. When his fishery was disrupted by the American Revolution, John Caldwell, as the sole support of his mother and sisters, sailed in a merchantman to the West Indies. On his return he sailed on a voyage to Quebec and was captured by the American privateer *Dolphin* and taken into Salem. In consideration of his youth and the fact that he had never sailed in an armed ship, he was permitted to return to New Jerusalem with William Greenwood in the schooner *Sally*. Elizabeth Caldwell and her family may have left Port Roseway about this time, as neither she nor her son received a grant of land with the other Scots-Irish settlers in 1785, and their names do not appear on the early assessment rolls.[58]

THE NEW ENGLAND SETTLERS

Shortly after the coming of the Scots-Irish settlers, others came to the shores of Port Roseway. They were chiefly New Englanders pushing their way along the shores from newly established communities to the east and west – from Liverpool and Barrington. By tradition, Anthony DeMings was the first New England settler. As with all traditions, the story varies with the raconteur. It is thought that he was Portuguese by birth, born in Oporto. The spelling of his name 'Domings' by Simeon Perkins suggests that his Portuguese name was probably 'Domingos.' When a child, he was kidnapped with his nurse by the crew of an American fishing vessel and was taken to Salem, Massachusetts. Years later, as a young man fishing out of Marblehead, he was put ashore at Port Roseway for quarrelling with the crew. Searching for a site where he could live, he sat down under a tree. While sitting thus, an apple struck him. He had been sitting under one of the old French apple trees. Pushing through the undergrowth, he came to an abandoned cabin where he lived until he later built his own house. The time of his coming to Port Roseway varies in the accounts from 1760 to 1767. In 1773 or 1774 he returned to Massachusetts for his wife and son, Anthony. Another story of DeMings is that in the spring of 1783 he piloted the Loyalist fleet up Shelburne Harbour to safe anchorage. Those recalling the old tales forget that the Loyalists sailed under the protection of Sir Guy Carleton's orders as Commander-in-Chief of the British forces in North America and were in vessels provided by the British Navy with pilots and competent master mariners.

The records of Anthony DeMings are sparse. In 1766 he was living in Manchester, Massachusetts, where his intentions to marry Elizabeth Belcher were published on January 2.[59] The earliest record of him being at Port Roseway is August 1776, when he bought yards of swanskin from Gideon

PROLOGUE TO 1783

White who was on a trading voyage along the coast of Nova Scotia, and recorded his name as Anthony 'Mings.'[60] Three years later, in September 1779, Simeon Perkins noted in his *Diary*, 'Nathan Doane and Domings shallop from Roseway – both bring me fish.' In June 1781, Demings and Nathan Doane delivered to Perkins several barrels of clay for the reconstruction of his chimney. A few months later, Perkins heard that two American privateers had put into Jones Harbour and had taken Anthony DeMings' sloop. In 1785 DeMings was among the old settlers who received a grant of land for the improvements he had made to the acres where he lived, between James Colville's and Joshua Snow's land, east of Dexter's Lake in what is now Carleton Village. He was listed on the tax rolls of 1786 and was assessed two shillings county and one shilling poor tax. In 1788 he was appointed by the Shelburne Court of Sessions as a fence viewer for the Carlton Village area.[61]

The land granted to Anthony DeMings was part of the reserve of 4,700 acres (exclusive of 500 acres reserved for Agnes McNutt, and 50 acres each for Donald McLeod, Savil McDonald and William Sutherland) granted in 1785 to Eleazer Doane and fifteen other old settlers on the west side of Port Roseway harbour lying 'between that port and Cape Negro.' The land stretched from the southern line of Gunning Cove to and beyond Round Bay and butted that laid out to Silas Perry and others. The sixteen grantees were: Eleazer Doane, Joshua Snow, Anthony DeMings, Ann Gilfillan, James Colville, Jesse Dexter, Jesse Nickerson, Moses Crowell, Benjamin Kirby, Thomas Doty, Asa Doane, Archelaus Crowell, Ansel Crowell, David Wood, Nathan Doane and Arthur McNutt.[62]

The first named grantee, Eleazer Doane, from Mansfield, Connecticut, first settled in Falmouth, Nova Scotia, in 1760. Later he came to Port Roseway and settled on the shores of the harbour opposite McNutt's Island in Carleton Village. An armourer by trade, appointed in 1758 as 'Armourer in the 1st Regiment raised in Connecticut Colony for this Campaign at an allowance of £6 per month,' he established himself in Carleton Village as a farmer. Two of his sons, Asa and Nathan, settled in Port Roseway – Asa in Roseway, Nathan at Round Bay. Asa Doane, born in Mansfield, Connecticut, in 1743, prior to coming to Nova Scotia served in a provincial corps in Montreal at the time General Wolfe captured Quebec. He was a farmer, his land assessed in 1786 for two shillings county and one shilling poor tax. Nathan Doane lived on the west side of Round Bay in a house near the beach. He was a farmer, fisherman and mariner, operated a ferry across Round Bay, and owned (with Anthony DeMings) a shallop that they used to deliver fish and other produce to Simeon Perkins in Liverpool. On one of his voyages he was brought to by two armed vessels, one a forty-gun ship, the other a ten-gun brig, and was detained for some time under their sterns, until (in the fog) he cut the cable and escaped. He supposed the vessels to be American privateers. Two years later he was one of the New England settlers helping distressed American privateersmen to find a vessel and a way to escape to the safety of their own shores.[63]

Archelaus, Ansel and Moses Crowell were from Barrington, sons of Barrington grantees. Moses Crowell came to Port Roseway with his stepfather, Benjamin Kirby, and settled in Roseway to the east of his stepfather. He later returned to Barrington and lived on Moses' Island (Hogg's Island). Ansel Crowell was a farmer and lived near Round Bay. He also had land on Cape Negro Island, which he sold when he returned to Barrington. Archelaus Crowell was a mariner, master of the shallop *Elizabeth* and the schooner *Betsey*. During the years of the American Revolutionary War he moved along the shores to Liverpool and Halifax and over the Bay of Fundy to Newburyport, Massachusetts, his schooner laden with fish and fish oil and salt to trade for provisions for himself and others at Port Roseway. On a voyage to Newburyport in the schooner *Betsey* in 1780 he was captured by an American privateer and taken into Salem. In consideration that Obediah Wilson of Barrington, who was with him, had, with his father, supplied provisions for the crew of the distressed American privateer *Mercury*, the schooner *Betsey* and her cargo of fish were released and permitted to return to Port Roseway. Archelaus Crowell and his family returned to Barrington sometime after 1785.[64]

Others who lived in Barrington and came to Port Roseway were Thomas Doty, Jesse Nickerson, Joshua Snow, Benjamin Kirby, and David Wood. Thomas Doty settled in the Roseway-Round Bay area near Benjamin Kirby.[65] He was a farmer and was associated with Archelaus Crowell in fishing. In 1786 his property was assessed 5 shillings county and 2 shillings 6 pence poor tax. Jesse Nickerson, a son of the Barrington grantee Eldad Nickerson, came to Port Roseway with his mother and stepfather Jesse Dexter in the 1770s. He was a farmer, and besides the land granted to him in 1785 on Crane's Point he had extensive marshland near Round Bay, land in Roseway, and acreage on Cape Sable Island.[66] Benjamin Kirby came to Port Roseway sometime prior to 1780, when he was captured with Archelaus Crowell by privateers on their way to Newburyport with a load of fish and fish oil. He settled on a large tract of land east of Round Bay where he had a farm with a fresh-water creek, Kirby's Creek, meadow and marshland for his cattle, and a sheltered cove, Kirby's Cove, for his fish boat. Here he built a house that he lost in a fire in 1781 with almost all he possessed. In 1790 he was listed on the assessment roll as a farmer at Round Bay.[67] Joshua Snow, a farmer with an interest in vessels, married Mary, the

PROLOGUE TO 1783

daughter of the Port Roseway grantee Eleazer Doane, and settled near his father-in-law in Carleton Village. He later lived in Shelburne, from where his son Joshua sailed as master of the schooner *Two Brothers* and other vessels, and where he and his son Joshua 3rd established a substantial business as shipowners, shipbuilders, merchants, importers and exporters. Joshua Snow 3rd was member of the House of Assembly for Shelburne Township 1847-1851[68]

David Wood, a son of the Rev. Samuel Wood, an early minister in the old Meeting House, Barrington, was by profession a master mariner, and sailed out of Barrington in the schooner *Endeavour* to Halifax and American seaports during the American Revolutionary War with fish to trade for supplies for the early settlers. In the early 1780s he came to Port Roseway and settled on a large tract of land, 500 acres on the east side of Round Bay. He and his family later returned to Barrington, and in 1815 his widow and children sold their Round Bay property with houses and other buildings to William Munro. David Wood's son Samuel, master mariner and shipowner, sailed in the schooners *Plato* and *Dashen*, his vessels laden with shingles and lumber for maritime ports. Great grandsons of David Wood, sons of Captain Elisha Wood, harbour master for the port of Halifax, were founders of the well-known Halifax business firm of Wood Brothers.[69]

Jesse Dexter, the only Port Roseway settler to come from Liverpool, had land bounded on the 'east by the west branch of Roseway River' (Dexter's Brook). He was a farmer and lumberman and shipowner, and coasted along the shore to Liverpool with hay and timber. He rescued two Liverpool men put ashore on one of the Ragged Islands by an American privateer in 1779, and two years later fell prey himself to a privateer out of Salem, but was released with his vessel laden with hay. A few years previous to his death in 1823 he sold his land to his son Jesse and came to Shelburne to live and work as a carpenter. His son, Elisha Dexter, was a master mariner. He lived on a well-stocked farm with cattle, sheep and horses, and had an interest in shipbuilding.[70]

Three other early settlers lived in the Port Roseway area but did not share in the 4,700 acres of land granted to the other settlers in 1785. These were Lemuel Bush (spelled 'Fush' by Gideon White in his account book in 1776); Simeon Edwards at Round Bay; Brayn Smallwood at Gunning Cove.[71]

Other early settlers, Ebenezer Berry and his son-in-law Jacob Locke, lived near the waters of Port Roseway Harbour, their land facing the entrance to Jordan Bay. They had extensive meadow and marshland and good farm land as well as wooded acres reaching up the hill above their farms. An old tale is told of Ebenezer Berry. When the transports bearing the Loyalists came into the harbour of Port Roseway, he, with other early settlers, clambered aboard the ships. When queried by one of the Loyalists why he had settled in Nova Scotia, he gave the gloomy answer, 'Poverty brought me here and poverty keeps me here.'[72]

Along the shores of the land given to Alexander McNutt and his associates, besides the settlers on the harbour of Port Roseway, were numbers of families who came mainly from New England. To the westward of Port Roseway beside the Cape Negro shores (that stretch of coastline later to be designated as Ingomar, North East Harbour, North West Harbour and Port Saxon) were families who had spread along the coast from Barrington and other areas: John Spinney at Cape Negro, Henry Bush, who also had a lot of land granted to him in the town of Shelburne, Isaac King, Joseph Smith, the brothers Theodore and Elisha Smith, William Greenwood, Ephraim, John and Chapman Swain. To the east of Port Roseway, across the waters of Jordan Bay from the point of land where Ebenzer Berry and Jacob Locke farmed their acres, at Green Harbour, were Joseph Huskins, Hercules Hewit, Sr., and his son Hercules Hewit, Jr.; John Hewit, Sr. and his son John, who had land on Green Island and shared 500 acres of land with his father at Green Harbour. At Ragged Islands were a number of families. With their houses perched on the high land of the peninsula in what is now the town of Lockeport were Jonathan Locke, Sr., and Jonathan Locke, Jr., and Josiah Churchill. On the western shore of the harbour above Western Head, in a sheltered cove, was Gilbert Benning. John Mathews, Thomas Hayden and William Porterfield were on the northwestern shores of the inner harbour. On the eastern shores (East Ragged Islands) were Christopher Cotman and Daniel Mathews, and somewhere along the shores were Joseph Hardy and John Hopkins, Job Huskins and Michael Turpin. Others at Ragged Islands in the early years were Jesse Atwood and Captain Martin. Little Harbour had two early settlers, Benjamin Arnold and Enoch Godfrey. The long river and the estuary of the Sable River were favoured shores of the New England settlers. On the first location lists which included Jones Harbour and Port L'Hebert under Sable River, there were eighteen families: John Colby, Ira and William Pride, Joshua Crowell (his name was also spelt Crowe), John Latham, William Porterfield removed from Ragged Islands, Robert Dickson (Dixon), Gilbert Wright, Duncan McMillan (in some records McMullen), Joseph Mills, Thomas Pierce, the widow Giffin, Jacob Jones, John Craige, with Jacob Rude, John Rider, Peter Frude, and John Lewis at Jones Harbour and Port L'Hebert.[73]

Others looked at Port Roseway as a possible site for the location of settlers. In October 1766, two gentlemen from England, one a Quaker and the other a Methodist preacher according to Simeon Perkins, looked at the township of Port Roseway, 'designing to purchase and bring settlers there from England.' The following year, in July 1767, a schooner came along the coast from Nantucket with several gentlemen looking for a location for fifty families. They, too, preferred Port Roseway. If any settlers actually came from England or from Nantucket there are no records of their coming.[74]

The New England settlers (like the earlier French families of Port Roseway) depended upon fishing and farming as their main sources of income, supplemented with products from their woodlots, green hides and dressed skins. In their gardens they grew vegetables, oats, barley, rye, flax, Siberian wheat; small fruits – strawberries, currants, raspberries and gooseberries; and had cherry, plum, apple and pear trees in their orchards. In their pastures were horned cattle, oxen and cows, and sheep and pigs. The women spun both flax and wool and wove linen and woolen cloth that they cut and sewed into clothes for their families. They made butter and cheese, candles and starch and their own yeast; brewed home remedies from the herbs they gathered in the fields and woods and along the shores or grew in their gardens; and boiled spruce boughs for a liquor to which they added molasses for spruce beer. Dried fish, salted fish, and fish oil were traded in New England seaports and in Halifax and Liverpool for the goods they needed, or they purchased supplies from traders who came their way in vessels, as Gideon White did from Plymouth, Massachusetts, in his schooner *Christian*, offering, for trade or cash, yards of swanskin, green baize, duck, and osnabridge (osnaburg), shoes, tobacco, earthenware, codlines, hatchets, rye and rum. Tons of hay cut on their inland meadows, and salt hay from their marches, they sold to Simeon Perkins in Liverpool, along with vegetables, beef, wild geese, clay for mortar, barrel staves, and hewn timber for houses. Shipbuilding was established in Port Medway as early as 1766. The early settlers of the Port Roseway area, if they did not build vessels, were equipped to repair vessels, to caulk them, and to provide masts and bowsprits.[75]

Although Alexander McNutt complained to the Council of Massachusetts Bay in 1778 that armed ruffians from an American privateer had robbed him of sword, pistol and firelocks, scarlet and 'Blew Cloaths,' drawing box, books, silver spoons, silver buckles, gold lace and diamond rings, few of the early settlers, when they came to the land they had chosen for their homes, had more than their two hands to establish a foundation of security for themselves and their families. That many established substantial foundations is evident from the settling of their estates and from the early assessment rolls. Ira Pride of Lewis Head, in 1828 left an estate valued at £269.11.0. In Liverpool, on Fort Point, he had a house and a town lot; in Lewis Head, a house, barn and store, and a one-third share in the schooner *Acadian*, boats and nets, a farm with cows and calves, hogs and sheep. His house was nicely furnished with birch and pine tables, chairs, a looking glass, bedsteads, bedding, a candle stand, waiters, tongs and dog irons, jugs, mugs, cups and saucers, bowls, a bake oven, tea pots and tea kettles, a churn and a butter tub, a well-worn carpet, glasses and plates, spoons, knives and forks, loom and spinning wheel, calico, prints and blue cashmere. Thomas Hayden, ending his days as a farmer at Ragged Islands, left an estate appraised in 1815 at £267.10.0. Property assessments for many of the early settlers indicate well equipped farms and sturdy homes: the widow McNutt, 10 shillings county, 5 shillings poor tax; Joshua Snow, Sr., and Simeon Edwards, each 5 shillings county and 2/6 poor tax; Ebenezer Berry, 14/– county, 7/– poor; John Hewit and Isaac King each 8/– county, 4/– poor; Martin McNutt, 10/– and 5/–. Alexander McNutt, despite his losses to the American privateersmen, was well endowed and was assessed 20 shillings county and 10 shillings poor tax.[76]

Salt marshes and meadows for their cattle, soil good for farming, sheltered coves and safe anchorage, determined where the early settlers built their houses. Where the land was poor and rocky and many acres were needed to provide a marginal income, houses were scattered. Where land was not as important and there was good fishing near good anchorage for their boats, small settlements developed, as in Carleton Village. The houses of Port Roseway were probably like the first homes of many of the New England settlers in nearby communities: low, gable-roofed, a central door flanked by a window at either side, a massive central chimney, two or three low-ceilinged rooms below and a loft above. Their first houses were likely of logs cut on their land, later replaced by houses of hand-hewn timber and boards. Sometimes they clapboarded or shingled their log houses, panelled the interior with planed boards or skirted the walls with a chair rail, wainscoted below, and plastered above with a course mixture of sand and pounded clam shells. The Port Roseway settlers had clay to shape into bricks or to use as mortar to hold stones in fireplaces and chimneys. Some, probably at first, had wooden chimneys daubed and coated with clay like those the Loyalists and disbanded soldiers constructed a few years later. They built their houses close to the shore as they cleared the land from the water's edge. Edging the shores were fish houses and fish flakes, and stone-filled crib landings for boats. Their vessels were sloops and shallops and small schooners.

The New Englanders, as observed by Robinson and Rispin (the Yorkshire farmers who, in 1774, wrote of the early settlers of Nova Scotia), were a stout, tall, well-made people, fluent of speech and remarkably courteous. The men wore their hair queued, and their clothing, except on Sundays, was home-made – in summer, long trousers with checked shirts; in winter, breeches with linsey-woolsey shirts, stockings and shoes. On Sundays they dressed in ruffled shirts and wore shoes and stockings even in summer, when they went barefooted the rest of the time. The women, on week days, wore petticoats and aprons and a loose jacket like a bedgown, and in the summer they, too, went without shoes or stockings, and many without caps. Their hair they tied close to the neck and brought up to the crown of the head. On Sundays they were no 'less gay than the men' with dresses of silk and calico with long ruffles, their hair dressed high on their heads and many without caps. When they went to church or meeting 'from the mistress to the scullion girls, they have all their fans.'[77]

Without church or meeting house, the ladies had no place to show off their fans, but they could use them to good advantage when an itinerant preacher came along the shores and meetings were held in the best room in their houses. The first settlers to come to Port Roseway, Alexander McNutt's Scots-Irish families, were Presbyterians. Shortly after their arrival came Mrs. Anthony DeMings from Massachusetts, a fervent Methodist. Early Methodist records suggest that she carried many into the fold of Methodism. Ministers from nearby communities and pastors of the New Light movement came from time to time, devoting a few days to each of the settlements. One of these was the Reverend Israel Cheever, from the Congregational church in Liverpool, who came to Ragged Islands 'to Baptize, Marry, etc.' His return to Liverpool a month later was greeted with concern. 'The Decons of the church,' Perkins noted in his diary, 'do not attend meeting on account of some Disgust, Mr. Cheever having taken upon himself to Receive a Confession, and receive into Convenant, Baptize, etc. at the Ragged Islands, without the consent of the Church.' With the growing fervor of the New Light movement in Nova Scotia the Reverend Henry Alline, 'a seperate preacher,' came along the shores, stopping at the scattered settlements from Barrington to Port Roseway, the Ragged Islands and Sable River. He found the settlers lost in 'midnight darkness,' some not having heard a sermon in fourteen years, but at Ragged Islands he wrote joyfully in his *Journal*, 'I found a dear child of God.'[78]

When the years of discontent in America with British administration broke into hostility, the peaceful occupation of Port Roseway and other New England settlements was disrupted. The rebellious colonists were their people, struggling for the right to develop and direct the destiny of their country. Remembering how their ancestors braved the seas in little ships to seek in the new land civil and religious rights denied them in the old, their sympathies were with the rebellious Americans. When they came to Nova Scotia as settlers, it was natural that they traded in New England seaports. With the increasing dangers from American privateersmen and the threat of American invasion, their contacts in America aroused the suspicion of the Halifax authorities. When Archelaus Smith and Samuel Osborne Doane of Barrington entered the port of Halifax, they were taken to the governor. Declaring themselves inhabitants of Barrington for fourteen years, the governor signed a certificate for them to go on a fishing voyage. They were the first New Englanders to declare themselves inhabitants, and the governor turned to the chief justice to define for him what 'constitues an Inhabitant.' About this time an Order-in-Council was issued 'that all persons in trade coming into this province... from any part of America, shall be required to take the state oath.' One of the first from America to take the oath was Gideon White, who later came as a Loyalist to Shelburne in the summer of 1784.[79]

Certificates for fishing voyages protected the New England settlers neither from the harassment of the American privateers prowling along the coast nor from the British ships when a sturdy sailor was needed to man a vessel. Nor were their homes safe from thieving Americans, seizing the opportunities of war, who came along the shores, many without letters of marque, and preyed upon helpless homesteads. The alarm of the early settlers for their safety was expressed by the inhabitants of Yarmouth in a memorial to the Nova Scotia government requesting permission 'to go to New England, come to Halifax, or to remain neuter.' Their plea to remain neutral was unanimously rejected. They were promised every possible measure for their protection, and a request was sent to the admiral to station a ship of war at Port Roseway to guard the coast. The governor had already proposed to raise a regiment of a thousand men, and by late December, 1775, he had appointed field officers and captains with instructions to recruit men.[80]

To protect the long coast of Nova Scotia and the scattered homesteads was an impossible task. Thieving American privateersmen continued to swarm over the land, and at sea the little fish boats, the sloops and shallops of the settlers, fell prey to their grasping hands. Benjamin Arnold lost two of his shallops. One he went after and took from the privateers and brought to her mooring. Anthony DeMings and Jesse Dexter lost their sloops; John Colby, Jacob Jones, and others lost theirs; and Archelaus Crowell had his schooner *Betsey* later returned to him. Not content with taking their sloops and schooners, the privateersmen robbed the settlers' fish houses, killed cattle and sheep, and went into their houses and well-stocked cupboards for molasses and sugar, butter and cheese. Such deeds were 'very surprising,' the settlers of Ragged Islands protested to the state of Massachusetts Bay, since they had helped three or four hundred escaped American prisoners 'up along to America and Given part of our Living to them, and have

Concealed Privateers and prizes too from the British Cruisers, in this Harbor.'[81]

News of the surrender of Lord Cornwallis at Yorktown, Virginia, in October, 1781, reached the New England settlements in Nova Scotia in early December. But it was not until June of 1782 that rumours of peace spread along the coast. Simeon Perkins must have expressed the feelings of the New England settlers when he wrote, 'We hope for a Peace with ourselves, which God of his Infinite mercy Grant, that our Nation may no longer Ly under the awful Judgment of Devouring one an Other.' That peace in America would affect them and perhaps threaten the occupation of their land was unforeseen. Those living in Port Roseway first knew there were Loyalists interested in their land in January, 1783, when in Halifax one of the McNutts met an agent for a group of Loyalists in New York who had formed an association to settle on the shores of Port Roseway harbour. The prospect of having Loyalists among them must have been greeted with mingled emotions. They, like the other New England settlers, immediately thought of their land. To quell their alarm the governor printed in the *Gazette* a statement to 'confidently assure those persons residing in the townships in this province, which are liable to forfeiture, that they shall have grants made them, suitable to the improvements they have made.' Taking no chances that the hard labour they had given to their land should be lost to themselves, Benjamin Arnold prepared a petition for himself and others of Hebron[82] for a grant to their land, sending £12 in cash by Alexander Morris to pay for escheating their township for allotment to themselves.[83]

In early May, 1783, the first of the Loyalist transports were sighted as they worked their way into the harbour and dropped anchor off the shores of McNutt's Island. The Loyalists were coming to a rocky and a wooded shore but not to a raw land where the foundations of civilization had not been well established. The impact of the Scots-Irish and the New England settlers of Nova Scotia on the cultural, political and religious life of the province was marked not only during the early years but in moulding the future texture of Nova Scotian life. Their insistence on religious toleration for all Protestant religions, and on a representative government, laid a solid foundation upon which later to build a responsible government. Apart from their influence on the religious and political life in the province, they laid the foundations of its main industries: fishing, shipbuilding, agriculture, commerce, lumbering, trading within the province and in foreign ports. Roads and bridges and ferries were well under way. Schools had been established and newspapers published since 1752.

However diverse the political affiliations of the old settlers and the Loyalists, living together on the shores of Port Roseway harbour they soon became as one people. Two centuries from their coming it would be difficult to find a family of Loyalist origin without an old settler lurking in the background, nor a descendant of the early settlers without a trace of Loyalist blood.

2
The Port Roseway Associates, the Provincial Regiments and the Freed Blacks

The surrender of Lord Cornwallis on the battlefields of Yorktown, Virginia, on October 19, 1781, was a heavy blow to those Americans who had not supported their country in its struggle for political independence from Great Britain. But it was not until the summer of 1782 that they knew that the war had ended with his surrender of the posts of York and Gloucester.

Having waited anxiously during a long winter for the British to renew hostilities, the Loyalists (those Americans who had desired a peaceful settlement of their differences with Great Britain and who wished to remain under the British Constitution) welcomed the arrival of Sir Guy Carleton as commander-in-chief of His Majesty's Forces in America. Carleton had served as governor in Canada and was commander-in-chief of the British forces in Canada during the American attempt to seize Montreal and Quebec in 1775. He was appointed to his new post on March 2, 1782, to succeed Sir Henry Clinton. They believed that he came 'to gratify his Majesty's Expectations, and the ardent wishes of his People' for 'Peace on equal and honourable Terms.' They assured Carleton 'that the pacific disposition of the Parent state will abate the prejudices of the deluded Inhabitants of America, and dispose them to listen with candour to that System of Reconciliation and union, which, under your Excellency's auspices is now to be offered them.' As devoted Loyalists they pledged their affection to their gracious and beloved Sovereign, their attachment to his Government and their best endeavours to promote 'the success of the great and benevolent Design which has brought your Excellency to this Country – to restore it to Peace and Civil Government – to reunite it to the British Empire, and make it permanently happy in the free and full Enjoyment of all those Priviledges and blessings which flow from the British Constitution.'[1]

They were soon to learn that Carleton's mission was not to reunite the rebellious colonies with the mother country but to recognize the independence of the 13 provinces. News of Cornwallis' surrender reached England on November 25. Lord North recognized it as the end of the war in America; but the King was all for pushing on 'though the mode of it may require alterations.' Parliament and a war-weary nation stood against him. Early in 1782 the Commons voted to authorize the King to make peace with America and on March 4 declared that it 'would consider as enemies to His Majesty and the Country all those who should advise or by any means attempt the further prosecution of offensive war on the continent of North America for the purpose of reducing the revolted colonies to obedience by force.' In accord with the decision to consider as enemies of His Majesty all those who should advise the further prosecution of the war, on March 21 Sir Guy Carleton and Rear Admiral Digby were appointed commissioners for restoring peace in America.[2]

The Loyalists first learned of the changed attitude of the British toward the war in America in a letter from Carleton and Digby to General Washington informing him that negotiations for peace had been opened in Paris and that 'His Majesty in order to remove all obstacles to that Peace which he so ardently wishes to restore has commanded His Minister to direct Mr. Grenville that the Independency of the 13 provinces should be proposed by him in the first instance instead of making it a condition of a general treaty. However, not without the highest Confidence that the Loyalists should be restored to their Possessions, or a full Compensation made them for whatever confiscations may have taken place.'[3]

The changed attitude of the British Government staggered the Loyalists. Those who had not assisted the British forces nor joined a provincial regiment and those who had not fled for protection behind the British lines nor menaced the patriots could look forward to peace. They could go on living in their homes, plow their fields, harvest the sea, turn the wheels of industry, build with their neighbours a new nation, and forget in their labour that they had not always shared the same ideals. They could make peace with the Patriots as the Associated Loyalists in the Province of Pennsylvania, Maryland, and the three Lower Counties of New Castle, Kent and Sussex on Delaware had already written Carleton what they would do if Great Britain withdraws 'her right and claim to the Sovereignty over these colonies and shall discharge her subjects from the allegiance they justly owe to His Majesty by withdrawing her protection or acknowledging the Independency of the colonies.' They were willing 'at the hazard of their lives and fortunes' to assist 'in restoring the King's authority – as repeatedly offered, to the last drop of their Blood.' But if Great Britain, 'from an inglorious and dishonest despondency,' withdrew 'her right and claim to the Sovereignty over these colonies,' they would 'consider themselves as a deserted People in a State of Nature and at Liberty to become the subjects and to pursue the protection of those whom they now deem their enemies.'[4] For those who had led the Loyalists in their stand against the Patriots, who had fought and laboured to preserve all that they cherished in their years of devotion to Great Britain, there was no going back. For them there must be homes in a land still British. They could not 'express the consternation with which we are struck,' they wrote Carleton and Admiral Digby, 'even on the probabilit of so calamitous an Event taking place as the independency of the 13 Provinces.' To preserve the British Dominions they had hazarded their lives and fortunes, 'firmly depending on the Justice, magnanimity, and Faith of Parliament, that we should never be deserted in a Cause so just, and in distresses so great and overwhelming.' The time when 'there yet exists a majority of the People throughout the Provinces who are ardently desirous to be again reunited under His Majesty's just Authority and Government,' when 'His Majesty's naval superiority has been gloriously asserted and regained,' when 'the most brilliant advantages have been obtained by His Victorious Arms in the East,' when 'the national commerce, Resources and Spirit' are rising 'far beyond those of our combined Enemies' may be 'the proper Hour to Treat of Peace,' but not 'to dismember an Empire.' But, if 'the independency of the thirteen colonies be determined' and we are 'forever cast out from His Majesty's Protection and Government,' we entreat 'your Excellencies Interpostion with His Majesty, by every Consideration of Humanity, to secure, if possible, beyond the mere form of Treaty, our Persons and Properties, that such as think they cannot safely remain here, may be enabled to seek Refuge elsewhere.'[5]

Carleton and Admiral Digby were well aware of the plight of the Loyalists and their need 'to seek Refuge elsewhere,' for the growing hostility of the Patriots toward those who had stood against them in their right to direct the destiny of their country was harsh and tumultuous. In his search for unoccupied land where the Loyalists could live in safety, Carleton turned to the vast areas of unsettled country in Nova Scotia. Shortly after his arrival in New York he wrote to Brigadier-General Campbell requesting general information about Nova Scotia such as where wheat and oats were grown and where there were pastures and hay. Thinking of the troops to be disbanded, he enquired about towns and villages where soldiers might be quartered and in what numbers without oppression to the inhabitants.[6] With the pressing needs of the Loyalists in mind, in late August Carleton wrote to Sir Andrew Snape Hammond, acting governor of Nova Scotia, that since it was difficult to foresee what events might follow the propositions made in Paris, it was certain 'that many Refugees will need and will have a just claim to establishments out of the 13 Provinces.' It was therefore an act of necessary caution 'to reserve as much Land as possible in your Province to answer demands which are so likely to press, both on the generosity and good faith of the public.'[7] This communication was followed a few weeks later with the recommendation by Carleton that each family should have a grant of 500 to 600 acres of land and each single man 300; that 2,000 acres should be reserved as glebe and church land and 1,000 for a school in each township; that all grants should be exempt from the payment of fees, quit rents, and other pecuniary obligations. Besides free grants of land, he urged that the refugees should be supplied with materials to build houses and artificers to assist in the work of building.[8]

THE PORT ROSEWAY ASSOCIATES

With the encouragement of Sir Guy Carleton many hundreds of Loyalists began to think of Nova Scotia as a land of hope. Among them were a number who wished to settle at Port Roseway, a place described by Carleton as 'about 10 leagues from Cape Sable.' For those who wished to go to Port Roseway, Captain Joseph Durfee, a merchant, farmer, seafarer and shipowner of Newport, Rhode Island (a man, no doubt, acquainted with the area) wrote from New York on August 20, 1782, to Sir Andrew Snape Hammond, requesting a grant of land at or near Port Roseway for fishing and agriculture for himself in association with a hundred heads of families. A few weeks later he received a cordial reply from the provincial secretary, Richard Bulkeley, informing him that the governor had given directions that an enquiry should be made 'in respect of Port Roseway or some other place fit and proper for to answer the views and intentions of yourself and other Loyal Associates so that the same may be reserved.' 'I am further to acquaint you that every possible attention will be paid to the Loyal Associates for which it is expected full instructions will soon be transmitted from His Majesty.' At the same time the Governor recommended that the prospective immigrants should not 'move hither before the spring on account of the many inconveniences that would happen on your arrival in any part of this season through want of a due provision of many indispensible necessaries, and it is further recommended that every person be furnished to the best of His ability with all the requisites for carrying your intention of fishing and farming into execution.'[9]

Bulkeley's letter and encouraging proclamations relative to land settlement drew many Loyalists to the ranks of those seeking homes in Nova Scotia. On November 16, 1782, those interested in Port Roseway as a haven of refuge met in Roubalet's Tavern in the city of New York 'that all things, Business, Negotiations, Regulations, relative to the Settlement of Port Roseway – shall for the future be determin'd finally by the Majority of Votes of the Company assembled and met together.' With the decision that a president should be chosen at each meeting from the company present, Joseph Pynchon, a farmer from Connecticut, was appointed president. John Miller, a farmer from New Jersey, was appointed secretary.[10]

Members of the Association were carefully chosen. No one was allowed to subscribe his name at a public meeting, but was obliged 'to attend for that purpose at the House of Captain Durfee, No. 125 Water Street New Slip – with a proper Recommendation from one of the Associators.' Only members could attend meetings, a ruling later amended so that those with a ticket of recommendation from one of the associators could be admitted 'and none Else.' In accord with the laws of England that Jews 'cannot possess any land,' they were not to be accepted as members in the Association.[11]

Members of the Association were 'chiefly of the number of those, who for their attachment to Government, and after numberless fatigues in supporting the Royal Cause – have been Obliged to quit their All and take refuge within the King's lines.'[12] They came from many places and were of many trades. From Boston there were Andrew Barclay, a Scottish bookbinder; Thomas, Richard and James Courtney, merchant-tailors; Peter Lynch, a hatter; William Hill, a baker; James Gamage, a trader; William Burton, a pump maker. Nathaniel Rae Thomas, a farmer, came from Marshfield, Massachusetts; Joshua Pell, a farmer, was from Pelham Manor, New York; Joseph Durfee, shipowner, sea captain, merchant and farmer, was from Newport, Rhode Island. From Albany came James Dole, merchant and seafarer, and William Castle, a farmer. Among the Philadelphians were Jasper Harding, a tailor; his brother George, a carpenter; and their brothers Richard and Robert. George Chisholm and Hugh Fraser were farmers from Kortright Township, New York; Joshua Hill, a farmer and member of the General Assembly, was from Sussex County on the Delaware. Charles Oliver Bruff, silversmith and cutler, from New York, was a native of Talbot County, Maryland. From New Jersey came James Frazer, a shoemaker of Rahway, and Nathaniel Munro, a carpenter of New Brunswick. From New Hampshire there were John Davidson, a carpenter, and James McMaster, a merchant of Portsmouth. From Virginia came James Miller, a trader from

Portsmouth, and Alexander Murray of Osborne, a trader in his own ships in the West Indies. Among the farmers were Soirle MacDonald from Ansonco County, North Carolina; Edward Ward from East Chester, New York; and Samuel Perry from Sandwich, Massachusetts. From the Ohio River in Pennsylvania was Alexander Robertson, farmer and trader. These men, like hundreds of others who had suffered in the Royal Cause, stood ready to leave their homeland to seek a foothold on British soil, to live under the British flag in Port Roseway.

To achieve their goal of homes in British territory, the Port Roseway Associates appointed a committee of seven to transact their business with Sir Guy Carleton. Those chosen, Joseph Pynchon, Joseph Durfee, James Dole, Fleming Pinkstone (on his retirement, a few days later, replaced by Peter Lynch), Thomas Courtney, Joshua Pell and William Hill were to have 'full and ample powers Until others be chosen in their Room.' To transact their business in Nova Scotia they sent Joseph Pynchon and James Dole to Halifax in His Majesty's ship *Garland* under the auspices of Admiral Digby.[13] With them went letters to the new governor, son of an Irish army officer, John Parr, and to the provincial secretary, Richard Bulkeley. The 'kind attention' they had received from his predecessor, Sir Andrew Snape Hammond, the Associates told Parr, 'had the Effect of greatly encouraging them.' They now looked to him in 'full confidence' that their cause would receive the same attention and every aid in His Excellency's power. With assistance, it was their fond hope 'the Associates will form a Settlement, not only Happy for themselves, but... an ornament to the British Empire.' The particular favours they had received from the provincial secretary, they assured Richard Bulkeley, 'had great Influence in increasing and forwarding their Association, which now amounts to the Number of Two hundred and twenty-four Subscribers.' Grateful for his patronage, they requested his attention to the business their agents were to transact for them.[14]

Of greater importance than their letters to Parr and Bulkeley were their instructions to their deputies, who were to consider themselves 'totally Invested with full and ample power from the Associators to settle and determine all matters, Grants &c of the Settlement of Port Roseway.' They were to obtain the best council in the province for their assistance in all matters affecting the association, and were to discover what instructions the governor had received from His Majesty for the settlement of distressed Loyalists.

In their talks with the governor, they were to request for the Associators the privilege of nominating all officers necessary for the settlement of Port Roseway; that all grants should be exempt from quit rents and should be laid out and surveyed at government expense, their grants to extend as far eastward and westward along the sea as possible. Within their grants they were to ask that the privilege of fowling and fishing in rivers and bays be reserved for them only; that landsmen and seamen should be exempt forever from impressment and the harbour and coast protected by a sufficient force by sea to secure the safety of the settlement. They were to acquaint the governor with the nature of the place they were about to settle – without houses, building material, and sawmills – and were to ask for assistance in these and some workmen to forward their settlement. They were also to arrange with the governor that every settler must cultivate his land, and that no one could convey his grant to another until actual improvements had been made. Above all, assurance must 'be given by Government' that their settling at Port Roseway 'shall no ways injure the claims and demands of the associated Loyalists for former losses and Sufferings – or be estimated as a Compensation thereof.' Since 'in every Infant Settlement, much depends on peace and Unanimity' at home and abroad, they were to request 'the privilege of a patent for a City, – as it will greatly prevent designing men from interrupting our Peace and Quiet.' They were fully convinced that in the instructions which 'we chearfully transmit to you Gentlemen – nothing will be wanting in your power to render the Port Roseway Associators a happy and Flourishing People.'[15]

With Pynchon and Dole went the good wishes of Sir Guy Carleton. 'The provision which it is necessary should be made for those Loyalists, who have sacrificed their properties and exposed themselves to hazards of every kind, in supporting the Union of the Empire, has induced me to look for a resort on the behalf of many, in the Province of Nova Scotia,' he informed Parr. 'Agreeable to this general design of affording a place of refuge... I am now to recommend to your protection Mr. Joseph Pynchon and Mr. James Dole,' commissioners for upwards of 220 families, 'likely to be joined by many more,' who solicit a grant of the land adjoining Roseway Harbour 'to be equitably distributed among them for the purpose of carrying on the fisheries, and establishing a commerce in that advantageous situation.' It was his hope such a settlement 'established by an industrious body of men, inured to hardships, accustomed to dangers, and acquainted with fisheries and trade, will bring a great accession of strength and wealth to the province, and give it suddenly that importance – that it should obtain.'[16]

On the arrival of Pynchon and Dole in Halifax, letters assuring the Associates of their favourable opinion of their cause were hurried off to New York by Parr and Bulkeley.[17] At the same time Parr wrote to Carleton that the 'singular merits from your recommendation' of the Port Roseway Associates 'have engaged my utmost attention and nothing in my power shall be wanting to them both on their account and in consideration of the

Silhouette of Governor John Parr. (Courtesy Public Archives of Nova Scotia)

considerable acquisition likely to be made to this province by the accession of so great a number of valuable people.' To accommodate the many who were likely to come he had 'made provision of a much greater tract of Land' than first applied for, so that 'His Majesty's gracious intentions towards them may neither be frustrated or delayed.' He had also taken measures to have a sufficient quantity of boards obtained 'to put them under shelter.' When His Majesty's authority is received, he assured Carleton, 'they shall not meet with any impediment whatever.'[18]

By January 23 Pynchon and Dole had not only talked with Governor Parr and his Council but with many others interested in their proposed settlement at Port Roseway. On that day Pynchon wrote the Associates in New York a long, rambling and important letter to go with Captain Dole on his return to New York. It was enthusiastic, overshadowed with doubts of Governor Parr's ability to handle their affairs satisfactorily. Although he was pleased with the prospect of their settlement and 'desired Us to state our wants, and he would do all in his power,' his instructions 'only respect the Grants of Lands.' He, however, had ventured 'to grant 400,000 of Boards to be ready' to be distributed 'at the rate of 1300 feet to a family.' If more boards were needed 'those who have signed after the allotment [is] taken up must depend upon the Saw Mills we are venturing to engage to be built, if the Association as such in a public way would be concerned to build.' He wished for instructions and the necessary money to pursue his plans for sawmills 'with some of the workmen from New York if it is thought best' or with 'a millwright here engaged to go with us.' He had talked with one of the McNutts from Port Roseway, who had assured him that the land back of Port Roseway and Jordan River was well timbered. With many places for mills 'we have concluded, provided I can't get Mills to be built otherways, to engage one or two of the first mills that shall be built shall be the Property of the builder forever' and '100 acres around it be one part of his right.'

In glowing terms Pynchon wrote of the enthusiasm of others for their chosen port of refuge. Although there were those who 'for interest are in Opposition,' the governor and others were of the opinion that Port Roseway 'will be one of the *Capital ports* in America,' not only for trade in lumber with other seaports, but as 'the best landfall in the Province to all European vessels' exceeding 'any port of the New England shore.' With such favorable opinions of the future importance of Port Roseway, 'we find many respectable Characters in this place very friendly and wishing to join with large Capital – and some unhappy Loyalists' who 'will petition [for land] for themselves at New York and this place.' Since there were to be escheated 'for our use about 400,000 acres,' Pynchon felt, 'we can't but on our part recommend them to partake with us in the share of Lands.' Others interested in Port Roseway were Colonel Hambleton, who was about to leave for New York, and some or all of his people from Carolina, who 'may join at least on the back of Us – but we had need to be careful of an absolute determination – as the Governor at present is in opposition to it as he proposes to settle them in another part of the country.'

Well aware that the Associates were eager to know the nature of the land surrounding Port Roseway, Pynchon had turned to the surveyor general, Charles Morris, who had assured him 'we have chosen the best situation in the province for Trade, Fishing, and Farming.' The land back of Port Roseway, Jordan River, and towards Annapolis was reported to be good, 'though he says we must expect some indifferent land in every part of the Province.' Of the four townships, each of 100,000 acres, to be escheated for the Associates (Port Roseway, or Jerusalem Township; Port Hebere; one at the back of Port Hebere; and one at the back of Liverpool), Port Hebere 'is broken and indifferent Land, and as to that back of Liverpool it is out of the way.' Land to the westward of Port Roseway harbour 'is indifferent'; that between Port Roseway and Jordan River 'is pretty good and well timbered.' 'Very few people here have any further acquaintance with the land than the heads of the Harbours,' Pynchon continued. 'For further Information I expect in a few days to make a Journey to Annapolis – expecting to send a Surveyor with chain and compass across the Country to Port Roseway – measuring the distance, and making remarks every mile or half mile of the size and quality of the timber, and the general surface of the country, till he comes to Port Roseway.'

Having learned from one of the McNutts that the soil at the back of Port Roseway was good for crops, small fruits, and fruit trees, Pynchon ventured to suggest a plan for the Port Roseway settlement. 'I think the grand object in our Settling at Port Roseway is to keep the whole of the force of the Settlement in one channel, and in no Shape divided that we should have all our trading Stock at one port – our Farming people so situated as their produce may naturally center at the Capital. This Occasions my own private opinion that good land on the back, on a Road to Annapolis, is to be prefer'd to another indifferent Port surrounded with Wasteland' which would 'divide our strength.' As to a patent for their city, 'I am in hopes a corporation may be obtained – I think it will unless the Jealousies of other parts of the Province make it necessary for the Peace and Quiet of the Governor to be [*sic*] otherwise.'

Certain items, Pynchon had discovered, were scarce in Halifax, and it would not do 'to depend absolutely on Supplies from England.' Nails must be purchased in New York and tools for building. Stoves should be procured 'at least every Family one - for it may be all our chimnies cannot be built before winter - in such case every Family with a little cooking Shed adjoining the back door, and a Stove in the Keeping Room, may be very comfortable during One Winter.' As to glass and windows, 'I like the fashion of many windows in this place, the Rooms are low and warm – the windows consist of 12 Squares of 8 by 10 or 10 by 12 Glass. They make a very decent appearance and much less expence in the Sash way.'

His long letter finished, Pynchon thought of other things and hastily added postscripts. He should have a letter of introduction to General Patterson, commander-in-chief of the British Forces in Nova Scotia, as troops might be needed for protection of the mills to be erected early in the spring before the arrival of the settlers. The governor had strongly recommended that they should apply to Carleton for a surveyor, as there was more to be done in Nova Scotia than the surveyor general 'can possibly do.' Thinking of the rough terrain to be traversed, he added, 'I hope it will be not only a man of skill in the Business, but of activity, and a good constitution.'[19]

To the Port Roseway Associates it was an alarming letter. That Loyalists other than themselves were pressing for land at Port Roseway and were considering the erection of sawmills was preposterous. To establish their position as the sole benefactors of whatever bounties might be given the founders of Port Roseway, they voted unanimously 'that all Lands, Bounties, and every other Emolument granted by Government, or the Governor of Nova Scotia, upon the arrival of the Associators at Port Roseway or other place of Settlement shall be *Equitably* distributed among such Associators as have Signed at New York, without favor or affection, and that the same be considered to any other bounties that may be hereafter granted.'[20]

With their resolution firmly in mind they answered Pynchon's letter. He was not to make any assignments or grants of streams to any individual to build a mill, nor was he to enter into any contract of any kind without further advice of the committee. Shingles, clapboards, lumber, and other material for building which might be prepared before their arrival he was to endeavor to hold for the New York Associators, 'who will pay the customary price of the Province for such Articles,' and he was to prevent 'their being monopolized or Ingrossed by the Halifax Associators or any other Person.' To emphasize the importance of their instructions they added: 'N.B. This matter merits particular attention.' He was 'to suffer no person to associate with Us – but such as you are clearly of Opinion, are in our Situation, and real Suffering Loyalists.'

As disturbing as having other Loyalists demanding land and privileges at Port Roseway, was Carleton's recanting from his former promises. They could expect nothing more from him than vessels for their passage to Nova Scotia and provisions. 'Men and Boys, upwards of twelve years of Age. Full allowance. No Rum. Women half allowance and Children One Quarter allowance.' Thereafter all applications for assistance were to be addressed to the commissionary general, who 'gives his answers thereto - Helas.' Carleton's cool response to their plea for assistance, and his 'injunction' that they were to leave New York on the first day of April, turned their thoughts to the favours they had received from the governor and secretary of Nova Scotia. 'We must look steadily up to those Gentlemen for our future Guardians. Every exertion must be made use of to merit their patronage.'[21]

As the work of the Association increased, the committee of seven appointed in November of 1782 required assistance. On March 1, 25 members of the Association were appointed 'to consult and advise the original committee.' They were men the associates trusted to serve them well: Thomas Hartley, James Potter, James Moffatt, Nathaniel Dickinson, John Tench, George Beattie, William Black, John Stuart, Robert Wilkins, Thomas Turnbull, Peter Parker, George Pashley, Nicholas Brown, James Lodge, William Murray, Benjamin Grosvenor, John Lownds, James Gautier, Alexander Robertson, Gideon White, John Hefferman, Peter Robinson, John Watson, Captain Cocken and John Walker.[22]

At this time the Associates decided that any person unable to pay his subscription, if approved, should 'be admitted to Subscribe - acknowledging himself indebted to the Association for the Subscription money - payable on demand.' With this resolution in effect, they accepted into the Association Luke Dorney, Owen Hughes, Rufus Handy, John Williams, William Sutherland, Alexander Parker, John Blackwell, Peter Stewart and John Davison. Then there was the unhappy family of William Johnson, 'unfortunately Kill'd in a late Battle with the Enemy,' whose son William, although under age, was to be allowed to go to Port Roseway 'as an Associate and be entitled to any privilege as such for the benefit of his father's family.'[23]

Preparations for Departure

Ships to convey the Loyalists to Nova Scotia were the responsibility of Rear Admiral Digby; victualling the transports was the duty of the commissionary general, Brook Watson. Private vessels, schooners and sloops, as well as transports from His Majesty's navy, were to be part of the flotilla to sail for Port Roseway. On private vessels, Brook Watson assured the Port Roseway Associates, provisions would be allowed for those who chose to sail in them, but no money for other expenses. In early March, to enable himself and Admiral Digby to prepare the number of ships required to go to Port Roseway, he requested an immediate count of the exact numbers of the Associators and their servants, who would receive the same rations as themselves and must be listed among the Associates; the number of private

ASSOCIATES, PROVINCIAL REGIMENTS AND FREED BLACKS

vessels going to Port Roseway and the numbers sailing in them; and an inventory of arms and ammunition in the possession of the Associators. To further assist the Commissionary and Admiral Digby, a committee of well-seasoned sea captains – Durfee, Watson, Cocken and Robertson, with John Tench – was elected by the Associates to determine the tonnage necessary to transport the baggage of the Associators. By March 20 the committees had their reports ready, and a few days later, on March 25, the membership roll of Port Roseway Associates prepared by Andrew Barclay was closed with 306 heads of families, 229 women, 557 children and 420 servants – in all 1,512 persons waiting to embark for Port Roseway. For these persons, whose numbers were to be soon augmented by many more as the captains of the companies were given permission to admit other worthy Loyalists to the ranks of the Associates, the committee requested 30 tons of vessel space for each family, an average family consisting of about six persons. It was an astonishing estimate to Brook Watson as was their request for the conveyance of 80 horses for the farmers going to Port Roseway. He could only assure them that vessels would be victualled and made ready for their transportation and referred their requests to Admiral Digby as his responsibility.[24]

Carleton's decision that they were to sail from New York on April 1 aroused a flurry of activity. The Associates voted unanimously to appeal to Brook Watson 'to prolong the Embarkation to the fifteenth day of April.' Watson did not agree. They should begin putting their goods on board by the twentieth of March. If they insisted on April 15, 'the procrastinators would prolong their departure until late in the Season.' As for provisions, 'he had orders to give no more than Six months provisions to the Body,' to be delivered from the day of landing in the proportions of 'all Males and Females above the age of 10 years – full allowance. Children under the age of 10 years half allowance.' The poor, as listed in their returns, he assured them, would be provided for.[25]

Six months provisions with a long winter before them dismayed the Associates. Previous to their conversation with Brook Watson they had prepared a letter of appreciation to Sir Guy Carleton for his 'constant attention to His Majesty's loyal Subjects,' and in particular to the distressed refugees of their Association. With the letter in hand, they approached their commander-in-chief. 'His Excellency,' Captain Durfee reported later to the Associates, 'was pleased to say in Answer to our Address that he wished us to Embark as soon as possible that we may reap the benefit of the Season. That transports would be ready for us – and those transports should lay at Port Roseway until we were under cover and in an easy situation.' As to the six months provisions, 'His Excellency was pleased to say that six months Provisions was Ordered – But he particularly express'd it could not be supposed that Government would set a number of people down' and say, "We will do nothing more for you; You may Starve." If they were in want, their needs would be supplied, 'and if any were dissatisfied they had better Not go, if they could do better for themselves.'[26]

While the Port Roseway Associates and those responsible for their departure from New York worked to have all in readiness for their embarkation, in Halifax, Parr was ordering large tracts of land escheated for the Loyalists. For the Port Roseway Associates he reserved a much larger tract then originally requested, setting aside for their accommodation 400,000 acres of land that reached from the eastern boundary of Barrington Township to the harbour of Port Mouton and the land at the back of the harbours and along the rivers far into the wilderness. The old settlers having been reassured that they would receive grants suitable to their improvements, the escheats went forward, and by March 7 the 400,000 acres destined for the Port Roseway Associates were ready for them to hold with a license of occupation until the land was surveyed for the grants. A few weeks later, on April 21, Benjamin Marston, a former merchant, shipowner and shipmaster of Marblehead, Massachusetts, was engaged by the surveyor general, Charles Morris, as deputy surveyor. He was to work under Morris' son, William, who was chief surveyor. They were to proceed to Port Roseway to lay out a town plot for the reception of refugees from New York 'agreeable to the design already approved for that purpose and according to such further Instructions as you shall hereafter receive.' On the same day the plan of the town to be laid out on the shores of Port Roseway Harbour was approved by Governor Parr.[27]

About the same time as Morris and Marston were engaged as surveyors for the new town of Port Roseway, Lieutenant William Lawson of the Royal Engineers was appointed by Carleton to be in charge of the engineers' department at Port Roseway. Instructions for the protection and settlement of the Port were prepared by Robert Morse, chief of the Royal Engineers, and approved by Carleton. They were to establish a military post for the defense of the town by sea as well as by land, having in mind a town, wharves, barracks, and other public buildings necessary for a great and permanent establishment. The refugee settlers were to be shown 'the spot intended for the town, upon which only they should be allowed to build, agreeably to a plan laid out for them.'[28]

As the time for their departure pressed closer, the Associates on the 19th of March adopted the recommendation of Sir Guy Carleton that they should form themselves into a militia. Each company was to consist of a captain, two lieutenants, four sergeants, and thirty-six rank and file, the

ASSOCIATES, PROVINCIAL REGIMENTS AND FREED BLACKS

captains to be authorized magistrates to settle all disputes until the government of Nova Scotia appointed others in their place. A few days later the Associates nominated twenty-four 'proper persons,' from whom they chose sixteen captains on March 30. Joseph Pynchon came high in votes, but, being in Halifax, he was declared ineligible for election and those chosen were: Peter Lynch, James Dole, Andrew Barclay, Thomas Turnbull, Benjamin Grosvenor, Alexander Robertson, George Pashley, John Lownds, James Potter, Richard Courtney, Alexander Murray, James Moffatt, Alexander Frazer, Stephen Shakespear, Thomas Hartley, John Stuart. They were commissioned captains by Sir Guy Carleton in New York on April 4, 1783. With the captains chosen, Carleton commissioned as first lieutenants: James Courtney, William Castle, Benjamin Wood, John McEwen, John Clisby, Henry Edward Knox, John Barr, Richard Wetton, William Hale, Dennis Kennedy, Timothy Prout, Peter Robinson, Thomas Hudson, Daniel Grandin, Nicholas Browne and George Dundass. The second lieutenants selected were: Weart Banta, Richard White, Thomas Duncan, John Cooke, John McAlpine, Alexander Frazer, Richard Brazel, Archibald Campbell, George Lowe, Charles Hart, George Patton, James Gamage, Archibald Nesbitt, Jesse Lear, Henry Elvins and Abel Thatcher.[29]

On April 5 the Associates gave each captain permission to complete his company with members of the Association. If any member withdrew from the Association, the captain was then at liberty to complete his company with others, not members, but he was to 'be particularly careful in those he may admit into the Association.' Later the Associates gave the captains liberty to augment their subscribers, to whom they must give certificates to be passed to Captain Durfee that each might have an opportunity to sign the membership book and be a Port Roseway Associate.[30]

The day set for their departure, April 1, found the Associates, as well as the officials, with many things still to be done. As the sailing drew closer, the Associates made arrangements for those who, for various reasons, would not be able to sail for Port Roseway on the day appointed. They decided 'that no Person shall be deemed or look'd upon as a member of this Association only those who embark with the Body at large from New York for Port Roseway. Those who have already subscribed, and not able to Emigrate with the Body – their reasons being found sufficient by the Association – will be admitted as Members upon their making personal appearance at Port Roseway four months from this date the dangers of the Sea Excepted.' There was to be no excuse for those who had subscribed their names as members of the Association, since the book was closed on March 20 – 'except in real cases of sickness.'[31]

About this time the Associates received a second letter from Joseph

Pynchon. It was their first intimation that the large grants of land Carleton had recommended, 500 acres to a family, 300 for a single person, were more 'than in the Governor's power to give.' Letters respecting Loyalist grants had been sent to Britain, and new instructions, 'every thing according to their wishes,' were expected. In the meantime the provincial secretary had assured him that, not only the township of Port Roseway, and the land back of Port Hebere and Liverpool would be reserved for them, but all the lands at the back of the townships to Annapolis County, some 700,000 or 800,000 acres. As this would give the Associates 'so great a Choice,' he thought it needless to send persons across the country from Annapolis to assess the land, 'as it would be attended with great Expence.' By March 7 Pynchon was able to inform the Associates that the escheats were finished for 400,000 acres. 'We may have a Licence of Occupation and go forward with the Settlement the same as if we had a Grant. The legal process is after we are in Possession – to procure a writ of *scire facias* to the former Grantees to shew cause why final Judgment shall not be given for vacating the Grant – for which they are allowed a year and a day for pleadings – A quicker decision maybe had by a petition to the Assembly – who by their authority can finally vacate the Grants and confirm our Title immediately.' Pynchon had rounded up a number of carpenters ready to proceed to Port Roseway to prepare timber for buildings 'and for some particular settlers from this Place' – some 100 settlers besides the Carolina Loyalists – who waited only for word from the Associates and convenient transportation, for, Pynchon told them, 'I would not have you disappointed to find Port Roseway taken Possession of when you come there.'[32]

As to the disappointment of the Port Roseway Associates when they learned that they were not to receive the large tracts of land they had believed would be theirs or how they felt toward the more than a hundred Loyalists besides the Carolinians waiting for land at Port Roseway, their records are silent. On April 12 they met together for the last time in New York to bid farewell until they arrived in their new land of hope on the shores of Port Roseway.

THE PROVINCIAL REGIMENTS AND THE FREED BLACKS

As Carleton prepared the way for the Port Roseway Associates to find a new homeland, he was busy looking for land for other refugees, many of whom also sought sanctuary in Port Roseway. These were the men of the Provincial Regiments, who, 'from the purest principles of Loyalty... took arms in His Majesty's Service' and 'persevered with unabated zeal through all the vicissitudes of a Calamitous and an unfortunate War.' As the negotiations for peace proceeded and it became evident that the offer of independence to the American Colonies by the British would 'terminate in the separation of the two countries,' the officers of the Provincial Regiments appealed to Carleton. It would be 'utterly impossible,' they told their commander-in-chief, 'for those who have served His Majesty in Arms in this War to remain in the Country,' civil dissensions having been 'so heightened by the Blood that has been shed in the contest that the Parties can never be reconciled.' In joining the Provincial Regiments, the officers reminded Carleton, they had sacrificed their property, their professions, and 'all their expectations from their Rank and Connection in civil Society'; and many had wives unaccustomed to hardships and children to educate. Among those who had served in subordinate capacities were many who had been 'respectable yeomen of good connections and possessed of considerable property, which from principles of Loyalty' they quitted. Others of the men had wounds and disorders contracted in service and were 'totally unable to provide for their future subsistence.' Many of the widows and orphans were reduced to extreme poverty and had no hope of relief except from the justice and humanity of the British government. On behalf of themselves and the men who had served with them, they asked for grants of land in His Majesty's American Provinces. They asked also for assistance in making settlements 'that they and their children may enjoy the Benefits of the British Government'; for permanent provision for wounded and disabled non-commissioned officers and private soldiers and for widows and orphans; and, as a reward for their faithful service, the permanent rank of officers in America and half-pay on the disbanding of their regiments.[33]

This was followed by a second memorial to Carleton by the commanding officers of the Provincial Corps in the event of a general peace and the independency of the thirteen American provinces, relative to the granting of land 'to such of His Majesty's Provincial Forces as shall be willing to remove to Nova Scotia or any other part of His Majesty's American Dominions for the purpose of making a Settlement.' In their opinion '300 acres of good land will be sufficient for each private soldier, 350 acres for each corporal, 400 for each sergeant, with the same allowance to commissioned officers and staff officers as was granted by His Majesty to the officers of His Troops who served in North America in the last war, and were at the conclusion of it reduced to half pay.' As well as ample grants of land, they suggested that non-commissioned officers and privates 'be allowed provisions, pay, and clothing for three years from the time of their taking possession of their Lands, that they be furnished with arms and ammunition for the defence of the settlements and a proportion of ammunition for hunting, and that the settlers be allowed a proportion of farming utensils, with tools and materials for building and for erecting mills.'[34]

KING'S BOUNTY

Accompanied by a letter requesting the attention of His Majesty's ministers to 'a measure I think necessary both for the dignity of the Crown and the interest of Great Britain,' Carleton forwarded the memorials to Thomas Townshend. The most cordial relationship, he urged, should be established with the provinces which had preserved their allegiance, and all grievances and 'every source of jealousy, or suspicion, should be done away forever.' Again emphasizing, as he had earlier for the benefit of the Loyalists, the importance of dispensing with quit rents and fees, he now urged that taxes should not be imposed by Great Britain nor permitted 'but for their own benefits, and for their provincial defence and security, till their strength become respectable, and their wealth will enable them to contribute to the general support of the empire.' 'I entertain the most sanguine hope,' Carleton assured Townshend, 'that the provinces which are to remain under His Majesty's dominion will suddenly become powerful, and objects of envy to those who in the present moment, madly renounce the most equitable and wise system of government, for anarchy and distraction.'[35]

At the same time as the officers of the Provincial Troops appealed to Carleton, they sent a memorial to Governor Parr requesting, as they had from their commander-in-chief, grants of land in British America, pensions and half pay. Parr had already proposed to Thomas Townshend that since the province of Nova Scotia was of great extent and thinly inhabited, it would

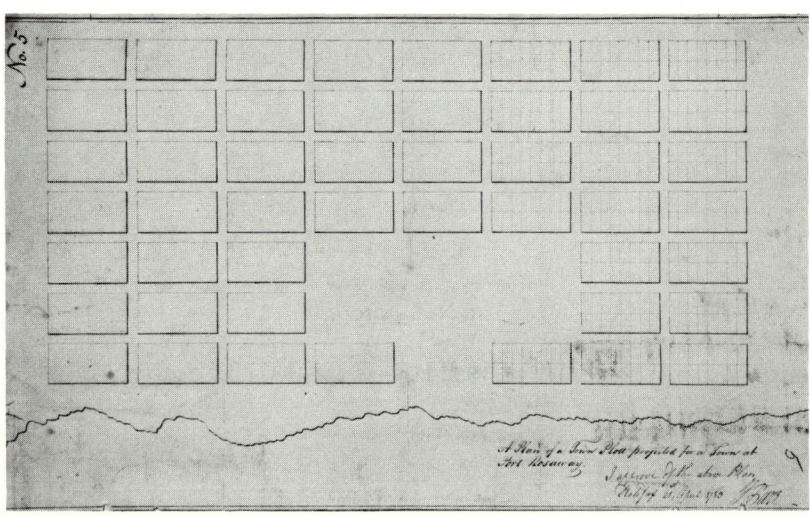

Photograph of "A Plan of a Town Plott projected for a Town at Port Roseway," approved and signed by Governor Parr, April 21, 1783. (Courtesy Land Registry and Research, Nova Scotia Department of Lands and Forests)

tend to augment the population, especially the working classes, 'were it left to the option of the men of any corps now here and which may be hereafter disbanded, to remain, and become settlers.' He now sent the memorial of the Provincial Troops off to London with suggestions for their settlement and the settlement of the Loyalists in Nova Scotia. His plans for their establishment in the province met with the approval of the British government, and on August 8 Lord North wrote to Carleton that 'Governor Parr's plans for establishing Provincial Troops and Loyalists in Nova Scotia appear so Judicious and so well calculated for the Security and general Benefit of the Province' it was 'strongly recommended his carrying them into Execution.'[36]

Along with the Provincial Troops and the Loyalist refugees, Carleton had to find a new homeland for the hundreds of freed slaves who had escaped their masters and had sought within the British lines the protection offered them by Sir Henry Clinton and General Howe. Of the 2,000 or more former slaves who had filtered into New York seeking the freedom they longed for, several hundred were sent by Carleton to Port Roseway and were allotted land on the North West Arm of Port Roseway Harbour in a settlement which they named Birchtown in honor of General Birch, commandant of New York City during the later years of the Revolutionary War.[37]

Departure
With the arrival in early spring of the preliminary articles of peace and the King's proclamation for a cessation of arms, Carleton had new responsibilities. Article 7 of the peace terms stipulated that no slaves or any other property belonging to Americans should be carried out of the country and that proper persons should be appointed to guard against such an eventuality. Carleton wasted no time in appointing a board of commissioners, with Colonel Abijah Willard as secretary, and issued orders couched in the terms of the treaty, a copy of which he sent to General Washington. Turning to the Loyalists, he issued a further statement to those intending to sail in the transports and those responsible for their embarkation, that no person should be admitted for passage who was not known to be a Loyalist in want of assistance and who had suffered from adhering to the royal cause. Furthermore, 'every being who shall go under the above description must be enrolled in some one company the head of which to be answerable for His or Her answering the description given of them to the Commissioners – such, who have been a year within the lines.' As a further precaution that only persons adhering to the royal cause should leave the new states of America, Adjutant-General Oliver De Lancey issued instructions that the

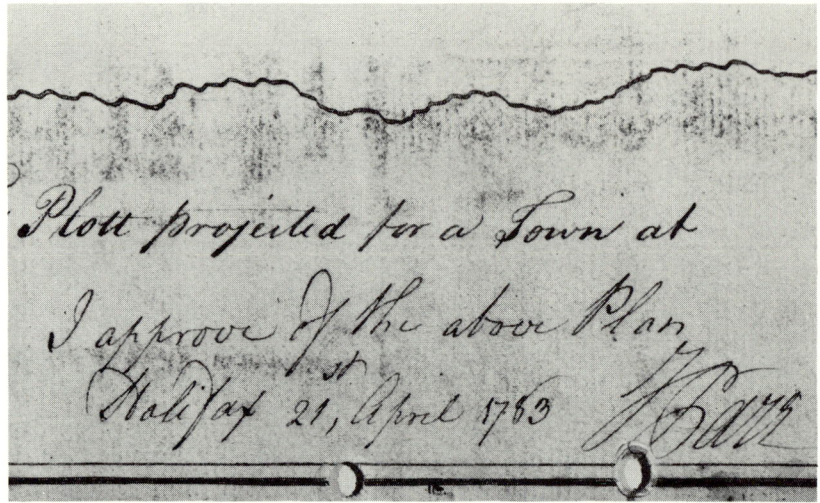

Enlargement of Governor Parr's signature approving the 'Plan of a Town Plott', April 3, 1783. (Land Registry and Research, Nova Scotia Department of Lands and Forests)

refugees themselves and the masters of the vessels were to take care that no person who had not resided within the British lines for twelve months should be permitted to embark as a refugee, unless he had special permission from the commandant, and that no person of bad character should be allowed to board the ships.[38]

As the ships were made ready for the embarkation of the Loyalists, Carleton directed W. Elliott, superintendent of exports and imports, to grant those bound for Nova Scotia permission to ship any article they might find necessary to carry with them without the customary bond, and to grant them a general clearance, 'as the enumerating of the variety of articles necessary for Family use would give the Adventurers much trouble and perhaps bring them into Difficulties should there be any omissions.'[39]

As the time drew near for their departure, the Port Roseway Associates, 'truly sensible' of Carleton's 'attachment to their interests,' solicited that 'his Excellency will be pleased (previous to his declining the command) to issue the necessary Orders for the conveniency of Embarkation and Settlement of Port Roseway.' A few days later, as they boarded the transports, a rough wilderness before them, they again turned to Carleton. 'In this arduous Undertaking we must encounter great difficulties, some of them perhaps surpassing our most Industrious Exertions to surmount, but from adherence to that Government for which we have risked our All we will chearfully combat every practicable difficulty,' they told Carleton, 'in

ASSOCIATES, PROVINCIAL REGIMENTS AND FREED BLACKS

Hopes and confident Expectation, that every relief and assistance will be afforded which the necessities of the people may require – much we most gratefully acknowledge has been done'; for the rest, 'we look forward through your Excellency's benevolent Representations to a hitherto generous nation – and will be happy to receive through you as the most Acceptable Channel every mark of public attention.'[40]

By April 12 the flurry of preparation was over; the Loyalists were ready, the ships waiting for their departure. On that day Carleton wrote jubilantly to Thomas Townshend: 'The Refugees who are going to Nova Scotia will embark tomorrow, and sail in a few days for Port Roseway and St. John's River, consisting of about four or five thousand in number.' With hundreds of Loyalists, men of the Provincial Troops, and Blacks still clamouring for a way to Nova Scotia, Carleton informed the secretary that a considerable increase in shipping would be necessary to accomplish the entire evacuation of New York in the course of the summer, as he would be more particularly informed by Rear Admiral Digby.[41]

The days from the time of their embarkation until the transports lifted their sails for Nova Scotia were long for the Loyalists. At last, on April 26, the transports moved away from their moorings. With the Loyalists went the good wishes of Sir Guy Carleton, who wrote on the day they sailed to Governor Parr recommending the whole expedition to His Excellency's protection. He had for some time been making every preparation in his power for their reception, Parr assured Carleton in his reply, and the chief surveyor, on his orders, had sent his deputies with proper instructions to every district which the agents for the Loyalists had pointed out for their settlements. 'Your Excellency may be assur'd that no attention shall be wanting to render their situation as beneficial, commodious and Secure as Circumstances can possibly admit.' Well aware that the Americans were impatient for the Loyalists to be on their way, Carleton on May 12 reported to General Washington that the 'fleet sailed about the 27th April for different parts of Nova Scotia and including the troops carried about 7,000 persons, with all their effects, also some artillery and public stores, so that you will perceive the evacuation began sooner, and was in greater forwardness than cou'd have been expected.'[42]

Of the 7,000 Loyalist refugees, provincial troops, and free Blacks who sailed in the spring fleet, about 3,000 persons were destined for Port Roseway. The promise of building material, grants of land and Pynchon's glowing expectations of the future importance of Port Roseway had drawn many unhappy Loyalists into the ranks of the Port Roseway Associates. From the 'upwards of 220 families' that Carleton reported in December, 1782, as eager to go to Port Roseway, membership in the Association had increased to well over 300 heads of families entitled by the membership in the Association to all the 'emoluments offered by the Governor to all distressed Loyalists.' Even without Pynchon's enthusiastic reports and the governor's promises, conditions in America were driving hundreds of Loyalists who longed to remain in their homeland to seek refuge from the victorious rebels. In Boston on the eve of their departure the legislature resolved with one dissenting voice, 'to oppose every enemy to the just rights and liberties of mankind; and that after so wicked a conspiracy against those rights and liberties, by certain ingrates, most of them natives of these States, and who have been refugees, and declared traitors to their country; it is the opinion of this town, that they ought never to be suffered to return, but to be excluded from having lot or portion among us.' Other towns were urged by the Bostonians to pass similar resolutions to prevent those who had not fought with them to free their land from British domination from reaping the fruits of the struggle. Despite the angry protests, many Loyalists clung stubbornly to their homes; still others left the ranks of the refugees they had joined to remain in the new America. The dilemma of their former friends was gleefully noted by the Patriots. In New York 'Independent Fever rages there in such a Degree among the Tories and Refugees,' the *Boston Gazette* informed its readers, 'that it carries off great numbers weekly; and General Carleton, in order to prevent the Infection from spreading, has ordered many away to New Scotland.'[43]

Those who chose New Scotland to the wrath of their neighbours watched their homeland fade into the distance as the ships moved into the open sea. For those who had wished as ardently as the Patriots to be free from British rule, to direct and shape their destiny, but had wanted freedom only if gained peacefully, and for those who had been happy and content under British administration, parting came with sadness. For those who had known only poverty and city streets, it was a shining adventure – land, material for a house, free rations. Those who had reaped benefits from the old regime, like those who considered the victorious Patriots as rabble, turned from the country in contempt. As one wrote, 'I quit this dam'd country with pleasure.'

3
Arrival and Early Days in Shelburne

SPRING AND SUMMER 1783

The ships bearing the Port Roseway Associates to their port of refuge had been nine days at sea when they came to the harbour of Port Roseway about four o'clock in the afternoon on Sunday, May 4, and came up into the northeast harbour and dropped anchor. The wind was a fresh northwesterly and the weather fair for their first glimpse of their new homeland. Looking toward the land the adventurers saw little to cheer them. For most it was their first glimpse of Nova Scotia, and to the many who had known only city streets or land opened to the plow, the great granite boulders, the rocky, tree-covered shores, the reefs and shoals they had passed must have looked formidable.[1]

In the fleet were 'upwards of 30 sail in all, in which there are 3000 souls (as an agent tells me),' Benjamin Marston, the recently engaged deputy surveyor for the new township of Port Roseway, noted in his diary, an invaluable chronicle of early Port Roseway. According to the commissionary general's returns, in the first fleet there were 1,686 men, women, and children (577 men, 452 women, 354 children over 10, 303 under 10) and 415 servants. In the ships with the Loyalists were 936 freed slaves listed as servants by John Miller, secretary to the Port Roseway Associates, in his returns to the commissionary general, 60 of whom had indentured themselves to the Loyalists. In all – Loyalists, servants, freed Blacks – there were 3,037 persons. They were organized in 16 companies under the 16 men the Associates had chosen as their representatives, who were commissioned captains and magistrates by Sir Guy Carleton to transact their business, to attend to the distribution of their lots of land, and to collect their rations from the King's bounty of provisions.²

William Morris and Benjamin Marston and their assistant surveyor, Charles Mason, along with a pilot and Joseph Pynchon, had arrived in Port Roseway from Halifax two days before the arrival of the fleet. On Saturday, May 3, they explored the land along the eastern arm of the harbour for a 'convenient situation for a town.' The land they found 'not much Broken, produces Spruce, Pine, oak, and some maple, the soil very Good and not many Stones, wants nothing but cultivation.' The northwest arm of the bay was found not as good a harbour as the eastern branch, but the land 'nearly the same.' To his dismay Morris discovered that Pynchon had no instructions to act 'in concert' with him 'in any matter respecting the People.' The choice of the town site was to be the decision of the Port Roseway Associates. Accordingly, Morris and Pynchon met the captains of the Associates on Tuesday, May 6, and 'with some difficulty persuaded them to appoint a committee of three or four to examine and Pitch upon a Spot for the Town.' It was the first of many confrontations with the Associates, and Morris' remarks were not flattering. 'Not the smallest appearance of that unanimity and disinterestness and sentiment which one would Expect to find from People who say they have Sacrificed their private Fortunes and Domestic Happiness in support of Gov: & which is of the utmost consequence in the fulfillment of a new country.'³

A long day exploring the shores of the harbour convinced the committee that the northeast side of the harbour was the most eligible situation for a town and it was agreed 'to lay out the Town agreeable to the original Plan sent to New York.' On Thursday, May 8, Marston and Morris surveyed the eastern shore of the harbour near the head of the bay. The Associates coming ashore were dismayed with the land chosen for the site of their town. It was rough, strewn with boulders, and covered with trees. They insisted that the land must be explored again and that they be represented by three men from each of the sixteen companies. 'That is to commit to a mere mob of sixty what a few judicious men found very difficult to transact with a lesser mob of twenty,' Marston commented. 'This cursed republican, town meeting spirit has been the ruin of us already, and unless checked by some stricter form of government will overset the prospect which now presents itself of retrieving our affairs.'⁴

The plan for the town of Port Roseway, as ordered by Governor Parr, drawn up in Halifax and sent to New York and approved by Sir Guy Carleton and by Governor Parr, was for a well-designed settlement to lie close to the shore and to be built around a large and impressive square. Streets 50 feet wide running north and south were to cut at right angles

ARRIVAL AND EARLY DAYS IN SHELBURNE

streets running east and west, dividing the town into 49 blocks, each with 16 house lots. It was an orderly, well-designed town plot, but gave no consideration to wharfs and warehouse lots for the commercial intentions of the town's builders nor for the fisheries. Neither Marston nor Morris discusses the changes made in the original plan.

Finding no location better than the land chosen by the committee, on Friday, May 9, Morris and Marston laid out the centre street for the town, and the people fell to work 'very cheerfully to cut down the trees – a new employment to many of them.' On the following day the line for Water Street was marked parallel with the waterfront along the level land above the sloping hill to the shore, and four blocks were surveyed, two on either side of the centre street (King Street).

On May 15, with a number of streets cut and blocks marked for house lots, Morris sat down to revise the plan. It would seem from the number of blocks marked off (28 recorded by him), that at this time he separated the town into two divisions, North Division and South Division, one on each side of the centre street. These were subdivided into 10 blocks south of the centre street and 11 blocks north, the blocks being separated by five long parallel streets running north and south (Water, Mowat, Hammond, Digby, Harriot) and cut by streets at right angles from the waterfront to the height of land above the lower town, their ends flowing into Harriot Street. Below Water Street, south of King Street, on the slope of land to the water's edge, lying between the ends of the streets, were to be three blocks of water and warehouse lots; north of King Street, north of the public block on the waterfront, three blocks of water lots were to be divided by lanes, as were those south of King Street. Unfortunately for the future peace of the town, he left the large public square (equal to four town blocks), bounded by Mowat, King, Digby and what is now Victoria Street, undivided into blocks and without streets. South of the town square was a public block (equal to two town blocks), bounded by King, Mowat, St. John's, and Digby Streets. North of King Street, the block bounded by King, Mowat, Bulkeley and Water Streets he reserved for public use, and the block west of Water Street, from Water Street to the waterfront and extending from King Street to Bulkeley, was also reserved for public use. In all, the land set aside measured seven town blocks (112 house lots) and one wide warehouse block on the waterfront equal to 80 and more of the narrow (25 feet wide) water and warehouse lots.[5] The settlers felt this land would have been better used for housing.

With a well-defined plan for the town, on May 16 Morris set about marking the blocks into house lots, each lot 60 feet by 120 feet, 16 lots to each block. For four days the Loyalists laboured, cutting trees, slashing the

KING'S BOUNTY

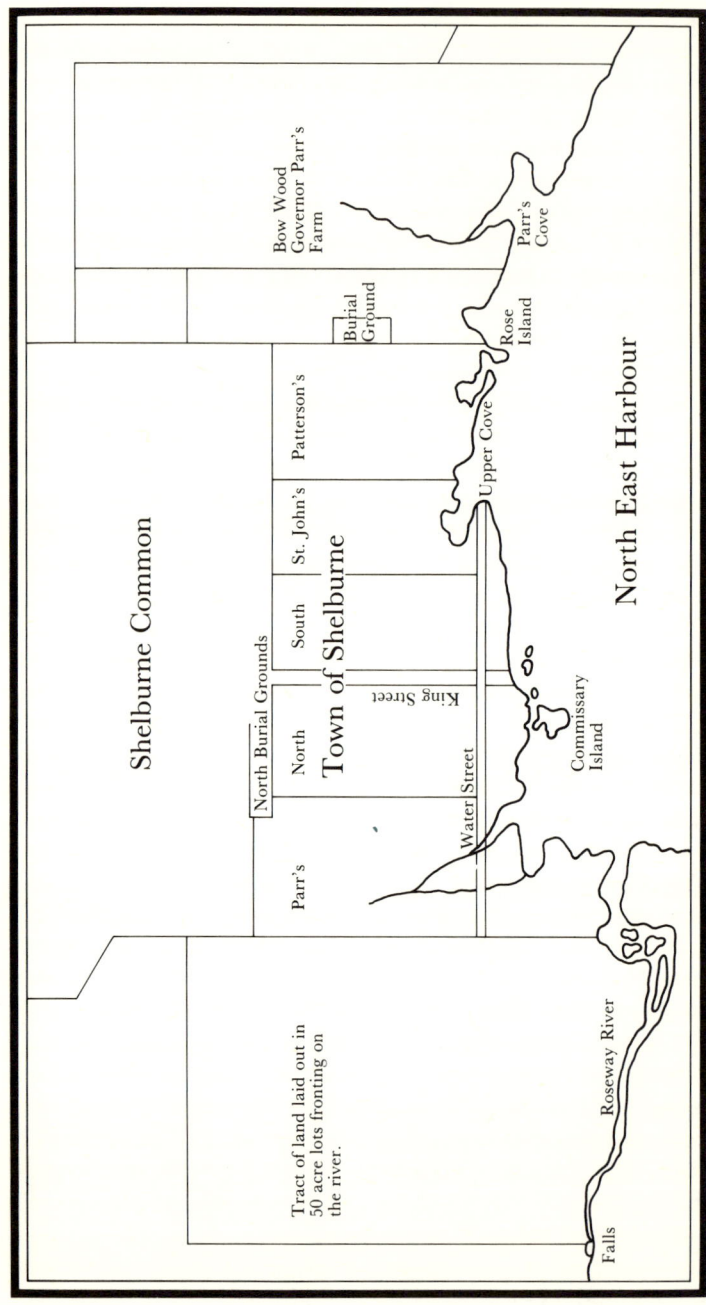

The divisions of the town as laid out by the surveyors Marston and Morris.

underbrush, assisting the surveyors. After that they were weary of trees and labouring. Some did not come to work until eleven in the morning; many did not come at all. 'From ½ past 5 to 8 and not a Soul in town to assist me,' Morris wrote irritably, 'the 3rd time I have been served so, if they catch me waiting on them again like a Lacky they'll have good Luck indeed.' With few of the Loyalists willing to work, Morris had to depend upon 'my own people to help me' and on William Lawson of the Royal Engineers, who surveyed many of the lines for the town, with the officers and working parties sent ashore by Captain Affleck from the *Duc de Chartres* to cut the streets. Marston considered that the war had provided the Loyalists with easy employment and they were impatient with arduous toil. Many were from the lower classes of large towns and it was difficult to deal with them. Some were beginning to suspect that their leaders had private intentions harmful to themselves, a suspicion which Marston had discovered was 'not without some reason,' for most of the captains were self-centred, and men 'whom mere accident has placed in their present situation.' Morris's opinion was equally harsh. 'Gentlemen, Barbers, Taylors, Shoemakers, Tinkers &c who have the Honor to wear Com. as Capt, &c a most Loyal Sett of . . . . ., who have neither the fear of God or man before them.'[6]

With numbers of the blocks divided into house lots, on May 22 the Loyalists began to draw for their town lots. Morris had already established on lots a number of carpenters from Halifax recommended by Governor Parr. Others, Loyalists from Marblehead and some from Halifax, who had sheltered there as the Associates sheltered in New York, were eager to be admitted as settlers. Most of these, the Associates insisted, should not share in the distribution of their land. From the beginning, the Associates wanted Port Roseway for themselves. They were unanimous in their decision 'that all Lands, Bounties, and every other Emolument granted by Government, or the Governor of Nova Scotia, upon the arrival of the Associates at Port Roseway or other place of Settlement, shall be Equitably distributed among such Associators as have signed at New York, without favor or affection, and that the same be considered to any other bounties that may be hereafter granted.' As the day drew near for them to draw for their town lots, to enforce their determination to keep Port Roseway for themselves and the few they might elect to share with them in the bounty of land, they nominated a committee of 16 to point out who were to draw lots. 'They say only 441,' Marston recorded, and to him they were 'a curious set' who 'take upon themselves to determine who are the proper subjects of the King's grant.'[7]

Beginning on May 22 and continuing for several days, the Associates drew for their small house lots, presenting their billets entitling them to their rightful share in the King's bounty of land. As they stepped forward to draw for their lots, Marston agreed with Morris that they were 'upon the whole – very unfit for the business they have undertaken. Barbers, Taylors, Shoemakers and all kinds of mechanics, bred and used to live in great towns, they are inured to habits very unfit for undertakings which require hardiness, resolution, industry and patience.' 'Indulging their cursed republican principles,' Marston noted, a number were left out of the first draft. He was annoyed with what he considered 'a set of Licentious villains whose only motive for coming here seems to have been the King's Provisions and a short respite from that Fate which ever must attend men of their character.' Morris set to work and prepared a list of his own and laid out two blocks for those omitted from the draft. Those who drew good lots of land were pleased; to those with wet or rocky soil Morris offered better lots; but most, finding they must go to the back of the town for better land, refused to move. Relocating those who would move, by the end of May Morris had most of the Loyalists on lots of land in tents and pole huts, clearing their land for log houses and permanent homes of sturdy frame construction.[8]

Until their arrival in Port Roseway the only characterization of the Associates was in their assessment of themselves as zealous Loyalists devoted to their King. Upon their meeting with the surveyors they immediately emerged in a very different light. As the days passed, Marston and Morris wrote many harsh words about the Associates, which might be dismissed as expressions of haughty and irascible tempers if others had not condemned them in as virulent terms. Where others failed to note that many were persons of refinement, Marston felt keenly 'for the distress of the sensible feeling part, who have come from easy situations to encounter all the hardships of a new plantation and who wish to submit cheerfully to the dispensations of Providence.' Morris also recognized that there were 'sensible good men among them.' The opinion the Port Roseway Associates held of themselves was as people who deserved consideration because of their loyalty to the British crown, and who were 'under no obligations' to government 'for the land nor the favors conferred on them.' Their attempt to place all their members on an equal footing, the losers of vast estates with penniless city dwellers, brought unhappiness upon themselves and others. The intention of the Associates to exclude the King's grant in Port Roseway from all but themselves; their determination that all decisions affecting their welfare should be settled by themselves in meetings of the Association; their discontent, mutinous inclinations, noncooperation and the frivolity and lack of responsibility of many of their numbers, angered those who strove earnestly to found for them and with them a lasting town on the shores of Port Roseway. Marston pinpointed a source of the confusion and unhappiness that developed in Port Roseway when he wrote, 'These people are like sheep without a shepherd. They have no men of abilities among them. Their captains, chosen out of the body at New York, are of the same class as themselves... they are the best men they have. Sir Guy Carleton did not reflect that putting 16 illiterate men into commission, without subjecting them to a common head, was at best contracting the mob.' Confident in their ability to govern themselves, to shape and mold their community in what Marston termed their 'cursed republican town meeting spirit,' they would have resented Carleton's appointment of one person to direct and supervise the founding of the town.[9]

During the weeks of June and July many hundreds of Loyalist refugees came to Port Roseway: in June came the companies of Moses Pitcher, with 177, and James Cox, with 188; in July came 162 with Robert Wilkins, 152 with John Speirs, 206 with James Miller. With Duncan Cameron came 169 and with Nicholas Dean, 116. Many who came did not associate themselves in a company but entered their names at the office of the Adjutant-General, Oliver DeLancy, for free passage in one of the transports. Others neither joined a company nor applied for transportation. They slipped away on the tide in ships lifting their sails for the ports where they wished to go. Masters of ships sailing to those ports advertised in the New York papers. On June 12 the sloop *Industry*, William Marquis, master, was about to turn her bow for Port Roseway and St. John. 'For freight or passage apply to Mr. VanDuzer, near the White Hall Stairs.' On July 31 the fast sailing schooner *Polly*, Adam Watson, master, was ready to sail for Port Roseway and St. John; on August 5 the brig *Tyger* was waiting to sail to Port Roseway. Those interested for freight or passage were to apply at the office of McAdam, Watson and Company. In October the brig *Lovely Lass*, John Keaquick, master, lay at Roache's wharf below the Coffee House with excellent accommodation for passengers destined for St. John and Port Roseway.[10]

Vessels to and from Nova Scotia during the months of May, June and July, as listed in the returns of the commissionary general's office, show that many had been to Port Roseway with passengers and supplies. Some made two and three trips during the summer and early fall. Among the first to sail to Port Roseway in May were the *Charming Nancy*, John Clark, master; the *Elizabeth*, commanded by Michael Hodgson; the *Hero*, George Budnet, master; *Three Sisters* under the command of John Wardell; and the *London Frigate*, 441 tons, with the company of Captain James Dole and under the command of Captain Hugh Watts. In June came the schooner *Betsey and Sally* with family effects; the sloop *Fanny* with merchandise; the *Apollo*, 361 tons, commanded by John Adamson. In July came the brig *Charming Polly*,

KING'S BOUNTY

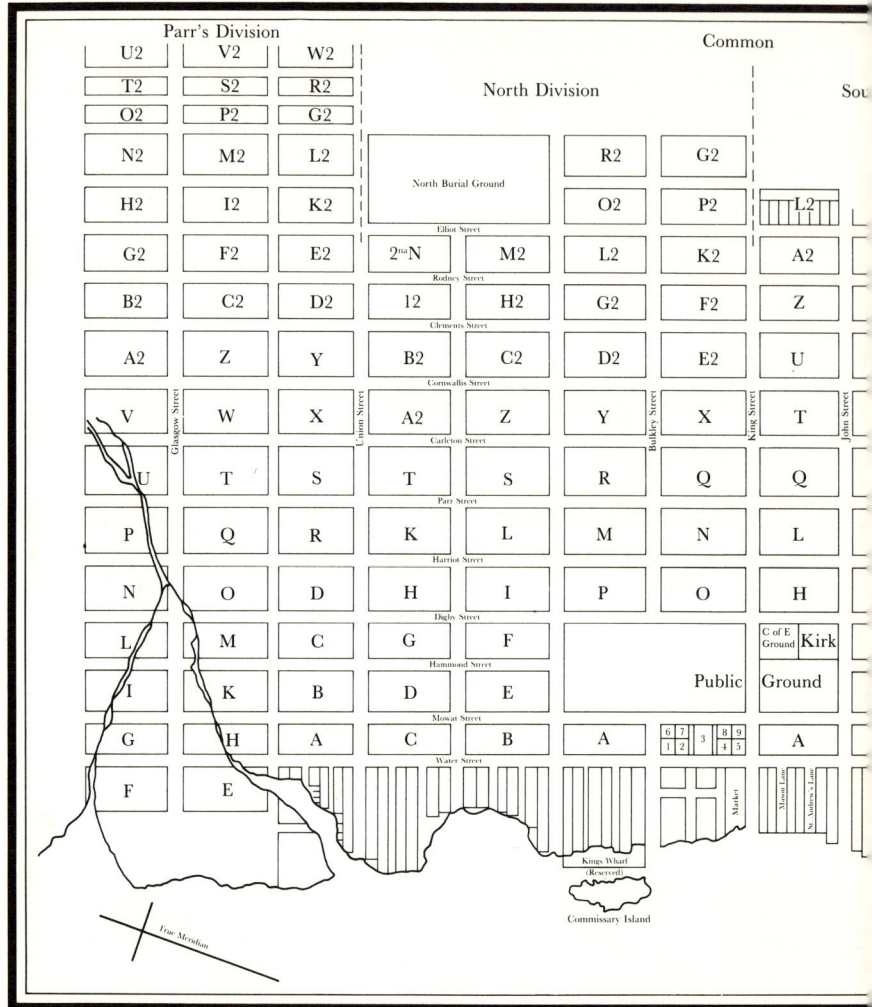

Map of Shelburne compiled from early plans of the town.

ARRIVAL AND EARLY DAYS IN SHELBURNE

C2	Q	R	S2				
X	P	O	I2	K2	L2	M2	N2
W	M	N	H2	G2	P2	E2	D2
R	L	K	Y	Z	A2	B2	C2
O	D	F	T	U	V	W	X
N	C	E	B	C	F	S	R
K	B	G	A	D	E	P	Q
G	A		G	H	I	O	N
E	H				K	L	M
C	I						

St. John's Division | Patterson's Division

South Burial Ground

St. George Street, Charlotte Street, Thomas Street, Fanning Street, Morris Street, Prince Street, Duke Street

St. John Square Market
Brew House Lane
Cove
Kings Ship Reserved
Battery Point
Rose Island Basin
Rose Island
St. Patrick's Lane
Rodney Lane
William Street

59

J.H. Burton, master; the *Diana*; the *Esther*, Captain Robert Gill, master. Topping all others in scuttling back and forth between New York and Port Roseway was the Kingston, of 338 tons, John Atkinson, master. She first sailed to Port Roseway in May, with 109 passengers, and was back and forth between Port Roseway and New York in May, June, July, September and October, making a final trip in November.[11]

THE CAROLINA LOYALISTS

In addition to Loyalists from New York were those from the Carolinas. They came to Halifax in November 1782, some 300 to 500 refugees, disbanded soldiers and Blacks, in the transports bringing the cannon from Charleston. They were the most distressed of the newcomers. 'The wretched situation that those poor people came in,' Parr wrote Evan Nepean 'has obliged me to apply to Mr. Townshend to represent to the Lords of the Treasury, the great distress they must be in at their first settling for want of Boards and Nails' and where 'there is not a Hutt or any kind of covering for them at the places they are to go to. Those from Charleston are in a much more miserable situation than those from New York coming almost naked from the burning sands of South Carolina to the frozen coast of Nova Scotia destitute of almost every necessary of life. Some Provisions must be made for them from home, or I must be allowed to make some for them here.' They 'stand in great need of clothing, and the whole for Tools, particularly those of Husbandry.'[12]

Shortly after their arrival in Halifax Colonel Hambleton,[13] spokesman for the Carolina refugees, met Joseph Pynchon and heard of Port Roseway. He was immediately interested in the proposed settlement and wished for some or all of his people to join with the Associates in its founding. Pynchon hesitated to give a definite answer, as Governor Parr had selected another part of the province for their settlement. Undaunted, Colonel Hambleton departed for New York to discuss with Carleton the settlement of his refugees. At the same time, some of the Carolinians individually asked Governor Parr for permission to join the Port Roseway Associates and for grants of land. He consented, provided that the Associates approved. In New York Colonel Hambleton was successful in his bid for land at Port Roseway. Provisions and other supplies were ordered for his refugees 'in the same manner and in an equal proportion' to the allotments to other refugees going to Nova Scotia, and 'as soon as the season renders it advisable' they were to be sent. The provisions were to be allotted to them for one year by the commisary at Halifax from His Majesty's stores in the proportions of a full allowance to 129 men, 130 women and youths, and 24 Black servants, and half allowance to 65 children, a total of 115,157 and a half rations

ARRIVAL AND EARLY DAYS IN SHELBURNE

without rum.[14]

There are no records as to how many of Colonel Hambleton's refugees came to Port Roseway nor is there a list of their names. From Loyalist claims and town records, some from the Carolinas can be identified. Most prominent among them was Colonel Samuel Campbell of the North Carolina Militia, who was already on his way to Port Roseway on May 7, when Simeon Perkins noted in his diary: 'Two small Schooners from Halifax, with people for Roseway, came in here in the Night. A Colonel Campbell is in one of them. He is said to be a man of Property, has several Black Slaves with him. They go out again this morning.' Others were John and Peter Blewer, John and Abraham Freitz, John McLeod, Soirle McDonald, Jacob Strhum, Daniel and Peter Michaeler, Conrad Marks, John Doris (Dores), George Long, and Adam Bower and his sons Charles and Philip.

EXTENDING THE TOWN SITE

With hundreds of Loyalists pouring into Port Roseway, many more town lots were needed for their accommodation. Despite the ruling of the Port Roseway Associates that only they and the few they chose to admit should have lots of land in their town, the hundreds of homeless families had to be provided with land. To the south of the town a new division, St. John's Division, was laid off and marked into house lots. By early August a second division south of St. John's Division, Patterson's Division, was surveyed and cut into lots; and a division named Parr, in honour of the governor, was marked off at the north of the town. To meet continued need for land, in September blocks were surveyed at the back of the town, extending it six blocks to the eastward, with six long streets running north and south (Parr, Carleton, Cornwallis, Clements, Rodney, and Elliott). In June, Morris and Lawson sounded the depths of the harbour in front of the town for wharf lots and good anchorage; and in early July, assisted by Benjamin Marston, Morris surveyed the shore in front of the town from north to south and marked off the water and warehouse lots for North and South Divisions and later for Parr's Division. In September Marston surveyed the shore south of George Street to the end of Patterson's Division and marked it into water lots to be given only to those with the ability to improve the lots and in want of places for stores and wharves.

Following instructions from Governor Parr to lay out in the township, ungranted land lying between Port Roseway and Annapolis in farm lots not exceeding 500 acres, Marston surveyed 34 fifty acre lots on the west side of the harbour and up the west bank of the river to Herring Falls. Above the 50 acre lots, a number of 500 acre lots were surveyed on both banks of the river. South of the town, Charles Mason began the survey in July for the 50 acre farm lots along the eastern shores of the harbour, around the point of land and up the western side of the Jordan to a little below the falls, a vast acreage of wilderness known as Mason's Division. By early fall the land along the western shores of the harbour (Gunning Cove and Churchover) was surveyed, and Oliver Lyman, one of the assistant surveyors, was busy exploring the river and land toward Annapolis. Below the town, south of Patterson's Division and the 100 acre allotment to the shipbuilder, David Thompson, Governor Parr ordered a large tract of land surveyed for himself, a 500 acre farm which he named Bowood, after the Earl of Shelburne's country estate in Wiltshire. Here he thought he might 'build a small house near a little cove, to which he could go once a year.' East of the town, butting the eastern boundary, a large block of land was marked for a common, which was later divided into small farm lots held by licence of occupation.

Burial grounds were set aside, comprising a small plot south of the town and a large plot east of Elliott Street in North Division. As the surveyors continued their work in 1784 and 1785, Alexander McNutt's New Jerusalem and land beyond its borders was cut into lots, along the river banks from the Cape Negro (Clyde) River to the Sable, around the harbours and the fishing coves, and far into the wilderness along the paths blazed into the woodlands, along the ways to Annapolis and to Tusket and to Barrington.[15]

From time to time Marston and Morris noted the dates on which the lots were drawn by the Loyalists. They drew for house lots in the centre of town beginning on May 22 and continued to draw as the lots were made ready. The first water lots below Water Street south of King Street were drawn in early July, and the first of the 50 acre lots, those on the west side of the harbour and along the west bank of the river, were allocated on July 12. Some lots in St. John's Division and in Patterson's were ready in July and early August, and a few were already allocated in Parr's Division by August 19. Tickets for the lottery were made by Marston from sheets of paper. On each he wrote the number of a lot and carefully twisted the sheet into a roll. As each applicant drew for a lot, the number on the ticket and the name of the person were noted by Marston in his book of locations, and the name of the applicant was added to the ticket he had drawn. 'The people yesterday drew for their 50 acre lots,' Marston wrote on July 12. 'They have left many out of the drawing who are equally entitled to a lot as those who have drawn. They want government, more knowledge and a small portion of generosity. They wish to engross this whole grant into the hands of the few who came in the first fleet, hoping the distresses of their fellow Loyalists, who must leave New York will oblige them to make purchases.' Then there were speculators to watch for, 'who get house lots in order to make money out of them... one... I suspect has already drawn a lot and sold it.'[16]

Marston's suspicions were well founded. 'Town lots at Port Roseway of 60 by 120 feet,' one of the Loyalists wrote a friend in New York, 'sell from 10 to 250 guineas.' Some of the speculators were not Loyalists but adventurers who inveigled the captains into adding their names to the lists prepared for Marston's guidance. One of these was a man from Penobscot, Maine, Henry Ross, who 'at the time of drawing was accidently here disposing of a cargo of lumber and was and is now a subject of the United States.' Three others were from Halifax. Spotting them for what they were, Marston struck their names from the list. One tried a bit of cajolery on Marston. 'A Capt. McLean has this evening sent me a green turtle, about seven lbs. I am obliged to him. He is to have a house lot, but this must not blind my eyes. He must run the same chance as his neighbours who have no turtle to send.'[17]

VISITORS, CELEBRATIONS AND FIRST IMPRESSIONS

Toward the end of June, on Wednesday the 25th, Major-General Patterson, Commander-in-Chief of His Majesty's Forces in Nova Scotia, came to see the new town of Port Roseway and to inspect the troops sent by Carleton to protect the town and harbour. 'General Patterson has been with us,' one of the Loyalists wrote enthusiastically, 'and promises every [thing] in his power.' He was well pleased with Morris' plan and report of the town, but to Benjamin Marston it was a day when 'not much business was done.' June was a round of events frowned upon by Marston and Morris, who were striving desperately to locate the hundreds of homeless people on their land: the King's birthday with no work on that day nor for several days after the festivities; dancing and bonfires in the streets at night; a ball somewhere in the town; a proposed duel between two of the captains narrowly averted; two boxing matches in which one of the captains was involved; a Free Mason festival on St. John's Day. 'The D___l is among these people... these things ought not to be here as yet.' A few days later Marston wrote with growing concern over the lack of order. 'The people here are suffering for want of a civil establishment, which to the shame of government is most scandalously neglected.'[18]

About this time James Courtney wrote of his first impressions of Port Roseway:

'On our arrival here dark woods and dismal Rocks Cover'd the ground (which belonged to the Associated Loyalists) on my first going on shore after travelling five of six hours, returned quite dismayed, and yet had in the Course of my Ramble knocked down two brace of Partridges and one Hare, next time went further [and] still returned dissatisfied, I tho't Hunger look'd every wretch in the face that could not hunt or shoot for his subsistance... boasted Land of Cannaan my stay here shall be very [short] but I will first look at the Fishery we went & [return]ed well satisfied. Providence in this Article has been exceeding bountifull, fish never was more plenty nor easeyer come at, than from this place.

'We have got our town Lotts which is just large for a good House and Small Garden... Since the Trees are cut/ good down the Ground looks... far preferable to any about Halifax [and] I think equal to any I have seen in the Province, if... Encouragement is given by Government it will in a time be a fine Settlement.... [I am no]w determined to stay and think to do exceeding well.'

In Halifax Parr was writing in an equally enthusiastic letter that upwards of 3,000 refugees, exceedingly 'well pleased with their situation and reception,' were 'clearing the country and building a Town, (agreeable to a regular Plan sent them) at Port Bosway [sic], a most excellent Harbour 33 Leagues from hence W:S:W.'[19]

'THIS PLACE, SHELBURNE'

In the midst of building, Governor Parr came to see the new town springing up on the shores of Port Roseway. On Sunday, July 20, he arrived off Point Carleton (Fort Point) in His Majesty's sloop *La Sophie* and, with salutes booming from his ship as he disembarked and from the fort as he landed, he was received by the officers and shown the fortifications. On Monday he sailed up the harbour, dropped anchor off the town, and interviewed numbers of the Port Roseway settlers. Among those who clambered aboard was Benjamin Marston, who had been recommended to Parr as 'a gentleman of liberal education... and one who always supported the character of a man of integrity.' He appointed justices of the peace and discussed with Marston the plan of the town. On the whole, he was pleased with the layout of Port Roseway but disliked the scheme of the water lots.

On Tuesday morning, a fine, warm July day, Parr landed at the foot of King Street to see the town. Greeted by a discharge from the cannon on the shore, he proceeded up King Street, which was lined on either side by Loyalists under arms, to the place appointed for his reception[20] and was welcomed with an address by the newly appointed justices of the peace and principal inhabitants. In a short speech he signified his intention of naming the new settlement Shelburne, in honour of William Petty Fitzmaurice, 2nd Earl of Shelburne, later created the Marquess of Lansdowne. He drank to the King's health, to the prosperity of the town and district of Shelburne and to the Loyalists, each toast greeted with three cheers and a rumbling boom from the cannons. He then named as justices of the peace, James McEwen, a Boston Loyalist; James Robertson, printer and publisher of the

ARRIVAL AND EARLY DAYS IN SHELBURNE

first Shelburne newspaper; Joseph Pynchon and Joseph Durfee, leading founders of the Port Roseway Association; and Benjamin Marston; Henry Edward Knox, as notary public; and as coroner, Alexander Murray. Accompanied by the magistrates, he returned to *La Sophie* for a dinner given by Captain Mowat, with loyal toasts to the King, to the success of Shelburne, and to the Loyalists of Nova Scotia, echoed to the shores by royal salutes from *La Sophie*.

On Wednesday Governor Parr and his suite, attended by Captains Mowat and Elphinston of the Royal Navy, dined with the leading Loyalists at the home of James Robertson. In the evening the town gave a public supper and ball, 'conducted with the greatest Festivity and Decorum,' which did not break up until five o'clock the next morning, when Governor Parr departed for *La Sophie*, 'as highly pleased with the entertainment as the company appeared gratified and delighted by his presence.'[21]

Before he sailed Parr wrote to Sir Guy Carleton, proudly dating his letter, Shelburne, July 25: 'I have the honour to inform your Excellency of my arrival here (late Port Roseway) in the *Sophia*, Frigate, and that I have named the Town and District SHELBURNE. From every appearance I have not a doubt but that it will in a short time become the most flourishing Town for Trade of any in this part of the world, and the country will for agriculture.' On the same day he wrote to Lord Shelburne, again proudly dating his letter as written in Shelburne, where on July 22 he had 'had the heart felt satisfaction of shewing a small mark of my gratitude, by naming the first Harbour in the world after Your Lordship, and I flatter myself that the Town will in a very few years, be worthy of so fine a Harbour.... The Harbour is about five miles long, and three and a half broad, the depth of water from five to twelve Fathom, a safe Bay without it for Ships to Anchor in, a deep bold Shore without Rocks or Shoals, and good holding Ground.

'The Town stands upon a gentle rising Ground the situation most beautiful, the Land Good, with a prospect of its being very fertile, some good Timber, the Streets of Shelburne are laid out very regular at Right Angles, the Houses in great forwardness, Industry is seen in every Quarter. My being so particular may seem trifling, but it proceeds from the joy and pleasure I felt, at the universal satisfaction that appeared, upon my naming Your Lordship aloud, and the immediate firing of the Guns in the Town, the Fort, and the Sophie Frigate.'[22]

The name Shelburne was a most unhappy choice for a Loyalist town. Many of the Port Roseway Loyalists resented it bitterly, for they had no desire to honour the man who, as prime minister of Great Britain, had failed to protect their interests during the negotiations for peace. Some refused to call the town Shelburne, and one referred to it ruefully as 'Port Roseway alias Shelburne.' Three years later there was one who still rejected the name because Roseway was the name in his warrant. The Port Roseway Loyalists were not alone in their dislike of the name Shelburne. Sarah Winslow in Halifax deplored its use. 'After every thing that has been done that's horrid, that any part of the only elysium the Suffering ones have should be called by the name of Shelburne is rather too bad.' Benjamin Marston's only comment was, 'The name of this place Shelburne.'[23]

LATE SUMMER AND FALL OF 1783

During Parr's visit in Shelburne important decisions were being made in London. The promised action to revoke old unimproved grants in favour of regranting the land to Loyalist settlers had not as yet been sanctioned. At last, in response to a memorial stating the injury to Nova Scotia caused by the lack of improvement to many acres of the land granted to the early settlers, on July 24, Lord North sent instructions to Governor Parr to revoke all orders made for grants prior to January 1, 1774, where the terms of the grants had not been carried into action.[24]

Loyalists continued to pour into Shelburne. During Governor Parr's visit three transports arrived from New York with about 90 families. These, with nearly as many more from other parts of the old British provinces, were clamouring to be located on house lots that had not as yet been surveyed nor cleared for their settlement. From time to time the surveyors still received help from William Lawson, but little assistance came from the Loyalists, now busy with their houses. On two occasions Governor Parr noted their indifference and lack of co-operation. 'Some of the Loyalists,' he reported to Nepean, 'refuse to carry the chain in marking their own land without exorbitant pay.' To Lord Sydney he reported, 'As many surveyors as possible were obtained but the people for whose benefit they were engaged refused to give assistance unless paid for it.'[25]

Surveying and laying out the land for the Loyalists was one of Governor Parr's first considerations. He acknowledged the arrival of the embarkation lists from Carleton with the assurance that he had for some time been making every preparation in his power for the reception of the Loyalists and that the chief surveyor had, 'by my order, dispatched his Deputies with proper instructions to every district wherein they may make settlements to the best Advantage.' Also, in early May he wrote to the secretary of state that surveying had begun and that, because of the great number of refugees coming into the province, the work would involve considerable expense. He asked to be enabled to discharge this outlay. In October Parr reported that in the district of Shelburne, Port Mouton, and the coast between the two settlements, six surveyors had been working at 10 shillings a day and that each surveyor had two chainmen and an axeman to assist him. In April 1784, Charles Morris submitted a bill for £1,838.4s for laying out the lands for the Loyalists. Of this account he had paid on September 14 for surveying and laying out the town of Shelburne, to William Morris and his expenses, for chain bearers, axemen, rum and provisions, £175.0.5½; Benjamin Marston, deputy surveyor, £84.10; Charles Mason £78.5; Oliver Lyman £70.3.6; Christopher Tully £14. To pay the account of the surveyor general, Parr informed Lord North he had been obliged to draw for the sum of £1,838.4.0 as the surveyors would not proceed in laying out the land for the Loyalists without their pay.[26]

Despite the lack of assistance from the Loyalists, Marston located 183 newcomers on house lots on August 7, and on August 28, 158 were allotted land in Patterson's Division. These, with several others located in various parts of the town, swelled the population by several hundred persons, many of whom were not members of the Port Roseway Association and were a growing concern to the original founders of the town. Then on August 10 a new plan of the town and environs arrived from the surveyor general's office. It distressed the Associates and Marston for the reserved land entirely 'deranges all that has been done towards settling persons in the farming line, who are as yet quite unprovided for.' Later in the month Colonel Robert Morse, chief of the Royal Engineers, and Major Pitcairn, arrived with instructions from headquarters to prevent any timber being cut from the King's Wood, which Marston remarked was as yet uncertain 'where about that will be.' They wanted the magistrates to prevent any cutting on the reserved lands and to publish orders to that effect. This the magistrates stoutly refused to do, contending that one purpose of the reservation was for a common.[27]

A rough sketch of Shelburne and environs in the late summer of 1783 shows the reserves that distressed the Shelburne Loyalists. On both sides of the Roseway River the land was marked reserved from the upper falls to the mouth of the river, and on the west side of the river from the lower falls along the western side of the harbour to the undivided land at the end of Hart's Point – land for which the Loyalists wishing to have farms near the town had paid 12/6 a lot to have surveyed. South of the town a block of land two-and-one half miles wide was reserved for a common, and below it (on Sandy Point) were reserved plots of land scattered among the 50 acre lots surveyed by Mason as farm lots for the Loyalists. On Roseway Island (McNutt's Island) were two reserves and at Cape Negro was a large tract of land marked the 'Governor wants to Reserve.'[28]

The alarm of the Port Roseway Associates over the reserves and the disreputable persons pushing into their town is expressed in their attempt to stem the flow of undesirable persons into Port Roseway. Although Marston and Morris considered many of the Associates irresponsible and many from the lower classes, and Governor Parr regretted that there were few 'men of education and abilities among the first adventurers,' the Port Roseway Associates looked upon themselves with respect and had admitted into their association only persons they considered decent and honourable. On September 19, James Dole, then in New York, wrote to Sir Guy Carleton on behalf of the Associates, deploring the situation that was developing in Shelburne. 'Among all the grieviances that the Associated Loyalists have from time to time met with, no one situation bears any likeness to the present, or that deserves your Excellency's compassion and advice half so much, and as our Patron and first friend we Humbly beg leave to lay before you with the assurances given us by Sir Andrew Hammond, the Honourable Mr. Bulkeley, and confirmed by your Excellency's recommendation to Governor Parr that the Lands in the Township of Port Roseway... should be resarved [sic] and Excheated for us and us only we in consequence thereof embarked with your Excellency's assistance and began to Clear, Build on, and Cultivate, and to survey and lay out fifty acre lots for each of us, convenient to water carriage, for our better accommodation having no other mode in our power of conveying Timber & firewood, stone, Brick clay, Fish &c in Boats from said Lots to Town'... which work 'we effected... at no less a sum then sixty thousand Guineas.' 'Governor Parr furnished us with three surveyors at the Public cost to lay out the Town lots, and to our great surprise has resarved Two miles length of the best ground along the side of our Town, and ordered his surveyors to lay out Town lots for all sorts and ranks of men that come here.... he has also of late sent a plan... marking a great number of miles of resarved lands, being part of the very lands we have Improved and paid for the Surveys at our own expence. We on our part could freely wish a resarve to be made of no more Lands then is wanted for His Majestys Public works &c and we have the well grounded confidence,' Dole assured Sir Guy, 'that your Excellency from your well known goodness and sound knowledge of Justice, will recommend that we are righted, and we in particular who made Port Roseway of Value, and gave life to the Immigration of the many Bashful subjects who is now obliged to march.'[29]

Carleton was indeed hard-pressed, with the Port Roseway Associates begging him not to allow 'all sorts and ranks of men' to have lots of land in their town, and the fact that conditions in America were such that the Loyalists were forced to flee from their homes and seek sanctuary in a land still British. Only a few weeks before James Dole's letter reached him, Carleton had written to Elias Boudinot, president of Congress, that 'the violence of the Americans, which broke out soon after the cessation of hostilities, encrease the number of their Countrymen who look to me for escape from threatened destruction,' and that 'these terrors have of late been so considerably augmented that almost all within these lines conceive the safety, both of their property and of their lives, depend upon their being removed by me.'[30]

As disturbing to the Loyalists as the hostility of the Americans and their resolves to 'oppose every enemy of the just rights and liberties of mankind from having lot or portion among us' was the 'inglorious peace' which recognized American independence and permitted Congress to agree only to 'earnestly recommend' to the States the restitution of Loyalist property and rights. To a Georgia Loyalist the terms were 'most shameful to Britain' for 'no other provision has been made than just recommending' the Loyalists 'to the clemency of congress, which is in fact casting them off altogether.' To a Loyalist of the northern states the terms of the peace were equally distressing. 'Our fate seems now decreeded and we left to mourn out our days in wretchedness. No other resource... but to submit to the tyranny of exulting enemeys or settle a new country.... In all our former sufferings we had hope to support us – being deprived of that is too much. Was there ever an instance – where such a number of the best of human beings were deserted by the government they have sacrificed their all for? The open enemys of Great Britain have gained their point, (and more than ever they could have had impudence to have asked for) – while their persevering Noble Friends, who have suffered and toiled for years and whom they were bound by every tie of honour and gratitude to assist, are left without friends, without fortune.'[31]

As the Loyalists suspected, Congress' agreement to earnestly recommend to the States that their rights and property should be restored to them went unheeded. Those who had suffered to obtain for themselves and their country the advantages they had envisioned would be theirs with their independence from Great Britain, were not willing to share those advantages with those who had stood against them. As the months passed and tempers cooled, the resolves to oppose all those who had opposed them were softened. As early as the fall of 1783 some of the southern states issued proclamations relaxing the laws of confiscation and banishment, and the sale of Loyalist estates was stopped. Measures, a few months later, were adopted to permit former residents to return from their years of enforced exile with the right to own property and with the assurance that their offences would be overlooked, all except that of murder. The spirit of forgiveness in the southern states induced many Loyalists to slip back to their old places of residence rather than face an unknown land.[32]

The relaxation of confiscation and banishment laws came slower in the northern states, and Loyalists dreading a strange land and the cold winters of Nova Scotia could not return to their former homes. The two miles of good ground along the side of the town, which the Port Roseway Associates complained had been ordered by Governor Parr surveyed into town lots 'for all sorts and ranks of men,' Parr had in mind for some of the hundreds of homeless refugees barred by the resolves of the States from returning to their homes. With these hundreds of distressed persons pouring into Nova Scotia, 'Government has not yet honored me with commands relative to this vast Emigration' Parr informed Lord Shelburne. 'I have hitherto acted in the dark, to the best of my abilitys; and flatter myself what has been done will be approved of, as they have proceeded from the best motives, humanity and justice.' As late as October 25, when the migration to Nova Scotia was almost over, Parr had still not received the instructions he wanted and he appealed to Lord Shelburne to honour him with 'some Instructions how to act in a Crisis which never happened to any Governor before.'[33]

The crisis which Parr feared to face without special instructions, the coming of the last shiploads of refugees, filled the streets of Shelburne with hundreds of people. Men who had fought in the provincial regiments, their wives and children; Loyalists who had tarried in New York hoping the evacuation of the city would be delayed; disbanded soldiers from the British army enticed to the shores of Nova Scotia by the offer of free grants of land; freed slaves for the first time in their lives making homes of their own.

Ships for the fall fleet and for the final evacuation of New York were in preparation by midsummer. A sufficent number of ships to carry the vast numbers going to Nova Scotia with their household effects was difficult to find. Brook Watson wrote to Adjutant-General Major MacKenzie on August 19, 'that great numbers of Respectable Loyal Families, driven from their homes for the part they have taken during the late war and now claiming the assistance of Government to move them to their intended asylum in Nova Scotia were in want of vessels to carry them' and which were 'not to be had unless His Excellency will be pleased to authorize me to hire them on the usual Terms and conditions, to be discharged in this Country, which will be attended with much less expence than should they be hired by the navy to be discharged in England according to their customs.' With permission to hire vessels in America, Brook Watson searched the American seaports, in Philadelphia and along the coast nearer New York. At the same time the British Government was 'continuing to procure every vessel that can be of use to you' Lord North informed Carleton, 'and the admiralty will see a considerable Quanity of Tonnage is on its way to you.'[34]

ARRIVAL AND EARLY DAYS IN SHELBURNE

As government officials laboured to acquire ships to carry them to their intended destinations, the Loyalists were busy getting themselves organized into companies, obtaining recommendations as to their loyalty and permission to sail in the transports and other vessels. In the month of August Carleton commissioned ten captains of companies going to Port Roseway to sail in the fall fleet: on August 26, Bartholomew Sullivan, John Van Norden, John Ackerman, Joseph Dowers, Joseph Bell, Samuel Kirk, Daniel Wright, James Hamilton, Valentine Nutter; and on August 31, Thomas Leonard, each captain to be assisted by two of their company's commissioned lieutenants. In September nine captains were commissioned: on September 9, John Minshull, John Huggeford; September 13, Joshua Pell, Robert Appleby, Edmond Ward; September 16, Nathaniel Rae Thomas; on September 20 John Aymar and Patrick Wall, and on September 23, Richard Jenkins. Five of these men, Daniel Wright, Joshua Pell, Edmond Ward, Nathaniel Rae Thomas and Valentine Nutter, with their companies, were Port Roseway Associates delayed in sailing with the others in the spring fleet. With these companies came the companies of Gideon Palmer and Hugh Breen. Also in the fall of 1783 came the companies of Goldsburg, Little, Neill, Hayden, Jones, Blanchard, Savage and Loring.[35]

In August and September the captains of the companies sailing in the fall fleet posted instructions for their associates. Those in John Van Norden's company were to have their luggage at the Fly Market ready for embarkation by August 13. On September 17 Thomas Leonard informed his company that the ship *Friendship*, then lying in the North River opposite the woodyard, was ready for their luggage. Daniel Wright, impatient with the laggards in his company, assured them 'their room' would be filled by people from the army 'as it is not expected that the ship will lye by the wharf for no other purpose than to indulge indolent people.' As the days passed for tarrying in New York, the captains in sharp terms urged their companies to board the transports. If they were not on board the ship *William*, Captain Potts, master, by three o'clock on September 20, Robert Appleby warned his associates, their names would be returned to the Board and they would be precluded from their passage at government expense. Similar warnings were issued by John Aymar sailing in the *Nancy* and Patrick Wall in the *Kingston*. Richard Jenkins cajoled his Loyalists: 'Notice to all those that are to be shipmates with me in my company not forget this night to drink to your Wives and Sweet-hearts, as I expect them, one and all, on board tomorrow morning to turn the windlass and have a pleasant sail to Staten Island, and there is no time to be lost. Wind and tide wait for none.'[36]

The fall fleet got under way from New York on Monday, September 15, and shiploads of refugees continued to come to Nova Scotia until the final evacuation of New York in late November. About 400 families of those sailing in the fall fleet were expected in Shelburne. Marston mentions the arrival of newcomers on September 24, 27 and 30; on October 10, 12, and again on the 14. On Monday October 13 he met with the captains of the five companies recently arrived who 'agreed to put their people below the town for the present.' The following day he went with others of the newcomers to show them the ground where they were advised to build shelters for themselves for the winter. 'They don't seem on the whole to favour the idea of hutting,' Marston observed and few were satisfied with the land available to them. 'They murmur and grumble because they can't get located as advantageously as those who have been working hard these 4 months.' Later he noted with satisfaction 'the last comers have at length taken the advice I first gave them to hut as soon as they could against winter.'[37]

Besides the Loyalists who came in organized companies in the transports, were others who requested grants of land at Port Roseway from Governor Parr or from Carleton. Among these were Nehemiah Hayden and Benjamin Griffith with others, chiefly ship carpenters, who wished to open a shipyard in Port Shelburne, and Samuel Burling, a New York merchant and shipowner, who was willing to relinquish his property in America for an asylum in Nova Scotia. With these groups of Loyalists came Lieutenant Colonel Abraham Van Buskirk, of the 3rd New Jersey Volunteers, with a number of settlers, mainly farmers, who wished to have farm land near Shelburne. Other families of Dutch ancestry came in the fall of 1783 in the schooner *Cherry Bounce* and lived in log houses they built near Robertson's Cove below Patterson's Division. Along with the Loyalist refugees were a number of New York merchants recommended by Carleton to be given grants of lots with a view to their commercial undertakings.[38]

THE KING'S PILOTS

Others who sought shelter in Shelburne were a number of pilots who had been employed by the British during the war. On July 4, Admiral Digby recommended 15 pilots to Governor Parr as deserving subjects of the King's bounty since they had lost all they possessed and dared not return to their homes. He requested land for them at Port Roseway or wherever they wished to go. By September the pilots were in Shelburne and Benjamin Marston sent them to Gunning Cove, and requested the surveyor general to send a deputy surveyor to mark off house lots for them, 60 feet by 120 feet. On October 2 Marston and Christopher Tully went to Gunning Cove and laid out house lots for seven pilots, and three weeks later Tully marked off five more lots in Pilot Town. An early map shows two blocks of lots for the

ARRIVAL AND EARLY DAYS IN SHELBURNE

King's pilots lying close to the shore and near the engineers' reserve on the north side of Gunning Cove.[39] Later the land was resurveyed and the shore from Robert Gow's lot beside the engineers' reserve to Isaac Wilkins' land was divided into 24 village lots lying like a fringe along the edge of the shore, with a 60 foot road, a lot for church and school, and a public lot for uses other than for church and school. Here seven pilots received village lots.[40] Westward, and at the back of the village lots, were six 50 acre farm lots for the six pilots, Gideon Boyce, William Rowland, William Hargill, Samuel Edwards, Henry Killigrove, and James Neal. There were other pilots. One who lived at Cape Negro, William Mullneaux; and five Black pilots on McNutt's Island: London and James Jackson, Richard Leach, James Robinson, Joseph Restine. For their services to government during the war the pilots were placed on half pay. 'No people among the Loyalists,' a visitor in 1787 wrote of the pilots, 'have exerted themselves more successfully than they in rendering their present situation comfortable.'[41]

DISBANDED SOLDIERS
The Provincial Troops

With the Loyalists who came in the fall of 1783 were several hundred disbanded soldiers from the Provincial or British American regiments and men from the British army who wished to settle in Nova Scotia. For none of the Loyalists was the recognition of the independency of the thirteen colonies a deeper blow than for the men of the Provincial Troops who had struck out at the Americans, had fought beside the British, and had harried and despoiled rebel property. As raiders and despoilers they were as feared by the Americans as the rebel raiders were by the Loyalists. To expect amenity from those they had injured was more than even the most sanguine could hope for. In alarm for their future safety, the men of the Provincial Troops appealed to Carleton to obtain for them grants of land in British territory; permanent provision for disabled noncommissioned officers, private soldiers, widows and orphans; arms and ammunition, clothing, farming and building tools; and the rank of officers to be permanent with half pay on the reduction of their regiments. They waited anxiously for word from Britain, but no word came. In August Carleton was informed of His Majesty's instructions that 'the abstracts for the British American Forces are to be made up to the day of their being disbanded and 14 days pay from that day without deduction is to be given to each of the noncommissioned officers, Drummers and private men.'[42]

The lack of concern for their welfare evoked 'the most serious apprehensions.' 'We flattered ourselves,' they wrote Carleton, that 'our memorials transmitted to His Majesty would be answered. The services of

On the right is the Stephen Shakespear house at the southwest corner of George (formerly St. George's) and Water Streets, built of logs in 1783 and later clapboarded. Watercolour by Mrs. Annie Bruce. (Courtesy Miss Marjorie Bruce)

the British American Regiments for the space of six years we forbear to mention. But lament at the end thereof we should be disbanded without any positive subsistance for the officers or a provision for the men equal to that of the American Loyalists in general.' Until there was a decisive answer to their application for assistance, they requested the continuation of pay to the different corps, a year's provisions to be granted from the first day of May, 1784, the earliest date when they could be allotted their land, and tools and implements of husbandry.[43]

In late August, Carleton received instructions that all the British American corps and some from the British regiments were to be disbanded 'forthwith in Nova Scotia.' Having received no special instructions respecting the British American Corps he suggested to Governor Parr, that in his opinion, they should be considered as refugees in the number of acres allotted each man for 'many of them certainly have equal pretension on account of the property they have been obliged to abandon.' Their having taken up arms and served during the war was an additional merit and Carleton recommended them to Parr 'in the warmest manner to your protection and favor.'[44]

The earliest returns from the commissary's office, without differentiating between the British American Troops and the men of the British Army choosing to settle in Nova Scotia rather than return to their homeland, reported 983 as gone to Port Roseway (704 men, 140 women, 139 children). By the summer of 1784, 17 British American Regiments were listed with disbanded soldiers in Shelburne. These were: 7 men of the 84th Regiment (Royal Highland Emigrants) raised in Canada in 1775 by Lieutenant Colonel Allen McLean; 24 from the British Legion; 15 of the King's American Regiment; 1 from the Royal Garrison Battalion; 3 from the Prince of Wales American Regiment; 2 from the Nova Scotia Volunteers; 6 from the 1st, 5 from the 2nd, and 13 from the 3rd New Jersey Volunteers commanded by Lieutenant Colonel Abraham Van Buskirk; 3 from the 1st and 5 from the 2nd Battalion DeLancey; 6 from the Queen's Rangers; 1 each from Emmerick's Corps, the New York Volunteers, the 60th Regiment; 3 from the King's Royal Regiment of New York, and 4 from the King's Carolina Volunteers. In all, this was a total of 100 soldiers – with their families, 213 persons (48 women, 65 children).[45]

British Troops
In February 1783, Governor Parr wrote to the Honourable Thomas Townshend, Secretary of State, suggesting that Nova Scotia being a province of great extent, the greater part unpeopled and the rest thinly inhabited, it would tend to augment the population, especially the working classes 'were it left to the option of the men of any corps now here... and which may be hereafter disbanded, to remain and become settlers.' In early May Governor Parr was informed that His Majesty 'very much approves of the proposal of leaving it to the option of the men of any corps which may be disbanded in Nova Scotia to remain and become settlers.' At the same time the officers commanding His Majesty's forces in Halifax were instructed that His Majesty had consented to grant to every noncommissioned officer who settled in Nova Scotia after his regiment was reduced, 200 acres of land, to every private, 50 acres 'exclusive of what he shall be entitled to in right of his Family,' to be discharged of all fees of office and quit rents for the first ten years. As a further inducement for them to remain and become settlers, each man was to be furnished out of the public stores with the usual ration of provisions for one year and was to be permitted to retain his arms and accoutrements. As plans for the disbandment of the troops proceeded, Carleton urged General Fox to have the disbanded men discharged as near

as possible to the lands where they were to settle and to impress on the governor the importance of determining the spots where each corps was to settle. By September 29 most of the men of the British regiments had received their discharge and those going to Nova Scotia were ready to sail. Their accounts were settled and paid to October 24 and each man had been given two pairs of stockings, two pairs of mitts, a pair of shoes, extra clothing and an axe and a spade. On their arrival they were to be victualled on board the transports until the day of their landing from which time the King's allowance of one year's provisions was to commence.[46]

With the troops ready to sail, Carleton reported to Lord North on October 6 that transports had been allotted for the men of the British regiments destined for Nova Scotia, for those 'desirous of settling in that Province,' and that they would sail in a few days. They were to remain in their regiments as a militia and their officers were to continue in their respective ranks and were to be obeyed as such until the governor of Nova Scotia made other arrangements.

Many of the men of the regiments were allotted to transports bearing companies of Loyalists. Men of the 17th Dragoons sailed in *L'Abondance* with Captain Valentine Nutter's Loyalists, and sailing in the *Clinton* with the soldiers of the 7th and the 37th Regiments was the company of Captain Joshua Pell. Men of the 22nd Regiment sailed in the *Nancy*, Robert Bruce, master, with the company of Captain Samuel Kirk and in the *Prosperous Armilla*, Thomas Atkinson, master, with the Loyalists of Captain Joseph Bell's company. In the *Castor* with Joseph Dower's company came 16 soldiers of the 43rd Regiment and in the *Friendship* with Thomas Leonard's Loyalists were 27 of the same regiment. Men of the 38th Regiment came in the transports *G.D. Russia* with John Minshull and his Loyalists and in the *Charming Nancy* with John Huggeford's company. In the brig *Hopewell* with Captain Edmond Ward's company of Loyalists and in the *Charming Nancy* came the 23rd Regiment, soldiers of the Royal Welsh Fusiliers, and in the *Congress* the men of the 57th Regiment.

By the summer of 1784 there were men from 23 of the British Regiments waiting in Shelburne for their farm land. With those listed above there were soldiers from the Artillery; from the 80th Regiment; and from the 76th or MacDonald's Highlanders. Others were from the 42nd, the Royal Highland Regiment; the 40th Regiment; the 54th; the 63rd; the 64th; and the 70th. There were soldiers who had fought in battles in the southern states – Fraser's Highlanders, the 71st Regiment; men of the 74th Regiment, the Argyle Highlanders; and men from the 82nd, the 65th and the 79th Regiments; and 22 from the Duke of Cumberland Regiment. With the British regiments were a number of disbanded Hessian soldiers who had served as

ARRIVAL AND EARLY DAYS IN SHELBURNE

mercenaries with the British troops mainly as 'jagers' or riflemen. On their coming to Shelburne they were allotted land in the north end of Shelburne in Parr's Division (block letter C). In the summer of 1784, in the muster of disbanded British troops there were 854 soldiers, with their wives and children, making a total of 1,272. Among the Hessians were 28 men and 29 women and children.[47]

The most desirable lots in the centre of the town already allocated, most of the disbanded soldiers were given lots in Parr's Division and south of the main town in Patterson's and in St. John's Divisions. Marston and Christopher Tully were staking off lots for disbanded soldiers and officers as early as September and continued in the assignment of land until November 22 when 383 soldiers drew for their lots. Inured to hardships, the soldiers cheerfully set about building winter huts on their small lots of land awaiting the day when their farm acreage would be ready for them.[48]

With the sailing of the last transports with the last of the refugees, the disbanded soldiers, and the freed Blacks, Carleton's work was finished. He had accomplished a phenomenal task efficiently and with integrity. Not all his decisions pleased the Port Roseway Associates, but they remembered him as a friend in their distress and named in his honour one of the long town streets, the point of land garrisioned and fortified to protect their town, and the small village on the shore south of the fort where men settled to fish and to farm.

LATE ARRIVALS

With the arrival of the last of the transports in early December the great influx of Loyalists, disbanded soldiers and freed Blacks was over. Others were to come in 1784 and in 1785. Isaac Wilkins was one who came in 1784, having remained in New York to settle his estates. Stephen Skinner was another who came later. He first went to England to plead redress for losses and did not settle in Shelburne until 1785. Others came from Florida and Jamaica and numbers moved in from Port Mouton where they had settled in the late fall of 1783. Among the arrivals in the spring of 1784 was Captain Gideon White from Chedebucto (Guysborough) where he had gone with men of the Duke of Cumberland Regiment. On April 6 he with 14 Shelburne Loyalists and disbanded soldiers petitioned Governor Parr for 15 fifty acre lots on the east side of the Port Roseway River which was land known to Gideon White from his days of trading with the early New England settlers. On the last day of April five companies of freed Blacks with the captains of their companies came from Port Mouton where they had wintered and had drawn their provisions with Colonel Molleson. They were given lots of land in Birchtown with other freed Blacks. Others, men of the British Legion and Loyalists, came from Port Mouton, driven to Shelburne by a disastrous fire that destroyed their new settlement of Guysborough, which had been laid out for them by William Morris in October 1783 on the shores of Port Mouton Harbour. Among those who came seeking land in Shelburne and acres to farm along the Jordan River and elsewhere were Captain Nathaniel Vernon and his son Lieutenant Nathaniel Vernon, Adjutant Michael Largin, Captain John Spencer, Francis Gilbert (Gildart), Donald McPherson, Lieutenant Donald McCrummon, Cornet William Robins, Private John Christy, and Privates Donald and John Cutt of the 76th Regiment.[49]

THE FLORIDA LOYALISTS

Few of the Loyalists who came from Florida were seasoned Floridians, for their homelands were Georgia and the Carolinas and even the northern state of Massachusetts. As the vigor of the Revolution pressed into the southern states and Loyalist adherents were harassed, Governor Tonyn of East Florida and Governor Chester of West Florida issued proclamations inviting Loyalists to leave the provinces in revolt and find a welcome and a refuge in the Floridas where they would receive grants of land and other advantages. The invitation drew hundreds to shelter in the wooded pine lands of the Floridas and on plantations along the St. John's and the St. Mary's Rivers. As distressed Loyalists they were given rations from the King's Bounty of provisions, from the storehouse of the commissary general in New York. On the surrender of West Florida by the British to Spain in 1781 and later when East Florida was ceded to the Spanish, many of the Loyalists who had sheltered there left for land still British. Of the many, several eventually came to Shelburne.

Transports bearing the Florida Loyalists to their chosen asylums sailed from St. Augustine in April, June and October 1784. Returns list 880 as gone to Nova Scotia: 725'whites, 155 negroes. Many, especially the Blacks, were destitute. Parr reported in late July '260 miserable wretches,' had arrived from St. Augustine, 'without a shilling, naked, destitute of almost every necessary of life.' To relieve the suffering of those who came to Shelburne, and were from West Florida, William Campbell received from Halifax on their behalf in February 1785, 56 yards of olive-coloured coating, 50 yards of wide baize, 3 ells of thread, 2 gross of buttons. Those 190 persons who came from Florida to Halifax in May 1785 were as distressed as those who came in 1784. They were ordered a year's provisions by General Campbell, and requested that each man should have a suit of clothes and a shirt, every man and woman and child a blanket and a pair of shoes, and each family a pair of sheets, a camp kettle and a proportion of wooden

ARRIVAL AND EARLY DAYS IN SHELBURNE

furniture. Campbell therefore sought donations to relieve their suffering. By the end of May numbers of these destitute Loyalists were in Shelburne, and in late July others from East Florida came in the transport *Spring*.[50]

For those who came from Florida to Shelburne there is only the sparse record of the number who came in 1784, in Thomas Courtney's company of 46 (19 men, 12 women, 5 children over 10, 10 under 10) from St. Augustine. From claims and town records emerge these few names: Patrick Lisitt, Samuel Anderson, John Fanning, William Campbell, George Rolleson, John and Richard Shave, Andrew Hewet, Jesse Gray, James Wright; Daniel Migler and Jean Henderson, formerly of the District of 96 in South Carolina; James Bruce and his family and John Allen Martin from West Florida. Some Loyalists who had lived in Florida came in private vessels. One of these brought Robert Ross, a West Florida planter and merchant who, with his brother George, established a flourishing mercantile business in Shelburne. Their old house and store is used today as a museum.

OFFICIAL LISTS OF PERSONS GOING TO PORT ROSEWAY

Parr's statement that there were upwards of 12,000 persons living in Shelburne in December 1783 perhaps explains the error so often repeated, of the vast numbers of Loyalists who came to Shelburne after fleeing their homes in the new United States. The earliest lists give 7,400 men, women and children going to Port Roseway, including 1,312 freed Blacks and servants. These lists were compiled from the returns of the commissary general's office, dated October 12, 1783, with the notation 'it is probable the numbers actually gone will fall far short.' Besides the 7,400 there were 83 in the engineer's department, 430 freed slaves that came in Black Companies, and 983 discharged men from the regiments with their wives and families, for a total of 8,896. In the same returns are the numbers who went to other locations: to St. John, 14,162; to Annapolis Royal, 2,530; to Halifax, 928. The earliest returns of the numbers of persons victualled in Shelburne as of January 8, 1784, gives a total of 8,645. This number included 4,700 Loyalists, 1,269 servants and freed Blacks living in Shelburne, 1,485 freed Blacks living in Birchtown, and 1,191 disbanded soldiers. The careful muster of Loyalists, disbanded soldiers, and Blacks made in the summer of 1784 under the direction of Colonel Robert Morse, chief of the Royal Engineers in North America, gives the total for Shelburne as 7,922. Of this number 1,521 were freed slaves living in Birchtown, 1,614 were disbanded soldiers which number included 72 Hessian soldiers living in Argyle, and 4,787 Loyalists. These numbers give 6,329 residents in the town of Shelburne in the late summer of 1784.[51]

THE ROYAL BOUNTY OF PROVISIONS

The importance of the Royal Bounty of Provisions to the Port Roseway Associates was emphasized in their arrangements with the officials. The fact that they were promised only six months provisions from the day of their landing induced many not to go to Port Roseway. That there would be a need for provisions beyond the six months was soon evident to Carleton, and on July 18 he issued directions to General Fox for the distribution of rations to the first of May next 'to those whose necessities may require it... to carry them thro' the winter.'[52]

Brook Watson, commissary general, anticipated a need for provisions long after the six months had expired and on June 10, 1783, submitted to Carleton a statement of provisions in storage and an estimate of the quantity of flour needed to May 1, 1784. Of beef, pork and butter there were sufficient quantities for every demand. It was necessary that he be given orders to issue contracts for flour. For Nova Scotia he needed 26,095 barrels, computed at 196 pounds per barrel. Flour was cheaper in America than in England. If, after waiting a reasonable time, he was not advised of a supply being sent out from Britain, he asked Carleton's approval to enter into contracts for sufficient quantities to be supplied in America.[53]

The Royal Bounty of Provisions in Nova Scotia was under the direction of General Fox and later was the responsibility of General Campbell, for distribution from the depot in Halifax to the various settlements of Loyalists and disbanded soldiers. In Shelburne two storehouses were built on the small island lying close to the shore of the town (Commissary Island). Edward Brinley was commissary. Some supplies were sent direct from New York to Shelburne by Brook Watson who, by July 22, had contracted for flour to be delivered at St. John and Port Roseway and requested orders for sending beef, pork and butter from New York in sufficient quantities to last until May 1, 1784. By late November 1,613 barrels of flour had been delivered on a contract for 2,000 barrels by Daniel Parker and Company, and 597 barrels on their contract for 1,500 barrels by Murray, Sansom and Company. The amount of stores in Shelburne on November 24 were given as 2,594 pounds of bread, 213,451 pounds of flour, 3,968 pounds of beef, and 277,736 pounds of pork. Of other provisions there were 32,744 pounds of butter, 512 pounds of rice, 3,912 pounds of oatmeal; of pease 85 gallons, vinegar 333 gallons, rum 3,196 gallons and molasses 7,672 gallons. These were being distributed at the rate of 6,939 rations per day, the figure updated a month later by Brinley to 7,089. On January 8, 1784, the numbers victualled by the Shelburne depot were 7,160 Loyalists, disbanded soldiers and servants, and 1,485 freed Blacks in Birchtown, a total of 8,645.[54]

ARRIVAL AND EARLY DAYS IN SHELBURNE

From the returns it was evident there would not be sufficient rations to meet the demands of all the settlers, and in late December Campbell requested a supply to be sent out from England in the early spring. He also ordered an examination of the claims of every individual to enable him to discriminate between those able to provide for themselves and those in distress. The examination revealed so many abuses of the King's Bounty, Campbell ordered a thorough investigation. This was known as the Muster of 1784, when 445 names were struck from the Shelburne list leaving a total of 7,478 recipients, still further reduced in 1785 to 6,520. In the meantime Parr joined with Campbell in requesting an extension of rations to the refugee settlements, and on March 31 Campbell issued a proclamation assuring those in need that the bounty of provisions would be continued until the King's pleasure was known. To meet the immediate needs of the refugees Campbell ordered a month's supplies, and in June came word from Whitehall that provisions would be extended for a year.[55]

In Shelburne there were special problems. Persons from Britain had arrived in the town with the intention of settling who were not within the description of refugees for whom the magistrates requested an allowance of rations. Without instructions for such emergencies, Campbell restricted rations to Loyalists and their servants, disbanded officers and soldiers and the freed Blacks until he was honoured with the King's command. A lack of sufficient rations to meet their needs plagued the Shelburne Loyalists. To relieve the distress in the new settlements, Parr permitted supplies to supplement the King's rations to be brought in from Boston and other American seaports, several of the provision-laden ships bending their course for Port Roseway. Even with extra supplies from American seaports to fill the larders of the King's storehouses, many suffered from a lack of adequate provisions during their first winter in Shelburne. They fared with less through the winter of 1785, when by early spring the cupboards were bare, 'no provisions of any kind in his Majesties Stores,' and without an early supply they were faced with the 'horrors of Famine.' Pinpointing a cause of their continuing need for provisions, after nearly two years of waiting, most of the settlers were still unprovided with farm land and 'the means of providing a future subsistance by agriculture' for themselves and others. Later, in 1785, to encourage the settlement of the farm lands, Alexander Leckie, with the first allotments of farm lots confirmed by grants, urged Brook Watson to obtain a continuance of one-third rations for three years 'to all people who shall actually settle on and improve the Farm Lands assigned to them,' but not to any others. One-third rations for farmers only, in the opinoin of the Shelburne Magistrates, was not sufficient. It was pointed out to Governor Parr that the difficulty encountered in securing land for cultivation had so long delayed the production of farm products for their support that all the Loyalists' savings had nearly, if not entirely, been expended. They requested, in a memorial to be sent to the King, a continuance of provisions for two years to all Loyalists. Provisions from the Royal Bounty continued to flow into Shelburne until the summer of 1787. By that time means of caring for the indigent had been established by the Court of Sessions and the taxable were assessed for their support.[56]

4
The Freed Blacks

A proclamation issued by General Sir Henry Clinton at Philipsburg, Pennsylvania, on June 30, 1779, offering protection within the British lines to Blacks who deserted the rebel standard and their rebel owners, gave to the slaves of rebels their first taste of freedom. As the news of the proclamation spread and was reaffirmed by the commanders of the British Army, hundreds of Blacks fled to the British lines. Of the hundreds who escaped, some 2,000 found sanctuary in New York; others reached Charleston and other strongholds of the British. By the summer of 1784, of those hundreds who escaped bondage, 1,531 were living in Shelburne and in Birchtown on the northwest arm of Shelburne Harbour.[1]

The proclamation issued by Sir Henry Clinton as the 'General and Commander in Chief of all His Majesty's Forces, within the Colonies laying on the Atlantic Ocean, from Nova Scotia to West Florida, inclusive,' stated, 'Whereas the Enemy have adopted a practice of enrolling Negroes among their Troops; I do hereby give Notice, That all Negroes taken in Arms, or upon any Military Duty, shall be purchased for a stated Price; the Money to be paid to the Captors. But I do most strictly forbid any Person to sell or claim Right over any Negro, the Property of a Rebel, who may take Refuge with any part of this Army: And I do promise to every Negro who shall desert the Rebel Standard, full Security to follow within these Lines, any Occupation which he shall think proper.'[2]

Once within the British lines the escaped Blacks were given certificates for their protection, declaring they came in consequence of the proclamations issued by the commanding officers of the British Forces. Blacks who reached New York were supplied with rations, and on the order of Brigadier-General Birch, commandant of the city of New York during the later years of the Revolution, they were provided with houses which had been abandoned by their rebel owners. As independent Blacks under the protection of the British, they worked on the fortifications, served the British officers, joined black military units, the Black Pioneers and other regiments. Skilled artisans hired themselves to employers; those with tools of their own worked for themselves.[3]

With the surrender of Cornwallis and the loss of America to the British, rumours that they were to be delivered to their masters, filled the Blacks with 'inexpressible anguish and terror.' For some the rumours became terrifying reality when their masters came from Virginia and the Carolinas and seized their slaves on the streets of New York and even dragged them from their beds. The proclamations, little more than bids by the British for cheap labour and a means of embarrassing the rebel owners of slaves, had offered only protection to the Blacks within the British lines. Faced with the despair of those under their command, the leaders of the British forces issued a proclamation declaring all Blacks free who had taken refuge in the British lines and had claimed the privilege of the proclamations respecting their protection and security. With the proclamation each was given a certificate from a commanding officer 'which dispelled all our fears and filled us with joy and gratitude,' Boston King, one of their number who came to Shelburne, was to remember.[4]

Proclamations freeing the Blacks did not deter their former owners from pouring into New York to claim what they considered their property. As the ships lay ready to sail, slave owners from Norfolk and Princess Ann Counties in Virginia protested that they had been to New York to collect their slaves (some 300 who had deserted their masters during the war); and that contrary to the treaty between Great Britain and America, in particular Article 7 which stated that negroes or other property belonging to Americans should not be taken from the country, they had found their Blacks on board transports bound for Port Roseway. Passports, they complained to Carleton, had been granted to them and the slave owners were informed they could not compel any of their slaves to return with them unless they did so voluntarily. They were apprehensive of a total loss unless their embarkation was stopped. Determined not to deprive the Blacks of their freedom, Carleton informed General Washington that he had given orders to prevent the carrying away of any slaves or other property belonging to the inhabitants of America and had appointed inspectors to visit the transports and

THE FREED BLACKS

enforce his orders. However, 'in the case of negroes who had been declared free previous to my arrival as I had no right to deprive them of that liberty I found them possessed of, an accurate register was taken of every circumstance respecting them so as to serve as a record of the name of the original proprietor of the negro and as a rule to Judge of his value.' By this method he hoped to prevent 'fraud and whatever might admit of different constructions is left open for future explanation or compensation.' Had the Blacks been denied permission to embark, he reminded Washington, they would have found various ways of quitting New York and their 'former owners would no longer have been able to trace them and would have lost in every way all chance of compensation.'[5]

Carleton's decision to allow the free Blacks to leave America was heartily approved by the British. 'The Removal of the Negroes whom you found in the possession of their Freedom upon your arrival in New York and who are desirious of leaving that Place,' Lord North wrote the commander-in-chief, 'is certainly an Act of Justice due to them from Us, nor do I see, that the Removal of those Negroes, who had been made free before the Execution of the Preliminaries of Peace, can be deemed any Infraction of the Treaty.'[6]

As Carleton had informed General Washington, before the embarkation of the Loyalists and Blacks on board the transports, he issued orders respecting Article 7 of the provisional treaty and the carrying of Blacks and other property belonging to Americans out of the country. Masters of vessels were cautioned, at their peril, 'not to commit any breach' of the article. To superintend the embarkation on board the transports, Carleton appointed Captain Chads of the Royal Navy, Captain Gilfillan and William Armstrong, assistant deputy quartermasters general, to represent himself; and on his request Messrs. Hopkins and Parker, Esquires, consented to attend for the Americans. Persons claiming Blacks as their property, either already embarked or about to be embarked on the transports, were to apply to those appointed, who were to call a board to examine the claims. Should doubts arise, the circumstances were to be noted as evidence for commissioners to be appointed on both sides to adjust and settle all claims.[7]

As the Blacks were ready to embark each was given a passport. One of these was for Cato Kannisay:

New York 21st April, 1783

This is to certify to whomsoever it may concern, that the Bearer hereof, Cato Kannisay, a Negro, resorted to the British Lines, in consequence of the Proclamations of Sir William Howe, and Sir Henry Clinton, late commanders in chief in America; and that the said Negro has hereby his

Excellency Sir Guy Carleton's Permission to go to Nova Scotia, or wherever else he may think proper.

By order of Brigadier General Birch[8]

Following the instructions of Carleton, as the Blacks boarded the transports with their certificates they were registered with brief descriptions of each: a healthy, stout fellow, scars, smallpox; stout and likely wench; an ordinary fellow, old and worn much, with the name of their former owners and their places of residence. As further protection they were given certificates to produce if seized by their owners and taken ashore for investigation stating they claimed the privileges of the proclamations issued for their security and protection.[9]

Once the Blacks were on board, the ships were inspected and a certified list of those sailing in each vessel, believed 'to be all the negroes on board,' was given the master of the ship. He was warned in writing that he was not permitted to land in Nova Scotia any Blacks other than those on his list or he would be severely punished, and the agents of the transport were to return to New York any Black not on the captain's list.[10] Most of the free Blacks sailed in the transports with the Loyalist companies; a few came in ships by themselves; 18 of the Black Pioneers came with the Royal Engineers; others came in vessels provided for them. One of these, a brig with 30 families on board, was seen to founder a few hours after sailing from New York. All on board perished, the roughness of the sea preventing the frigate accompanying the brig from rescuing those on board.[11]

On their arrival in Shelburne the Blacks were given land to live on until the governor issued instructions for their settlement. Many of those who arrived with the Loyalist companies indentured themselves as servants and artisans for various periods of time for wages of 50 or 60 dollars a year and clothing. Their provisions were to be drawn for them by the person for whom they worked, or they were to receive their rations from the captain of the Loyalist company in which they came to Shelburne. Some unfortunate Blacks hired themselves to unscrupulous employers who paid them only in part for their labour or failed to pay them at all; gave them less than their quota of rations and even turned them away without provisions, keeping their rations for their own use. Although the Muster of 1784 to investigate the abuses of the King's Bounty of rations reveals many instances of dishonest conduct toward the Blacks, not all their employers were ruthless and for many of them the months of their indenture proved a profitable experience.[12]

With hundreds of Blacks already in the town, Governor Parr wrote Lord Shelburne in July that he expected a 'Brigade of Blacks,' (some 1,500 negroes) to arrive in the province. However he still had no instructions as to their permanent settlement. His orders for the placement of Edward Elliott as late as August 15 were to allow him 'a lot amongst the negroes at the Black Quarter laid out for them at Shelburne,' and that he was to receive 'the same allowance of land, tools, provisions, etc. as are given those people.' A few days later, with the arrival of hundreds of Blacks imminent, the provincial secretary informed the Shelburne magistrates that those who obtained their freedom 'must have an accommodation of land for their habitation and gardens for the present, as to the rest the Governor waits the King's pleasure and the determination of the Legislature of this Province for their final privileges and settlement.'[13]

By August 27 hundreds of Blacks had arrived at Shelburne, and at last orders had been received from Governor Parr that they were 'to be placed up the North West Harbour.' On the same morning Benjamin Marston went on board the *Cyclops*, which had accompanied the transports, to discuss with Captain Christian the placing of the Blacks on the shores of the northwest arm of Shelburne Harbour. The following day he went with their leader Colonel Bluck, to show him the land allotted to his people. Marston had found, at last, someone pleased with the rocky land and he noted in his records that 'They are well satisfied with it.[14]

Colonel Stephen Bluck was a man of upright character, intelligent, and of good education. He was a mulatto, originally from Barbados, his mother a negress, as was his wife. In Birchtown he built a spacious house and laid out an excellent garden. On September 7, 1784, he was commissioned by Governor Parr lieutenant colonel of the Black Militia in the District of Shelburne. There are old tales that Stephen Bluck was accused of misappropriating funds entrusted to him for the use of the Blacks. He disappeared and sometime later his torn clothing was found on Pell's Road leading to the belief he had been killed by a wild animal. Later the funds entrusted to him were found and his name cleared, but too late to save a man who gave many years of devoted service to the welfare of the Blacks of Birchtown. With Colonel Bluck came six companies of Blacks: those of Captains Hutchins, Nathaniel Snowball, Cesar Perth, York Lawrence, Francis Jones and Robert Nicholson; in all, some 499 free Blacks.[15]

By August 30 Benjamin Marston was ready to lay out the land for 'Colonel Bluck's black gentry.' The following Monday he surveyed and ran lines for house lots. On Wednesday, September 3, the Blacks made their settlement, receiving from that day their rations at Birchtown. They had named their community to honour the man who had sheltered them in New York, Brigadier General Samuel Birch. It was a joyful day. 'Every man had a lot of land,' Boston King wrote years later, 'and we exerted all our strength in order to build comfortable huts before the cold weather set in.'[16]

With the Blacks busy building their huts, Marston sent Lyman and Tully to continue the survey of their land. A rough sketch of the Shelburne area of about this time has written on the west shore at the head of the northwest arm of Shelburne Harbour, 'Negroes landed here.' Maps of a few months later by Charles Mason show Birchtown compressed into a block of land on the west Birchtown Brook measuring 1,350 feet by 1,160 feet with a base of 1,056 feet and an irregular west boundary bordering the marsh. Still another map has Birchtown as a block of land straddling the west Birchtown Brook with 35 ten-acre lots extending northward above the village along either bank of the west brook. A chart of 1785 of the tracts of land granted by Parr in 1784 has Birchtown a small block of land surrounded by land granted to Loyalists – on the west to Hugh Kennedy and 95 others; on the east to George Pashley and 57 others. From these maps it seems that the original intention of a black settlement on the shores of the northwest harbour was considerably altered. Benjamin Marston indicates that such was the case. A number of Loyalists, anxious for their 50 acre lots, on September 19 sent Peter Sparling off with a pocket compass and codline to survey the western side of the harbour to Cape Negro. 'He has taken into his survey Birchtown which will utterly ruin it,' Marston commented in his diary, since it would shift the Blacks at least two lots as Sparling had laid out that many 'on the Black men's grounds.' That the small block of land left to them was far too small to accommodate the number of persons requiring land must have been immediately evident to the surveyors. Later maps indicate that they soon spread along the shores at the head of the northwest branch of the harbour, to the west and to the east of the two brooks.[17]

Despite the small portion of land allotted to them, the free Blacks continued to pour into Birchtown. By January 8, 1784, there were 1,485 on the victualler's list; by the late fall of 1784 the muster of free negroes listed some 1,531 Blacks. How many lived in Birchtown on the land set aside for them and how many in Shelburne is impossible to know. It would seem from the muster of 1784 that the companies of Captains Hutchins, Snowball, Perth, Lawrence, Jones and Nicholson, numbering 499 persons, lived in Birchtown from the beginning of the settlement. Those in the company of Adam Dixon (22 men, 14 women and 13 children) drew their rations in Birchtown from February 24, 1784. Then on May 1, 1784, came five companies of free Blacks, those of Captains Scott Murray, Robert George Bridges, James Read, George Fraction and Jacob With, numbering 308 persons, from Port Mouton where they had wintered and drawn their provisions with Colonel Mollison. Some 105 others, part of the company of Levin Johnson, who were formerly indentured servants to the inhabitants of

THE FREED BLACKS

Shelburne, were located on lots at Birchtown by Benjamin Marston. As late as August 15, 1784, free Blacks were arriving in the company of John Hamilton – 40 persons from London, mustered at Birchtown on September 7. Of the other companies of Blacks and the 66 who came by themselves and were not in any company, there were well over 1,100 receiving their rations in Birchtown. Many of these worked in Shelburne as indentured servants to the Loyalists or to the officers of the regiments or the Royal Engineers.[18]

During their years of slavery most of them acquired skill in a trade which they could offer in service to an employer. Their trades were as varied as those of their white competitors vying as they were for the work available. Among the Blacks were: ship carpenters, boatbuilders, caulkers, anchorsmiths, sailmakers, rope-makers; sawyers and millers; shoemakers, coopers, blacksmiths, tanners and skinners; carpenters, painters, a chairmaker; gardeners, farmers; fishermen, pilots, sailors and seamen; bakers, a cook, weavers, tailors, a seamstress, a clothier, a hatter; chimney sweeps, a coachman, carman; labourers and one doctor.[19]

Since they were skilled and able workmen, proposals were made by military personnel as well as by the Shelburne magistrates for their employment. In August, 1783, Lieutenant Colonel Robert Morse of the Royal Engineers suggested to Brigadier General Fox that the Blacks at Port Roseway for whom 'lands are not yet located nor other provisions made,' should be enlisted for one year with the same pay and on the same terms as the Black Pioneer Company (the 16 who came with the Royal Engineers), and be employed and paid in the Engineers' Department to the number of 40 Blacks, if they so chose. A year later Colonel Morse suggested raising a corps of Blacks to be clothed and fed by Government, to be employed on public works or, 'that by law of the Province, a certain proportion from out of the whole should be annually called upon for such services.' This, he continued, should 'prove a benefit to the negroes, as well as the Province, for it is known from experience that these persons brought up in servitude and slavery, want the assistance and protection of a master to make them happy; indeed to preserve them from penury and distress.' At this time the Shelburne magistrates were considering the Birchtown Blacks as a source of labour to build a log jail, each carpenter to have one shilling, each labourer eight pence per day, and Colonel Bluck to be asked to send a company each week to Shelburne to work.[20]

Even as skilled workmen, the free Blacks found it difficult to maintain their existence. To obtain work they lowered their wages and this brought them in conflict with the disbanded soldiers competing for the same jobs. By the summer of 1784 the conflict resulted in riots and the free Blacks living in Shelburne were forced to quit the town. The soldiers pulled down 20 of their houses in retaliation for trepassing upon their means of livelihood.[21]

LIFE IN BIRCHTOWN

In Birchtown, where many of the Blacks fled from the soldiers, living became increasingly precarious. To a stranger visiting Birchtown the place was 'beyond description wretched, situated on the coast in the middle of barren rocks, and partly surrounded by a thick impenetrable wood. Their huts miserable to guard against the inclemency of a Nova Scotia winter, and their existence almost depending on what they could lay up in summer. I think I never saw wretchedness and poverty so strongly perceptible in the garb and the countenance of the human species as in these miserable outcasts.'[22]

For those who had fled their masters in the warm South, from the banks of the Santee River, from the District of Ninety-Six, from Charleston, from St. Augustine and from Georgia, living in huts on a bleak shore in Birchtown was a gruelling existence. But looking back to the kindest masters they had known – even those who had given them meat once a day and milk for breakfast and supper, and had sent them to school at night to learn to read

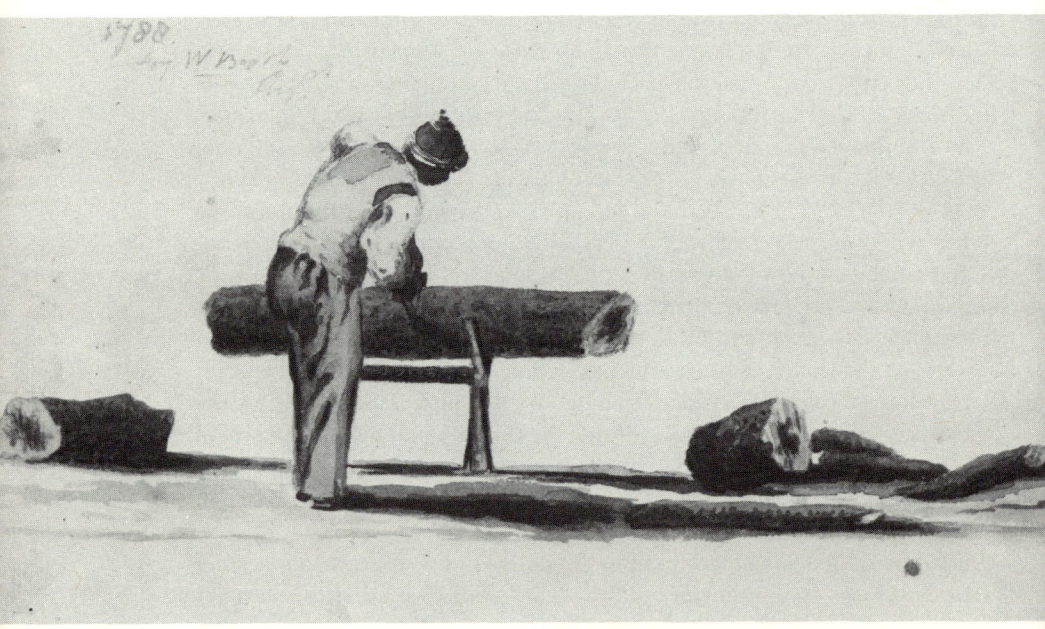

Black woodcutter at Shelburne, 1788. Watercolour by William Booth. (Courtesy Public Archives of Canada, C-40162)

the scriptures – one of the Blacks was to declare, 'could not satisfy me without liberty.' In those years of suffering and starvation, Boston King recalled years later that 'when they had parted with all their clothes, even to their blankets,' several fell dead in the streets from hunger, and 'some killed and ate their dogs and cats; and poverty and distress pervailed on every side.'[23]

Many causes contributed to the continued suffering and despair of the Blacks: the rapidly dwindling population of Shelburne with fewer and fewer each year to engage their services; their own inexperience in providing for themselves and their lack of money to establish comfortable homes; and above all the long delay in grants of farm land. During the years when provisions were provided, when they should have been clearing and preparing their land for cultivation against the withdrawal of their rations, they had no farm land to clear. When at last they were granted acreage for farms in late November 1787, the land was poor and strewn with boulders. As distressing as the rocky soil and the wet savannahs, was the distance of their land from Birchtown, since their lots bordered the shores of Beaver Dam Lake and extended westward to the eastern boundary of the Clyde River grants. Fishing was a possibility for the Blacks and was for those who could engage in it 'the chief and most profitable employment and which they follow as far as their circumstances will admit, for it must be known that even fishermen require a little yellow and white earth (what is commonly called cash) to commence his business.' Those who were as fortunate as Boston King to be hired for a summer's fishing in the Bay Chaleur, fared well. Fishing was not to his liking, but with £15 and two barrels of fish for his labour 'I was enabled to clothe my wife and myself; and my winter's store consisted of one barrel of flour, three bushels of corn, nine gallons of treacle, 20 bushels of potatoes which my wife had set in my absence, and the two barrels of fish; so that this was the best winter I ever saw in Birchtown.'[24]

Few fared as well as Boston King who had known, as the others, the pangs of hunger and the despair of seeking for work where there was no work to be had. In July 1788, with the growing needs of the Birchtown Blacks, two of their own men, James Young and Tobias Johnson, were appointed overseers of the poor at Birchtown to assist the overseers of the poor for the township of Shelburne. By early February 1789, the overseers for the township were in an impossible situation. They petitioned the Shelburne magistrates for assistance for the Blacks of Shelburne and Birchtown 'who are in the most distressing circumstances.' Many they had relieved, 'otherwise it is highly probable that some of them, during this inclement Season, must have perished. But as the Number of White People whom we have constantly to supply, are very considerable, it is not in our power to afford the Blacks that assistance which their pressing necessities loudly call for.' It was evident that the poor would become each year a greater burden and they hoped 'through your interest with His Excellency the Governor, or by such other means as to your Honours Wisdom and prudence may seem best, some mode may be adopted that may be favourable to the distressed Blacks and free this Infant Settlement from a Burden which it is by no Means in a Capacity to bear.'[25]

Poor and distressed Blacks were still a burden on the town in 1802, when a motion was passed in the Court of General Sessions to tax the Blacks toward the maintenance of their own poor. Steps were taken in the early years to care for the children of the poor, particularly those of the Blacks, by binding them as apprentices 'that they may be brought up useful, and not burthens to the Community.'[26]

For many of the children bound to masters there was unhappiness for themselves and their parents. One of these was the boy Robert Gammel, bound to John Harris to learn 'the art and Mistery of a Butcher.' In 1791 his mother discovered that John Harris was about to leave the province and intended taking her son with him. On her appeal to the General Sessions the Court cancelled the boy's indenture and restored him to his mother. On the complaint of Peter VanTile that Robert Clerk, to whom his child was bound, had put her out to service to Thomas Tully, and that he wished her to go to school in Birchtown, the Court ordered, that if VanTile could support his child she should be given to him; otherwise she was to be bound out by the overseers of the poor according to law. Then there was Sarah Neilson, apprenticed to William and Sarah Milby. She entered a complaint that her mistress often beat and abused her and withheld from her a sufficient quantity of provisions. On the testimony of Hannah Coffin that Sarah Neilson was more than two years of age when she came to Shelburne in 1784, and it was now 1800, the Court declared she had served the terms of her indenture and ordered her release. On the complaint of Margaret Clippen that Sarah Neilson came down her chimney at one o'clock in the morning and stole bread, she was confined to jail for petit larceny. Brought before the Court she was sent to the house of correction unless she could be hired to some person.[27]

SLAVES AND INDENTURED SERVANTS

The unhappy fate of many of the Blacks who indentured themselves as servants or labourers is revealed in the muster of the free Blacks ordered in 1784 to investigate the abuses of the King's Bounty of provisions. Day after day the commissioners scratched with their fine quill pens across the pages of the muster as the blacks gave their names and occupations and answered

THE FREED BLACKS

questions as: in whose company they came to Shelburne, to whom they were indentured and the amount of rations they had received. Many of the indenters honoured their contracts; others turned their servants away without pay or the provisions they drew in their name from the King's Bounty. Thomas London, a cooper, indentured to Alphea Palmer was given only two and a half months of his year's provisions. Jacob Wickfall, carpenter, was indentured to Joseph Wheaten for two years at £40 a year. When ill he was turned away without provisions. Betsey Rogers came in the company of Robert Turnbull who drew her rations for a year, but as she was not indentured to him, he never gave her any provisions. Cyrus Williams, a barber, indentured to Alphea Palmer for one year at $50, served the term of his indenture 'and instead of receiving any wages obliged him to pay 12/ a week for drawing his provisions.' Samuel Wiley bound to Daniel McLeod of the British Legion for three years at $40 and victuals and clothing, was 'turned off at the end of one year as he was troubled with rheumatism.' Marion Primus hired by Doctor Kendrick at $2 a month, 'lived with him a year – never paid her.' Henry Jones lived for two months with Mr. Nugent, after which term of service he never received his ration of provisions 'which he imagines was kept by Mr. Nugent.'

Disobedient Black servants could be ordered punished by the magistrates before a court of law was established. Later they could be committed by the court to 'hard labour, to fetters and shackles and moderate whipping (not exceeding ten stripes at once) in case of their being stubborn' or idle, or neglecting to perform the tasks assigned them, and their food withheld 'as the case may require until they be reduced to a better behaviour.' Isaac, the slave of William Young, for an assault and battery upon his master was confined to jail, publicly whipped in King Street with 39 lashes, and was kept at hard labour for two months with a monthly whipping of 10 lashes in the house of correction during the time of his confinement. On the complaint of Robert Summerville that his slave, Joe, stole sundry articles from him, the court ordered 39 lashes on his bare back in a public manner.[28]

Indentured servants could be hired to others and slaves were sold at their master's will. On their arrival in Shelburne in the company of Stephen Shakespear, Anthony and Hagar Loyal indentured themselves to Daniel Grandine for two years at £10 a year, and victuals and drink. After six months of service they were hired to Simeon Perkins of Liverpool from the first of December 1783, to May 1, 1784, for $50.00. On their return to Shelburne they were hired to Mr. Lear, a carpenter, again to their master's advantage. Documents hiring a slave to another were witnessed by justices of the peace. One such document was for George Jolly, the slave of James Cox, who hired him in August 1800, to Captain Samuel Mann of the brig

Greyhound for a coasting voyage to Newfoundland and back at the rate of $14 a month.[29]

As unhappy as the indentured servant may have been when hired to another, he was free and with the expiration of his term of service he was at liberty to go his own way. The slave suffered the indignity of sale without hope. At least one slave was sold in Shelburne as advertised by the auctioneer in the *Port Roseway Gazetteer* on August 11, 1785. 'Public Auction... at the Merchants Coffee House, will be sold a likely strong Negro Wench. About 18 years of age; she was brought up in a genteel family, is well acquainted with all kinds of house work, and can have an undeniable character; is sold for no fault but want of employ. The property warranted. John Hughes.' Some were seized and taken to the West Indies and sold. One of these was Benjamin Trost, who lived in the household of Mr. Gough, and was carried away and sold in Jamaica by a Mr. Miller. Others were bought by captains going to the West Indies for resale or were sent to the Islands for sale. Lord Dunmore, Governor of New Providence in the West Indies, allowed the captains of ships bringing Blacks into his Government two guineas for each negro or negress. Mr. Rowland sold a negress for £30 who, it was speculated, would fetch $300 at New Providence. Captain William Booth, of the Royal Engineers, before his departure from Shelburne, having no further use for his negress Betty Anna sent her to Grenada. He started her off with her wardrobe well replenished: 'I gave her two shifts, a complete white dress and a new striped (Red and white with flowers on the stripes) short Gown. Blankets, nightcap, Bread and cheese &c. She had also an old yellow striped short Gown and Peticoat of the same with a hat.'[30]

Slaves were disposed of in wills according to the wishes of their master and were listed among the goods and chattels of the deceased, valued according to the appraisal of the executors. In 1787, Thomas Robinson, 'formerly of Sussex County on Delware, at present of Nova Scotia,' a resident of Shelburne, willed to his eldest son Thomas £500 in cash in Nova Scotia currency, his pinchback watch, chain and gold seal, his negro boy Manuel, and 'the bed and furniture I sleep on, with my Silver Spectacles and Case.' To his daughter Arcada Cannon, £200 in cash, Nova Scotia currency, together 'with my negro women Priscilla, and her Child Sally.' To his brother Peter Robinson he bequeathed his negro boy named Philip, by trade a blacksmith. John Herbert of Shelburne, in his will recorded in 1799, gave and bequeathed to his wife, Sarah, his negro woman Venus; to his son, Thomas, 'a slave named Isaac.'[31]

Many slaves attempted to escape their masters; others strove to free themselves from bondage. One of these was a slave named Richard who ran

THE FREED BLACKS

away from his master David Hurd and entered the service of William Hill at Port Roseway, who would not release him until his master proved he was his property. Even then David Hurd was without his slave, for the Shelburne magistrates 'conceive he was made free by your Excellency,' Hurd complained to Sir Guy Carleton. From Annapolis came Mertilla Dixon, the slave of Major Barclay, seeking refuge in Birchtown. On petition to the Shelburne Court of General Sessions she was declared entitled to 'all the protection of the Law, and should have the same.' In 1789 came four slaves of the Earl of Dunmore from Nassau, New Providence. Roger was soon apprehended in Shelburne by Dunmore's appointees, George and Robert Ross, and was sent on board the brig *Providence* to Nassau; Jack managed to get himself in jail with a 'trumped up account against him to the amount of £15' which the Ross brothers refused to pay. Kate eloped and Bett took herself off to Halifax. They would be sent to Nassau when found, George Ross assured their master, and they would send Jack when they could persuade his creditors to let him off, for half the £15. Indentured servants as well as slaves ran away from their masters as did the servant of James Cox who advertised in the *Nova Scotia Packet* in November 1786: 'Runaway. An indented negro man named Henry Jones. He is a tanner by trade, has a remarkable impediment in his speech, is very artful and will probably say he is a free man.'[32]

For Mary Postell and her children there was no respite from bondage. As the slave of a rebel officer, Mary Postell took refuge within the British lines and worked with other escaped Blacks on forts and public works. She was given a certificate of protection, but it was taken from her by one who pretended he wanted to see her papers. On the evacuation of Charleston she was persuaded by her husband to go to St. Augustine in the service of Jesse Gray. Here Jesse Gray claimed he sold her to his brother Samuel, having purchased her from a man named Rea. When he came to Nova Scotia he bought her back from his brother. Suspecting that he intended selling her after her arrival in Shelburne, Mary quitted his household taking her children with her. Proving he had owned her, Gray again took possession of her by an order from the Shelburne justices of the peace, carried her and her children to Argyle and sold her to William Maugham for 100 bushels of potatoes; her daughter Flora he sold to John Henderson, and Nell he kept as his slave.[33]

Other Blacks struggled to free themselves from masters who illtreated them. Most of these were from the deep South where, without the firm stand taken by Sir Guy Carleton to protect those who reached New York, many fell into the hands of ruthless men who ignored the protection offered them by the British commanders. One of these was the 'negro wench Molly,' a slave to the same Jesse Gray who sold Mary Postell for a load of potatoes. Her claim to liberty was ignored by the Shelburne Sessions, as was the plea of the Blacks, Pero and Tom, the property of Joseph Robin who gave a mare and eight guineas to purchase Pero. James Singletory's master, Samuel Anderson, late of St. Augustine, when called before the Court, claimed he had lost the bill of sale for James, his wife and child, for whom he paid £50. He was given a year to prove his ownership. In the meantime the three Blacks were to live with him as his servants. If he could not prove they were his slaves they were to be paid wages as hired servants.[34]

'FROLICKS.' IDLE VAGRANTS, CRIMES AND PUNISHMENT OF BLACKS

'Negro frolicks' were a constant annoyance in the town. In May 1785, the Court ordered 50 handbills immediately printed forbidding Black dances and Blacks frolicking in the town. A few days later seven women were brought before the Court accused of riotious behaviour and were ordered to the house of correction. A year later, dancing and frolicking still unabated, the constables were ordered to pick up the Blacks found dancing and gambling at night and to lodge them in the house of correction. Still they frolicked, 'to the prejudice of the Inhabitants in the back of the Town,' and a publication was issued restricting the assembling of Blacks for gaming, frolicking and dancing. The disorderly house of Hysem Leeds and his wife and Silvia Howel, 'giving encouragement to other Black People assembling there,' was a noisy disturbance to their neighbours, and the Court ordered the 'Worshipful Bench do Reprimand them.' 'Bad Houses by which man servants were induced to frequent to the great prejudice of their masters' were complained about by James Cox. At least one 'bad house,' a hut occupied by Blacks on Charlotte Lane, was ordered vacated.[35]

Idle vagrants and rogues like Pompey Donaldson and his chum Thomas Gould were administered corporal punishment and told 'to go to Birchtown, and not be seen in Shelburne.' For John Windsor punishment was more severe. For running away from the workhouse he was sent to the house of correction as an idle vagrant to be kept at hard labour with a log chained to his leg, with ten lashes on entering, and ten lashes on his bare back every Monday morning for two months. For loitering around Captain Miller's potato patch, Joseph Warren was ordered to the workhouse as a vagrant, he protesting he was employed by Mr. Cox to watch his potatoes and that he never stole a potato from Captain Miller.[36]

Some Blacks, for trifling crimes, were punished with brutal severity. Dianna, convicted for two petty larcenies (a theft under twelve pence), was sentenced to 200 lashes at the cart's tail on Saturday at noon for the first

THE FREED BLACKS

offence; 150 lashes at the cart's tail the following Saturday for the second offence. For petty larcenies, a Black named George was sentenced to 39 lashes at eleven o'clock a.m. and at one p.m. to stand in the pillory one hour; Light Horse Jack was given 100 lashes at the hands of the common hangman – 20 lashes in front of the jail, 20 lashes at the corner of King Street, 20 at the corner of St. John's Street, and 20 each at the corners of Ann and St. George's Streets on Water Street. Following the lashing he was ordered confined to jail and bound out. Patty Brown, for stealing a calico gown and wearing it to meeting on the Sabbath, was taken to the whipping post on Stanhope Hill in Water Street and there whipped on the bare back 10 lashes with the cat-o'-nine tails and told to leave the township immediately. David Anderson, for stealing towels valued at one shilling, was flogged 39 lashes and was confined in the house of correction. For a watch he borrowed 'to equip him for a negro dance' and which he sold to a soldier for seven dollars, Thomas Bell was confined 30 days in jail; John Green, for stealing rum from the jailer, received 39 lashes.[37]

Many of the thefts committed by Blacks reflected their poverty, their hunger and suffering from cold. For a pair of shoes he stole in the winter of 1785, Prince Frederick was given 39 lashes on the bare back and was kept at hard labour for a month. At the expiration of his sentence he was again lashed 39 stripes and was obliged to pay the jailer his lawful fees. For the theft of a bed quilt, another Black man named was Prince was committed to the house of correction for a month. For a similar offence, for the theft of a blanket and a hog's skin, a culprit named Windsor was committed to the house of correction for one month with hard labour and 39 lashes with a cat-o'-nine tails. Thomas Shepherd, for stealing two pieces of pork from the *Charming Sally*, was sentenced to two months in the house of correction with hard labour and 12 lashes on the bare back.[38]

One of the free Blacks was hanged for stealing: Britain Murray in 1786. As a felony punishable by death, his crime is included in the section on the judicial responsibilities of the Court of Sessions.

MINISTERS AND RELIGIOUS AFFILIATIONS

Among the Blacks, Boston King remembered, 'the work of the Lord prospered greatly.' Together they built a meeting house in Birchtown where all denominations met for services of worship.

There were a number of religious leaders, among them David George, the outstanding founder of the Negro Baptist Church in Nova Scotia and later in West Africa. Born the son of slaves, he knew the bitterness and suffering of slavery. When he was about nineteen he ran away from his master. Awakened to a deep religious concern by the words of a Black named Cyrus he began to preach to the slaves to repent of their sins. During the Revolution he and his family found their way to Charleston where they sheltered behind the British lines. In the fall of 1782 they came to Halifax. Here David George found few opportunities to preach to people of his colour, and in the spring of 1783 he came to Shelburne and on the first Lord's Day he held a meeting 'in a valley, between two hills, close by the river.' He met bitter opposition and was told by the magistrates he could not stay in the town. But a white man, one he had known in Savannah, gave him permission to build a pole house on his land. With the arrival of Governor Parr in July, bringing with him David George's wife and children, they were given six months' provisions and a quarter of an acre of land in the north end of the town for their subsistence. With the governor's good will, George was preaching again, and as he cleared his land and built a meeting house, others besides Baptists came to cut the trees into timber and helped with shingles and a few coppers to buy nails. Others heard of David George, and he was asked to extend his preaching to Ragged Islands, Liverpool, Preston and into New Brunswick where the lieutenant-governor gave him a special license to instruct the Blacks in the knowledge and practice of the Christian religion. In 1791 he and his family were among those who accepted the offer of land in West Africa by the Sierra Leone Company and there he continued to preach the word of God.[39]

Among the Blacks were many followers of Methodism. Moses Wilkinson, a blind cripple (long remembered as 'Old Moses') was leader of the Wesleyan Methodists. Cato Perkins, who was also blind, William Ash and Richard Ball were leaders of the Calvinist Methodists, followers of the Countess of Huntington Connexion, and the Reverend John Marrant, an ordained Black, who was sent from England by the Countess of Huntington to work with the Black people in Nova Scotia. Associated with Moses Wilkinson in preaching Wesleyan Methodism was Boston King, who struggled to find in the Lord that 'all His paths were peace.' The Blacks of Birchtown were an abiding interest to John Wesley who wrote 'that they need never want books while I live,' and urged the Wesleyan Methodists in Shelburne 'to give them all the assistance you can.'[40]

A number of Blacks in Shelburne and Birchtown were Anglicans. On August 1, 1784, the Reverend George Panton reported to the Society for the Propagation of the Gospel that he had baptised 44 infants and 81 adults and had married 44 couples among the Blacks of Shelburne and Birchtown since December 20, 1783. He held services occasionally in Birchtown where he found 'the people very desirous of the ordinances of religion.' Also in Birchtown at this time was the Black known as Limerick who officiated as a preacher and exhorter and catechist.[41]

THE FREED BLACKS

SCHOOLS AND SCHOOLMASTERS

A charity or free school for Black children was established in Birchtown by the Associates of the Late Doctor Thomas Bray in 1785. Two schools had already been established in Nova Scotia by the Associates, one in Halifax and one in Digby, and in February, 1785, the Associates requested the Reverend Doctor Breynton of St. Paul's Church, Halifax, to establish a school at Birchtown under the instruction of Colonel Stephen Bluck.

Schools founded by the Bray Associates for the children of slaves, as well as for those of the free Blacks, gave these children their only opportunity to learn to read and to spell. The Associates provided books for the children's studies and the teacher's stipend; the Blacks themselves provided a school house. The school year was from Lady Day to Lady Day with classes in session until 5 p.m. In 1787 Stephen Bluck had 36 pupils in his school which was inspected by Isaac Wilkins, and other justices of the peace, who gave very favourable reports of the children's progress and the conduct of the schoolmaster. The children's ages ranged from five to eleven years. For the beginners, there was the first reader; for others their reading lessons were from the New Testament or from the Bible or from the psalter, with spellings. For the girls there were lessons in sewing. In their slender library, provided by the Associates, were copies of Bacon's *Sermons, Collects* and *Catechisms,* the *Sermon on the Mount,* books including *Religion Made Easy,* with Watts' *Hymns* and Foxe's *Lessons.* In 1790, for teaching his class of 44 children, Stephen Bluck was paid £28.10.

In 1796 with the number of children to go to school reduced to 14, Stephen Bluck closed his school in Birchtown. Two years later on November 19, 1798, the Society for Promoting Christian Knowledge opened a school for Black children in Shelburne under the direction of the rector and church wardens of Christ Church, with Richard Brazel, master. In 1799 the Society extended its charity to a school for white children and Richard Brazel was appointed master of the school, and Joseph Ingram took his place as master of the school for Blacks under the patronage of the Associates of the Late Doctor Bray. He continued as master of the school until his death in 1813 when William King became master, succeeded a few years later by Roswell Brown.[42]

SIERRA LEONE

The Blacks who were settled in other parts of Nova Scotia at the end of the Revolutionary War on the same terms as they were settled in Birchtown, were not given the good farm land they were expecting on their arrival in the province. Without land to farm for their subsistence, and forced to labour for wages that left them in misery, they were as destitute and as unhappy as the Birchtown settlers. In their despair, in the summer of 1791, their suffering found expression in the action of Thomas Peters of Annapolis. A freed slave like themselves, his courage and fortitude carried him to London to present the plight of the Blacks and to ask for redress of the wrongs they suffered. In England he met Granville Sharp of the recently incorporated Sierra Leone Company. Originally an association to relieve distressed, freed Blacks in England who had escaped their masters in America and had found their way to England during the Revolutionary War, the newly incorporated Sierra Leone Company was looking for likely settlers, both black and white, to found a Christian settlement in Sierra Leone and to promote trade in the natural products of Africa. Encouraged by Granville Sharp, in a memorial to William Grenville, one of His Majesty's chief secretaries, Peters told of the suffering of his people because they had not been given the land promised to them. Some, in spite of their distress, earnestly desired to obtain their rightful allotment and remain in America; others were 'ready and willing to go wherever the Wisdom of Government may think proper to provide for them, as free subjects of the British Empire.' For both, he asked, 'that they may be afforded such relief as shall appear to be best adopted to their circumstances and situation.'[43]

The memorial was given the immediate attention of the British Government. A letter to Governor Parr, enclosing the memorial, ordered an enquiry into the alleged circumstances, and if the promises of the Government had not been fulfilled, grants were to be made immediately in 'a situation so advantageous as to make them some atonement for the injury they have suffered.' Those who wished to accept the proposals of the Sierra Leone Company were to be offered a free passage to Africa. When the numbers wishing to go were known, he was to order sufficient tonnage for their removal – about two tons for each man or woman, one and a half tons for each child – to enable them to take with them any article which might be useful in their new settlement. As a third alternative they were to be offered an opportunity to enlist as soldiers for service in the West Indies, with the promise of British pay and a bounty of one guinea per man on enlistment.[44]

As the instructions of the British Government were being prepared for Governor Parr, the Sierra Leone Company issued a proclamation relative to their proposed free settlement on the coast of Africa. Lieutenant John Clarkson of the Royal Navy, who had long been concerned about the suffering of the Blacks, and who was a brother of Thomas Clarkson, a director of the Sierra Leone Company, was appointed to go to Halifax to explain the terms of the Company to them and to superintend the embarkation and voyage to Africa. At the same time Lawrence Hartshorne of Halifax was appointed an agent of the Company to assist Lieutenant

THE FREED BLACKS

Clarkson in interviewing those wanting to go and in providing each person accepted with a certificate of approbation as to his 'Honesty, Sobriety and Industry.'[45]

Clarkson arrived in Halifax on October 7. Two weeks later he set sail for Shelburne. News of the Sierra Leone Company had already reached Birchtown and Stephen Bluck had written to Hartshorne for further information respecting provisions and transportation to be 'furnished for the encouragement of Adventures.'[46] Many in Shelburne were adverse to having the Blacks leave. Those who had used them to clear and cultivate their land were opposed, aware that no white man would labour on the same terms as the helpless Blacks; others, 'actuated by the vilest motives persuade them to go that they may purchase their property on the most shameful terms.' Still others objected that only the best type of Black – honest, sober and industrious – was being accepted by the Company, leaving the shiftless, the sick and disabled. Stephen Skinner, who had been appointed by Parr as the agent in Shelburne to receive the names of those emigrating to Sierra Leone and afterwards to convey them to Halifax, was discovered by Clarkson among those 'disinclined to the present undertaking.'[47]

To inform the Blacks of the proposals offered them, they were assembled in their meeting house in Birchtown. For them it was a momentous day. Clarkson was distressed by the evidence of suffering and misery in the faces of those waiting to hear him speak. Determined not to influence them to make a decision adverse to their welfare, he carefully explained the intentions of the British government and the offer of the Sierra Leone Company. They had the choice of the government's offer of land in Nova Scotia, the full proportion promised them, 'in a situation so advantageous that it might make them some atonement for the delay.' Or, they could enlist as soldiers in the West Indies under the protection of the British Army and be entitled to the same privileges as others serving under arms. A third alternative was the offer of land in Africa by the Sierra Leone Company along with which, if accepted, the British government would provide free transportation to the river of Sierra Leone. That every Black should know the terms, he read to them the proclamation for a free settlement on the Coast of Africa:

'The Sierra Leone Company, willing to receive into their Colony such Free Blacks as are able to produce to their Agents, Lieutenant Clarkson, of His Majesty's Navy, and Mr. Lawrence Hartshorne of Halifax, or either of them, satisfactory Testimonials of their Characters, (more particularly as to Honesty, Sobriety, and Industry) think it proper to notify, in an explicit manner, upon what Terms they will receive, at Sierra Leone, those who bring with them Certificates of Approbation from either of the said Agents, which Certificates they are hereby respectively authorized to grant or withhold at Discretion.

'It is therefore declared by the Company

'That every Free Black (upon producing such a Certificate) shall have a Grant of not less than TWENTY ACRES of LAND for himself, TEN for his Wife, and FIVE for every Child, upon such terms and subject to such charges and obligations, (with a view to the general prosperity of the Company) as shall hereafter be settled by the Company, in respect to the Grants of Lands to be made by them to all Settlers, whether Black or White.

'That for all Stores, Provisions, &c. supplied from the Company's Warehouses, the Company shall receive an equitable compensation, according to fixed rules, extending to Blacks and Whites indiscriminately.

'That the civil, military, personal, and commercial rights and duties of Blacks and Whites, shall be the same, and secured in the same manner.

'And, for the full assurance of personal protection from slavery to all such Black Settlers, the Company have subjoined a Copy of a Clause in the Act of Parliament whereby they are incorporated, viz.

'PROVIDED ALSO, and be it further enacted, that it shall not be lawful for the said Company, either directly or indirectly, by itself or themselves, or by the agents or servants of the said Company, or otherwise howsoever, to deal or traffic in the buying or selling of Slaves, or in any manner whatsoever have, hold, appropriate, or employ any person or persons in a state of slavery in the service of the said Company.

'Given under our Hands, LONDON, the 2d Day of August, 1791. Henry Thornton, Chairman, Philip Samson, Dep. Chairman, Charles Middleton, William Wilberforce, Granville Sharp, John Kingston, Samuel Parker, Joseph Hardcastle, Thomas Clarkson, Vickeris Taylor, William Sanford, Thomas Eldred, George Wolff, Directors.

'N.B. For the convenience of those who are possessed of property which they cannot dispose of before their departure, the Company will authorize an Agent, who, on receiving from any Proprietor a sufficient power for that purpose, shall sell the same for his benefit, and remit the Purchase-money (through the hands of the Company) to such Proprietor at Sierra Leone.'[48]

Despite Clarkson's efforts to have the Blacks consider the proposals carefully before their decisions were made 'these poor creatures assured me they were unanimous in the desire for embarking for Africa, telling me their labour was lost upon the land in this country and their utmost efforts would barely keep them in existence – being now sunk to the lowest pitch of wretchedness they had made up their minds for quitting this country,' and 'would not be diverted from their resolution though disease and even death were the consequence.' Concerned by their response and the evidence of suffering and abuse that prompted the response, Clarkson urged them to consider the advantages and disadvantages of each proposal, then, 'those who after serious reflection were determined to embark for Sierra Leone' could call on him at his lodging house, the Merchants' Coffee House in Shelburne, the following three mornings and he and Major Skinner would enter their names to go to Sierra Leone.[49]

Early in the morning of October 27 Clarkson and Major Skinner began enrolling the names and history of each family, 'advising them to dispose of their property though they might not get the full value, reserving a sufficient proportion to maintain them till the first week in December,' when Major Skinner would provide victualled vessels for their transportation to Halifax to await their departure for Sierra Leone. It was soon evident that many of the Blacks were leaving not 'with the idea of improving their own condition, but for the sake of their children, whom they wished to be established upon a better foundation.' One, a slave, came with his wife and children who were free, with tears streaming down his face, begging to have them enrolled for Sierra Leone, where, in his 'wretchedness he could at all times cheer himself with the pleasing reflection his wife and children were happy.' Clarkson offered to buy his freedom, only to be told by his master that 'the intricacy of the law' prevented him from selling his slave. Clarkson had better success freeing a young boy indentured to a butcher who was leaving Shelburne and who intended selling the boy a slave in America. Clarkson had his parents steal their child and brought the case to trial after the butcher had sailed for Boston. When no one appeared against him he was restored to his parents.[50]

Clarkson was overwhelmed with the numbers wanting to go to Sierra Leone. In three days so many enlisted their names he feared there would not be ships to convey them to Halifax. Still they continued to come and he enrolled them conditional on there being enough ships to carry them to Halifax. Their tragic circumstances overcame his determination not to enlist their names. One, who had lived on the coast of Africa and spoke English indifferently, expressed the feeling of others. To Clarkson's query if he knew the nature of His Majesty's proposals he replied, 'Mr. Massa, me no hear, nor no mind, me work like slave, cannot do worse, Massa.' Clarkson reminded him of the many difficulties in a new settlement. 'Me well know that Massa, me can work much and care not for climate. If me die, me die, had rather die in me own country than this cold place.'[51]

By November 6 Clarkson had enrolled 156 families, 540 Blacks. On that day he set sail for Halifax in the schooner *Deborah* accompanied by Major Skinner and Lieutenant Miller, who had been sent to Shelburne to enlist those wishing to join the Black Corps in the West Indies, with his 14 recruits and their families. With Clarkson's return and his report of the numbers wishing to leave Nova Scotia, Governor Parr issued orders for upwards of 1,000 tons of shipping to be engaged to convey them to Africa, and appointed Michael Wallace, government agent, to purchase provisions and other necessary items for the voyage and to engage the ships and to superintend the general equipment of the fleet. At the same time he authorized the agents at Annapolis and Shelburne to hire good and sufficient vessels, properly victualled, for transporting the Blacks to Halifax about the first week of December, and assured them provisions would be provided in Halifax until their departure. On Clarkson's suggestion that every Black should have a medical examination before embarkation, Dr. William Burns of Shelburne was appointed for the Shelburne district. A few days later Lieutenant Wickham of the navy was appointed to go to Shelburne to supervise the embarkation of the Blacks and to conduct them to Halifax.[52]

On December 9 the first of the departing Blacks arrived in Halifax in eleven overcrowded vessels. Two or three of the vessels sailed from Shelburne with only two days' provisions and they were on board five days. Most were in a deplorable condition. Clarkson had been assured by the Council of Nova Scotia that clothing would be supplied to those in distress. He wrote immediately to the president and ordered shifts, shirts, petticoats, jackets,&c. 'to be got ready *immediately*, for more than half the people from Shelburne are entirely naked.' During their days in Halifax they were housed in storehouses and the Sugar House Barracks, aired and made clean and comfortable with stoves and with laths laid on the floor for their beds to be put upon, and a sentinel was posted at the door for their safety at night.[53]

As the Blacks gathered in Halifax they were ordered into companies with a captain for each company. As the days passed and the ships were made ready for their embarkation, each Black, head of a family, was given a certificate to receive his proper proportion of land in Sierra Leone; passenger lists and a master of each company were prepared and the Blacks were assigned to the 15 vessels waiting to take them to Africa. Of the 1,190 Blacks fleeing a cold land, a country 'whose inhabitants treated them with so much barbarity,' 544 were from Shelburne, 151 men, 147 women, and 220 children who came in the vessels from Shelburne, and 26 who got to Halifax by stealth and were permitted to sail with the others.[54]

Many were returning to the land of their birth. From Birchtown were 47 who had known the terror of seizure in Africa and the long, painful voyage to America. Many were leaving small plots of cultivated land, some had even ventured to their 40 acre farm lots and had cleared land for crops. All were taking with them their skills and years of experience as farmers and artisans.[55] In Sierra Leone they made a lasting impression on the town (Freetown) which they helped to found. David George, soon after his arrival in Sierra Leone, had a meeting house constructed of posts driven into the ground with a roof of poles thatched with grass. As he founded the Black Baptist Church in Nova Scotia he was the founder of the Baptist Church in West Africa, and as a chosen representative in the Legislative Council his influence in shaping the future colony of Sierra Leone was considerable. Boston King's concern for the native Africans and his attempt to teach them in a small school he established won the respect of the directors of the Sierra Leone Company and he was sent to England to study in Kingswood School. On his return he was appointed schoolmaster in the colony to teach the English language to the native Africans. Others of the Shelburne Blacks who had concerned themselves with the spiritual welfare of their brothers continued to preach and to lead the people in their services of worship – Moses Wilkinson among the Wesleyan Methodists; William Ash and Cato Perkins among the followers of the Countess of Huntington Connexion.[56]

The cost of transporting the Blacks to Sierra Leone far exceeded the expectations of the British government. With the first returns to arrive in London, word was hastily sent to Richard Bulkeley to prevent any further expense in collecting and transporting them from the province. If any were in Halifax of those collected before or since the embarkation, he was to grant land to those willing to settle and induce those best qualified to enter the corps for the West Indies.[57]

The loss of so many Blacks was of serious consequence to the province as in the towns where they had lived. Shelburne, this 'new and unfortunate Settlement,' Stephen Skinner grieved, 'has been deprived of upwards of Five hundred good and efficient Citizens,' including 'labouring People and Servants who have been flattered by imaginary prospects of happiness to leave a comfortable and decent maintenance.' The loss of Black labour was bewailed by Gideon White. 'The 800 Negros who were carried to Serea Leone was a serious loss but more so to me than any One – I had Eight Negro Families Tenants which had each a quantity of my Land and allowed me rent – each had his House &c. those are all gone.'[58] But not all the sturdy and reliable Blacks had gone to Sierra Leone. There were still some 50 men and their families living in Shelburne and Birchtown and in the county, who had accepted Clarkson's advice that those who had in 'great measure surmounted their difficulties and were getting up in the world and possessed of some little property' should remain and not 'resign a certainty for a prospect extremely precarious.' Stephen Bluck was one of the 50. In a petition to Governor Parr he and the others declared they were convinced their brethren 'so infatuated as to embrace the proposals of the Sierra Leone company' had done so to 'their utter annihilation.' They requested a share of the assistance promised to Thomas Peters and his associates, 'that the whole may be benefited by his Royal clemency,' to enable themselves to live in comfort on their farms, and a sufficient sum to purchase a cow and two sheep.[59]

Many of those left in the province suffered distressing hardships. Governor Wentworh, in a letter to the King, deplored sending the Blacks away when one eighth of the expense of their removal would have made all of them perfectly happy. It is strange 'for government to spend so much to remove laborious people and will spend nothing to help those who remain.' Without funds to assist them he knew that many would perish during the winter.[60]

Indigent Blacks continued to be a problem in Shelburne long after those who left were in Sierra Leone. In 1802 the committee for the poor urged the town to find some means of taxing the Blacks themselves for the support of their poor and relieve the increasing financial burden on the town which had advanced at the astonishing rate of some £64 in two years [61] To establish themselves in comfortable homes was a long struggle, but one which most of the Shelburne Blacks did achieve for themselves and their families.

5
The Army, The Navy and Fort Elliott

With the decision in the spring of 1783 to establish a military post at Port Roseway for the protection of the town, Lieutenant William Lawson of the Royal Engineers was appointed to establish the post and to secure ample reservations for all military purposes. Instruction for his guidance were prepared by Robert Morse, chief of the Royal Engineers, and were approved by Sir Guy Carleton.

'Upon your arrival you will in conjunction with the commanding officer of the troops, the superior officer of the navy and such persons as you may find authorized by the Governor of the Province, carefully examine the harbour with a view to find a proper place to land the troops, provisions, ordnance and all the King's stores, and to establish a military post which may afford a protection to shipping and be capable of defence toward the sea as well as by land, having in contemplation a town, wharfs, barracks and other Public buildings necessary to a great and permanent establishment, for all of which purposes ample reservations of lands should be made, and the Refugee Settlers shewn the spot intended for the town, upon which only they should be allowed to build, agreeably to the plan laid out for them.

'When the several situations shall have been made choice of for these purposes, the troops should be encamped or enhutted upon such a plan as may be hereafter extended and improved.'

Provisions and perishable ordnance stores were to be covered as soon as possible; the heavy cannon planted to give immediate protection to vessels and the surrounding country carefully explored and cleared for the materials first wanted. To assist him were Ensign Lambton of the 33rd Regiment as assistant engineer; a foreman and eleven carpenters; a mason, a smith, artificers with their entrenching tools; a sergeant, a corporal and sixteen of the Black Pioneers, who, with the artificers, were to be employed 'in His Majesty's service only.' For use at the post were provided a whale boat, a gun boat and a sailing boat with tackle, rigging, oars, &c., for which, with other articles provided, he was responsible, as he and his assistant engineer were responsible for the weekly reports of the artificers' labor. He was to apply by letter to the commissary to purchase lumber and other material, 'putting a fair and just value upon the same.' He was to incur no expense, except for covering the provisions and ordnance stores, until further orders were given by the commander-in-chief, the general officer commanding the district, or the chief engineer.[1]

With the fleet sailing for Port Roseway in late April went some of the artillery with public stores and supplies. At the same time Carleton requested General Paterson, commander-in-chief of His Majesty's Forces in Nova Scotia, to apply to the governor for an ample reservation of land for a military post for the defence of the settlement of Port Roseway, but he was not to permit any works to be constructed nor incur any expenses without further orders. Captain Hare of the Royal Artillery was to be sent to command the post and to 'give every assistance in his power to the settlers.'[2]

The strategic position of the point of land jutting from the western shores of the harbour, known to the early settlers as Scarborough Point, and marked by Durell for its 'good wooding with white oak,' was evident to Lieutenant Lawson. To house the provisions and military supplies he had suitable buildings erected. The detachment of artillery, consisting of five companies of the 37th Regiment, was landed and the point was renamed Point Carleton in honour of the commander-in-chief. On August 1 Carleton appointed Mr. James Auchumty on 'his bond for £500 sterling for the faithful discharge of the trust reposed in him,' to be ordnance storekeeper at Port Roseway. Working with the land surveyors sent from Halifax by Governor Parr, Lawson assisted in choosing the site for the town, and with William Morris, carefully sounded the harbour for rocks and shoals and for good anchorage. Captain Hare arrived on May 17 to take charge of the post and a few weeks later General Paterson inspected the new town and proposed military sites. With the appointment of Brigadier-General Fox in July as commander of His Majesty's Forces in Nova Scotia, Carleton again stressed the importance of reservations 'of such lands as may be judged proper' for the erection of buildings and storehouses and for fortifications, as it may be necessary 'to erect works for the defence of some of the new

THE ARMY, THE NAVY AND FORT ELLIOTT

Shelburne Harbour, showing the Barracks. Watercolour by H. Pooley, approximately 1818. (Courtesy Special Collections, Killam Library, Dalhousie University)

settlements now forming in Nova Scotia.' He was to send a battalion to Port Roseway if he found it an advantage to the inhabitants to do so, but' in all cases where the Province is concerned' he was to consult with the governor.[3]

With the necessary reservations in mind for the defence of the town by land and by sea, the distribution of provisions, the storage of ordnance and military supplies, for naval as well as for military use, a vast acreage of land was reserved. For the war department there was an engineer's reserve of about 197 acres at Point Carleton (Fort Point). North of Point Carleton, at Burnt Head, was a reserve of 112 acres. On the opposite shore to Point Carleton, on Sandy Point, where the harbour light now guards the narrows, a large reserve was made cutting back into the land and along the shore. South of it at the rock known as the Tea Chest, 241 acres were set aside, and south of the Tea Chest, at the end of Lower Sandy Point (Government Point), 225 or more acres were marked reserved. On McNutt's Island, then known as Roseneath, across the harbour from the Tea Chest, was a reserve of 11½ acres. Farther south along the eastern shores of the island, on North East Bluff, 12 to 15 acres were reserved, and at the southern end of the island 100 acres were set aside for a lighthouse. The largest of the engineer's reserves was that of 876¾ acres on Hart's Point. It extended inland and along the eastern shores of the point and cut across the land to Pompey Point on Birchtown Bay.[4]

On Point Carleton, by the summer of 1784, good log barracks had been built for a hundred men with rooms for four officers, and buildings had been erected for military stores. The garrison was well equipped with brass and iron ordnance and small arms, with brass and iron guns, with English 3 to 24 pounders, with carronades and howitzers. There were: wooden mortar beds and carriages for guns and carronades; paper cartridges for muskets and carbines, flannel for mortars, barrels of corned powder, shots and shells.[5] One twelve pounder was mounted as a signal gun.[6]

A plan of Point Carleton in 1786 shows 13 buildings, an artillery park, and a flag staff, its flag whipping in the wind. Facing the harbour and back from the shore were two long, gable-roofed barracks, a smaller house and work shop for artificers. Below the barracks stood the ordnance storehouse, the bake house, the guard house and the artillery park. To the south from the cluster of garrison buildings were two small houses built by William Lawson, and on the land set aside for John King, the assistant engineer and deputy storekeeper, were three houses he had built, and edging the shore, a log hut occupied by Black people.[7]

REGIMENTS

In the summer of 1783, when Carleton suggested a battalion should be sent to Port Roseway if to the advantage of the settlers, Parr did not consider soldiers were necessary 'from the present good disposition of the Inhabitants.' However, with dissensions over the distribution of land and labour problems in the spring of 1784, he requested troops to be sent to Shelburne. General Campbell ordered the 17th Regiment to embark immediately. Land on the opposite side of the harbour from the town, 150 acres (lots 29, 30, 31), already allotted as farm land, was purchased by the war department. Good log barracks, their hearth stones set with slabs of granite, were constructed for 300 soldiers. (Lieutenant William Booth's records say barracks were built for 258 soldiers and a number of huts near the barracks for married men). A barracks of 12 rooms was built for officers, the yard of which was enclosed with painted pickets, and well-framed quarters were constructed for the commanding officer. Storehouses were built near the barracks road leading to the boat landing and a house south of the barracks was purchased for a hospital. The work of construction was by contract by order of General Campbell, 'because I am convinced by my own observation and experience that it is a more economical method than retaining in the Pay of Government a great number of artificers on great wages and who are generally indolent.'[8]

An early impression of the barracks was of extremely good buildings set in a wretched situation of stumps and rocks and in a poor location in relation to the town. With nearly a mile of water separating the area from the town, the ice in the winter prevented small boats from crossing the harbour, and when the ice was broken and hazardous for walking, there was only the rough road of a mile and a half hacked through the woods to the river where the bridge was still unfinished. The Shelburne citizens urged that other buildings should be built nearer the town. Of their request General Campbell wrote Lord Sydney: 'The expence of those Barracks has been enormous, owing, principally to the situation they have been built upon, but at the sametime, tho it appears the wish of the inhabitants of Shelburne that they should be removed, I do not think it advisable to recommend the incurring that additional Expence, as I understand the spot was originally fixed by Lt-Col Morse at their express desire.'[9]

The 17th Regiment under the command of Colonel Johnson remained in Shelburne until the summer of 1786 when five companies of the 6th Regiment (the 1st Warwickshire Regiment of Foot) commanded by Major Edwards, arrived from Ireland with others from England in the transport *Mary Ann*. Prior to the arrival of the 6th Regiment and the departure of the 17th, soldiers from the 33rd Regiment were in Shelburne. They cleared the forest near the barracks to remove the danger from fire and were recommended for compensation for their labour by General Campbell. The 6th Regiment remained in Shelburne longer than any of the King's soldiers. In 1788 Prince William Henry in a flotilla of His Majesty's ships, the *Andromeda*, the *Thisbe* and the *Brisk*, arrived in Shelburne to review the 6th Regiment. Accompanied by his officers, he landed at the barracks ground. 'The morning was so boisterous,' William Dyott recalled, 'it was with difficulty we could get on shore, and blew so hard that half the Grenadiers lost their caps, so that it was impossible to judge of the discipline of the regiment. They made a handsome appearance, but their ground was so limited (having nothing but a parade of about 120 yards by 50) that they laboured under every disadvantage of time and place.[10]

From time to time advertisements appeared in the Shelburne newspapers for supplies for the regiments; for 600 cords of firewood for the 17th Regiment to be delivered contiguous to their barracks; for five or six tons of hay for His Majesty's troops 'for which a generous price will be paid.' The boredom of a soldier's life and the temptation to escape are revealed in the

Shelburne Court of Session records and in advertisements in the newspapers, ordering, on the request of Major Johnson, the immediate cessation of encouragement to soldiers to desert their posts of duty and seamen the ships of war. An old story is still remembered of an escaped boy who had been impressed into His Majesty's navy. Reaching the homestead of a settler he discovered himself pursued. An old grandmother sitting by the fire lifted her long full skirts and he ducked beneath. Spreading her shirts wide she was just an old woman sitting by the fireside and the soldiers passed on. But not all had an old lady's skirts to hide beneath and for the capture of one of His Majesty's soldiers of the 6th Regiment, Thomas Whiting was paid ten shillings. Mary Hughes, on her written confession that she had harboured a midshipman from His Majesty's ship *Mercury*, was pardoned by Captain Stanhope and was dismissed from court.[11]

Except for the assistance given by civilians to deserters, there were few complaints made by the military to the Shelburne magistrates. Adam Bower, for purchasing 'necessarys' from a soldier, had his tavern license cancelled, and a sharp order was issued to all civilians of the town and district not to purchase necessarys from any soldier or credit a soldier more than a day's pay. Orders were soon forgotten and Abigail Roberts was fined five pounds for buying a soldier's regimental clothing for a few shillings and a quart of rum. There were likewise few complaints by the Shelburne magistrates, with one exception, when a soldier lifted a fisherman's net and on his protest struck him to the ground with a scoop net. Captain William Booth gave pleasing glimpses of the soldiers: chipping holes in the ice to fix branches to be used as guides across the harbour-ice to the barracks; planting small gardens; repairing the wharf for their boat; marching three miles to church and, when they went armed, piling their muskets with fixed bayonets beside the church; dancing and dining with 'much drum beating and claret drinking.' The band of the 6th provided music for many of the services of the churches, and on the consecration of Christ Church and burial ground the playing of the band added 'solemnity and pleasure.' Tragedy came to the 6th Regiment in July, 1790, when Lieutenant Nicholas Ball and Ensign Patrick Maxwell were drowned on their way to Point Carleton when their sailing boat upset near Hart's Point. They lie beneath a stone in Christ Church burial ground.[12]

By the spring of 1789 the 6th Regiment had expectations of leaving Shelburne and even Major Edwards, Booth remarked, was not 'dressing-up his garden.' But it was not until 1791 that orders came for the departure of the regiment. The 6th had been resident in Shelburne for five years. With the approbation of the Court of Session and Grand Jury an address of farewell, a 'Tribute of Our Gratitude... for the numerous instances of

THE ARMY, THE NAVY AND FORT ELLIOTT

polite, and friendly attention wherewith you have honoured the Inhabitants of this Settlement the whole time of your being Stationed among them' was presented to Colonel Whyte at the barracks on the evening of the regiment's departure. A company of the 4th Regiment was sent to Shelburne and on its removal soon after, the military establishment was broken. Point Carleton was dismantled and the barracks opposite the town fell into decay, all except the commanding officer's quarters lived in for years by Donald 'Barracks' McKay. The departure of the last of the soldiers to fife and drum beat was long remembered in Shelburne as they disappeared into the forest over Pell's Road on the way to Annapolis.[13]

THE NAVY

As Carleton made plans for a military post at Port Roseway, he made arrangements for a provincial naval force as 'it becomes of great importance and highly necessary that these Provinces should be covered by a naval force at least until the new arrangements have taken place and that the troops arrive at their respective destinations.' As senior officer of the naval station at Port Roseway he sent William Affleck, commander of His Majesty's ship *Duc de Cartes*, who remained at Port Roseway until October when he was succeeded by the Honourable Edwin Henry Stanhope, captain of His Majesty's ship *Mercury*.[14]

With the expectation that Shelburne would be an important naval base, eight reserves were set aside. Opposite the town, the islands called the Navy Islands were reserved for naval purposes. On the town side of the harbour, Provision Island (Commissary Island) was set aside for the storage of the King's Bounty of provisions. Opposite Commissary Island, the waterfront area designated by block letter A, North Division, beginning at the north side of Bulkeley Street, and the water between the island and the shore, were reserved for the King's wharf. The shore and water at the south end of Water Street were reserved for the King's slip, and in Roseway River, the wooded island, near and above the falls, was marked for the use of the navy. Other reserves were set aside by John Wentworth, the surveyor general of His Majesty's Woods, because he believed 'from its situation, extent and goodness of its harbor,' Shelburne would be 'of great consequence to the safety and supply of Halifax' and a safe retreat in the hurricane months for the fleets employed in the West Indies. Furthermore, and of still greater importance, Shelburne was 'peculiarly adapted for all naval operations that may ever be necessary for the defence or offence on the Coasts of America,' he assured the commissioners of His Majesty's navy. With the impending importance of Shelburne as a naval and repair base, he marked large tracts of timberland with the King's broad arrow. In the Roseway River he reserved Long Island with its 3,000 acres of pine timber 'sound from 18 to 25 or 26 inches diameter and of proper lengths'; spruce for smaller spars and hardwood for repairing timber, for planks and for fuel. About twelve miles from Shelburne, on the east side of the Roseway and including the river, he set aside a tract of land 160 chains on the river and 160 chains back into the wilderness, with an allowance for a road 40 rods wide. On the west bank of the Jordan, a few miles above the falls, he marked 2,400 acres of fine timberland as the King's Forest. As his deputy surveyor, Wentworth employed David Thomson, shipwright and shipbuilder, who considered the reservations 'to be perfectly commodious for all naval purposes,' as did also Sir Charles Douglas, chief of the King's navy in North America, who marked 'these places to be essentially useful to the King's Service.'[15]

Wentworth's optimistic opinion of the future prominence of Shelburne as a naval base and repair centre was not shared by Colonel Robert Morse. After careful investigation he was of the opinion that, 'with all the advantages attending the harbour I do not think it an eligible one in a military view, for though there is a fine situation for careening wharfs and a naval yard upon the tongue (Hart's Point) it would be difficult to defend this harbour against a superior naval force, without extensive and expensive works. The entrance into it at the Narrows is too wide to be secured by batteries; nor does there appear any single situation within, favourable to the protection of naval and military arsenals.'[16]

Although Shelburne did not achieve importance as a naval base or as a repair center, ships of the King's Navy came into the port and naval officers visited the town. Captain Mowat of *La Sophia* was among the first to view the town, in June 1783, when one of the long Shelburne streets was named in his honour. In early May 1784, Sir Charles Douglas, commodore and commander-in-chief of the King's Navy in North America, visited Shelburne in H.M.S. *Assistance* and H.M.S. *Hermione*. He was favourably impressed with the town of Shelburne and its possibilities as a naval base and supply centre for heavy pine timber for the King's ships. By the summer of 1788, when Prince William Henry inspected the military installations, the rapid decline of Shelburne was everywhere evident – in its deserted houses and places of business. The Naval Office reports of ships entering and departing the port of Shelburne indicate the decline in the importance of Shelburne as a naval station and as a place for trade and commerce. In 1787, July 1 to December 31, 65 ships entered the port and 69 were cleared; 1789, January 1 to June 30, 30 ships entered port, 32 cleared; October 1, 1789 to March 31, 1790, 6 ships entered, 7 cleared. The concern of the Shelburne citizens with the decline of their town was perhaps nowhere more poignantly expressed than in their appeal to Sir Richard Hughes, vice-admiral of the Blue, to represent to His Majesty and his ministers the advantages of the situation of their port for the fisheries and the West India trade and the safety of their harbour for large shipping. In the reduced state of their 'once populous and flourishing settlement' they were in need of the 'protection and encouragement of our munificent parent country.'[17]

FORT ELLIOTT

On the suggestion of Sir Guy Carleton that the Port Roseway Associates should form themselves into a militia, they had nominated 16 of their leading men to be their captains. At the same time, they listed their arms and ammunition and provided the commissary general with a return of the armaments they needed. Similar arrangements were made with the men of the British and British American regiments destined for Nova Scotia, their officers to continue as militia officers and to be 'obeyed as such until the Governor of Nova Scotia, shall make other arrangements.' On Parr's arrival in Port Roseway in July 1783, he appointed justices of the peace for the new settlement of Shelburne, but did not commission officers for a local militia. He perhaps considered a militia unnecessary at that time and it was not until after 1793, when war was declared between England and France, that a volunteer company was mustered and officers were commissioned to serve under the command of Captain Jacob Van Buskirk. Without official recognition from Governor Parr, it seems that the captains of the companies of Loyalists and the officers of the disbanded regiments persisted as officers of militia and erected a small fortification on the hill near the end of Water Street, south of William Street, then known as Watson's Point (Battery Point). The date when it was constructed is uncertain. In September 1784 the members of the Court of Quarter Sessions were 'of opinion that a magazine ought to be erected in some convenient place for the purpose of receiving in and delivering out all Guns, Powder that may be brought to this settlement.' This perhaps resulted in the building of Fort Elliott at this time. Two year later, in September 1786, on the anniversary of His Majesty's coronation which was celebrated 'with every possible demonstration of loyalty and joy,' a royal salute was fired from Fort Elliott by the inhabitants of the town at 12 noon and at 1 o'clock from His Majesty's sloop of war *Weazel* and from Point Carleton.

During the war with France and again in 1812 when French and American privateers prowled along the Coast of Nova Scotia, Fort Elliott was reconstructed. Barracks were built for the militiamen, and a gun and a tar barrel on a pole (to be used as a beacon) were mounted near the mouth of the harbour above the sandspit at Sandy Point. When these were fired and the drum and fife sounded in the streets, the miltiamen raced to the fort. As a means of defence Fort Elliott was insignificant. 'Indeed an enterprising man, commanding a frigate,' commented Lieutenant Napier of HMS *Nymphe*, 'by taking advantage of a side wind, might destroy fort and town, or take any vessel from the harbour.' But the militiamen were well trained by the bombardier in charge of the battery and fired a royal salute with their two field pieces as smartly as the gunmen on HMS *Nymphe*. As a civilian fortification, Fort Elliott stood on the hill overlooking the long reach of the harbour until it fell a victim of disuse and was lost in grass and a tangle of wildflowers.[18]

6
Building the Town

The building of Shelburne was a remarkable achievement. Where there were 'dark woods and dismal Rocks' in the spring of 1783, there stood hundreds of houses, stores, inns and taverns eight months later. Parr boasted to Lord Shelburne that of the new towns almost completed, 'the most considerable, most flourishing and most expeditious that ever was built in so short a time is Shelburne. 800 houses are already finished, 600 more in great forwardness, and several hundred lately begun upon, with wharfs and other erections.' Benjamin Marston, from information gathered by the Royal Engineers, reported in September 1784, 1,127 buildings constructed between May 23, when the first house lots were allotted, and February 1, 1784. Of the houses, 80 were temporary structures for the winter only, 231 were framed houses; the remaining were log houses 'built of pieces of timber framed together at the ends' which, with clapboards, could be made permanent buildings. From February 1 to September 1784, Marston estimated that some 250 to 300 houses and stores were built, 'and these later buildings are altogether framed houses and most generally large, commodious, and some of them elegant buildings.'[1]

A long remembered sight of Shelburne during the first winter was of many tents and marquees, sheds made of boards for shelter, log cabins, houses being built, the sound of hammer and saw, and bare rocks and moss when the snow melted. Houses were built 'from the very wood that grew where the town now stands.' To build a log house some large stones or rocks were chosen to serve as a firehearth and for the lower and back part of the chimney at one end of the house. Trees were felled, their branches lopped off, the trunks cut into proper lengths and piled one upon another horizontally, so as to form a quadrangular building. The ends of each log, forming the front and back walls of the house, were set into a groove (cut toward the extremities of the logs used in the two ends of the building), in such a manner as to project six or seven inches beyond the end logs. The roof was thatched with dry twigs and hay and the spaces between the logs were chaulked with moss. A small cellar or excavation in the earth for the storage of potatoes was reached through a small hole in the floor covered with loose planks. A better finished log house was of squared logs framed together at the corners as mentioned by Marston and as depicted by William Booth in one of his drawings of early Shelburne. In larger buildings using hewn or squared logs erected vertically, a sturdy horizontal beam was placed between the logs of the first and second storey as in the store of the Ross-Thomson House. Huts were made of poles covered with strips of bark.[2]

Early drawings of framed Shelburne houses are of rectangular buildings, of one storey or one-and-one-half storeys high, with a few two storey houses, with peaked gable ends or gambrel roofs, like the bottom of boats turned turtle. Most houses had few embellishments to relieve the bareness of eaveless gables and of plain finish boards for door and window casings. A few houses had narrow, close-fitting eaves with shallow overhang that gave neatness to their appearance. The sturdy, straight-forward simplicity of the early Shelburne houses and their style of architecture mark the background of most of their builders as New England.

The frames of the early Shelburne buildings were of sawn or handhewn timber marked with Roman numerals as an aid to the builder; rafters of heavy hewn oak or pine, their ends cut and lapped, were held with oak pegs. Both gable-ended and gambrel-roofed houses were constructed without ridgepoles. Buildings were covered with shingles or with clapboards, the ends of the clapboards bevelled and lapped rather than butted as in later construction; or wide, heavy weather boards were used, lapped one over the other to exclude the rain. In some buildings, pine needles were used as insulation between the walls.

The placing of doors and windows gave to most houses an appearance of symmetry in relation to their proportions. Exterior doors were of four panels or were six-panelled Christian doors neatly finished with moulding, or were constructed of heavy planks studded with hand-forged, square-headed or rose-headed nails. They swung on butt or strap hinges, were barred or were secured with massive rim locks or with mortise locks, some requiring two turns of a key to unlock. Some doorways were topped with a transom set with four or five panes of glass for light in dark hallways.

BUILDING THE TOWN

Doorsteps were of great blocks of cut gray granite or were of 'pudding stone' (conglomerate). Interior doors were similar in style to the exterior doors and had iron thumb latches, rim or mortise locks (some with small brass knobs) and swung on H and L or L hinges or on light butt hinges. Small houses had single sash windows fitted with small panes of glass; larger houses had windows of two sashes, the lower usually with eight or twelve lights, the upper with twelve or sixteen lights of five by seven inch panes of glass, or six by eight inch panes. Many of the early houses had heavy wooden shutters to their windows held with iron clasps or with iron bars when closed.

The interior walls were panelled with pine or oak boards or were plastered with a coarse mixture of lime and sand to which crushed shells were sometimes added, and the rough surface was coated with a smooth wash of lime. Instead of laths, in some houses, stout stems of witherod were nailed to the studs and given a thick coat of plaster, an old method known as 'wattle and daub.' Most rooms had a chair rail 28 to 30 inches from the floor or had a panelled wainscot. Some wall paper was available, one merchant adver-

Part of the Town of Shelburne in Nova Scotia, with the Barracks opposite, 1789. Wash drawing by William Booth. (Courtesy Public Archives of Canada, C-10548)

tising his as a plain blue paper with a very handsome border. Few of the early Shelburne merchants mentioned paint, and unless it was imported by individuals, paint was home-made from lime, skim milk and caraway or linseed oil, and was coloured with red or yellow ochre, with Spanish white made from chalk, Spanish brown, or lamp black. A paint for houses and fences was made from resin melted in oil and added to a mixture of lime and milk. From fine sand, ashes, and slaked lime mixed with oil, a sturdy fireproof paint was made and was used on the roofs of houses.

Deep cellars were excavated for many of the houses. They were walled with field stones in dry-stone construction and were usually topped with cut granite blocks for the foundation of the house. Massive chimneys of granite supported three and four fireplaces for living rooms and bedrooms. Great slabs of neatly dressed granite or pudding stone formed the hearths of first floor fireplaces; hand-made bricks or clay tiles were generally used for second floor hearths. Fireplaces had wooden mantels supported by fluted pilasters with decorated or plain capital and base and usually had a narrow mantelboard. With the addition of a panelled wall, deep closets and cupboards were created beside the fireplaces where housewives stored their choicest jams and cakes. Kitchen fireplaces were equipped with chains and hooks, swinging cranes and an iron baffle board to reflect the heat to bubbling pots dangling beneath the board. Bake ovens were part of kitchen chimneys or were in a cellar kitchen where in some houses the cooking was done. Many of the first Shelburne homes had wooden chimneys daubed with mud. High board fences enclosed house lots providing privacy and protection for small gardens. Wide gates set in the fences swung on strap hinges and were secured at night with padlocks.

The Loyalists brought some lumber for their houses with them in their vessels. Other lumber they bought from the New England settlers living along the shores of Nova Scotia and from traders from the New England seaports, paying from 30 to 36 shillings to £4.10 per thousand feet. Parr supplied what lumber he could to the various new settlements, but the 400,000 feet of boards promised the Port Roseway Associates in the winter of 1783 fell far short of the lumber needed even to build the houses of the Associates. In their own saw pits and sawmills the Loyalists cut most of their own lumber from trees on their land, whipping out boards to cover six to ten houses a week. 'In conformity to his Majesty's most gracious Instructions,' John Wentworth as the surveyor of His Majesty's Woods wrote the Duke of Portland, 'I have permitted the Inhabitants settling at Shelburne to cut such pine timber growing upon their respective Lots, as were not fit for the public Service, that were injurious to cultivation and the want of which to cut into building material was extremely distressing.' All of which was

BUILDING THE TOWN

accomplished 'without the loss of any tree, that could be ever used for mast, yard or Bowsprit.'[3]

Tools to assist the Loyalists in clearing their land and building their houses were slow in reaching the settlements. In the spring of 1783 Lord North advised Parr that 'His Majesty's Servants having taken into consideration the distress of His Majesty's faithful Subjects now in Nova Scotia' they were sending them several articles for the erection of their houses. The King left the distribution to his judgment to be given to: 'proper objects only... that Government will not from this mark of Liberality be put to any u⟶nessary Expence.' There were tools to clear land, to till the soil, to fell trees, to saw and trim boards, to build houses. There were hammers, gimlets, bits and stocks, planes, chisels, gouges, augers; saws, carpenter's squares, files and wood rasps. There were whip saws, wedges, broad axes, felling axes, helved hatchets, adzes, drawing knives; grindstones, rub-

Town of Shelburne from the Barracks. Watercolour by H. Pooley, approximately 1818. (Courtesy Special Collections, Killam Library, Dalhousie University)

stones, oilstones, files for whipsaws; broad and narrow hoes, spades and pickaxes. For their houses were: garnet hinges, hooks and hinges, locks, padlocks, hasps and staples, hooks and eyes for windows, window bolts; spikes, nails, brads and screws. In August more tools were sent from England. These Governor Parr acknowledged in late November, assuring Lord North that they would 'be distributed without loss of time.' Few of the tools and other supplies sent for distressed Loyalists reached Shelburne. When surprised by Governor Parr's statement that he had sent ironmongery to Shelburne that he valued at £1,000, Alexander Leckie asked permission to examine the returns. He could find no vouchers and only one account of sixteen casks of nails and five casks of spades, hinges, etc. sent to the town. It was the same with the distribution of other gifts to the Loyalists and to the Blacks – never enough to meet the needs of all. For some, there was cloth for a dress or for a shift, for a coat or for a pair of breeches; for others there was a pair of shoes; for a few, an axe or a spade or a pair of hinges; for others, less or nothing from the King's Bounty. The cry soon arose of gifts to favourites. In the summer of 1784 the Board of Agents appointed to distribute the lots of land were asked also to distribute the clothing, farming utensils and other supplies not yet given out and to prepare returns of items already released. With not enough for all to share in an equal distribution, only 'Individuals whom the exigency of the times have reduced to extremity' were to apply, their proverty vouched for in certificates.[4]

The Minshull house, northeast corner of Ann and Water Streets, sketched by the owner, John Minshull, approximately 1784. Farther down Ann Street was the Minshull stable and the home of Rev. William Walter, an Anglican clergyman. Next to the dwelling on Water Street was Mr. Minshull's warehouse. In the 1920s the house was moved to a new site and remodelled by Mr. John J. Cox.

7
Distribution of the Land

From the beginning, the Port Roseway Associates were not pleased with the setting aside of their intention that Port Roseway was to be for them only and not for all ranks and conditions of men who might come among them. They insisted that only 441 heads of families were entitled to have lots of land in the town and that all should share in an equal distribution of the land. That many came and elbowed them from choice lots and obtained special concessions for allotments of farm land rankled deeply. Governor Parr was soon aware of their discontent and that of other Loyalists in other settlements. 'Some few discontented Rascals,' he complained to Lord Shelburne, 'begin to be clamorous and seditious... there are some not to be pleased or satisfied.' That the grievances of the Shelburne Loyalists and the disbanded soldiers huddled in shacks of logs and boards ran deeper than discontent was to stir even Parr into action.[1]

The Port Roseway Associates, as the others who came to Shelburne, believed on their arrival that land would be given to them – lots in the town and farm land where they could immediately begin to prepare the soil for crops. Something like this might have happened if *only* the Associates had come to Shelburne and if only a few weeks had been required to survey the town and countryside to meet their needs. With hundreds of others pushing their way into the town, the boundaries of the modest settlement planned for the Associates had to be more than doubled in length and breadth, still without enough good land for house lots.

With the great need for land, Benjamin Marston, with the responsibility of acting-chief surveyor thrust upon him by William Morris' departure as surveyor for other Loyalist settlements, turned his attention to marking country lots for farm land. As he worked and explored the wilderness, he made many suggestions to Governor Parr and to the surveyor general for the future development of the land. The 200 acre farm lots for grazing and raising of produce planned for the outskirts of the town could be as profitably situated on public roads 12 miles inland from the town where there was good land available. Lyman had discovered Long Island in the Roseway River: 3,500 to 3,600 acres of rich meadow and 'tolerably good upland.' It, he suggested, should be reserved for glebe and school land. Captain Nicholas Dean, 'a man of some property... with other persons of property' wished to establish a fishing settlement at Green Harbour. Here locations need not exceed in general more than a lot convenient for a house and garden for 'those whose livelihood was the Hook and Line'; employers and curers of fish should have larger grants.

As the first winter turned into spring, Marston marked lots in the town for the 770 to 800 persons still unlocated. These were well north of King Street in Parr's Division on the eastern boundary of the town. They were cut into blocks by Glasgow and Minto Streets and were divided by Temple, Pitt and Devonshire, and were bounded on the east by Back Street. They were more than a mile from the waterfront and the centre of the town and of little value to persons whose occupations required their being near their places of business. The Loyalists protested they did not want them for lots. To relieve the tension, Marston proposed that in lieu of lots in Shelburne 'locations be made of town lots at Cape Negro Harbour for as many as choose to go there and more at Gunning Cove.' Following Parr's instructions, he had, by the end of April, distributed the last of the water lots at the lower end of the town to owners of vessels, merchants, boatbuilders, smiths and blockmakers. The number of lots fell far short of the demand. Disappointed in not receiving water lots, some requested lots of meadow land along the eastern boundary of the southern half of the town to drain and convert to grass land. This land Parr had already agreed should be laid off into lots and sold, and the money applied to levelling the streets. Marston now suggested that it should be given instead, in lieu of water lots, to those who would improve it. Most of the Loyalists, by the spring of 1784, were indifferent to Marston's plea for chainbearers to assist him in measuring the land. Their indifference sprang partly from the inconvenient location of the only land left to be divided into house lots, and partly because they wanted the great squares of the town (set aside for public buildings) divided into house lots for 112 families 'similar to the other squairs.' During the first days the surveyors gave permission to land baggage and to build temporary shelters on the public squares until town lots were provided. Some immediately proceeded to construct 'midling houses for themselves.' Resentment was rife when it was discovered they were to be moved 'not for public Buildings, but for a more valuable end, to accommodate sons of Favour . . . that go to Halifax with full pockets of a mettle well know in Mexico.'[2]

By the spring of 1784 the displeasure of the Shelburne Loyalists and the disbanded soldiers was being expressed in more forceful ways than indifference to Marston's request for assistance and by demands that the public squares be divided into house lots. With strife already breaking into violence, the magistrates wrote to Parr through their agents Joseph Alpin and James Clark. As Loyalists who had 'sought in the Deserts of His Majesty's province of Nova Scotia an asylum from Republican Tyranny,' they had 'by immense Labour and Industry and at a very heavy Expense built the Town of Shelburne.' Before their arrival in the province they were promised certain portions of land 'which were understood to be but a Small and very inadequate Recompence for their past Sufferings, Loss of Time and Loss of Property.' After many months, few had any assurance by grant that the land allotted to them was indisputably theirs. Parr and his Council immediately ordered grants to be issued for the lists of locations already made. And, 'could we be possessed of every necessary return from Mr. Marston,' they informed the magistrates, 'the whole of the Town shall be immediately located and the Inhabitants fixed in quiet Possession.'[3]

On May 27, 1784, the first of the grants, those for warehouse or water lots in the south division of the town, were registered on the approval of Governor Parr and were issued under the seal of the province. On June 7 the grants were entered at the auditor's office by Francis Shipton, deputy auditor, and were attested to as a true copy of the original returns by Samuel Burling, assistant agent for the Shelburne Loyalists. By the terms of the grants, the land was to belong to the grantees with the payment to His Majesty of a free yearly quit rent of one farthing for each lot, payable at the expiration of ten years from the date of the grant. By the end of June grants were ready for a number of the town lots. They were granted on the same terms as the water lots except that the payment of the quit rent was to commence in two years from the date of the grant. At the time these grants were issued came the grants for Mason's and Marston's Divisions surveyed in the summer of 1783. Mason's Division of 12,780 acres, divided into 50 acre lots, lay along the eastern shore of Shelburne Harbour (Sandy Point) and the western shore of Jordan Bay and Jordan River to the falls. Marston's Division was the block of 50 acre lots on the west side of Shelburne Harbour at Churchover; the point of land in the Jordan River, Jones' Point

(McLean's Island), and a 200 acre lot at the back of the 50 acre lots nos. 221-225 in Mason's Division. As for the town and water lots, the land belonged to the grantees with allowance for public landings and roads: 'all woods, underwoods, timber, and timber trees, lakes, ponds, fishings, waters, and water courses... with privileges of hunting, hawking, and fowling, in and upon the same, and mines and minerals' except 'all white-pine trees' and 'all mines of gold, silver, copper, lead, and coals.' The lots were given 'in free and common soccage [tenure]... yielding and paying yearly at the Feast of Saint Michael, after the expiration of ten years, two shillings for every hundred acres.' The land was given to be improved. In three years, for every 50 acres of plantable land, three acres must be cleared and worked, or three acres of swampy or sunken or marsh land cleared and drained, and upon every 50 acres accounted barren must be three neat cattle. To hold land unfit for cultivation without manuring and improving, the grantee had to erect 'one Good Dwelling House to be at least 20 feet in length by 16 feet in Breadth' and three neat cattle for every 50 acres. To hold stony or rocky ground not fit for planting or pasture, one good and able hand employed for three years digging any stone quarry or mine would be considered sufficient cultivation and improvement. Every three acres cleared and worked or cleared and drained would be sufficient to save forever from forfeiture 50 acres in any tract granted. Rent unpaid for one year and no distress found on the land or the grant not duly registered within six months 'every part and parcel thereof shall revert to Us, our heirs and successors.'

ANARCHY AND CONFUSION

Despite grants for town and water lots and 50 acre lots along the shores, only the Loyalists who had applied for special allotments, and none of the disbanded soldiers, had any substantial grants of farm land, nor were there any orders from the governor to survey land for farms. This was at least partly because Parr himself had not received instructions from the British government for the establishment of townships and the allotment of land. His plea to Lord Shelburne in the fall of 1783 to honour him with some instructions as how to act in a 'crises which never happened to any Governor before,' was still unheeded in late March of 1784, and he was obliged 'to act in the dark in many matters, for want of proper answers.' Still acting 'in the dark,' since by June 5 the belated instructions he was to receive had not arrived, Parr, on the representation of the Shelburne magistrates, agreed to have 200 acre farm lots surveyed and laid out in the district of Shelburne. These were to be assigned to all persons who had a proper claim on government, 'with the advice and opinion of the magistrates and Grand

DISTRIBUTION OF LAND

Jury' in places 'suitable proper and convenient' for their accommodation.[4]

To people dependent on what they had discovered was a skimpy royal bounty of provisions, farm land was a pressing necessity. In the summer of 1784, their land needed to yield produce to eke out what might be given them from His Majesty's pork barrels. By the first of January 'the spirit of exploring and getting on the land in ye country is becoming very general' Marston informed Governor Parr. Joshua Pell, a founder of the Port Roseway Association, was 'in a good measure the first promoter of the present enterprizes.' He had cut and cleared a road 20 feet wide within a full three miles of the town. Here he found good land and set about surveying it for farm lots. By May 18 he had lots for 234 persons and with Marston's assistance was ready for the lottery. Persons who had stopped Pell before in allotting 15 twenty acre lots edging the road he had cut into the wilderness, 'prevailed against the drawing.' 'This cursed levelling spirit,' Marston stormed, 'must be crushed by every means or we shall be for rebellion soon.' The determination of the Port Roseway Associates that all should share alike in the distribution of the land was to be a rough stumbling block to the peaceful settlement of the issue. When they looked around them and saw lots edging the harbour and the river, some of 500 acres, given to persons, as one disgruntled Loyalist wrote, who could go to Halifax with money to pay for special favours, they turned rebellious and demanded an equal distribution in what they considered their rightful share in the King's Bounty of land. They also resented the large tracts of land reserved for the King's Forest and the land marked by the Royal Engineers for military and naval purposes. Joseph Pynchon, who had been appointed an assistant to mark the reserve of timber for the King's Navy, found 'the spirit that at present prevails' rendered 'a general survey and marking the Timber... a most dangerous undertaking and without Effect as no attention would be paid to it... and no prosecution practicable for want of Information.'[5]

It was at this time in late May that Governor Wentworth, as he was still referred to by the Loyalists who remembered him as the governor of New Hampshire, arrived in Shelburne as the surveyor of His Majesty's Woods in Nova Scotia. He was conducted up the harbour by HMS *Mercury* and was saluted by a discharge of cannon.

No contemporary document describes or sets the date of the first public protestation over the distribution of land and over the military and naval reservations. It perhaps occurred shortly before the arrival of Wentworth on May 25 or during his stay in Shelburne, for shortly after his return to Halifax, General Campbell sent a regiment of soldiers to Shelburne. With mounting concern the Shelburne magistrates watched the uneasiness spreading among the people, 'from the land not being Located to them.'

'Unless some mode was adopted for immediate relief,' they informed Governor Parr, 'this settlement must fall through and the Large Sums of money already expended be entirely Sunk, added to this – Anarchy and confusion must be the inevitable consequence.' They suggested that the Lieutenant-Governor should be invested with full power to sign grants and that he should reside in Shelburne 'until the Business of Locating be completed.' Or, that a Board of Agents, consisting of the magistrates and grand jury of the Court of Sessions, should be given full power to locate all persons having just claims with the immediate possession of their land.[6]

This was on July 23. On July 26 the anarchy they feared gripped the town. Simeon Perkins, learning of the riot, wrote in his *Diary*: 'An Extraordinary mobb or Riot has happened in Shelburne. Some thousands of People Assembled with Clubbs, and Drove the Negroes out of the Town and threatened Some people.' A few days later he heard that the disbanded troops were under arms. That it was more than people held idle from lack of employment rising against the free Blacks 'because they labour cheaper than they' is evident from Marston taking refuge in the barracks and fleeing to Halifax. Although the large allotments of land to individuals were made on the recommendation of the governor and the surveyor general, it was inevitable that Marston should be accused of partiality. One who obtained 500 acres on the Roseway River for a sawmill was Thomas Courtney, with another 500 acres allotted to his brother James. As the tension mounted, Thomas Courtney became a victim of violence and during the riots his house was guarded by citizens who did not side with the rioters. A leader of the discontented in the first rumbles of disorder in the early spring of 1784 was Ephraim Smith. He was convicted 'of disturbing the Peace in propagating reports of intended opposition to the laws of the Province and of cruel punishment determined to be inflicted by riotous Persons, to the Terror of His Majesty's Subjects.' The records are silent on the names of those who in the month of July fomented the riots from which Marston fled and which caused Governor Parr to come to Shelburne to restore peace and order.[7]

THE BOARD OF AGENTS

Until the violent eruption of discontent, Parr considered the reports of unrest as trivial. Several families were unlocated, he wrote Lord Shelburne, 'owing to disputes among themselves, quareling for the same spot, all wishing to be upon the Sea Coast, great partialitys commited by their Agents and Surveyors, the principal of the latter at Shelburne,... in short my Lord there are many of them like sharks preying upon each other.' Of the rumours he had heard of the vast acreage he had reserved for himself, he protested it amounted to only 'a 500 acre Lott, at the distance of a Mile and a half from Shelburne, where there is a small Cove, I purpose building a little House on it, and to go there every Year for a short space of time, the Land just there is of very little value, another reason for my fixing upon this spot is, the probability of the seat of Government being removed there, one day or other.' If Parr had wanted vast acreage for himself, his wishes were curbed when he remembered the reaction to the 55 Loyalists who had petitioned Carleton for 5,000 acres each in Nova Scotia (altogether 275,000 acres), considering themselves entitled because of 'their special services and the dignity or importance of their former positions in Society.' Many who protested the '55' in 1783 and had demanded 'that they may be all put on an equal footing' in the summer of 1784, faced Governor Parr with the demand for a just distribution of the land promised them.[8]

When a Board of Agents was suggested to Parr to allot the land and get the settlers on their acreage, he considered such a Board as unconstitutional and felt its appointment 'might prove a dangerous tendency.' But with the eruption of violence, he put aside his reservations and Parr appointed a Board to assign land to 'all persons entitled thereto according to His Majesty's Instructions.' All controversies and disputes over the assignment of land were to be investigated and reported to Parr; and all persons applying for grants were first to apply to the Board and only on its recommendations were grants to be issued. They were to encourage the association of families for farming settlements, assigning to them a quantity of land appropriate to their needs in any part of the county not exceeding 15,000 acres to be divided among 40 families, reserving 600 acres for future appropriation. They were also to locate the Blacks at Birchtown in a manner most conducive to their welfare and the interest of the settlement. The men chosen by Parr were substantial Shelburne Loyalists: Isaac Wilkins, James McEwen, Abraham Van Buskirk, Joseph Brewer, David Thomson, Joshua Watson, Benjamin Davis, Charles McNeil, Ebenezer Parker, Alexander Leckie, Joshua Pell, Nicholas Ogden, Robert Gray, justices of the peace; Valentine Nutter, John Miller, Peter Lynch, William Harvey, Charles White, John Lownds, Alexander Robertson, Patrick Wall, Michael Largin, 'gentlemen inhabitants of the township of Shelburne,' and Joseph Alpin, an agent for the Shelburne Loyalists.[9]

Shortly before Parr appointed the Board of Agents, he had finally received His Majesty's instructions for the distribution of land; for the setting up of townships with reserves for military and naval purposes and for the growth and production of naval timber; for the establishment of custom-houses and the reservation of land for churches and schools; and for the sowing of hemp and flax seeds. To every person, master or mistress of a family, was to be granted 100 acres plus 50 acres for every white or black man, woman and child, 'such person's family shall consist [of] at the actual time of making the Grants.' To the men of the British Forces disbanded in the province, were to be granted for their 'Services and Bravery,' 200 acres to a noncommissioned officer, 100 acres to a private, which were to be exclusive of the quantity of land each man was entitled to receive for each member of his family. Those loyal subjects who took up arms and those who associated themselves together in the support of the British government and its authority under the name of the Associated Loyalists 'without being put upon any particular Establishment,' were to receive the same allotment of land as that given to noncommissioned officers and privates of the disbanded British Forces. To commissioned officers of the provincial forces on their application, 'indicating their willingness and intention to settle and improve land': a field officer was to be given 1,000 acres, a captain 700 acres, subaltern, staff and warrant officers 500 acres, exclusive of the usual acreage for each member of a family. Privates and officers, noncommissioned and commissioned, where practicable, were to be settled in corps 'as contiguous as may be to each other... that the same may be united and in case of attack be defended by those who have been accustomed to bear arms together.' No grants were to be made until the surveyor general of the King's Forest had viewed and marked reservations for timber for the Royal Navy and no grants were to be issued to land within the reservations. Farm grants were to be made only in proportion to the grantee's ability to improve the land. Those capable of improving more than granted to them, on application, could be granted 1,000 acres over and above that which they were entitled to receive as Loyalists or as disbanded soldiers.[10]

With the King's instructions for his guidance, Parr arrived in Shelburne in late August 'to quiet the minds and apprehensions of the settlers.' In a list of their grievances, the Board pointed out to Parr that the first Associators, having no instructions from the provincial government for the allotment of land, 'adopted the equal measure of laying out certain districts of the Soil into 50 acre lots,' not from 'any Passion or Fondness which they bore to a levelling principle,' but rather 'they considered the Lands... not as a compensation for the Losses which they had sustained... but as a Reward for a Mere Mental Quality. A man who never possessed property of the value of £200 Sterling... [being] as capable of the Virtue of Loyalty as a man possessed of Ten Thousand.' 'This equitable Idea' was of short duration, for several who came after the lottery, as well as several of the original Associators, applied for and obtained separate grants of 500 acres. From 'this impolitic conduct,' the Board assured Parr, sprang 'in some measure, the want of Lands in the vicinity of Shelburne,' and those deprived of the land they considered should be theirs, 'will never be at Heart's

DISTRIBUTION OF LAND

Ease, till the original Plan is restored, or till some adequate compensation is awarded them.' The town and water lots, as the 50 acre lots, were drawn on an equal basis, each considering himself 'indefeasibly entitled to what his number blindly promised to him.' Those with lots on the waterfront were considered the owners of the soil to the high water mark and 'equally the owner of the water in front of his lot.' Under the guise of an 'unequal Distribution,' some having more valuable lots than others, there began to be rumours that the water was distinct from the soil and grantable to anyone who might apply for it. Perceiving an altercation, they reminded Parr that on his first visit to Shelburne, he had proposed that the lots adjacent to the water should be sold and the returns from the sales applied to some public use. Since the sale of lots would 'altogether Destroy the Effect of the Lottery,' he had then suggested 'a Sort of Tax' to remedy the Inequality complained of by proposing a 30 foot street be built by the owners of the waterfront lots across their land for public use. To this they had agreed, believing grants to the water would be given to them. But certain persons, late comers to Shelburne, who knew that the water did not go with the land, had applied and had obtained grants to the various pieces of water. The rights of the draw had been annihilated and until the offended were appeased there would be no peace in the town.

His pen scratching across the pages, Samuel Burling, secretary to the Board, recorded their decisions as Parr and the Board sought measures to bring peace to the town. Those in dispute over wharf and water lots were to leave their contentions to arbitration; those losing lots were to be compensated for their improvements. Grants for 50 acre lots actually made in favour of those who were not the original locatees, were to have their grants confirmed and the original locatees were to be compensated with 50 acres in some other location. Disbanded soldiers, in lieu of water and town lots, were to be given 200 acre allotments. Marston's locations and returns, where regular, were to be confirmed except in cases of absentees and forfeitures. Those who had purchased land from absentees or were upon lots where no prior location interfered, and had erected buildings, were to be given grants to the land. Unneccessary reservations made by the engineers' department were to be surrendered and given to the unlocated, and Wentworth, as the surveyor of the King's Forest, was to be requested to relinquish such parts of the reservations of glebe and other lands as appeared unneccessary to the Board.

The magistrates of the first Association who had been promised 500 acres by Parr, if unprovided with their allotment, were to have their land on the island seven miles up the Roseway River, provided that Wentworth relinquished the island already a reservation. Lutheran and other churches

KING'S BOUNTY

acknowledging the King's supremacy were to be given land on the reserved blocks in the town at the discretion of the Board. The surveyor general, with Marston, was to make an exact return of all unlocated land, and those unprovided with land were to draw for the lots available in a general lottery. Those they were unable to locate within the district were to be given a greater proportion of land outside the district 'to put them all, indiscriminately on the Foot of Equality, respect being had to Quality and Quantity.' Surveyors were to be employed by the Board to locate the Loyalists on their land 'to which they are, by every Tie of Honour and Humanity entitled,' and where necessary to interfere with Marston's locations. Those dispossessed were to have land in new locations 'consonant to equity and Substantial Justice.'[11]

On his departure Parr issued a proclamation demanding submission to the authority of the Board, 'to the end that people disposed to faction may avoid the Penalties which the Law inflicts on all Contempt offered Public and lawful Authority.' Parr was alarmed with the anarchy in Shelburne. In early August, with the reports of violence, he had ordered additional soldiers and on his return to Halifax he immediately requested one of His Majesty's frigates to be stationed in the port to cooperate with the troops in

House built by Robert Wilkins on the northwest corner of St. John's and Water Streets. It was later the house of Alexander Houston, an early Shelburne schoolmaster. Watercolour by Mrs. Annie Bruce, painted approximately 1906. (Courtesy Miss Marjorie Bruce)

supporting the authority of the magistrates. Two days after his first request, considering the danger 'to which the inhabitants are hourly expos'd from the Turbulence and unruly disposition of a very considerable number of disbanded soldiers with Arms,' he again urged a frigate 'or some other of the King's ships of force to proceed as soon as possible,' and to remain in Shelburne until the arrival of the *Mercury* to prevent the mischief he had 'so much reason to apprehend.' Many in Shelburne considered Parr's coming more harmful than good. Anarchy continued. By November it had spread to the assault of a number of Indians for which Edward Cavan, as ringleader, was committed to stand in the pillory one hour and remain in prison six months.[12]

With the first suggestion by the Loyalists in Nova Scotia of dissatisfaction with Parr and his administration of their affairs, he was quick to repudiate their complaints. He had shown no partiality in the granting of land or in the distribution of the King's Bounty of provisions. He had not assigned vast acreage to himself. He had always acted to the best of his ability. As the unrest built up he turned his comments to the Loyalists themselves. 'Some few discontented Rascals, at the most distant Settlements, begin to be clamorous and seditious, expecting more than possibly can be done in so short a time,' he informed Lord Shelburne in January 1784. However, 'tho they plague me with complaints, and quarrel among themselves &c, I shall continue to render them every good office in my power.' As the complaints continued, Parr shifted his comments to the magistrates. 'The most liberal of the Loyalists would not go to Shelburne and the River St. John,' he wrote Lord Sydney, and in these settlements he had to make magistrates 'of men whom God Almighty never intended for the office, but it was Hobson's choice.' At the same time, he informed Nepean he feared 'that at Shelburne the magistrates have not conformed to their oaths.' That few of the Shelburne Loyalists had had experience in government, in the administration of law and order and the shaping and moulding of the towns where they had lived, is evident in their claims for losses during the American Revolution. They had been content to go their ways as farmers and seamen, shoemakers and tinsmiths, as merchants and traders, and leave the administration of civil affairs to others. Although inexperienced in government, the magistrates on those first rosters of officials were upright men who strove diligently to perform their duties with honour. The butt of Parr's displeasure was Benjamin Marston. He was discharged with no recourse to justify himself. As a Master of Arts and a graduate of Harvard University, Marston was one of the best educated of those who came to Shelburne, but it is not likely that he had formal training as a surveyor. It was not that he erred in his work – rather Parr was convinced that he had accepted bribes. That few supported Parr's opinion of Marston became evident in June 1785 when he was appointed deputy surrogate, and the deputy surveyor of the King's Woods, and the first sheriff of Northumberland County in the province of New Brunswick.[13]

THE WORK OF THE BOARD

With Parr's departure, the Board set to work preparing lists of those who were already located and those who were without land. A house was hired as a meeting place, and Samuel Burling and George Thomas were elected secretaries; Robert Gray was appointed chief surveyor with John Van Norden, Isaac Hildrith and Robert Morris deputy surveyors. The people themselves looked for the land they wanted. Grouping themselves into companies of associates they prepared lists of locations where they wished to settle and presented their returns to the Board. If their returns were accepted, with the approval of the Board, the land was ordered surveyed at government expense, and the locations were drawn for in a lottery supervised by the Board with the assistance of the surveyors and the captains of the Associates.

As the work of the Board progressed, hundreds of acres of land were allotted along the banks of the rivers and the shores of the harbours and far into the wilderness with reserves for glebe and school use, for public ground and for village lots. On the east side of the Jordan, above the falls, land was allotted in three locations: along the river northward into the forest land extending to and above Lake John – a tract of land known as Campbell's Location, for men mainly from Scottish regiments; a second line of lots east of the river lots was also for men chiefly from the Scottish regiments; and striking off eastward from the second line of lots was a location for discharged artillerymen. Below the falls to the end of East Jordan were large farm lots varying in size from 200 to 600 acres for Loyalists and for disbanded soldiers of the British Legion. South of the East Jordan farm lots, a tract of wilderness extending to the Green Harbour locations was requested by men of the British Legion. Only a few appearing for the draft, the land was left unassigned. On the east side of Jordan Bay, the land on the west side of Green Harbour and around the head of the harbour was allotted to Richard Jenkins (also known as the Deane Location) and to 50 others, who were farmers and fishermen. Along the eastern shores of Green Harbour to the end of the land (Western Head), 5,046 acres were allotted to Loyalists and others, with 1,400 acres reserved from Turpin's Cove to Osborne Harbour for six of the old settlers – John Matthews, Thomas Hayden, Jonathan Locke, Sr., and Jonathan Locke, Jr., Josiah Churchill and Gilbert Benning. The Alexander Murray location (the Ragged Islands

DISTRIBUTION OF LAND

grant) extended from Osborne along the shores and to a point well inland and across the land to Little Harbour and to the back line of the Sable River lots, with land reserved for old settlers (Christopher Cotman and Daniel Matthews at East Ragged Islands; Benjamin Arnold and Enoch Godfrey at Little Harbour). The Sable River location which included Jones Harbour and Port L'Hebert and which was surveyed by Isaac Hildrith, was divided into six locations. The east side of the Sable was for Captain John Spier and his 22 associates; Sable River, and the west banks of the Sable were for Francis Boole and his 22 associates and Patrick Phillips and his 20 associates. Jones Harbour was allotted to George Harding and 27 others; the west side of Port L'Hebert was assigned to the company of Captain James Moffatt and 65 associates; and to Daniel Cameron and his 31 associates was allotted the east side of the bay. To the east of the Sable River locations were the Great Port Jolly (Port Joli) lots of Sergeants John and Neil Robertson of the 76th Regiment and 10 others, their 12 lots legally laid out by Captain Van Norden. With 11 others also choosing the shores of Great Port Jolly, the bay was surrounded with settlers.

As the months passed, few acres in the township and beyond the old lands of Alexander McNutt and his settlers were left unexplored. Along the west side of the Roseway River two locations were laid out above the eight 500 acre lots near the town. These were for Duncan Cameron and his associates, thirty 200 acre lots, and further up the river thirteen 250 to 500 acre lots to Andrew Barclay and others. On the east side of the river, beginning at the falls and along the northern boundary of the town, were fifteen 50 acre lots, assigned to George Thomas and his associates; six 500 acre farm lots to James and Alexander Robertson and four others; and above the farm lots, 7,510 acres were allotted to Peter Blewer and 39 others who were mainly families from the Carolinas and Georgia, their location listed by the Board as on Wright's Road. South of Shelburne, wedged between the lots of Mason's Division, were lots of various acreages to the north and south of Lake Rodney, with those south of the lake allotted to 13 sergeants. East of the town were five farm lots extending northward to the land of Joshua Pell and his sons on the shores of Lake George. On the west side of Roseway River from the Herring Falls to below the lower falls were thirteen 50 acre lots; on the western shores of Hart's Point the lots along the shore continued as a location along Birchtown Creek and westward to Harper's Lake. Along the western shores of the harbour, in Churchover and in Gunning Cove, large tracts of land were allotted to Joseph Durfee and others. To the north of their land were thirty-eight 50 acre farm lots; to the south, with other lots of farm land, were the village lots at Gunning Cove for the pilots who assisted the British navy – in all, a plantation of 6,700 acres including 200 acres for a glebe. Beyond the land set aside for the old settlers from the southern boundary of Gunning Cove to and beyond Round Bay were the Cape Negro Shores where numbers of the Loyalists received their allotments, and in back of the old settlers, acreage was assigned to farmers interested in meadow land. On both banks of the Cape Negro River, soon to be known as the Clyde River, lots were assigned to George Douglas and 88 others. The islands along the shores were divided into lots. Gray Island in False Passage was divided into two lots for John Jones and James Pryor for fish flakes and the curing of fish; McNutt's Island was marked into 35 lots for farmers and fishermen; and on Blue or Green Island, 130 acres were assigned to Samuel Marshall and William Hale for a brickworks.

As roads were marked through the wilderness, the land along the way was cut into lots. On the north and south sides of the Barrington road, west of Birchtown, the land was surveyed for men of the 7th Regiment. Along the course of the Tusket-Argyle road and on Pell's road to Annapolis the lots were drawn in a lottery by subscribers who received 50 acres for every twenty shillings subscribed toward the opening of the roads or for work on the roads at two shillings six pence per day for each labourer. The Argyle location was set aside for men of the 42nd and the 74th Regiments and for 49 Hessian soldiers and their wives and children. Other soldiers of the 42nd and the 74th Regiments asked for land at Cockawhite (Woods Harbour) in Argyle Township. The Tusket River Associators drew for their land on July 20, 1785, at the Merchants' Coffee House in Shelburne, under the inspection of their agents, Colonel Abraham Van Buskirk, Captain Thomas Leonard and Captain Nathaniel Richards. With the pressing need of garden lots for those living in the town, the Board had the Common on the east boundary of the town set aside for small farm lots. For these lots they issued licences of occupation for two and three acres of land to be laid out at the expense of the licencee by a deputy surveyor, the land to be improved within a month from the date of the licence.[14]

It was soon evident that even with careful scrutiny of the returns, there were many conflicts – two families claiming the same lot of land, and some, on going to their country lots, found them already occupied. A further frustration was the long delay before government grants were received for their land. Jasper Harding wrote in his family Bible, '1785 April 16 I come to Jons Harbor.' Grants to the land in Jones Harbour were not issued until 1790 which meant long years of anxious waiting when he could be ousted from his land as he had been from a town lot where he had built his house.[15]

As disturbing as the confusion over the distribution of the land and the unhappy months of waiting for grants was the cry of 'undue partiality.' Isaac Wilkins, president of the Board, was one of the offenders. He had by

DISTRIBUTION OF LAND

his 'avaritious claims' obtained 'a grant of ten fifty acre lots, intended, as the inhabitants have ever supposed, for that number of original settlers.' Further he had taken a warrant of survey 'for 5,000 acres more within six miles of the town on or near the Jordan river; a tract of land amply sufficient for the settlement and accommodation of twenty-five of those industrious farmers and their families who are yet without their land.' Isaac Wilkins repudiated the insults to his integrity. The 5,000 acres were given to him by the governor as compensation for the same quantity, but more valuable land, which he had purchased 15 years before on the St. John River and had relinquished 'for the accommodation of my fellow Loyalists.' By accepting the land 'I injured no man – It was out of the district of Shelburne; and by no means within the assumed claim of the first Associators.' The 500 acres near Point Carleton were in compensation for 750 acres in the township of Conway, near Parr Town, 'which I had relinquished for the same generous purposes.' Without referring to Isaac Wilkins, Parr stoutly supported the members of the Board and assured them he was well-satisfied with their 'zeal and integrity.' He was later to write that by 'steadily supporting a Board of Agents established there, they are now quiet.' It was an uneasy calm. Those watching the unhappiness that lingered over the distribution of the land recognized it as a major factor in the rapid decline of Shelburne. Disillusioned Loyalists left, many for their former homes in the new United States, and embittered soldiers turned away from promises too long unfulfilled.[16]

8
The Courts of Sessions and the Courts of Justice; the first Members of the House of Assembly

COURTS OF SESSIONS
Court of General Quarter Sessions; Court of Special Sessions

It was the earnest wish of the Port Roseway Associates that 'the privilege of a Patent, for a City, be granted, to the Associators, as it will greatly prevent designing men from interrupting our Peace and Quiet.' Such a patent, securing for themselves the sole rights and privileges of the town of Port Roseway, they believed would provide the 'peace and Unanimity' they desired, 'both as to the Internal Settlement at home, as well as our Commercial Interest abroad.' Governor Parr demurred. The Associates were to be under the laws of the province. With the patent they desired denied them, the Associates sailed for Port Roseway. The 16 men they had chosen for the captains of their companies who had been commissioned magistrates by Sir Guy Carleton were to settle all disputes that might arise among them and were to look after their affairs until others were appointed to replace them by Governor Parr.[1]

Believing that they had the right to direct the founding of Port Roseway, to shape it in accord with their decisions formulated in their meetings in New York, the captain-magistrates were at once in conflict with the surveyors and those who pushed their way into the town. As magistrates they had no legal means of enforcing the wishes of the Associators and no courts or constables to maintain order. The surveyors sent by Parr to lay out the town were soon aware that most of the Port Roseway Associates were humble people, inexperienced in leadership and government, and that most of their captains, chosen from among themselves, were incapable of authority. With no one appointed by either Carleton or Parr to have authority over the Loyalists, the people without leadership turned indolent and unruly. To those who strove to work with them they were 'like sheep without a Shepherd.'[2]

In July, on Governor Parr's arrival in Port Roseway, setting aside the sixteen magistrates, he appointed as justices of the peace: James McEwen, James Robertson, Joseph Durfee, Joseph Pynchon and Benjamin Marston. Joseph Durfee and Joseph Pynchon were commissioned justices of the Inferior Court of Common Pleas and James McEwen, judge of probate. Henry Edwin Knox was named notary public and Alexander Murray was appointed coroner. They were magistrates without a court, receiving their instructions from Parr and the provincial secretary. Until the meeting of the legislature, when they were promised that a separate jurisdiction would be established for the town, they were given 'all the powers that can be granted to you' to punish the disobedient and to erect a log jail. They were to examine the lists of the lots already assigned to future grantees to weed out those who had no intention of settling in the town, and were to prepare returns of all the persons and their families in Shelburne, their former occupations and their intentions of future business, to accommodate them according to their needs. They were to recommend 'persons of ability and property to have the privilege of building wharves,' setting aside thirty feet for public access from wharf to wharf. They were also to point out a proper place on the public ground near King Street for a public market for fish and flesh.[3]

In the meantime, with no Court of Sessions or Court of the Inferior Court of Common Pleas in Shelburne, the magistrates were subpoenaed to attend the meeting of the Sessions of Queens County in Liverpool on the third Tuesday in September. On October 10 an act was formulated to be sent to the House of Assembly to establish an Inferior Court of Common Pleas and General Sessions of the Peace in the township of Shelburne on the last Tuesday of March and the last Tuesday of October in every year. It was accepted and approved by the Council and the House of Assembly on October 27 and was assented to by Governor Parr on December 2, 1783. The Court of Sessions, a method of local administration long established in England, enabled the central government to extend its influence into local affairs. The court consisted of justices of the peace, appointed by the Governor and Council, and a Grand Jury, their names drawn by lot from a box of names prepared by the county sheriff. The executive officer of the Court was the county sheriff appointed by the Governor and Council. The

Grand Jury represented the people. They were freeholders with property of a yearly value of ten pounds or personal assets of £100. Officers of the Court were nominated by the Grand Jury and from their nominations the Court chose and appointed officers. Besides nominating a list of officers, the Grand Jury presented to the Court for its approval a summary of the things needed to be done and an estimate of the sums necessary to finance the work of the Court and the carrying out of the duties of its officers. The Court had administrative and judicial functions: the licensing of taverns and ferries, fixing certain fees and prices, the levying of poor and county taxes, the ordering of precepts for roads and the management of roads and bridges, the erection and maintenance of jails and workhouses and other public buildings, the care of the poor and the distressed, fire prevention, regulation of the river fisheries, and in its judicial capacity, the enforcement of law and order.[4]

Since a Court of Sessions in the district of Shelburne was as yet not established, Governor Parr in January 1784 appointed as additional justices of the peace for Queens County: Abraham Van Buskirk, David Thomson and Joseph Brewer. A few days later he appointed James Gautier notary public and reaffirmed James McEwen as judge of probates and wills for the district of Shelburne. On February 6 Parr issued commissions appointing James Robertson, James McEwen, Joseph Durfee, Joseph Pynchon, Benjamin Marston, Abraham Van Buskirk, David Thomson and Joseph Brewer, Esquires, justices of the peace for the district of Shelburne in Queens County, empowering them to hold Sessions as by law directed, the justices to swear each other into office. On March 30, 1784, the first meeting of the General Quarter Sessions of the Peace for the district of Shelburne was held in the house of James McEwen near the Cove with five of the justices, Joseph Pynchon, Abraham Van Buskirk, James McEwen, David Thomson and Joseph Brewer, in attendance. The Sessions were proclaimed, the commissions read, the Grand Jury called and sworn into office, the Acts read pursuant to ordinance, and the deputy sheriff Robert Fox made his returns. John B. Scott was appointed attorney for the King, *locum tenens*, and James Gautier was sworn clerk of the peace. Four days later Joseph Tinkham of Liverpool, high sheriff for the County of Queens, attended the Court, and on April 6 the first business was transacted and the first officers appointed. To meet the needs of a new town in the making, the officers were: Benjamin Davis, treasurer, Archibald Cunningham, town clerk; Benjamin Davis, Valentine Nutter, Peter Lynch, Joshua Watson, Archibald Cunningham, surveyors of lines and bounds and overseers of the poor; Hugh Hayes, William Hill, Thomas Powers, Michael Gordon, John Davison, Samuel Oldsworth, Thomas Jenner, Patrick Donnough, James

COURTS AND FIRST MEMBERS OF THE HOUSE

Littlewood, Peter Earle, constables; Alexander Robertson, William Briggs, fence viewers; George Beattie, clerk of the market; Charles Oliver Bruff and Thomas Denham, poundkeepers; cullers and surveyors of fish, Captain Peter Jenkins, Peter Parker, Ebenezer Parker, Lemuel Goddard; surveyors of lumber and cordwood, Nathaniel Munro, George Harding; John Mann, sealer of leather; Alexander Gay and Thomas O'Brian, gaugers; John Peck and Jonathan Baxter, hogreaves; surveyors and weighers of hay, Charles Church and Alexander Robertson; surveyors of the highways, Joshua Pell, George Rapalie, Alexander Dunlop, Thomas Pendergrass, Abraham Lent; Daniel Jessop, John Miller, cullers and inspectors of hoops and barrels; assessors of provincial rates and taxes, Gregory Springhall, Richard Townsend, William Milby, Ebenezer Parker, James Dole and James Leckie with Robert Appleby and Samuel Kirk collectors; William Harvey, John Minshull, Patrick Wall, assessors of Shelburne township; John Craig, George Bowman, overseers and directors of public buildings; Daniel Neale and Peter Jenkins, viewers and gaugers of fish barrels and surveyors of pickled fish; Abraham Lent, Henry Elvins and Nicholas Ogden, overseers of the river fishery; Abraham Ellison and Robert Bruce, measures of coal, grain and salt; Alexander Cocken and Robert Sommerville, wardens of the port. Fire wardens for each of the five divisions of the town and for Ann Street were appointed; regulations and fees were set for the sweeping of chimneys and a penalty of 20 shillings established for failure to comply with the regulations and a chimney catching fire. With a well-established Court of Sessions the town had the means of directing and shaping its course in accord with the wishes of its citizens in so far as the authority of the Court extended.[5]

As a Court of General Quarter Sessions, meetings were scheduled for the months of March, June, September and December. With many affairs to consider and judgments to be rendered, the Court met many times out of regular sessions. These meetings were recorded simply as meetings of the Court. To meet the demands of specific occasions, orders were issued for the meeting of a Court of Special Sessions. The first of these were for a meeting of the Court held in Birchtown on Saturday, August 21, 1784, when Colonel Stephen Bluck was ordered to assemble the captains of the various companies of freed Blacks and other officers – magistrates, overseers of the poor, constables and regulators – under his command. As the meetings of the Court of Special Sessions gained in importance, they were recorded in a book apart from the records of the Quarter Sessions. The meetings were attended by the same justices of the peace as those commissioned for the General Quarter Sessions with the addition of the four justices of the peace, Alexander Leckie, Charles McNeil, Nicholas Ogden and Valentine Nutter.

George Thomas was clerk of the Special Sessions, Benjamin Davis was treasurer and William Shipman was the clerk of licenses. The Court of Special Sessions attended to the same business as the Court of Quarter Sessions, but met more frequently – sometimes as often as three times a month. To meet emergencies, as when Captain James Napier came into the town and liberated convicts from the snow *Despatch* or when the county sheriff was to read proclamations from the governor, Extraordinary Courts of Special Sessions were convened and were recorded in the book of Special Sessions.[6]

County Court of General Sessions

With the boundaries for the county of Shelburne, as struck off from Queens County, defined by the Governor-in-Council on December 16, 1785, as comprising all the country from Port L'Hebert on the east to the District of Clare on the west, including the townships of Shelburne, Barrington, Argyle and Yarmouth, preparations were made for the founding of a Court of General Sessions for the County of Shelburne. By February 1786, the commission, under the great seal of the province, had arrived from Halifax constituting the justices of the peace for the new county of Shelburne. At a meeting of the Special Sessions of the Peace on February 6, the commission was read, and those present, who were named in the commission, were sworn into the office of justices of the peace by Nicholas Ogden and Isaac Wilkins by right of a writ of *dedimus potestatem* from the governor empowering them to administer the oaths of office and of allegiance, supremacy and abjuration. Orders were issued to all the magistrates of the County and to the grand and petit jurors to attend the General Sessions of the Peace for the county in the court house in Shelburne on March 28.

The Court of General Sessions for the county was staffed with justices of the peace, a petit jury, a grand jury and officers and constables drawn from the county, and a court crier. Its functions were similar to those of the Court of Quarter Sessions – precepts for roads, regulations for swine and goats and the river fisheries, the licensing of taverns and ferries, care of the poor, the assessment and collecting of taxes for the townships, the enforcement of the laws and regulations set by the Court. Like the Court of Quarter Sessions, the Court of General Sessions was a body of local administration which enabled the central government to extend its influence into local affairs. As for the Quarter Sessions, the justices of the peace and the sheriff for the county were appointed by the governor. Extending its influence still further into the County Court, twelve of the justices were members of the House of Assembly or were members of the Council and were not residents of the county. Since none of these attended the sessions of the Court, the work devolved on the county magistrates. These were for the townships of Argyle and Yarmouth: Ranald McKinnon, Francis Cook, Thomas Durkee, Joshua Frost, Samuel Sheldon Poole, Benjamin Bernard, and John Crawley. For Barrington township the magistrates were: Isaac King, Archelaus Smith, John Homer, John Coffin, and John Sargent; for the township and the town of Shelburne: Isaac Wilkins, *custos rotulorum,* the keeper of the rolls, James McEwen, Joseph Durfee, Benjamin Davis, Nicholas Ogden, Abraham Van Buskirk, David Thomson, Charles McNeil, Ebenezer Parker, Alexander Leckie, Joshua Pell, Robert Gray, Valentine Nutter, Mathew Cahill, Gideon White, Samuel Campbell, John Tench, and Gregory Springall. Officers for the town and for the county were appointed by the magistrates to attend to county affairs, to guard and to protect the welfare of its citizens and its resources. As watch dog for the town and county, at the first sessions of the Court, the grand jury presented 39 carefully worded proposals designed "to lay the Corner Stone for a happy, and permanent System for the Public Business of the County in its Infancy, and for the preventing of future disquiets, and Uneasiness."[7]

COURTS OF JUSTICE
The Inferior Court of Common Pleas

Although there were three Inferior Courts of Common Pleas in Queens County – in Barrington, Yarmouth, and Liverpool – because of the lack of roads and the inconvenience to the inhabitants of the township of Shelburne to attend the sessions of the court, an act was passed by the House of Assembly in October 1783, for an Inferior Court of Common Pleas to be held in the township of Shelburne on the last Tuesday of March and the last Tuesday of October every year. Abraham Van Buskirk, already a justice of the peace, was commissioned first justice of the Inferior Court of Common Pleas, and James Gautier was appointed clerk of the Common Pleas. With the justices of the Inferior Court of Common Pleas and justices of the General Quarter Sessions, the two Courts met in joint sessions on the last Tuesday in March, 1784, with James Gautier clerk of both Courts. As clerk to the Sessions and the Court of Common Pleas, James Gautier recorded in the records of the General Quarter Sessions, as part of the business of the Court, the indictment of prisoners, the verdicts of the jurors and the sentences imposed by the Court, making no distinction in his records between the meetings of the two Courts. Before the Court came indictments for assault and battery, petit larceny and forgery, with John B. Scott attorney for the King, or Richard Combauld as prosecutor for the Crown. Additional justices were appointed to the Court in December 1784, when Isaac Wilkins was commissioned first justice, and Benjamin Davis and

Nicholas Ogden justices of the Common Pleas, with Samuel Burling later appointed clerk of the Pleas. Joint meetings of the Inferior Court of Common Pleas were also held with the County Court of General Sessions, and indictments from many parts of the county were presented to the Court by the grand jury. Trials for the indicted were pleaded before the petit jury summoned by the Court, which in turn rendered its verdict to the Court for the sentencing or release of prisoners.[8]

Court of Oyer and Terminer
Serious crimes committed with violence came before a Court of Oyer and Terminer. For the first Oyer and Terminer held in Shelburne, Governor Parr commissioned a special court and sent judges to try the offenders. Later, in 1786, for other serious offences, he appointed by a special commission the Hon. Isaac Wilkins, the Hon. Benjamin Davis and the Hon. Robert Gray judges for a Court of Oyer and Terminer and 'general gaol delivery,' with the Hon. Isaac Wilkins as presiding judge.[9]

JUDICIAL RESPONSIBILITIES OF THE COURT OF SESSIONS
The Administration of Justice and Punishment of Criminals
Important functions of the Court of Sessions were the administration of justice, the punishment of criminals, the maintenance of law and order. With many hundreds of undesirable persons pushing into Shelburne who, the Port Roseway Associates protested to Carleton, were the dregs of humanity and should not be sent to their town, the magistrates appointed by Parr in July 1783 were soon aware of their limitations. They had neither a Court of Sessions nor a Court of Common Pleas to administer their decisions, nor did they have a jail for the confinement of criminals. They were assured by the governor that he had endowed them with all the power necessary to punish the disobedient, but as long as they lacked a jail in which to confine the unruly their authority was futile, so a building was constructed (or one was purchased) for a jail. It was condemned by Joseph Tinkham, high sheriff for Queens County, as insufficient for the confinement of prisoners. With the establishment of the Court of Sessions in the spring of 1784, the Court was urged to raise £300 to build a jail and £25 to erect stocks, pillories or pounds, and to purchase bolts and shackles.

In the meantime, the jail on Provision Island (Commissary Island) was guarded by men from the disbanded troops under the direction of the sheriff. Ten constables were appointed and were provided with staves, and an unnamed person was the common executioner to administer the lash. With the decision to build a log jail, Stephen Bluck was asked to assemble the Blacks of Birchtown into companies to build the jail, each carpenter to

COURTS AND FIRST MEMBERS OF THE HOUSE

Charles Mason-James Humphrey house, built 1783-1785, as it appeared in the 1930s. (Photograph courtesy Eldon Whynot)

receive six shillings, each labourer eight pence per day. For some reason, a jail was not built, and on November 1, 1784 the house of Mr. Selkrig was rented for a jail and court house. Joseph Rice was appointed jailer and £100 was voted for the use of the prisoners (prisoners then having to provide their own food and those who were destitute and without friends or relatives were allowed a few pence a day for bread).[10]

Besides the Selkrig house near the centre of the town, in 1785 the house of John Silby in the North Division was rented for a jail and a house of correction, and the hulk of a vessel was purchased for the confinement of prisoners. Rented houses failed to be adequate jails – one was even without a chimney, and in 1789 the house of John Ewing, near the Cove at the south end of the town, was purchased. It was repaired and the jail yard picketed with a stout fence. In one jail were a dungeon and a debtor's room in which debtors were held until their obligations were discharged or until their creditors failed to provide bread for their subsistence. Michael Cooling, jailed for a debt of £1 and 15 shillings in 1785, begged the Court for an allowance of bread or that he be discharged, he having no property except a jacket, waistcoat, breeches, short shoes, stockings and two old blankets. He was ordered discharged, his creditor at liberty to recommit him if he provided the eight pounds of bread per week the law demanded. Elisha Bragh presented a similar plea, he possessing only the clothes on his back. As late as 1796 debtors were held in jail in a starving condition. One of these, Mary Johnson, is recorded as begging the Court to provide her with some means of subsistence.[11]

The House of Correction, Work House, Whipping Posts and Pillory
Closely connected with the jail were the house of correction, the work house and the poor house, at times one building serving the purposes of all four. With the first meeting of the Court of Sessions it was proposed that 'a suitable and Sufficient workhouse, House of Correction' should be built upon the public grounds in Shelburne. However, a house was not built and part of the jail was used as a house of correction. James Moffatt was appointed keeper, succeeded in December 1784 by John Miller, and later by Hugh Walker. In 1785 the house of George Pashley was hired at £16 per annum as a house of correction and in 1789 that of Alexander Frazer for £2. In addition to the house of correction, in 1785 the house of Philip Lenzi on the corner of King and Harriot Streets was purchased for £70 for a workhouse and almshouse. On complaints of irregularities committed by the keeper of the house of correction, superintendents were appointed by the Sessions – three magistrates of the Court to inspect the house weekly, and regulations were formulated stipulating the power of the keeper. Misdemeanants committed to his custody were to be set to work and were to labour as long as they were in the house. The disobedient were to be punished by placing them in fetters and shackles, if necessary, and with moderate whippings, not exceeding ten stripes at a time 'in case of their being Stubborn, or idle, and Neglecting to perform such Necessary Tasks as shall be Assigned them, and to abridge them of their Food, as the Case may require, until they be reduced to better behavior.' No person committed to the house was to be chargeable to the government for any allowance, on entering or on leaving or during confinement, but were to maintain themselves with their earnings. Any surplus from the earnings of those committed to the house was to be used by the keeper to purchase tools for their employment, for their keeper's wages, and for the relief of those unable to labour. No one was to be permitted abroad after dark. Besides the jails and house of correction for the punishment of criminals, there were the whipping posts and the pillory. A plot of land was reserved, but not used, for a whipping post and a pillory on the public square, on what is now the northeast corner of Bulkeley and Mowat Streets – a site then referred to as Stanhope's Hill, after an incident that occurred during the riots of 1784.

COURTS AND FIRST MEMBERS OF THE HOUSE

When other sites were chosen, the pillory was placed on the corner of Ann and Water Streets, and the whipping posts were erected in the house of correction and on the hill in Water Street, between King and Bulkeley Streets (which was also known as Stanhope's Hill as it was on the grant of land given to Henry Edwin Stanhope).[12]

Miscreants were committed to the house of correction for petit larceny, for lewd and riotous behavior, for keeping disorderly houses, for vagrancy. Sylvia Gracey was sentenced to the house of correction for a petit larceny and to forty lashes save one with a cat-o'-nine-tails on her bare back; William Davis, for stealing a half bushel of flour from his master and dividing it between two mulatto women, was scourged forty lashes on his naked back and was sentenced to remain in the house of correction; for stealing, John Mason was committed to thirty days at hard labour. As an idle vagrant and for running away from the workhouse, John Windsor, a free Black, was sentenced to ten lashes on his entering the house of correction and ten every Monday morning for two months, and was kept at hard labour, a log chained to his leg to prevent his running away. Other more fortunate vagrants and disorderly persons were ordered from Shelburne never to be seen again in the town.[13]

CRIMES

Felonies Punishable by Death
The first serious felony, robbery with violence, punishable by death, occurred in the summer of 1784 when four men robbed a vessel and wounded the captain. Justice Brenton of the Supreme Court, and several other persons were appointed by Governor Parr in a commission of oyer and terminer to hear the trial. The four men were sentenced to hang. Joseph Tinkham, as the high sheriff for the County of Queens, came to Shelburne to carry out the sentence. One of the criminals escaped from the jailor the night before the execution. He was captured the following day, but the hour for the execution having passed, Tinkham did not hang him, and the others were reprieved until the governor's wishes were known. Two were pardoned and the remaining two were hanged on Stanhope's Hill. Their names recorded in the burial records as 'Shannon and Doyle, two criminals.'[14]

There were two felonies in 1786, one committed with violence. On March 22 James Westley charged Brittain Murray, a Black, with robbing him of a large wooden chest containing wearing apparel and an old stocking stuffed with half joes (Portuguese coins) and guineas, besides $217.00 in silver and some money, the property of his Black servant Cinder. He suspected that three others, Cato Mentes, Anderson Moore and William Green were concerned in the robbery. They admitted their guilt, naming Brittain

Murray as chief offender. The four were convicted and were sentenced to hang. Three were pardoned by Governor Parr, to suffer death 'agreeable to their sentence' if found within the province three months after the expiration of their pardon. Britain Murray was hanged on King Street hill by Simon Proff, 'a man of his own colour,' John Davison being paid £1. 7 for erecting a gallows.[15]

On the day the three were pardoned, James Murray was brought into court and confessed that he and James Mitchell and John Kennedy had robbed, with violence, the home of Josiah Johnston where Kennedy knew there was money in a chest. Mitchell struck Mrs. Johnston with the butt of a gun and Kennedy threatened to kill Johnston. They took money from a basket, a gown and jacket, a coat and two handkerchiefs and escaped across the river into the woods where they hid for two days before they went on toward Barrington to the house of a man named Murray where they separated. They were captured and chained in jail to await trial in a special court of oyer and terminer commissioned by the governor, appointing as judges Isaac Wilkins, Benjamin Davis and Robert Gray. On the night of September 20, in the violence of a storm, the three escaped and went off without shoes or hats, dragging heavy chains on their ankles. In the hue and cry that followed, Murray and Mitchell were apprehended. They and the escaped Kennedy, who was never captured, were charged with felony and jail breaking and were sentenced to be hanged. Again Governor Parr put aside the verdict of the judges and pardoned James Murray. On December 29 James Mitchell was hanged, the Court paying the hangman £18.3.10 for his services.[16]

A trial for felonies committed in Argyle involving the killing of sheep and cattle came before the Shelburne Court in 1787 and the culprits were hanged in Argyle or Tusket. Also in this year James Reath was convicted of murder. The last of the early sentences to hang was decreed for Alicia Wiggins, a free Black labouring woman. She was convicted of stealing and was ordered to jail for 39 lashes with the cat-o'-nine-tails on her bare back. She left Shelburne but was soon back, breaking into the house of Archibald Reth. There she stole nine Spanish-milled dollars, a cotton petticoat worth a shilling, a child's white shift, a cotton shawl, a white neckcloth, a pair of women's gloves, some purple silk ribbon and a paste silver brooch. She was sentenced to hang. She pleaded she was with child, 'a Quick child.' On examination by Doctor Hoose and twelve discreet women this was disproved and her indictment was signed by Andrew Bruce, deputy clerk of the Crown, and two justices, Nicholas Ogden and Benjamin Davis to 'be hanged by the neck until she be dead.' She was later pardoned on condition that she leave the province.[17]

COURTS AND FIRST MEMBERS OF THE HOUSE

Lesser Felonies and Petit Larceny
For a lesser felony and for felonies without violence and for larceny, the penalty was the lash administered at the street corners, at the cart's tail or at the whipping post. For some it was banishment; for others it was confinement. For Joseph Daniels it was 39 lashes with the cat-o'-nine-tails at the public whipping post; for Alselm Howard it was 39 with the cat-o'-nine-tails at the foot of King and John and Ann Streets. For the theft of a goat Elizabeth Sleator was ordered into confinement. Phyllis Westley, the servant of Gideon White, for stealing a petticoat and shift was given 60 lashes at the whipping post; Hannah Johnson for a felony was dragged at the cart's tail along Water Street, and lashed 39 times at the corner of the streets from King to George. William Galougher, for stealing a brass kettle, was given 39 lashes on his bare back and banished; John Russell for the theft of a bed quilt, 100 lashes. Rogues suspected of stealing were lashed at the street corners as incorrigibles and confined in the house of correction until the usual fees of the Court were paid. Suspicious vagrants were whipped at the whipping post on Stanhope Hill in Water Street and ordered out of the township.[18]

Assault and Battery, Defamation of Character, Malicious Libel
With hundreds of unhappy persons crowded into shacks and huts in unpleasant surroundings, tempers flared, and lawlessness and drunken brawls among the lower class citizens plagued the town officials. Charges of assault and battery and defamation of character fill many pages of the town's records. Sentences varied from a fine of a few shillings to the £10 for the 'use of our Sovereign Lord, the King' imposed on Mary Stonehouse for an assault and battery on Sarah Jones, and three stripes with a cat-o'-nine-tails at the cart's tail at eight street corners for her contemptuous behavior. For three drunken assaults in Brew House Lane and for smashing window shutters and the door of Susan Hatch's house, Thomas Tully was committed to jail. Finding no security for his good and peaceful behavior, he was fined £20.10 and to stand committed until this was paid. For assault with intent to ravish, the penalty was £10 and to stand in the pillory one hour.

Defamation of character irked the magistrates in the performance of their duties, and as private citizens they were also insulted by the dissolute. Fines for such insults were remarkably light: twenty shillings for the defamation of Justice Tench's character; one shilling for calling Justice James Robertson a rascal. Women were the victims of loose-tongued men who called them whores of hell and faggots, who shouted in the streets that they had been drummed out of the army in New York and were whores in Shelburne. Husbands, in the defense of their wives, sought judgement against the lewd and vicious remarks of the debased, against women as against men, as did Joshua Hill for his wife, Mary. She was called a whore and a 'muslin thief' and her children bastards, by Isabel Fraser, who spat in her face. For a libel, Margaret Tallant and Elizabeth Brown, Junior, were hoisted into a cart bearing on their backs placards marked 'Convicted of a Scandelous and false Libel.' It was a long-remembered tale that after being driven along Water Street, accompanied by the constables to prevent abuse of the culprits, the elder of the two, as she clambered down from the cart, thanked the driver for a very pleasant drive and for the fine, elevated view of the town.[19]

Forgery and Fraud, False Tokens and Counterfeit Money
For forgery, Matthew Hobbard was sentenced to sit in the pillory at the corner of Ann and Water Streets, there to have one of his ears cut off and to be remanded to jail without bail. for one year. On his humble petition and for his good behavior all of the sentence was remitted except to stand in the pillory for one hour. For a similar offence in which he involved the name of Gideon White, Jonathan Carman was committed to jail for an unspecified term; another, for fraudulently obtaining boards from Greggs Farish, was scourged publicly in the street and was afterwards kept at hard labour for a week in the house of correction.

False tokens and counterfeit money were made and issued 'to the great prejudice of this Town and County and His Majestys Leige Subjects.' George Beatty, a coppersmith, brought before the Court, declared that his boy told him that Samuel Kirk 'did make coppers' and thought that they might make them likewise. This they did, and sold them to the amount of about ten shillings; but he had forbidden his boy to make more. Believing him to be ignorant of 'the attrociousness of his crime' he was dismissed. Samuel Kirk, Shelburne merchant, was sent for. He informed the Court he had passed no coppers of his own making, except such as bore his intitials, in order to make the same good whenever they were brought to him. This he had done for the want of small change, and pledged himself for the amount he had issued. Other base half-pence coins had been issued by Mr. Black – about seven dollars worth of the fifty dollars he had brought from the United States. These he was willing to take back, and the Court ordered an advertisement to be published forbidding the issuing of false coins. Not heeding the warning of the Court, Jontham Carman was committed to stand in the pillory one hour for using false tokens.[20]

COURTS AND FIRST MEMBERS OF THE HOUSE

THE ADMINISTRATIVE DUTIES OF THE COURTS OF SESSIONS

The administrative duties of the Courts of Sessions involved most aspects of public concern and welfare. As well as these sections on the marketplace, care of the poor, fire protection, roads, bridges and ferries, the involvement of the Sessions emerges in other chapters as the resources of the town and district were developed, industries were founded and foundations were laid for a lasting community.

The Marketplace: the King Street Market; the Cove Market; St. John's Square
In October 1783, Governor Parr ordered the Shelburne magistrates to 'appoint a proper place on the public ground near King Street for a public market for fish and flesh.' Following the instructions of the magistrates, Marston marked a strip of ground along the north side of King Street, from Water Street to the water front. In the spring of 1784 the Court of Sessions appointed George Beattie clerk of the market and ordered that all buildings should be removed from public ground where permission had been given by the surveyors to land luggage and to build temporary shelters. James Robertson was one who had built on the market ground, on the northwest corner of King and Water Streets, a building which he used for his printing office and for the accommodation of his employees. For his improvements, Governor Parr granted him a license of occupation to remain on the land where he had established himself. A public market house, however, was not provided by the town, and the butchers and fishdealers acquired one for themselves, and Patrick Steele was appointed by the Court to be clerk of their market 'agreeable to an Act to prevent Fraud by Butchers and Fish-mongers,' and the butchers were obliged to purchase licenses at forty shillings each.[21]

In the spring of 1785 the grand jury of the Court of Sessions recommended that the Governor should be asked to grant to the town a block of land for a public market. The land they wanted was a block of land on the Cove in St. John's Division, measuring 150 feet on William Street and 208 feet on Mowat Street to the waterfront. At the same time, the jury urged that the governor should be requested to grant to the town the entire public block on the north side of King Street, from Water Street to the water and the water in front of the block, for the sole use of the public as a marketplace. The Court approved, with reservations, as long as the Cove market would not interfere with the just claims of any individual and the King Street market with special deference to James Robertson's interest in the premises. With land for markets tentatively arranged for, the Court ordered that 'no meat, fish, vegetables or articles of provisions be henceforth exposed to public sale, on any shambles or in any street, lane, or on the strand or shore of this Town other than in the markets, or places established by the Sessions, as markets in King Street, and at the Cove.' Accordingly, liquid measures agreeable to the Exchequer of England were ordered for the use of the clerk of the markets.[22]

Governor Parr did not concur with the requests of the Court of Sessions. Asking for less land, the magistrates again petitioned Parr in February 1787. In 'consequence of the inconveniences the Inhabitants labour under for want of a public market,' they asked for a grant to the lot of ground north of King Street originally reserved for that purpose, 'to erect a market house for the benefit and use of the Town of Shelburne.' A few weeks later a grant was issued, the land to be held in trust by Isaac Wilkins, Benjamin Davis, Matthew Cahill, Nicholas Ogden, Justices of the Common Pleas, and Thomas Braine, William Hale, John Graham, Charles White and James Collins, overseers of the poor and survivors of them. The boundaries were defined as: westerly by the harbour and Samuel Donaldson's lot, easterly by Water Street, southerly by King Street, and northerly by a street 60 feet wide running the full length of the market. An early map of this area gives its width as 100 feet wide from Water Street to the water front.[23]

With land for a marketplace, the Court granted permission to John Hardy to erect a fish market at the foot of King Street at his own expense, he to have one-half the rent for the stalls for seven years at which time the building was to be purchased by the town for its approved value. Stalls were rented and fees paid to the Court. How long the market survived is uncertain. In 1797 the Court deplored the lack of regulations respecting the fish market laid aside for several years, to the nuisance of the people living near the wharves where halibut and other fresh fish were exposed for sale. In 1800 the Court of Sessions was urged to provide a market for the country people, for the sale of their produce to prevent others from purchasing their products and reselling at a shameful advance. It would seem from the records that no steps were taken to re-establish the marketplace, and the old market house and the market wharf fell into disrepair and the land was acquired for other uses.[24]

There was still another square planned for a market — St. John's Square in St. John's Division. Marston marked it to the east of the Cove, widening Digby Street, between Charlotte and Thomas Streets, for the market house. From the lack of references to the Square in the town records it seems that it was not under the judisdiction of the Court. That it was used for a number of years is evident from advertisements in the early Shelburne newspapers and in other records.[25]

COURTS AND FIRST MEMBERS OF THE HOUSE

Care of the Poor
Care of the poor was a heavy burden on the town for many years. At the first meeting of the General Quarter Sessions in April 1784 it was recommended that a poor house should be erected on public ground to be under the direction of the overseers of the poor. Aware that there were many indigents in the town for whom they would be responsible, the overseers requested that the town should be assessed for the sums necessary for their relief: £200 to erect a poor house, £100 for a public school house, £10 for past disbursments, £100 for the poor to the first of October 1784. Instead of erecting a poor house, houses were rented, and in 1785 a house on Harriot Street next to the corner of King Street was purchased for an almshouse and workhouse. It was a two-and-a-half storey building, twenty-seven by twenty-five feet, with seven rooms, the walls finished with boards. It had a 'snug kitchen,' an excellent well and other conveniences, and a good dry cellar. Other buildings were also used as almshouses, the same premises usually being used as workhouses or jails. In 1788 one of these was at the Cove in St. John's Division, and in 1802 a small house adjoining the large poor house on Water Street was purchased for £25 as an additional home for the poor.[26]

Lunatics, with the poor, were lodged in the poor house under the care of a surgeon and a caretaker who was responsible to the overseers of the poor. Paupers who could labour were put into service. Those who would not work were refused the necessaries they stood in need of for their subsistence. Children of the poor were bound out 'that they may be brought up useful, and not burdens to the community' – boys to learn a trade, girls to learn housekeeping. For many children it was a happy and a profitable experience; for others bound to a brutal master, it was a painful existence. Cloe Redick was one of the unfortunate children bound by the overseers to John McQuaid, an innkeeper, to learn the art and mystery of a house servant. On many occasions he beat her immoderately, illegally sent her to jail and confined her in a dungeon, and held her in irons in his dwelling house and otherwise ill-treated her. The justices, aware of John McQuaid's barbarity, discharged her from her indenture 'to go without a day and so forth.'[27]

Rations for the poor consisted of three quarts of Indian meal, three pounds of salt fish and six pounds of potatoes a week, with some bread at times and a pint of molasses when there was money for extras. When there was no money for any provisions, the poor were told to beg for their subsistence, 'which they did.' On occasions the overseers themselves advanced the money needed for the poor, and in February 1792 they appealed to the Court to reimburse them for the £27.11.9½ they had expended from their own pockets to support the 92 Whites and Blacks under their care, many of them sick. They pleaded with the Court to point out some mode of providing them with the funds they required in the coldest season of the year – amounting to three pounds a week. Catherine Smith, afflicted with a nervous disorder, was one who suffered from the lack of food and adequate living conditions. She was allowed the usual rations for the poor, later reduced to three or four quarts of corn meal and a pint of molasses. The corn meal was bitter and the last days of her life she had no food. She lay upon the floor on a piece of blanket with some slight covering over her. She had neither shift nor gown nor a cap on her head. At night she lay in darkness, for no oil was provided for a light for the paupers who cared for her, until the keeper himself gave oil from his own meager supply. When the plight of Catherine Smith was brought before the Court, the overseers pleaded that they had 'not any money.'[28]

Some relief was given the poor by those who knew of their suffering and were in a position to share what they had with others. William Booth of the Royal Engineers was one of these. From the rations allowed an engineer, he had his servant Graves distribute to thirty distressed persons a tierce of pork and two bushels of rice: 'Twas very easy for me to spare it... the servants nor myself never eating any salt provisions.'[29]

The heavy expense of supporting the poor increased rather than lessened with the declining population. Besides the poor in the town, the overseers were responsible for the poor Blacks of Birchtown. To assist them in their duties James Young and Tobias Johnson, two Black men, were appointed as ovesrseers of the poor for Birchtown. With the growing numbers of indigents among the Blacks, added to the growing numbers of whites dependent upon assistance, the overseers in 1789 petitioned the Shelburne magistrates to appeal to the governor, or by some other means, to find a way to free the town from a burden it was not able to bear. With the departure of hundreds of the freed Blacks for Sierre Leone there were fewer to care for but no lessening of the expense of maintaining the poor. The rapidly increasing costs thrust upon a shrunken population, and one still decreasing in numbers, pressed heavily on the taxpayers. In 1802 it was pointed out that in 1799 the expense of the poor was £73.16.6; in 1800, £93.0.0; in 1801, 'the enormous Sum of £137.1.3½.' Until this time the Blacks had not been taxed for the support of their paupers. They were now taxed as the whites, their assessments showing each paid a shilling or two for the poor and a few pence each toward county expenses.[30]

FIRE PROTECTION
Firemen and the Fire Engines
With the first meeting of the General Quarter Sessions in April 1784, fourteen firemen were appointed for the five divisions of the town and two

COURTS AND FIRST MEMBERS OF THE HOUSE

additional firemen for South Division, for Ann Street. These were: for Parr's and North Division, Robert Appleby, Abraham Ellison, Joseph Bell, George Paton, William Silby; for South Division, Ebenezer Parker, Valentine Nutter, John Miller, Henry Guest, John Keeley, Bartholomew Bowers; for Patterson's and St. John's Divisions, John Cooper, Thomas Whiting, John Paton; for Ann Street, James Moffat and Samuel Davenport. At the same time, David Henry Mallows and William Hill were appointed directors of chimney sweeps. Prices were set for sweeping chimneys at six pence for a one or a one-and-a-half storey building, nine pence for a two or a two-and-a-half or a three-storey building as fees for the chimney sweep. For failure to have a chimney cleaned, and it catching fire, the penalty was a fine of twenty shillings. Chimneys were swept by small boys under the direction of the licensed chimney sweep, Edward Elliott. The funnels or flues for chimneys were examined by the chimney sweep during construction to determine if wide enough for his boys to ascend. Wooden chimneys and wooden funnels, stove pipes through the walls and roofs of houses, and fires in houses where there were no chimneys, were a constant menace to the safety of the town. In June 1785 the Court ordered the sheriff or his deputy, with the constables of the town, to remove all defective funnels and wooden chimneys in the town. Many were removed; others remained, along with pipes through the walls and the roofs of houses without iron or tin plates as 'dangerous nuisances.'[31]

In early 1785 two wooden fire engines were ordered by the Chamber of Commerce for use in the town. On their arrival, firemen for the engines were appointed and the Court of Sessions was asked to find suitable places to house the engines and to appoint proper persons to care for them, who would be exempt from serving on juries and in public offices. The engines were ordered through two of the Shelburne merchants, Benjamin Davis and James Robertson, each importing one engine. It was soon evident that the Chamber of Commerce was unable to complete the payments on the engines, and they were purchased by the town for £56.2.10 - £24 to the Chamber of Commerce, £16.1.5 to James Robertson and an equal sum to Benjamin Davis. The engines were kept in different parts of the town – one in the North Division with specially appointed firemen, and the other in the South Division under the care of its appointed firemen. The engines were in use until at least 1834 when one was repaired by the blacksmiths William and George McGill, perhaps the one which has survived and is a unique reminder of early Shelburne.[32]

The Friendly Fire Club
Shortly after the town was divided into fire districts and firemen were

Fire engine purchased by the town of Shelburne in 1786.

appointed, on August 5, 1784, the Friendly Fire Club was organized by a number of citizens, the association to be limited to forty members dedicated to assist each other in time of a fire. Each member was to provide for his own use: two three-bushel bags, each with a stout string to bind it, two buckets marked with his name and a round, black-brimmed hat with a white crown bearing the letters 'F.F.C.' Bags, buckets, and hat were always to be in readiness, hanging in the member's house, under the penalty of a fine of twenty shillings if not in readiness. At a time of fire, each member, with his bags, buckets and his fire hat on his head, was to go to the houses of the members most in danger, where only members were allowed to enter on giving the watchword to the sentinel at the door. For non-appearance at a fire, except for sickness or absence from town, the fine was forty shillings, with a fine of two shillings for failure to give the watchword. As a useful organization the club survived until at least 1795, when its membership numbered sixteen.[33]

Wells and Pumps
In the spring of 1785 it was recommended to the Court of Sessions that a

number of public wells and pumps should be provided in convenient parts of the town 'as well for the service of the Inhabitants, as the Safety of the Town, in case of Fire.' A year later it was again pointed out to the members of the Sessions that 'not only for the Convenience of the Inhabitants, but for the preservation of the Town in cases of Fires' a number of pumps should be fixed in proper places, particularly in Water Street. Pumps were not provided by the town and in May 1790 the firemen urged the Court to take under its direction those which had been privately installed. Two months later the Court accepted the pumps as public property, the town to be charged for their upkeep. Maintenance of the pumps was costly. In 1791 the Court ordered a warrant on the collector of rates and taxes for money which had been voted for the use of the poor and for other town expenses for their upkeep. Such methods of obtaining money for pumps and wells were contrary to the laws of the province. James Humphreys, as the member of the House of Assembly for Shelburne County, introduced a bill, passed by the House, to enable the inhabitants of Shelburne to raise money by taxation for the sinking of wells and for pumps and for keeping them in repair. With the privilege of assessing the taxpayers for the upkeep of the pumps, the assessors budgeted for £20.5.2 with an appropriate pump tax added to each assessment. A few years later, to assist in their maintenance, the Court fixed fees for transient vessels watering at the pumps at four pence per hogshead of 65 gallons and all other casks in proportion. David Whipple, blockmaker, was engaged by the Sessions to keep the pumps in repair at 15 shillings each pump per year, with an additional fee, not to exceed 20 shillings, for pumps requiring coring, iron work and reaming. Pump stems were cut with a five inch bore and all pipes were reamed from pine wood.[34]

Fires
The town and district of Shelburne escaped serious fires until the 1790s when forest fires devastated miles of woodland from Port Mouton to the banks of the Clyde. The most serious of these fires was in June 1792, when 50 farm houses along with barns and other buildings, a mill, and bridges were destroyed, chiefly along the Jordan River. The Court of Sessions met briefly in July to arrange for assistance to the victims of the fire, and the House of Assembly voted £300 in aid of the distressed. Mindful that such fires could again sweep across the land, the Sessions ordered that there should be no burning of brush, meadow or marshes after May 15 and not again before October 15.[35]

ROADS, BRIDGES, FERRIES

Roads to the new Loyalist settlements, to the older New England communities, as well as a way to Annapolis, were a major concern of the Shelburne Loyalists. Such roads required forethought and careful planning. As a first step toward the construction of roads, Joshua Pell, George Rapalie, Alexander Dunlop, Thomas Pendergrass and Abraham Lent were appointed surveyors of highways at the first meeting of the General Quarter Sessions in April 1784. A year later they were ready to begin their first highway – a road to Annapolis.[36]

Annapolis or Pell's Road and Wright's Road
The importance of a road to Annapolis was first noted by Joseph Pynchon when he was in Halifax to arrange for the settlement of Port Roseway. Learning that the best farmland lay at the back of Port Roseway, between the Jordan and the Roseway Rivers, he proposed to the Associates that this land should be settled by farmers along a road to Annapolis. This would provide them with a compact settlement, with a town supported by farms, which was to be preferred to opening scattered communities along the shores to accommodate all who wished to join them at Port Roseway. Charles Morris agreed with him. Money could not be laid out to better advantage than in opening a road between the two settlements – a distance of about 65 miles. The work, he suggested, could be done by the men of the Forces, should it be necessary to send troops to Port Roseway.[37]

Not long after their arrival, the Loyalists began to plan for such a road, and on July 30 Oliver Lyman set off across the land toward Annapolis. He was back in six days. He made a second attempt. It, too, failed. On September 12 he set off again with two men in a boat, using the river as a way across the land. A month later he had reached his objective and had returned to Port Roseway. On Monday, December 8, he, with Captain Wright and a party of men began to cut a road to Annapolis, directed by Marston 'to steer the most direct course only avoiding such grounds as are naturally impassable and would take much labour to make them otherwise.' A map of 1783 marks the road they cut striking off from the north end of the town, running roughly parallel with the Roseway River and petering off in the wilderness – the road now known as Wright's Road.[38]

Interest in the road was not confined to Shelburne. In Halifax, Sarah Winslow wrote to her cousin, Benjamin Marston, that her brother Ned 'desires I would tell you he intends to have a road between Port Roseway and Annapolis, and many other great and wondrous things is he to do.' As secretary to General Campbell, Edward Winslow was in a good position to put in a word for Port Roseway. He himself wrote to Marston of his intended proposal to General Campbell, that the 300 men of the 57th Regiment at Annapolis and the five companies of the 37th at Shelburne should be employed in the construction of a road between the two settlements. A few days later, General Campbell informed Governor Parr that he had received instructions to assist in making roads, and that he intended to open a road from Annapolis to Port Roseway. Parr heartily agreed with him as to the importance of a road between the two towns. The road was also well recommended by Colonel Robert Morse, who suggested, that if it was not considered proper to employ men from the troops upon such communications, that from among the freed slaves a corps, raised, clothed and fed by government should be employed on public works, or, by provincial law, a certain proportion of the whole should be annually called upon for such services. Post houses, which should be the property of the Crown, should be established and small reservations of land made 'in case it should ever become necessary to place troops at them' to maintain communication in time of danger.[39]

With these favourable recommendations, the Court of Special Sessions on February 24, 1785 appointed Joshua Pell, John Lownds and Richard Hall, freeholders, 'to inquire into the necessity for a Road leading from King Street across the common to the north line of the 15 (20 acre) lots and from thence to the South line of Justice Robertson's farm and so in a direction to Annapolis Royal.' On March 10 the committee reported that such a road would be of 'great utility to the public at large,' and the sheriff was ordered to summon a jury to lay out the road.[40]

By the end of June, Joshua Pell, as the surveyor and overseer of the road, had completed the line through the woods to Annapolis. On July 4, he, with 20 men started to cut the road. To meet his need for labourers, and to continue work on the streets and on other roads, the Court of Special Sessions ordered, agreeable to the laws of the province, that 'Every householder and laborer not being a hired servant for one year, must work six days every year on the Public Roads when summoned by a constable by order of the overseers of the Highways.' A similar order was sent to Stephen Bluck, later amended to read that the Blacks 'be obliged to work on the Roads... on Tuesdays, Thursdays, and Saturdays, the other days being allowed for themselves towards a Subsistance.' Other sources of labour came from vagrants and able-bodied criminals compelled by the Court to work on the streets and roads.[41]

In early September the Shelburne magistrates were able to report to Governor Parr 'the completion of the great road from Shelburne to Annapolis, which has been cut with great labour.' A few weeks later it was proudly announced in the *Nova Scotia Gazette:* 'The Enterprise and Exertions of the inhabitants of Shelburne exhibits the strongest proofs that perserverance and industry when judiciously applied will rise superior to every difficulty and discouragement and perhaps in no part of America is there an instance of cutting a road through an almost impassable forest nearly the distance of 80 miles in as short a time and at so small a cost as Captain Pell and his party have effected the Road to Annapolis and rendered it passable for Cattle.'[42]

The road, as planned by the magistrates, turned off King Street, struck across the common and the 15 twenty acre lots to the boundary of James Robertson's farm and from thence in a northerly direction toward Annapolis. It ran roughly parallel with the Roseway River, to the east of it and to the west of Lake George, and followed the high land between the Jordan and the Roseway Rivers to save the construction of heavy bridges. A century later, on his map of Shelburne County, Church traced the road as it crossed Black's and Mark's Brooks, passed to the east of Lake Deception, to the west of Aspect Lake, and to the east of Trap, Cranberry, Round and McAfee Lakes. Continuing on its way, it skirted the eastern foot of Bald Mountain, passed between Scoodiac and Silvery Lakes, and on to the west of Wainwright, east of Roseway and Handsled Lakes, and passed through the peak of Queens County and from thence on to Annapolis Royal.[43]

To encourage interest in the road to Annapolis, a plan was proposed in early 1785, which was approved by Governor Parr, offering fifty acres of land on the road for every twenty shillings subscribed, plus seven shillings six pence to have each fifty acres surveyed. By the end of March, 250 persons had subscribed and had drawn for their lots along the projected highway. In May, with the cutting of the road well in progress, the associates of William Parsons and Levin Levi, and the men of Captains Savage, Thomas and Wall's companies, and the disbanded artificers of the engineer's department, were ordered to hold themselves in readiness to assist the surveyor in laying out the land along the highway into lots for settlers.[44]

The road was completed 'passable to cattle' at a cost of £450. Of this sum £100 remained as a debt. To entice settlers into the wilderness to live along the edge of the road, the Assembly offered £200 in premiums to those settling on the highway. In June 1786, the sum of £500 was voted by the Assembly to complete the road and in December 1787, a further grant of £500 was voted, one half to be spent on either end of the road. At the same time the sum of £100 was voted to repair the causeway and the stretch of the highway between Marshall's and Bower's taverns. Two separate grants were issued on April 6, 1786: one for 40 lots on the west side of the road with lot no. 30 reserved as glebe land; one for 125 lots on the east side of the road. Other lots along Pell's Road were the 15 twenty acre lots north of the common granted prior to the construction of the road, making a total of 179 lots granted to prospective settlers.[45]

The road, as cut by Joshua Pell, was little more than a rough track through the wilderness. But it was used often enough to encourage the opening of a halfway house, and a Mr. Williams was appointed keeper. With the taverns of Marshall and Bower there were points along the way for rest and refreshment. It was a journey of three days from Annapolis to Shelburne, and when a gentleman and his servant traversed the 76 miles in two days it was worthy of comment as 'certainly very great walking on so new a road.'[46]

In 1790 the Shelburne magistrates reported to the House of Assembly that further sums were needed to complete the road 'lately opened to Annapolis,' and in October they voted from their own funds £5 to be given to Samuel Davenport to repair Pell's Road. Money continued to be voted, from time to time, by the Court of Sessions, but in such small amounts as to suggest that the road soon fell into disuse. Statute labour continued to be done on the road, under the direction of Alpheus Palmer in 1799 and Robert McQuhae in 1801, both of whom lived on Pell's Road. At least one small log house stood beside the road on three acres of cleared land in 1786 when it was offered for sale by Samuel Kirk.[47]

Although the road soon lost its identity as a way to Annapolis, and by 1814 it was overgrown with trees, the importance of a road to Annapolis was in the minds of the people of Shelburne long after it disappeared as a usable route. As late as 1848 Shelburne citizens were endeavoring to have the road re-opened, only to be informed by the local member for the township, then in Halifax, that there could be nothing done that year except 'it may be to have it surveyed and as far as expecting any special grant for it, the thought may as well be abandoned at once, as there appears a decided objection here to anything of the kind.'[48]

The Liverpool Road

A road to Liverpool was an early consideration of the Shelburne settlers. By the winter of 1784 they were pushing their way through the wilderness to the eastward, Perkins noting on February 3, 'Capt. Scott and one Mr. Hopkinson came through the woods from Shelburne.' But it was not until May 1786, that Captain Robert Gray surveyed a line for a road from Shelburne to Liverpool. Perkins, recording his arrival in Liverpool, gave the distance as 36 miles and the intended road to be well back from the seashore 'so as to leave the mouth of Port Mutton Great River about 4 miles to the Southward.' The course of the road having been blazed, the House of Assembly, in 1787, granted £350 for its construction. The road was mentioned occasionally in the minutes of the Court of Sessions. In 1788 overseers of the road were Samuel Davenport and Jonathan Pell; in 1797, Andrew Barclay. In 1800 a grant of £2 was given for work on the road from the sale of land for default in performing statute labour and the sum of £9 was set aside for John Martin to repair the bridges on the road. A year later 15/6 was granted to complete the bridge near Barclay's farm on Purney's or Swansburg's Brook.[49]

Tragedy came to one of the first to travel the road. In December 1786, William White, accompanied by his dog, set out from Liverpool for Shelburne and perished from the severity of the weather. His dog found his way back to Liverpool and led a party to his master's body. In 1795 James Munro described bits of the road as he went from settlement to lonely settlement. From Port Joli to the harbour of Port La Bear it was 'three miles still going westward; small path and much cumbered with brush wood which retards, and wets the traveller either with dew or rain.' Port La Bear to Sable River was 'five miles no road nor paths nor any marked out and is an entire Barren scarce any timber but underwood. Scar[c]e is it fit for pasture Huccle Berrie Bushes and Brakens are its chief growth, and which serve to entangle the traveller.' From Sable River, as the road struck off for the Jordan it was '8 miles cut road and of a great Breadth and once in good order, but now out of repair not only by length of time but also by reason of a fire that went over it and burnt the Bridges which makes it worse than if it had not been briged, that and the brush wood growing up makes disagreeable travelling.' Once in Jordan, the way to Shelburne was 'westerly 6 miles good road.'[50]

The Tusket or Argyle Road, and a Way to Yarmouth
A road through the wilderness from Shelburne to their proposed settlement on the Tusket River was first discussed by the Associates of the Tusket Location in Mrs. Lowrie's tavern on Ann Street on March 25, 1785. It was to be cut in a west by north course 'or as near thereto as maybe,' and was to be at least 20 feet wide and not to exceed 35 miles in length. Each member of the Association was to subscribe toward the expense of opening the road, and was to receive 50 acres butting and bounding the road for every 20 shillings subscribed and paid either in money or in labour at the rate of 2/6 per day each labourer.

A month later, on April 26, the Associates of Colonel Abraham Van Buskirk, who had drawn their lots on the Tusket River, met at the Merchant's Coffee House to consider the cutting, clearing, bridging and the building of causeways on the road 'run and blazed' between Shelburne and Tusket. The road they now proposed to build was to be '30 miles long or thereabout and 12 feet wide at least.' Those willing to undertake the cutting and clearing of the road were to contact Valentine Nutter on Water Street.[51]

The importance of extending the Shelburne to Tusket road to Yarmouth was soon apparent, and in July 1786, Messrs. Poole and Butler and Captain Richards 'came through the country to lay out a road... and have no doubt... but that the road will be shortly accomplished.' A grant of £50 was voted from the provincial funds in 1787, and in 1790 a petition was presented to the Yarmouth Court of Sessions for a road from the southwest corner of Alexander Bain's land 'past the Fish Pond and Narrows' as far as it shall be thought best, thence north-easterly until it runs into the 'Shelburne Road.'[52]

In 1790, with Greggs Farish overseer of the road, the Court of Sessions approved that he should have a number of men to work for him, and the sum of £5 was voted for repairs. In 1795 a further sum of 40 shillings was paid for repairing a broken bridge reported to the Court by William Robertson. It was in this year that the Rev. James Munro, travelling the wilderness trails of the southwestern townships, wrote of the Tusket Road and the land along the way: 'Between Shelburne and the Tuscate is 40 miles thro the woods and No Dwelling Houses on the road but one. A person of the name of Hamilton, who lives on a branch of the Clyde 14 miles from Shelburne and 26 from the Tuscate. There is none other Family nor likely to be as the land seems in general to be poor. Its continued forest, and yet of no great importance it being mostly soft wood.'[53]

Despite the poor soil and only one house in 40 miles, the Court of Sessions agreed to have the road re-surveyed in 1799 under the direction of William Robertson, and voted 'that a resonable sum be allowed for that purpose.' The road, as it crossed the land, was some 54½ miles long. It was sufficiently well travelled for James Hamilton to use his house as an inn and tavern and to keep a ferry on the Clyde. The road continued to be used until the early 1820s when, from the slender population of Shelburne, there were few to travel its way and it fell into disuse. Few roads have been known by as many names. In Shelburne it was the Argyle, the Tusket, or Farish's Road; to the westward it was known as the Shelburne Road, as Richard's, and as Nigger Road (for the Cape Negro River, as the Clyde was called by the early settlers.)[54]

Roads West of Shelburne
As roads were being built to distant places, others were being cut to nearby settlements. The first of these was a public road ordered by the Court of Sessions in March 1786, from 'Birchtown to Gunning Cove and from thence along the village of the Old Settlers to the head of Round Bay.' On the

petition of Isaac Wilkins and others that it should be a private rather than a public road and that it should be 60 feet wide, the Court recorded it as such and a warrant was issued for £10 from the license fund for Joseph Durfee to cut the road. Private or 'pent roads' with gates and bars enabled the early settlers to keep cattle from straying. One of the old pent roads in Roseway survived until fairly recent years.[55]

With a road along the shore to Round Bay, the Court in 1787, on the request of William Mollineaux and 24 others, ordered a precept or warrant for a road from 'Round Bay to the Head of North East Harbor to Cape Negro Harbor called Birch Point.' In 1794 a road was ordered from Captain Perry's at Black Point to join the Cape Negro Road near Sutherland's meadow, the same 'being laid out agreeable to law and duly advertised be allowed and recorded' as a public highway. With £15 recommended from the license fund in 1802 for the road from Barrington to Cape Negro, the long way from Birchtown along the shore to Barrington was completed.[56]

A shorter way to Barrington was across the land on a public road ordered by the Court in October 1785, to begin at the public landing near the falls on the west side of the Roseway and to proceed to Barrington, for which the House of Assembly granted £200 in July 1786. It would seem the road was not at this time completed or its old line of survey abandoned, as in 1796 the Court issued a precept to William Adams to lay out a road from Shelburne to Barrington. In the meantime, the Court ordered a road from the Roseway River to Clyde River. It was little more than a path and wayfarers were guided by the stumps of trees marked with red paint.[57]

Roads East of Shelburne
Precepts for roads to the eastward from Shelburne were issued during the first years of settlement. The first of several roads to Jordan River was one from King Street to the banks of the Jordan. At the same time, on January 3, 1785, a road was proposed from King Street to the head of the northwest arm of the Jordan and from thence to the point (Enslow Point) of the northwest arm, and from the head of the arm to the landing opposite McNutt's on the east side of the Jordan. Three years later in November 1788, the road was extended to Jordan Falls, forming a loop from Shelburne with the Shelburne-Jordan highway leading from King Street to the Jordan. Precepts for other roads to the Jordan were prepared in 1785 and 1786. These were for a public road leading from Rodney Street to 'Johnston's Ferry on the Jordan River,' a road later known as Morvan's and still remembered for its ghostly tales of a man who walked the road in a long brown duster; for Eagle's Road which was 'from Ann Street to Eagle's 50 acre lot on the Jordan River'; and one which turned south from King Street

across the Common to John Thomson's farm and on to the Jordan. As settlers went to their land on the west side of the Jordan, a road was cut across the peninsula beginning at the southern tip of Jones' Point (McLean's Point) and, running between lots 124 and 125, continued to Lake Rodney and on to Shelburne. With precepts to lay out a private road from Digby Street to Sandy Point in the summer of 1786 and for one on the west side of the Jordan from the northwest arm to Berry's Point at the southern tip of the peninsula in 1788, the land lying between the water of the Jordan and Shelburne harbour was well provided with roads.[58]

The first road on the east side of the Jordan was one from East Jordan to Ragged Islands Harbour, ordered by the Court on March 10, 1785. A year later a second road along the east side of the Jordan was ordered from Jordan River to Green Harbour. At the same time, on March 29, 1786, a precept was issued for a road from French Brook to Green Harbour. North of the falls on the Jordan, rough roads were cut on either side of the river. On the west side, the road ran 400 feet west of the river to the King's Forest and on into the wilderness. On the east side, the road began at the falls and cut through the forest to Lake John and on to the end of the lots granted to

The Joseph Bell house, built 1783-1784. (Photo by Nancy Hart)

disbanded soldiers and others for farm land. On the petition of Benjamin Arnold 'praying a road from Little Harbour to the head of the Great Bay (called Ragged Island Bay) and from thence to Jordan River,' a precept agreeable to his petition was ordered on May 19, 1790. It was not until much later, in November 1801, that a precept, on the petition of John Thorburn and others, was ordered for a road from the east side of Sable River to Port L'Hebert.[59]

Roads Beside the Roseway

On the east side of the Roseway River a road known as Lynch's had already been cut by Peter Lynch when, on September 29, 1785, the Court issued a precept for a road leading from the north end of Shelburne and up the east side of the Roseway River. The road on the west side of the river ran from Ackland's Landing, followed close to the river and ended at the 100 acre lot no. 75. A year later, in 1786, a precept was ordered on the request of Colin Campbell for a road to be laid out from Shelburne through the land granted to him and to others on the west side of the Roseway, a road that became known as Campbell's Road. With a bridge over the Roseway completed in 1787, James Courtney was granted a precept for a private road 30 feet wide 'from the new bridge across the Roseway River leading up the West side of the Roseway River.' James Dole protested. It would pass through his potato field. Others protested the road. They wanted it to follow the road already cut in front of Dole's house. The Court waited. If the precept was changed, it was not recorded.[60]

The McNutt Island Road

As a final road to open the land for those who farmed and fished, the Court of Sessions on March 12, 1791 ordered a public road not to be less than 100 feet wide to be cut across McNutt's Island from the lighthouse to Ross' Landing on the northern tip of the island.[61]

Shelburne Streets

For the streets of Shelburne, surveyed and cut in 1783 before there were town records, there are few references other than for their maintenance by statute labour and that the hills at the head of Rodney Lane and St. John's Street and Stanhope Hill in Water Street were nuisances. In 1784 the Court approved that John Lahey should be a public bellman to cry the news in the streets of the town, establishing his fees as one shilling each for crying the arrival of a vessel with provisions, for the sale of a house, lot, furniture, vessels and goods at public auction; for stolen, strayed or lost cattle, horses and goods. For the peace and quiet of the town, for 'its actual Safety and

Security,' the Grand Jury requested the Sessions to appoint watchmen to patrol the streets at night and have lamps properly placed to deter 'designing and evil minded Persons from executing their malepractices.' Clean streets were an early consideration of the Sessions and six wheelbarrows and six handbarrows were ordered for use in cleaning the streets. Later it was requested that the town should be cleared of all timber and carts and other obstructions standing in the streets preventing the free passage from one part of the town to the other. With the rapid decline in population many of the streets fell into disuse. The stumps of trees were left even in the main throughfares of the town, and with grass growing in the streets visitors were soon reporting 'a most desolate appearance' of the once bustling town of Shelburne.[62]

Bridges
As roads were cut, bridges were constructed over brooks and small streams. Larger bridges, requiring careful planning and grants to assist in their construction, were not built as the roads were slashed through the wilderness. For the construction of the first large bridge – one across the Roseway – arrangements were completed by September 1786, when Valentine Nutter was voted £20 toward the building of the bridge. In October a further sum of £20 was voted from the license fund 'toward the Bridge Building across the River Roseway.' A few months later it was proudly announced that the bridge across the Roseway was 'completed other than laying the planks on the top, the place of which is supplied by slabs over which carriages pass with great safety.' Still considered 'incomplete and dangerous' by the Court of Sessions, in 1789 and in 1790 money was appropriated from public collections and later from the sale of absentee estates for the completion and repair of the bridge.[63]

Bridges were not built across the Jordan and the Sable Rivers nor across the Clyde until the 1800s. It was not until 1818 that there are references to the Sable and the Clyde bridges when they, with the Jordan River bridge, were carried away in a spring freshet, and the sum of £200 was voted by the House of Assembly to rebuild them. It is perhaps of this freshet that the story is told of Robert Barry and his horse and a broken bridge. Having ridden through heavy rain from Liverpool on his way to Shelburne, Robert Barry came to the Sable River at night. He pounded on the door of the only inn in the village and was greeted in astonishment. When told the bridge was gone he assured the innkeeper, 'I had no trouble crossing the bridge.' On going to the river they found a single, foot-square stringer reaching across the river. In the mud were the footprints of Robert Barry's horse as he stepped from the stringer and on the far side of the river were his footprints as he stepped from the mud to that one beam of safety above the swirling water.[64]

Ferries
Ferries were used across the rivers and harbours until bridges were built, and for many years after bridges were constructed, to shorten the long distances by land. In 1784 and 1785 four ferries were established by the Shelburne Court of Sessions to ply across Shelburne Harbour. The first of these was from the west side of the Roseway River below the falls to a landing in North Division a little north of Commissary Island. Joseph Hiat was ferryman, and he received 3½ d. for each passenger. A second ferry from the west side of the Roseway, from the landing at Captain Dole's 50 acre lot near the falls, plied across the harbour to the foot of King Street, with Philip Ackland as ferryman. His fees were set at two pence for each passenger; for a horse or cow, one shilling; for a hogshead, two shillings; a barrel, three pence; a keg, two pence and 'every thing else in proportion,' and he to 'have a Licence Gratis, for keeping a House of Public entertainment.' Two additional ferries were established in 1785. One to Commissary Island left from the foot of Fanning Lane. David Watson, as the ferryman was to have for 'his trouble, each passenger, a halfpenny; each barrel, 1 penny, and so in proportion for a greater quantity, and a half penny for any quantity less than a barrel.' The other ferry, with two boats in operation, crossed the harbour from the foot of Mason's Lane to the landing near the Barracks with James McGrath and Michael Gordon as ferrymen.[65]

Public ferries were in operation on the Jordan by 1785. The first was John Johnston's across the river from the west side to the east 'he paying the sum of Forty Shillings for one year for the use of the district.' In 1786, as many of the disbanded soldiers and Loyalists went to their farm land along the banks of the Jordan, other ferry licenses were granted: to Nicholas Ogden for a ferry from French Brook to Farer's Landing; to Lieutenant Donald McCrimmon across the river from his landing on the east of the river (lot no. 2 East Jordan); and a joint license of operation to George Patton and Thomas Farer for a ferry across the Jordan from Jordan Ferry to the east side to Farer's Landing. Eagle's ferry plied across the Jordan from Hugh Eagle's landing at Jordan Ferry, from lot no. 186, to the upper and east side of the Jordan. With his license to operate a ferry he was granted permission to keep a public house of entertainment.[66]

A ferry was in operation on the Clyde in 1788 where the Tusket Road came to the banks of the river and where Alexander McDonald was given permission to have a tavern for wayfarers. James Hamilton was the licensed ferryman on the Clyde in 1795, and was to provide 'two good Skiffs, at his

COURTS AND FIRST MEMBERS OF THE HOUSE

own expense, and keep them in proper repair, one on each side of the River, for which he shall be entitled to receive from each person that crosses the River, without returning the Skiff, Two shillings. From every person that ferries themselves over, and returns the Skiff, Six pence.' If he went from his house with a passenger across the river, the fee was one shilling. An early ferry at Round Bay, known as Doane's Ferry, crossed the bay from Nathan Doane's landing on the west shore of the bay.[67]

FIRST MEMBERS OF THE HOUSE OF ASSEMBLY

Having achieved a Court of Quarter Sessions for the town and district of Shelburne, the magistrates turned their attention to achieving representation in the House of Assembly. They were assured that with the dissolution of the Assembly to be called in June 1784, writs would be issued for a return of members from all of the new settlements. But first there were problems to be solved. Royal instructions forbade an increase or diminution in the number of representatives. The province, then consisting of Nova Scotia and New Brunswick, was divided into eight counties and sixteen townships represented in the Assembly by 36 members. To comply with the wishes of the new settlers an additional 20 members would be necessary to the existing 36. Parr laid their problem before Lord North. In August 1784, came word that the province was to be divided, the land lying north of the Bay of Fundy to be administered by a new government and to be known as New Brunswick. On November 29, 1784, acts were passed, assented to by Governor Parr on December 8, to increase the number of counties and townships in the province to accommodate the accession of new settlers and to authorize the freeholders in the counties named (Digby, Sydney, and Shelburne) to elect members to the General Assembly: for the county of Shelburne, two members, for the town of Shelburne, one member. By the late winter of 1785 there were no prospects of an election. Impatiently the Shelburne Loyalists pointed out to Parr that neither they nor their 'fellow Loyalists in the Province' were represented in the Assembly, 'whose branches are known to contain individuals of principles ever inimical and whose conduct has at times been hostile to His Majesty's interest,' and 'from such men your memorialists can look for nought but oppression.' They were blandly assured that Shelburne as a new county and the town as its chief settlement 'will have due representation.' But it was not until October 20 that the governor and council by proclamation dissolved the House, which had existed since 1770, and issued writs for a new House returnable on December 1. In the election Alexander Leckie and Charles McNeil were returned members for the county and Isaac Wilkins for the town. They were declared duly elected on December 17 and took the oath of allegiance and their seats in the House of Assembly. In Shelburne stories were long remembered of that first election when the streets were crowded with voters and, it was said, one could walk to the polls on the heads of the people. Without political party affiliations to claim their allegiance it was friends voting for friends, the opposing sides known as the Blues and the Greens, the Blues taking the polls.[68]

For a number of years Shelburne Loyalists served in the House of Assembly for the town and county of Shelburne. The first elected, Alexander Leckie, Charles McNeil and Isaac Wilkins, were members until 1793, when Stephen Skinner and James Humphreys were elected members for the county and Colin Campbell for the town Colin Campbell, who served the town in many capacities, in the Church of Scotland, in meetings of the Sessions, as collector of customs, was elected to four terms in the House and was member for the town until his retirement in 1819. In 1798 George Gracie, and in 1800 James Cox were elected members for the county; in 1806 and again in 1812 Jacob Van Buskirk represented the county and was the last of the Shelburne Loyalists to serve in The House of Assembly. One other Shelburne Loyalist was a member of the House – Gideon White who was elected as member for Barrington Township in 1790 when the encumbent member, Joseph Alpin, vacated his seat for a leave of absence from the province. Three years later, in 1793, when a general election was called, John Sargent, who was also a Loyalist and who had settled in Barrington, was elected by acclamation. He was elected again and again as member for the township of Barrington. On his retirement in 1820 he was succeeded by his son William Browne Sargent and in 1836 his son Winthrop was elected member for Shelburne County.[69]

9
Churches, Schools and Social Life

Among the Loyalists and the disbanded soldiers were adherents and members of various religious groups: Sandemanians, Baptists, Lutherans, Methodists, Presbyterians, Anglicans, Calvinists, Congregationalists and persons interested in the Society of Friends.

Of the smaller groups of religious adherents to congregations apart from the older established churches were the Sandemanians, who were followers of the Scottish religious leader Robert Sandeman. Sandeman came to America in 1764 and taught independence in church government and justification by faith alone. There were at least six Sandemanians among the Shelburne Loyalists: Benjamin Davis, a prominent Shelburne merchant and magistrate; John Howe, a printer, and the father of Joseph Howe, who remained in Shelburne for only a few months; Joseph Pynchon, a founder of the Port Roseway Association and an agent for the Associates for the settlement of Port Roseway. Others were William Richmond, Benjamin Smith and Isaac Mansfield.

There may have been a few Quakers or members of the Society of Friends among the Loyalists, as on two occasions in 1786 preachers belonging to the Society of Friends were in Shelburne – Mr. Townsend from London and later Joseph Moore of New Jersey and Abraham Gibbon of Philadelphia. They preached in the Court House 'to very respectable audiences' and were well received by the people of the town. Among the Loyalists were a few descendants of the early Huguenot settlers of America – the Crocheron,

Guyon and Rapalie families, with others reputed to be of Huguenot background – the Sorrel, Purney, Bode and Bougert families. For these persons and for others of the Calvinistic communion, land was reserved on Clements Street (lot no. 7, letter O, St. John's Division) for a Low Dutch Calvinist Church. For those of the Lutheran faith, land was reserved near the southeast corner of Carleton and Charlotte Streets (lots no. 14 and 15, letter D, St. John's Division). There is no record that either the Calvinists or the Lutherans built a church on the lots of land reserved for them.

There were a number of Congregationists among the Shelburne Loyalists but where they held their services of worship is unknown. Their minister was perhaps the Rev. Joseph Brown, who came to Shelburne in 1783 and was given a lot of land on Hammond Street. In March 1784 he visited Liverpool and was entertained by Simeon Perkins, who spoke of him as 'a Genteel young man from Cheshire, England.'[1]

Baptists
The founder of the Baptist congregation in Shelburne was David George, the remarkable Black preacher who founded the Negro Baptist Church in Nova Scotia and later the Negro Baptist Church in West Africa. He preached his first sermon in Shelburne on June 25, 1783, the first Sunday after his arrival. His first meetings were mainly with Blacks. Later, with the arrival of William and Ann Taylor from London where they had been members of Dr. Rippon's church, a number of Whites joined his congregation, until the little church he had built at the north end of the town numbered 50 members. Others came from nearby settlements to be baptised. Among them were William and Deborah Holmes from Jones Harbour and Mrs. Jonathan Locke, Sr. and her sister from Ragged Islands. With David George's departure with many of the freed Blacks for Sierra Leone, most of the members of his Shelburne congregation went with him. The few Baptists who were left were formed into a church a few years later by the Rev. John Burton, founder of the Baptist church in Halifax. About this time, in 1794, he ordained John Craig of Ragged Islands a Baptist minister. On November 3, 1795, John Craig stood before the Shelburne Court of General Sessions as 'Preacher to the Baptist congregation in the Town of Shelburne – and took the State Oaths, and subscribed the Test, as enjoined by Law.' A native of Ireland, born in Dublin, John Craig emigrated to America before the Revolution and settled in Maryland as a weaver. With peace in America, he came to Nova Scotia and began his ministry as an itinerant preacher in Cornwallis and Horton. Travelling with a friend, he came to Ragged Islands where he met and married Mary Locke, a daughter of Jonathan Locke, Sr. During his pastorate in Shel-

burne, with the help of William Taylor, a meeting house was built by the Baptists on William Taylor's property on Mowat Street with William Taylor a deacon of the church and its caretaker. It served as a place of worship for a number of years. Later, a small church was built on Charlotte Lane, succeeded in 1874 by the present Baptist church on Mowat Street.[2]

Methodists
With the first Loyalists to arrive in Port Roseway came many Methodists. With them was Robert Barry who was to be a leader among the Methodists in Shelburne and a firm supporter of Methodism in Nova Scotia. The son of a Portsmouth merchant, he was invited as a young boy on board a man-of-war for a short coastal cruise. When at sea, orders were issued to proceed to America. Not favourably impressed with life on a man-of-war, he escaped when they reached New York. During the British occupation of New York he was the managing partner in a small business. With the first Loyalists to sail for Nova Scotia he came to Port Roseway. In his tent among the stumps and fallen trees, William Black, the representative of Yorkshire Methodism in Nova Scotia, found him on June 6, 1783. On the following Sunday, William Black is reputed to have preached the first sermon in Shelburne to a congregation gathered at Robert Barry's lot, from a table placed among the stumps.

With his departure, Black left the Methodists in the care of Robert Barry. They met on Sundays in a room in his log house (which he used on week days as a schoolroom) when he read a sermon by Wesley and discussed Wesleyan doctrines. In the fall of 1783 many more Methodists came from New York. Among them was John Mann, a Methodist preacher. By the spring of 1784, with a rapidly growing congregation, a large room in one of his buildings was given the Methodists by Charles White. Here on Sunday mornings and evenings they held services of worship with John Mann as their pastor. With his departure for Liverpool, where he continued his work, two itinerant preachers came to Shelburne. These were James Oliver Cromwell and Freeborn Garretson, the latter a man of great physical energy and spiritual vigour. Garretson's preaching met with immediate success. The room Charles White had given the Methodists was no longer large enough to accommodate all who came to hear him preach. Remembering the kindness of the Methodists in sharing their place of worship before their temporary building was erected, Garretson was offered the use of the Episcopal Church. His fervent preaching drew so many, after three Sundays the vestrymen became alarmed. They demanded his immediate withdrawal. Leading his congregation to the shore, he stood on a rock at the edge of the cove below the town and spoke to the multitude. Charles White's building was enlarged to hold 400. It was still too small. Garretson suggested to his Black listeners that they should erect a small church of their own, which they did on the brow of a hill at the north end of town where land was available.

During the summer of 1786 Garretson called James Mann to the ministry as an itinerant preacher. A brother of John Mann, he became one of the most highly esteemed and beloved ministers in the province. He and James Cromwell were given charge of the Shelburne congregation and the new Methodist society at Barrington. On their departure, when James Mann took up his duties as an itinerant, William Jessop, the son of a Quaker plantation owner of Delaware, served in Shelburne with the assistance of James Boyd. Later, Isaac Lunsford and Richard Stocket ministered to the Shelburne Methodists, with assistance in the work of the congregation from Robert Barry who acted as the recording steward for the circuit. Working with Robert Barry was his sister Elizabeth, who came from England to be with her brother, and married Dr. John Hoose. Dr. Hoose came to Shelburne as surgeon to the disbanded Hessian soldiers. Their home was always a meeting place for the Methodists and a home for the minister. Services at this time were held in a sail loft on Ann Street converted to a chapel with pulpit and benches.

In 1799 James Mann was stationed permanently in Shelburne, which included Barrington in his ministry and the settlements along the shores. Five years later on September 4, 1804, the cornerstone for the first Methodist Church in Shelburne was laid on the southeast corner of Ann and Water Streets by the Rev. John Mann. On February 16, 1806, the church was opened for worship by the Rev. James Mann. Its solid bare simplicity and its shapely gothic windows were long remembered by those who had worshipped within its walls. A larger church was built on the same site in the 1870s.[3]

Presbyterians
Among the Port Roseway Associates were many Presbyterians who brought with them (in the first fleet to sail for the new settlement) the Rev. Hugh Fraser as their minister. Shortly after their arrival they began to plan to build a church and asked for a grant of land. By early September of 1783 Benjamin Marston had marked a lot of land on the public square for a Church of Scotland. On July 22, 1784, His Majesty George III 'granted unto James McEwen, David Thomson, William Harvey, John Boyd, and James Duncan their Heirs and Assigns a tract of land or cite for a church or meeting House in Shelburne... for the use of the Inhabitants... as now are or hereafter shall be of the Protestant Profession of Worship approved

CHURCHES, SCHOOLS AND SOCIAL LIFE

by the General Assembly of the Church of Scotland.' The land was bounded on the east by Digby Street, measuring 240 feet; on the south by St. John's Street, 240 feet; and on the north and on the west by public ground, 240 feet both north and west. On the brow of the hill of their land, near the corner of Digby and St. John's Streets, the Presbyterians built a rough temporary building, 40 feet by 24 feet, for a meeting house and fenced their land for a burial ground. The Rev. Hugh Fraser was a native of Scotland who came to America in 1777 as chaplain to the 71st Regiment or 'Fraser's Highlanders.' Stricken with a fever, he was unable to accompany his regiment to Georgia and on his recovery, before he could reach the Highlanders, he was captured by the Americans and was held captive in Boston. At the end of the war, with the approaching disbandment of the 71st Regiment, he came to Port Roseway as minister of the Church of Scotland.

It was soon apparent to the Presbyterians that they lacked the financial resources, after years of warfare, to support a minister and build a sturdy church where they could assemble during the winter. Petitions for assistance to build a church were addressed to the members of the General Assembly of the Church of Scotland and to the Rt. Hon. William Pitt, Commissioner of His Majesty's Treasury. From these sources financial aid was not granted. Without assistance they were unable to construct a substantial building and in the winter months they used the court house as their place of worship. Mr. Fraser remained in Shelburne until about 1793. About that time the building erected as a temporary church was demolished in a heavy gale. Two years later, in 1795, when the Rev. James Munro visited the Shelburne Presbyterians, they were without a church and resident minister and held their services among themselves in a dwelling house fitted for the purpose.

In 1803 the Presbyterians of the township of Shelburne and places adjacent, united into a society to carry on the work of the gospel, and, 'having duly considered the need we have of an able and faithful minister to be Settled amongst us to the Eternal welfare of our immortal Souls,' they called the Rev. Matthew Dripps to 'take the charge of us. By preaching the Gospel, catchizing, visiting our families, administering the Sacraments and Exercising Discipline and doing by instructing, comforting, admonishing and Rebuking whatever is incumbent on a faithful pastor.' They, as members of the church 'in the Lords Strength promise to receive the word from your mouth, Subject ourselves to the several parts of your ministry to give you all due encouragement and do what is incumbent from a dutiful people to their faithful minister.' Rev. Matthew Dripps came from Kilmarnock, Scotland. He was ordained in 1797 and was sent by the Associated Synod of Scotland to serve in the Nova Scotia mission. Following years as an

St. John's Kirk, opened July 4, 1805, during the ministry of the Rev. Matthew Dripps.

itinerant missionary, he accepted the call of the Shelburne Presbyterians and served as a faithful and respected minister of the church until his death in 1828. In 1804 he married Margaret Ross of Sable River. They and their family of seven children lived for many years in the sturdy old house on the waterfront at the corner of King and Dock Streets.

With the arrival of Matthew Dripps, the congregation was reorganized and the corner stone for a church was laid on June 25, 1804, on the site of the first Presbyterian meeting house. The building of the church was under the direction of Rev. Dripps, pastor, Colin Campbell, Esq., president, George Gracie, Esq., vice-president, and Archibald Cunningham and David Walker, elders. The church was built by subscriptions from the Marquess of Lansdowne, the Earl of Shelburne, and others devoted to the Presbyterian church. A receipt for one subscription has survived, acknowledged by Archibald Cunningham to Gideon White for 'his-two-third subscription of £16.13.4 towards the building of the Church of Scotland in this town,' and for his subscription of £3.15 'towards the support of the Rev. Matthew Dripps as minister of that church.' The new church, St. John's Kirk, was opened on July 4, 1805. It was to stand a sturdy symbol of the Presbyterian faith for many years, until, no longer large enough to accommodate the Presbyterian congregation it was used as a church hall, and a new church was built below it on the slope of the hill.[4]

CHURCHES, SCHOOLS AND SOCIAL LIFE

Anglicans

The Port Roseway Associates were, for the most part, members of the dissenting churches. When those who were of the Church of England requested that one of their clergymen should go with them to Port Roseway, although the motion 'appeared in the Affirmative,' it was referred to another meeting. It was later again 'agreed to refer the Question, till [we receive] advice from our Agents.' The first clergyman to indicate his willingness to go to Port Roseway was the Rev. George Panton, and on the invitation of two of the Associates he agreed to go with them as their clergyman. A native of Scotland, he was ordained by the Bishop of Down and Cannon in 1771. He came to America and in 1773 he was inducted rector of the church in Trenton, New Jersey. When trouble began in America, he, with Dr. Charles Inglis and Dr. Chandler and other leading clergymen, wrote and published essays in support of the British government. He joined the British Army as a volunteer and was appointed by Sir William Howe as chaplain to the Prince of Wales Regiment. Unfortunately for George Panton, and for the peaceful founding of the Church of England in Shelburne, he was stricken with a fever and was unable to sail with the first fleet of Loyalists for Port Roseway. When he was ready to leave, he was informed by the admiral that the Rev. William Walter was sailing for Shelburne as cleryman of the Church of England. Although they sailed in the same fleet, the seas favoured Walter and on Panton's arrival he had already established himself as the rector of Shelburne and wardens and vestrymen had been elected, calling themselves the Vestry of Trinity Church.

An unhappy and disastrous conflict immediately developed. As a native of Massachusetts, the Rev. William Walter was known to many of the Shelburne Loyalists. He graduated from Harvard in 1756 and was ordained by the Bishop of London in 1764 and was appointed assistant-rector and later rector of Trinity Church, Boston. With the evacuation of Boston, he and his family went to Halifax and later to England. On his return to America he served as a chaplain in a British regiment. Shortly after he came to Shelburne he departed for England to present his claim for losses during the Revolution and to consult with the Society for the Propogation of the Gospel about his appointment as rector of the Church of England in Shelburne. During his stay in England he received the degree of Doctor of Divinity from King's College, Aberdeen.

Undeterred by Walter and his vestry, the supporters of Mr. Panton accepted him as their minister and elected officers of the church. On the division of the town and district of Shelburne by Governor Parr into three parishes – St. George, St. Patrick, and St. Andrew – Panton was inducted by the governor to the parish of St. Patrick. The boundaries of the parishes, later altered to two by an act of the Assembly in 1789, were defined as beginning at the high water mark midway between Ann and St. John's Streets and from thence eastward across the land to the Jordan River. St. George's parish extended northward along the Jordan to the King's Wood, westward to the Roseway River and south to the point of beginning. St. Patrick's ran southward along the banks of the Jordan to Berry's Point, from thence eastward along the shore to Shelburne Harbour and northward to the line of beginning. Dr. Walter insisted that the governor had no authority to allocate parishes or to induct a minister until one was presented by the people. Without regard to boundaries or to parishes, land was purchased by the vestry of Trinity Church in St. Patrick's parish and a temporary church was erected. It was opened on January 23, 1785, and a petition was sent to Governor Parr asking that Dr. Walter should be inducted into the church at Shelburne. They would 'not presume to enquire as to why the Parish was divided into two,' for a great number of those who invited Dr. Walter to be their minister lived in the part designated as St. Patrick's. They hoped His Excellency would order Dr. Walter inducted into the church they had erected 'in as central a part of the town as could be found' and that the church might bear the name of Trinity after one in New York and for Dr. Walter's church in Boston. Governor Parr demurred. Dr. Walter's conduct was 'repugnant.' He had encroached on St. Patrick's parish in erecting his temporary church and he refused to induct him. 'His disposition towards the authority of the Government countenanced a spirit of popular opposition,' Parr wrote the Society for the Propagation of the Gospel, and 'I consider the matter of some importance to the future of the Church in the Province.'

Earnest efforts were made by Mr. Panton and his vestry toward a reconciliation, to set aside 'all animosities and jealousies of each other, and pledge themselves each to other for that Christian-like purpose.' Dr. Walter and his vestry agreed to certain proposals; others they returned unanswered. Mr. Panton offered his resignation that 'someone unconnected with the unhappy disputes might harmonize the Settlement.' He hoped Dr. Walter would do likewise. To the censure of his actions by the S.P.G., Walter wrote that he had not sought to give uneasiness at Shelburne and had complied with Mr. Panton's proposals as far as they were acceptable. But to give up his church to another is 'an Height of Charity' which no member of the Society 'could expect him to rise to.' Walter further encroached on Panton's parish when he 'officiated at a Funeral in a Lot of Ground adjoining his Schism House in the Center' of St. Patrick's Parish. Although memorials and petitions show Dr. Walter had many more adhe-

CHURCHES, SCHOOLS AND SOCIAL LIFE

rents and that many from the dissenting churches favoured him to Mr. Panton as clergyman of the Church of England in Shelburne, most of the substantial citizens of the town supported Mr. Panton. As judges and justices of the peace, they deplored Walter's action in erecting a meeting house in St. Patrick's parish where he held services to the prejudice of Mr. Panton, their legally inducted rector. They condemned his converting land adjoining his meeting house into 'a burying ground in opposition to that assigned by public authority in another part of the town' and styling himself rector of an imaginary parish – the parish of Trinity Church – combining the parishes of the town and district of Shelburne. They urged that Walter should be suspended from further duties. No attempt was made by Walter or his vestry to amend their trespass and on September 15, 1785, Panton sent his resignation to Governor Parr. Walter, soon after, wrote the S.P.G. that his troubles were over – Panton had resigned and his vestry dissolved. He felt that the governor could give him no further trouble and his parishioners had gained the right of presentation. Parr did not agree. Instead, he wrote to the Bishop of London upholding his appointment of George Panton and asked for the removal of Walter from Shelburne.

Panton's departure from Shelburne did not restore peace among the Anglicans. Nearly a year after his resignation Walter reluctantly proposed to the S.P.G., with the approval of Governor Parr, that the district of Shelburne should be divided into two parishes and that the Rev. John Hamilton Rowland should be the rector of St. Patrick's. A native of England, Rowland came to America in 1768 and in 1775 he was appointed by Lord Dunmore to the living at Great Bridge in the parish of St. Bride near Norfolk, Virginia. In 1777 he was appointed chaplain to the 2nd Battalion of New Jersey Volunteers. On his coming to Shelburne on the invitation of a number of Anglicans, his application to Governor Parr for presentation was very favourably received. With his coming, happier relations developed between Dr. Walter and his vestry and the parish of St. Patrick. In May 1788 the two parishes met together for the first time with Dr. Walter the rector of the parish of St. George and Mr. Rowland the rector of the parish of St. Patrick. It would seem at this time that the temporary church built by Dr. Walter in the parish of St. Patrick was used by both congregations. With the meeting of the parishes, plans were made for the building of a 'permanent and church-like Structure' and land was purchased from Lemuel Goddard, Jr., then living in Jamaica and from Richard Hall (lots no. 2, 3, 4, 11, 12 letter G, South Division). On June 6, 1788, tenders for the erection of the church were received and the plans submitted by Isaac Hildrith and Aaron White, master builders, were accepted for their 'Strength, convenience and beauty.' In December 1789 the church was finished and the first

Shelburne Harbour, sketched from the town, showing Christ Church, by John Elliott Woolford, July 1817. (Nova Scotia Museum Collection)

service of worship was held within its walls on Christmas day. On July 30, 1790, during a visit to Shelburne by Bishop Charles Inglis, the church was consecrated as Christ Church and the sermon of consecration was preached by Mr. Rowland, Dr. Walter being at that time in Boston where he and his family soon afterwards returned to live and where he served as rector of Christ Church until his death in 1800. Bishop Inglis was later to write of the church: 'It is a plain neat well constructed building, and capable of holding 1000 persons. I consecrated the Church – the first ever consecrated in British America.[5]

SCHOOLS AND SCHOOL MASTERS

A first consideration of the overseers of the poor for the town of Shelburne was to obtain money, through assessment of inhabitants, for the construction of a public school house for which they requested £100 from the Court of Sessions on April 7, 1784. Money was not alloted nor a school house provided, and the only early school for the poor in the vicinity of Shelburne was one for Black children in Birchtown, founded and maintained by the Associates of the late Doctor Thomas Bray.

In 1793, after many families of the industrious poor had migrated to parts of the United States where charity schools were provided and where their children could be educated, the magistrates of the Court of Sessions appealed to Bishop Inglis to request the Society for the Propagation of the Gospel in Foreign Parts 'to extend their bounty in the allowance of a schoolmaster' for a charity school in the town of Shelburne. The bounty was granted and two schools were established, with Thomas Coattam master of the boys and his wife mistress of the girls. In 1798 the Society for Promoting Christian Knowledge founded a free school for white children in Shelburne under the direction of the Rev. Thomas B. Rowland and the wardens and vestry of Christ Church, with Richard Brazel, a former merchant, master of the school. In 1800 the town itself established a charity school, to be supported at public expense. Alexander Houston was engaged as schoolmaster to teach reading at six pence per week for each child; reading, writing and cyphering would be taught at nine pence. Children to attend the school were recommended to the magistrates by the overseers of the poor on the application of their parents.

To encourage education in Nova Scotia, in 1811 an act of the Assembly, to be in force for seven years, provided bounties for grammar schools. The master of a grammar school was to receive £100 from the provincial treasury, and the assistant master £50 when over 30 pupils attended. For the town to qualify for the bounty, by order of the Court of Sessions, a school house was provided and £50 was subscribed for the support of the school. Henry Guest, the Rev. Matthew Dripps and Jesse Lear were appointed trustees, and on November 4, 1811, the school was opened with John Cowling, described as 'decent, sober and with abilities to teach youth in Orthography, Reading, writing and arithmetic,' as schoolmaster. In 1814 two schools in Shelburne were granted bounties of £12.10 each half year from the duties on imports and excise appropriated by the Act of the General Assembly. These schools were Thomas Coattam's, which was partly supported by the S.P.G., and the school established in 1811 with Richard Brazel, schoolmaster, who had succeeded John Cowling on this decease. By 1819 the two schools had been merged into one.

There was, besides this school, a subscription grammar school opened about 1819 attended 'by the children of the better class' whose parents could afford to pay for their children's education. These schools did not begin to meet the needs of the many in want of an education for, although several were taught gratis in the subscription school, nearly two-thirds of the children in the town were unable to attend school because their parents were too poor to pay their tuition. Regretting their situation, the Rev. Thomas Rowland, in 1823, had built a schoolhouse, near Ann Street, measuring 32 feet by 14 feet, and of two storeys – one for the boys and one for the girls. Here the 85 children unprovided with schooling, on the consent of the teachers, were to attend. The teachers were to depend upon the parents who could pay toward their children's education and upon the allowance granted by the province.

Private schools, for those whose parents could afford to pay a schoolmaster, were in operation from the beginning of the town, with Robert Barry the first known schoolmaster. He opened his school in the summer of 1783 in the room in his log house where he also held services for the Methodists on Sundays. The assessment rolls of 1786 and 1787 list eight teachers: six schoolmasters, Thomas Coattam, John Cowling, John Charles Strueve, George Paget, Jeremiah Connor and Alexander Murray, music teacher and dancing master; schoolmistresses, Mrs. Carson and Christian Hefferman. Three schoolmistresses, in 1789, were Mrs. Newton and Mrs. Johnston and her daughter. Somewhere along the way was Mrs. Barry who taught her pupils polite manners, meeting in the schoolroom with bows and curtsies. In 1785, two teachers of a private school were W. Leary and Edmond Fogarty. Their school was on Mowat Street near the northwest corner of St. John's Street. They taught 'Reading, Writing, Arithmetic, Book-keeping, Navigation, Mensuration, the use and Construction of Maps and Sea-Charts, the Greek and Latin Languages, &c.' Edmond Fogarty on 'the request of several respectable families' also taught dancing, Tuesday and Friday evenings from six to nine o'clock, when he expected the young ladies and gentlemen to favour him with their company.

It was reported in 1790 that there were twelve such schools in the town of Shelburne, nine kept by men, three by women, with 257 scholars. It was believed that there were 770 children in the town, the parents of two-thirds of the children being too impoverished to bear the expense of their tuition. Probably most of the early private schools, if not all, had disappeared by 1802 when a grammar school for boys was established, with Robert Rogers of Cambridge, Massachusetts, preceptor at a salary of £150. Here seventeen boys struggled with the principles of Greek and Latin.[6]

SOCIAL LIFE

The delight of the Shelburne Loyalists in dancing, card playing and wearing pretty clothes decorated with ribbons and lace drew many harsh and uncharitable comments from those who knew them, and from those who were struggling to establish a stable town and had little time or patience

CHURCHES, SCHOOLS AND SOCIAL LIFE

with their dances. Others who met them wrote more kindly of those they knew 'who in general are an industrious sober set of people . . . some genteel people live in a decent manner, and live Sociable. The Gentlemen in the Town dine together in a decent genteel manner upon Beef and mutton . . . in fulness without superfluity, and cheerfulness without levity, and a hearty glass without intemperance.'

Their fondness for dancing in the streets and in their homes and in the taverns marked the Shelburne Loyalists with the long remembered epithet 'the dancing beggars,' bestowed upon them by one of the early Shelburne merchants. Their first dance, or 'ball' as they called their dances, was danced among the stumps in the streets with bonfires at dusk to celebrate the King's birthday. In July there was a ball to entertain Governor Parr when he named the town for his patron Lord Shelburne, and 'the Ladys danc'd till nearly five.' For the Queen's birthday in January the ball was in McGragh's Tavern where 'About 50 gentlemen and ladies danced, drank tea, played at cards in a house which stood where six months ago there was

House and store of George and Robert Ross, Shelburne merchants and ship owners, built circa 1785, photographed approximately 1958. The building is now operated as a branch of the Nova Scotia Museum.

almost impenetrable swamp.' There were private parties for dancing in homes among friends, parties given by the military officers, and the subscription assembly for dancing in the Long Room in Steel's Tavern beginning at half past six in the evening.

Royal anniversaries and saints' days were occasions for festivities. The King's birthday in 1785 was heralded with a royal salute at Point Carleton, echoed by the firing of guns at the barracks, and at half past twelve a royal salute boomed from the island at the foot of William Street, accompanied by royal toasts and three cheers. In the evening the barracks were illuminated and the houses in the town were bright with lights 'and the night was spent with that conviviality and decorum that marks the character of loyal subjects and good citizens.' On St. Andrew's Day 'old style' in 1786 'the Sons of that sage and ancient Saint... gave an elegant Ball, at the Merchant's Coffee-house, to the Ladies and Gentlemen of this place; perhaps the ball-room was never more crowded or a company made more happy than on this occasion; and the order and decency with which it was conducted, with the social harmony and good humour of the company, passed away the hours of the night in the most pleasing manner.'

At least one entertainer ventured to Shelburne to amuse the Loyalists and the disbanded soldiers. In the *Port Roseway Gazetteer* of May 12, 1785, he advertised:

> At Mr. Steel's Long Room
> on Friday Evening, May 13, 1785,
> Mr. Moore will deliver
> FASHIONABLE RAILLERY
> With Alterations,
> To be Preceeded by
> An ELOGIUM on FREE MASONRY.
> In which Mr. Moore will discover to the
> Ladies the SECRETS of that art
> The Evening's Entertainment will conclude
> With a Poetical Vision, Called
> THE COURT OF MOMUS;
> In which will be initiated the following
> Dramatic Characters:
> Falstaf LORD POPPINGTON   Scrub,
> Pistol   JOHN MOODY   and
> Fribble LORD OGLEBY   Mungo.
> Miser   MAWWORM

Tickets were one dollar each and the evening's entertainment began at half past seven o'clock.

Along with pleasant evenings spent dancing or listening to Mr. Moore and his fashionable raillery, there were four public billiard tables for entertainment, and for the men there were the dinner meetings of the Friendly Fire Club and of the Masonic lodges. There were six Masonic lodges during the first years of Shelburne's settlement. These were: Parr, No. 3 Provincial, Ancient York Masons, warranted in Shelburne September 29, 1784, and which continued until 1805; Lodge No. 4, warranted in 1784 and abandoned a few months later; Solomon's Lodge No. 5 Provincial, warranted September 29, 1784. Its warrant was surrendered to the Grand Lodge on June 4, 1788, and it subsequently took rank as No. 5 Grand Lodge in New York. Hiram Lodge, No. 10, originated from the Irish Lodge No. 143 in the 6th Regiment of the British army. It was warranted in Shelburne on March 3, 1785, and was withdrawn from the province with the departure of the regiment in 1791. Lodge No. 643 of His Majesty's 6th Regiment and Lodge No. 136, which was of Irish origin, and of the 17th Regiment, were in Shelburne from 1784 to 1786. The first St. John's Day after the arrival of the Loyalists, as a Free Mason festival, was celebrated by those 'of that Worshipful fraternity' who had arrived in the first ships. On another day of festival, on the anniversary of St. John the Evangelist, the brethren of Lodge No. 643 and those of Parr Lodge entertained at Brother Steel's tavern 'all ancient Masons with dinner at 3 o'clock.' On the same day, the master and brethren of Hiram Lodge celebrated with dinner at half past four at Brother McGragh's tavern in Mason's Lane.[7]

10
Taverns and Inns, Post Offices and the Cape Roseway Lighthouse

Many inns and taverns and grog shops were part of early Shelburne. The assessment rolls of 1786 and 1787 listed 29 tavernkeepers, but many who were enrolled under other professions also had taverns, as had George Harding, who was listed as a carpenter. Besides the many taverns, most of the merchants and shopkeepers had licenses to sell spiritous liquors at their places of business. A few of the taverns were also inns with accommodation for guests. The best known of the inns was the Merchant's Coffee House on Water Street facing Charlotte Lane. It was also known as Steel's Tavern after its owner and operator, Patrick Steel. It was not only a tavern and inn, but a meeting place for the Shelburne Court of Sessions, a centre for entertainment and for public auctions of vessels and of Blacks. It was also the location for the display of an oversize turnip that 'induced a Number of Gentlemen to try its weight' – twelve and a half pounds and said to be still growing! It was here, in the Tavern's Long Room, that the elegant St. Andrew's Day Ball took place in 1786.

A popular meeting place for the members of the Masonic Order, Hiram's Lodge, was McGragh's Tavern on the south side of Mason's Lane, also a popular place for parties, for dancing and for cards. Other taverns were Rodney's Victory, on the south side of St. Patrick's Lane; the King's Arms on St. George's Street; Campbell's Tavern, with George Campbell, proprietor, on Ann Street; Whiting's Tavern near the Cove operated by Thomas Whiting; and the British Coffee House on King Street opposite James

TAVERNS, INNS, POST OFFICES, CAPE ROSEWAY LIGHTHOUSE

Robertson's printing press. In Ann Street was Mrs. Lowrie's Tavern. Numbers of others, their names unrecorded, edged the sidewalks of the streets. Among them were: Patrick McDermott's on Rodney Lane, Jeremiah Crawley's and Peter Taylor's on Maiden Lane. Francis Wood was on Dock Street, John Johnston and Hugh Hayes were on St. Patrick's Lane, Mary Smith on King Street and Mrs. Brandon was on St. John's. Along with the taverns and inns was Mrs. Patterson's Boarding House on Charlotte Lane.

Prices to be charged by the innkeepers for a night's lodging, and for tea and dinner, were established by the Court of Sessions: for a comfortable bed, one man or woman, six pence; a servant, three pence; for stabling and hay for a horse, one night, one shilling; oats per quart, six pence; for a man or a women, breakfast of bread, butter, tea, coffee, or chocolate, with loaf sugar, eight pence; for a servant, breakfast, four pence; for a man's or a woman's dinner of good wholesome meat, with bread and vegetables, ten pence; a servant's dinner, six pence; for a man's or woman's supper of good wholesome meat with bread and vegetables, eight pence; a servant's supper, five pence; tea, or coffee, in the afternoon, with bread, butter, and loaf sugar, eight pence; a man's or a woman's breakfast or supper of bread and milk, four pence. Sufficient hay 'to bate [sic] one horse' while his master breakfasted or dined was four pence. Pasture for a horse for one night was three pence.

Licenses to operate a tavern and to sell spirituous liquors in a shop were issued for five shillings by the clerk of licenses on the approval of the Court of Sessions. A few licenses were granted free to the poor and to those who operated public ferries for the convenience of travellers. Selling liquor without a license was an offence liable to a fine of two shillings. William Mullneaux, a half pay pilot of Cape Negro, refused to buy a license, declaring the money supported a set of people who walked the streets with their hands in their pockets. Ordered into Court, he was fined forty shillings 'for the use of our Sovereign Lord, the King.' Taverns used as disorderly houses were ordered removed or closed. For misdemeanours in administering the privilege of selling liquors, licenses were temporarily cancelled as was Adam Bower's in 1785, for accepting a soldier's necessarys in lieu of money for the liquor he sold him.

The number of licenses issued to sell spirituous liquors is astounding. In two-and-a-half months in 1785 twenty-five tavern and eighteen shop licenses were granted in addition to the many already issued. The grand jury of the Court of Sessions deplored the number of dramshops and houses selling liquors as 'a grievance of so serious a nature that if not redressed the total extinction of every virituous principle in the rising generation will not be the least of the many ill consequences that must result from them.' They were still deploring the numbers of taverns in 1800 as 'an Evil of the first Magnitude.' Observers who wrote of early Shelburne attributed in part the rapid decline of the town to the intemperance of its citizens, a vicious evil the Court of Sessions was unable to curb and made no determined stand to eliminate.[1]

POSTMASTERS AND POST OFFICES

The first postmaster in Shelburne was James Donaldson, Shelburne merchant and master mariner. He was appointed to act as deputy postmaster at Shelburne by the British postmaster general in New York in the fall of 1783. Having no place of his own at that time, he kept his post office in the house of James Dole on the southeast corner of King and Water Streets. Here, he advised the people of Shelburne, until a regular post was established, all letters put into the office for Halifax or New York would be made up and sent to those places by sea every week or as often as a safe opportunity offered. Later, with his place of business established on the southeast corner of Ann and Water Streets, he transferred his post office to Ann Street. On July 12, 1785, Alexander Fernandes was appointed postmaster and the post office was removed to his house on Water Street near the Merchant's Coffee House. With the appointment of Archibald Cunningham as deputy postmaster on September 5, 1786, the post office was in his house on the west side of Mowat Street near the corner of St. George's Street.

Restating the importance of an act passed in the fifth year of His Majesty's reign to safeguard the collection of revenue from mail carried in vessels, orders were reissued in 1788 to all custom officers in His Majesty's Plantations 'not to suffer any vessel to break bulk or make any Entry, until the masters have delivered their Letters to the Post Office.' Further, they were to demand from 'mariners, Passengers, and all other Person or Persons belonging to such vessel... previous to their Vessel's being admitted to an Entry, all Letters and Packets brought by them', which were to be delivered to the deputy postmaster general in the port of entry. To administer these instructions, James Bruce, as customs officer, was appointed by the General Post Office, London, to be deputy postmaster for the port of Shelburne. As the portmanteaux and bags of mail were received from the vessels by James Bruce they were taken to the post office and opened. In his meticulous handwriting, Archibald Cunningham, as postmaster, carefully recorded the name of the vessel from which the bags of mail were delivered, the letters received and the amount due from each recipient. Postage varied from one to two-and-one-half pence to five-and-one-half and six and eight pence and sometimes was as high as two shillings three pence and three shillings.

TAVERNS, INNS, POST OFFICES, CAPE ROSEWAY LIGHTHOUSE

Some paid for their postage in ways other than in shillings and pence. In his records Archibald Cunningham noted:

May 14, 1792, David Walker 1 house Brush (damaged a little)

May 23, 1792, Alex^r Cocken 3 Bush^s potatoes a $\frac{1}{3}^d$ - $\frac{3}{9}^d$

By 4 doz. Eggs 5^d - $\frac{1}{8}^d$

Postage on letters outward bound was one penny. Roderick McKenzie, mail courier for the 6th Regiment, is recorded as paying seven pence for seven letters destined for Europe.

In 1792 the post office, under the authority of the London office, was closed. Archibald Cunningham continued as postmaster under the supervision of the post office in Halifax. The decline of Shelburne is poignantly remarked in his records. On January 19, 1802, 'The English November mail from New York to Halifax per the Hiram Rixby was opened at the office, and only four letters in it for Shelburne,' and on a later date, 'Only one letter for poor Shelburne.'

Sometime after Archibald Cunningham was postmaster, Jacob Weiser was appointed to the position. He had his post office on St. Patrick's Lane in a house remembered for its long, dark rooms. In 1836 Robert Ross Thomson was appointed postmaster for the town of Shelburne and operated from his store on Charlotte Lane – now open to the public as the Ross-Thomson House, a branch of the Nova Scotia Museum. Evidence of the post office is still to be seen: the slot in the window shutter in Charlotte Lane where letters were mailed at night and on Sundays when the store was closed and the door barred; and the small window cut high in the wall in the old dining room, to emit light at Robert Ross Thomson's desk in its corner by the chimney where he did his post office accounts.[2]

THE CAPE ROSEWAY LIGHTHOUSE

In the summer of 1784 Colonel Robert Morse of the Royal Engineers recommended that there should be a chain of lighthouses along the shores of Nova Scotia from Cape Canso to Cape Sable. The houses should be distinguished by the number of lights, 'one light at the first and increasing the number of lights with the number of Light houses.' He also recommended that there should be cannons, the same number as the lights, to be discharged in thick fog, and that the pilots who came to Nova Scotia after the evacuation of New York should care for the lighthouses and the cannons.[3]

In accordance with Morse's recommendations, one hundred acres of

The original Roseway Lighthouse, first operated in 1792, as it appeared in the 1930s. It has since been replaced by a modern structure. (Photograph by Eldon Whynot)

land, lots no. 21 and 22, were reserved for a lighthouse at the southern tip of McNutt's Island, the point of land known as Cape Roseway. No steps were taken to erect a lighthouse and in the spring of 1786 the grand jury presented to the Court of Sessions the complaint of strangers bound into the port of Shelburne as also 'those who daily frequent it, of the want of a Light House to enable them to distinguish the Port at night... for the want of which vessels have been blown off that would otherwise have made Port in time to avoid the Gales.' Action was taken by Isaac Wilkins. On his motion in the House of Assembly, the sum of £500 was granted on July 8, 1786, for the erection of a lighthouse leading into the harbour of Shelburne, the money 'to be paid and applied under the Direction of Commissioners to be appointed by the Governor.' William Hale, Joseph Durfee, Stephen Skinner, David Thomson and Robert Gray were appointed commissioners, with William Hale treasurer and contractor. Stone cutter and stone mason, John Thomson,[4] formerly of the parish of Belhelvie, Aberdeenshire, was engaged as builder of the light; Thomas Burnside and Peter Andes were carpenters, and Alexander Cocken was in charge of the building material.[5]

By January 1787 the commissioners were ready to order the construction of the lighthouse and other buildings and advertised for proposals in writing for the building of a frame dwelling house to be 32 feet by 16 feet and 8 feet high in the posts, and for 50 hogsheads of lime for the building of the lighthouse. With the work well underway, the House of Assembly in December 1787, voted a further sum of £500 to complete the structure. The cost of construction far exceeded the £1,000 voted for its erection. Warrants for £975 were voted to be paid to William Hale between the years 1787 and 1791. With a considerable sum still owing to Hale and others, in May 1793 the House of Assembly finally voted £232.16.5 to cover the demands against the lighthouse.[6]

By late fall of 1789 the first 35 feet of the building had been constructed. It was of great slabs of granite, octagonal in shape, tapering to the top. Construction was completed by October 1790 but the lights were not fixed until two years later. Fear was expressed that they would never be fixed 'so long as they continue to pay' the light money without actually having a functioning light. Shortly after the decision was made to build a lighthouse at the entrance to Shelburne Harbour, the Legislature passed an Act for collecting fees for its maintenance, from the first day of January 1788. For all vessels coming into or leaving the harbour, other than coasters and fishing vessels belonging to the province and transports or vessels employed in His Majesty's service, the fee was four pence per ton. For vessels wholly belonging to any person who was a freeholder and an inhabitant of the province, three pence per ton was the fee. Coasting vessels, in lieu of fees, were to pay twenty shillings per annum and one shilling for every ton above twenty tons. A surplus over necessary funds for the support of the lighthouse was to be 'applied to the use of the Government.' Michael Largin and Randal McKinnon were collectors of the fees. Their accounts from December 16, 1788 to November 8, 1790, show the sizable amount of £95.2.4 collected, with Jesse Hoyl, master of the ship *Loyalist*, outward bound for Jamaica, paying £2.7, Captain Gray for the schooner *Charlotte*, Portsmouth bound, paying five shillings, and others as their tonnage demanded.

By 1790 the collecting of light duties when there was no light was protested by the Shelburne Court of Sessions. They demanded a representation to Governor Parr of the injustice inflicted on 'the trading part of the Community, who despair of ever seeing a Light.' They had still nearly two years to wait until the lamps were lit for the first time by Alexander Cocken on September 7, 1792. Anticipating that the lamps would be lit long before 1792, Cocken, a native of Glasgow, Scotland, was commissioned lightkeeper on March 27, 1788, with a salary of £20 per annum. A man of sturdy dependability, he and his son Alexander gave 75 years of service to the Cape Roseway light.[7]

A model of the lighthouse, on the first Christmas it sent its beams of light across the water, decorated the supper table of Governor and Lady Wentworth at their Christmas ball. A few years later the Rev. James Munro wrote the first description of the Cape Roseway light. 'It is built upon a solid rock. Its height from the surface of the water to the foundation is 75 feet, from the foundation to the top is 92 feet making in all 165 in height. Its form is octagon or [an] eight sided figure about 10 feet each square at the bottom or base gradually decreasing to the top, built of Stone in the Strongest manner. Hath two lights. The upper and lower. The Lower hath three Lamps, the upper 9 all properly placed so that the whole of them shall face the windows. In each lamp there are twelve lights, so that the whole make 12 Lamps, and 144 lights. And from its great Height from the surface of the water and the window lights kept clean and the lamps well trimmed gives an excellent light which hath been seen at the distance of seven yea at the distance of ten Leagues off. . . It spends in a year near 7 tons of oil if not 7 Ton Altogether. It was first lighted 7th September 1792.'[8]

Although in a few years 'it was contemplated,' by the House of Assembly, 'to extinguish the light, either through the early decline of Shelburne, or the smallness of the revenue at that Period,' the light continued to shine and the original lighthouse stood on the headland overlooking the entrance to Shelburne Harbour for more than a century and a half until replaced by the present lighthouse.[9]

11
Early Industries, Trades and Professions

EARLY INDUSTRIES

Numbers of industries were in operation almost from the beginning of the town, from the small industries with one man working alone or two or three together, to shipbuilding and the fisheries, lumbering, saw and grist mills. Of the small, one man industries, there were: the pomatum maker, Mr. Bright; William Warden, brewer of essences of bark and spruce; soapboiler, Charles Hart; filemaker, Thomas Smart; ropemaker, Benjamin Hart, whose rope walk on the point of land opposite the town gave it the name of Hart's Point. There were the brewers, John Appleby and John Roberts on Hammond Street, near the Cove, whose brewery resulted in the lane east of the Cove becoming known as Brew House Lane, and John Stevenson on Ann Street, whose tavern license was given to him gratis, 'he having undertaken a mault brewery at great expense.' Of the two brickmakers, George Warden and Samuel Marshall, Warden was given a license of occupation to land near the government reserve at Sandy Point (below the Sandy Point lighthouse) for the making of bricks until it 'shall be wanted for His Majesty's use.' Samuel Marshall, in partnership with William Hale, was granted Blue Island, 130 acres, where the clay was know to be the best in the area. Listed as a potter, Samuel Marshall made excellent bricks and pottery from the Blue Island clay. With fishing and the curing of fish among the foremost early Shelburne industries, there was a demand for barrels and work for many coopers. Among these were David Nairn who, with William Black and John McCullum, had a cooperage on King Street. Richard Hall and Joseph

Oliver had their cooper shop on Ann Street. Among other coopers were Richard and Peter Jenkins, Thomas Lawrence and Archibald Campbell.

Important early industries were Joseph Bell's tannery and his shoe-making firm of Bell and Company. Joseph Bell came to Shelburne in the summer of 1783 and was alloted ten acres of land for a tannery at the north end of Shelburne on the northern branch of Black's Brook. Here he established the firm of Bell and Company for the manufacture of boots and shoes, and built his gambrel-roofed house (still standing on its stone foundation). In 1785 Bell and Company advertised boots of the best material for £1.15, men's strong shoes for 7/6, and women's leather shoes lined and bound for 7/6. Perhaps because of the rapid decline of the town and the fact that there were many shoemakers, Joseph Bell was soon in financial difficulties. In 1786 he pledged his land and houses and other buildings as security on a bond to Valentine Nutter for £262. In 1790 he sold his land and its buildings to Nutter for £150 and about this time he went to Yarmouth.[1]

Saw Pits and Sawmills

Sawmills and saw pits in early Shelburne provided not only lumber for many of the first buildings erected in the town, but were an important means of establishing trade in the West Indies and in other seaports. Until sawmills were constructed, timber was cut in saw pits. These were private pits and when it was discovered that the captains of the companies had put aside the boards for their own use, the Associates, in accord with their decision before they came to Port Roseway that all shingles, clapboards, lumber or material for buildings were to be reserved for the New York Associates, 'voted to seize all the boards... and convert them to the public use.' With this decision of the Associates, the saw pits continued to be operated, cutting during the summer and fall of 1783 sufficient boards to build six to ten houses each week [2]

The first lot of land ordered set aside for a sawmill was lot no. 1 of 500 acres on the west side of the Roseway River, well above the falls, in what is now lower Welshtown. It was surveyed and marked as a mill site for Stephen Shakespear. Below the falls, on the east side of the Roseway on McGill's Point, then known as Campbell's Point, land was surveyed in the late fall of 1783 for a mill site of about twelve acres for Joshua Pell. In March of 1784 Marston divided Pell's property into two lots, A and B. Lot A was assigned to the mill company of Miller and Others, and was granted on April 12 to John Miller, Stephen and David Shakespear, William Castle, James Dole, Valentine Nutter, Thomas and Matthew Pendergrass, Peter Lynch and John Lounds, each of whom were granted 500 acres on the west and on the east banks of the Roseway as mill and farm lots. Lot B, of about

EARLY INDUSTRIES, TRADES AND PROFESSIONS

five acres, was alloted to Joshua Pell. On the east side of the Jordan River, well below the falls, large 600 acre tracts of land were granted to Joshua Watson and Company and to Nicholas Ogden and Company, for saw mills.[3]

Not all who received grants of land as mill sites built sawmills. In the summer of 1784 Benjamin Marston recorded that there were two mills in operation. Unfortunately, he did not give the names of the owners. In 1785 there were five mills. These were listed by Alexander Leckie as: Courtney's, Dole's, Pell's, Hall's, Ross's and Hannah's. James Courtney's mill, a combination grist and sawmill, was on the west side of the Roseway River above the lower falls (50 acre lots no. 6 and 7, Marston's Division). In 1790 he sold his mill to Amos Williams for five shillings and '1 peppercorn upon the last day of the said time if the same shall be lawfully demanded.' Dole's mill was also on the west side of the river on lot no. 4 of the 500 acre lots. Pell's and Hall's mills were on Pell's Mill Brook (Purney's or Swansburg's Brook), Joshua Pell's near the bridge (Route 3), and Richard Hall's on the same brook north of Pell's mill on his land bordering Lake George. Ross's and Hannah's mill was on the Jordan River and if on Nathaniel Hannah's land, lot no. 233, it stood on the west bank of the Jordan below the falls.[4]

By 1786 and 1787 there were a number of other mills in operation: James Cummins' in Cape Negro; John McPhail's in Sable River; and in Shelburne, Richard Townsend's on the west side of the Roseway north of the road, now Route 3, and near the falls. Well above Richard Townsend's mill, on the west side of the river on the 500 acre lot no. 2, originally granted to William Castle and obtained by Stephen Shakespear on a mortgage deed, was a mill owned by several persons, Shakespear selling his one-sixth interest in the mill to James Cox, a Shelburne merchant, in 1787. Still other mills operating during the early years were John Miller's built in 1787 and John Walker's also built in 1787. Miller's mill was probably on his 500 acre lot on the west side of the Roseway near Lake Courtney. The location of John Walker's mill is uncertain but it was likely on the east side of the Roseway River and part of his gristmill. These mills and John McPhail's and Nicholas Ogden's, on Ogden's Brook in East Jordan, each received a bounty of £20 which was the premium allowed by the General Assembly from the duties of impost and excise to encourage the erection of sawmills. During these years there were three competent millwrights in the settlement: Martin Marshall, Robert McQuhae and Robert Drummond.[5]

Trade in Timber
In 1784 Governor Parr, aware of the importance of the sale of timber in the development of a stable pattern of trade between Nova Scotia and the West

*Mill on the Roseway River, by John Elliott Woolford, July 1817.
(Nova Scotia Museum Collection)*

Indies, was hopeful that in less than two years, with sawmills in the process of construction, the province would 'be able to furnish the West Indies with all the Lumber they may want.' Less than a year later shiploads of timber were being shipped from Shelburne and the Jordan River to the West Indies and elsewhere, the *Prince William Henry* taking on a cargo of squared timber at Jordan River for London in June 1785. The Shelburne settlers, unaware of the trade in timber established between Halifax and England as early as 1751, proudly but erroneously announced that 'Capt. Meader who is owner as well as commander of said ship has the honor of being the first gentlemen who carries a cargo to England of the produce of this Province.' By 1787, 29,900 feet or ranging timber, 447,805 feet of boards, 584,000 shingles, 20,476 staves and headings, and an unrecorded number of black spruce and birch ship's knees, anchor stocks and spars were exported from Shelburne in the holds of her outward bound ships. To ensure that only lumber of excellent quality was exported, the Court of Sessions in 1784 appointed

EARLY INDUSTRIES, TRADES AND PROFESSIONS

Nathaniel Munro and George Harding surveyors of lumber and cordwood. Boards and planks split one-sixth of their length or otherwise damaged were to be declared refuse and only merchantable lumber and no other was to be passed by the surveyors. The same standards were to be observed for ranging timber or ton timber; only that which was sound and well squared was to be shipped.[6]

The prosperous trade in lumber was short lived. By 1791 all the timber of easy access had been cut. Without deep water carriage into the woodlands and without roads into the interior where there was timber to cut, the price of lumber soared and was too costly for the shippers to continue their trade in the West Indies. Faced with a rapidly decreasing commerce and a declining population, an appeal was sent to the Rt. Hon. Lord Grenville, His Majesty's principal secretary of state. It was proposed that 'permission be granted by Law for Lumber cut in the late Province of Main to be brought to the ports of Entry in Nova Scotia in American coasting vessels, thence to be reshipped in British Bottoms to the West India Markets.' Such a free port of entry for American vessels, besides providing lumber for trade, would eliminate the heavy tonnage duty imposed on British ships loading lumber in American seaports for the Islands. (This duty was an important source of revenue for the American government, raised without any expense to American citizens, which fell ultimately on the consumer in the West Indies.) The British hesitated. The town was not named a free port, and consequently Shelburne merchants were without timber for the West Indies trade.[7]

Gristmills and a Snuffmill
There were four gristmills to serve early Shelburne farmers. The first of these was James Courtney's on the west side of the Roseway River and was part of his sawmill which he sold in 1790 to Gideon White who resold it in 1797 to Amos Williams. On the east side of the river, near the falls, was Gideon White's gristmill which was burned in the disastrous fires of 1792. Richard Townsend's and Joshua Wise's gristmills were on their farm land on the west side of the river. John Walker's mill was on the east side of the river. It came into operation in October 1787 when Alexander Houston took buckwheat and corn to be ground in Walker's mill. It seems he later had a gristmill in Lower Sandy Point on Stokes Brook where there was a gristmill left in the care of David Walker, from which, after his death, the mill stones were given to Richard Wall of Ragged Islands. With gristmills to grind grain into fresh flour and meal, it soon became more profitable for the merchants to import grain than to import flour from American merchants for resale in Shelburne. Rules were established by law in 1787 for the toll to

be taken at all gristmills in the province. Each miller, who kept a good bolting (sifting) machine, was allowed to take one quart and no more of each bushel of grain brought to the mill to be ground and bolted. For refusing to bolt grain that was clean, dry and in good order, or for taking a greater toll than allowed, the penalty was 40 shillings to be recovered before two of His Majesty's justices of the peace and paid to the overseers of the poor, plus the amount of the value of the grain or meal taken above that allowed by the toll. No miller was to be required to receive or to grind any corn that was not clean, dry and in good order.[8]

In June 1789 the Shelburne merchant David Black entered into a contract with John Gordon, stone mason, to dig a millrace for a snuffmill for £25. The race was to be cut a length of 700 feet from Woodside Pond with a breadth of six feet, and was to be built up and secured with stones in a four-foot ground digging. The mill stood near Wright's Road, where it struck off from Water Street, and was near the bridge over the brook which now bears Black's name.[9]

TRADES AND PROFESSIONS

With the Loyalists and disbanded soldiers came their trades and professions, their means of earning a living and maintaining a town. Among them were skilled artisans, competent shipbuilders, workers in iron and wood; merchants and shopkeepers; sailors, master mariners and fishermen; farmers, gardeners and labourers; doctors, attorneys, schoolmasters, ministers of the gospel. From the early Shelburne newspapers, from assessment rolls, from account and letter books, from letters, deeds and diaries, the trades and professions of the early Shelburne settlers have been compiled.

Merchants and Shopkeepers
Merchants and shopkeepers far outnumbered all other trades and professions, numbering more than 150 between the years 1783 and 1787. For 'Wholesale or Retail, very low for Cash, Bills of Exchange, Fish, Fur or Lumber,' they offered their customers a wide selection of goods. Much of it was reminiscent of the well-established towns from whence they came rather than merchandise for sale in a new town planted in a wilderness on a rocky shore. In their stores were boxes of green and black tea: hyson, singlo, soushong and bohea; barrels of coffee, puncheons of molasses, brown and white loaf sugar and 'the very best Muscovado sugar in hogsheads and barrels from Barbadoes.' They sold vinegar in 40 gallon casks, Florence oil, ketchup and pickles. On their shelves and in bins were spices, fresh limes and dried fruits and grains; cheese, flour and firkins of butter; Poland starch, pearlash, saltpeter, turpentine and soap. Porter came in hogsheads

and barrels as did high proof rum 'of excellent flavour,' shrub, red port, white wines, Jamaica spirits and Windward Island rum.

For ladies of fashion there were violet and plain hair powders and perfumery. For the men there were pipes, fine Virginia tobacco and snuff; shoe buckles, canes and walking sticks; silk, morocco, and black leather swordbelts; round and cocked hats, cockade and black hair ribbons; velvet and leather stocks; London-made boots and shoes and blacking balls and shoe brushes to clean them; silk and worsted hose and stockings; white kidskin, buckskin and beaver gloves; oiled skin and silk umbrellas. In ready-made clothing there were Irish great coats, jackets, trousers and shirts, fine velvet and superfine camlet (camel hair) cloaks lined with green baize, calamancoes in fine satin fabric, sourtouts, slops (loose garments) 'of sundry kinds.' Yards of choice 'Irish linen, cambricks, velvets, corduroys, fustians, jeanets, queen's cord, tammy, durants and shalloon' waited to be sewn into cloaks and jackets and fine dresses.

There were tools for carpenters and joiners; painter's oils and colours; oakum, sheet and bar lead, pumice and rotten stones; fishermen's and hunter's equipment, powder and shot. For the fireside there were shovels and tongs, pokers and bellows, and rolls of brimstone. For the dining table pewter dishes were offered, along with earthenware and glass plates, 'basons,' knives and forks. Candlesticks were japanned or plain, of tin or iron; candles were moulded or dipped. There were chairs and tables and bedsteads; blankets and quilts and carpets; copper scales and weights; brass cocks (weather vanes) and horn 'lanthorns.' For writing one could obtain writing and blotting papers, wax and wafers, ink powder and inkstands, pen and jack knives. For schoolchildren there were slates and pencils, Pew's and Ennick's dictionaries and spelling books. For Shelburne's first gardens and open fields were seeds of clover and grass, vegetables and herbs.

Edging the long main streets of the town and the lanes to the waterfront, were the stores and warehouses of the merchants and shopkeepers. Beginning at the northwest corner of King and Water Streets was the store of Robertson and Rigby housed in the same building as James and Alexander Robertson's printing press. Across the street, on the southwest corner of King and Water, was the store of Sullivan and Mills. Below Sullivan and Mills, on the south side of King Street and opposite Robertson's printing office, was William Cunningham's place of business. His stock in trade differed from most of his competitors, with women's stays and calimanco shoes, brown soap, brass shot moulds, Queen's ware in the newest fashion and 'a neat selection' of children's books. Below William Cunningham's store and near the waterfront was the firm of McLean and Bogle, importers of goods from the West Indies and from London. Near Sullivan and Mills, on Water Street on the corner of Mason Lane, was the store of Valentine Nutter. He sold fishermen's and hunter's supplies, mess pork and beef in barrels, quintals of fish, ship bread, kegs of crackers, cherry rum, brandy, orange juice by the gallon, Scotch snuff in small bladders. Turning his back on his cod and mackerel lines, his barrels of pork and beef, he stocked his shelves with violet-scented hair powder, Turlington's balsam, Harlem-oil, Anderson's pills, Stoughton's bitters, oil of lavender and of bergamot. For livingrooms, he had rolls of plain blue paper 'with a very handsome bordering for ditto.' For the musically inclined there were 'very excellent violins, voice flutes, musick and musick paper, violin strings and bridges, houtboys and bassoon reeds.' Along Water Street south of Valentine Nutter, on the southwest corner of St. John's Street, stood the store of Lynch and Keeley. South of Lynch and Keeley on the corner of Charlotte Lane, Mactier, Mackie and Company had their house and store. Still further along on Water Street was the store of George and Greggs Farish on the corner of Ann Street, and on the northwest corner of St. George and Water Streets was the business house of Gay and Lowe.

On the east side of Water Street, a little north of King Street, Andrew Barclay had his book and stationery store. South of his store, on the northeast corner of King and Water Streets, Richard Hall sold in his place of business Jamaica spirits, Holland geneva (gin), and fine Baltimore flour by the barrel and in large quantities for cash. Near Richard Hall, and to the east of his store on King Street, was Stephen Skinner's paint and hardware shop. Across King Street from Richard Hall's store, and two doors south on Water Street, was William Hale's store. He sold nuts and plums and 'spring patterns in callicos.' On the northeast corner of Water and St. John's Streets was the business house of MacKaness and Harvey stocked with black silk lace and bombazines, satins, persians, fine gauzes, jewellery and hosiery, hats and Yorkshire cloth. With their satins and silk lace they had beds, bolsters and mattresses, and chests of drawers, hardware and superfine Philadelphia flour. Further along Water Street near the northeast corner of Ann and Water Streets, was John Minshull's depository where he sold 'all kinds of merchandise.'

On the southeast corner of Ann and Water was the store of James Donaldson and Company stocked with 'barrels of mess pork made up for family use, tierces of Irish mess beef, Firkins of Irish Rose Butter.' Near the centre of the town on Water Street were the stores of Gregory Springall and of Robert Barry who, in partnership with his brother Alexander in England in the firm of A. and R. Barry, became one of Shelburne's leading merchants and shipowners. There were many others with stores on Water

EARLY INDUSTRIES, TRADES AND PROFESSIONS

Street. Among them, Thomas McPhail, tobacconist, Hugh Fraser, trader and shopkeeper, and near the northern end of the street were the shops of Adam Bower and Catherine Fretz.

Following along the streets to the waterfront, on the south side of St. John's Street below the southwest corner of Water and St. John's, was the store of William Robertson and below his store and near the waterfront was the ship chandler and hardware merchant, Charles Whitworth. Across the street from his store were the insurance brokers and ship chandlers, Tench and Taylor, Andrew Bruce and Company. On the opposite side of the street from William Robertson's store, near the slope of the hill, was James Cox and Company with Joshua Wise's store on the northwest corner of St. John's and Water above James Cox and Company. Ann Street had its quota of merchants and shopkeepers. Among these was Samuel Campbell a former merchant of Wilmington, South Carolina, on the north side of the street near the waterfront with his wharf at the end of the thoroughfare.

On the north side of St. George's Street, near the corner of Water St. was the store of William Moses. Halfway down the hill to the waterfront, Joseph Burton, captain of the *Charming Polly*, had his place of business; and 'At His House... bottom of George Street,' Charles Keeling sold, 'fresh flour, cod fish, and old Madeira wine of the first quality.' Across the way from Charles Keeling's, on the south side of the street, was Stephen Shakespear's store. James Humphreys, publisher of the *Nova Scotia Packet*, had a store in the former tailor shop of Richard Courtney, on the northeast corner of St. George's and Water Streets. He sold fine shoes and beaver gloves; knives and forks with ivory and camwood handles; warming pans, coffee mills, chaffing dishes, grid irons, tin coffee pots and tea kettles, sad and flat irons; parchment, black and red sliding pencils, spelling books and primers; and velvet corks. Joseph Brewer, east of James Humphrey, specialized in 'oznabrigs' (burlap), carpeting, and 'cast iron stoves of the common kind and those with ovens.' At the lower corner of Walsmley Street (William Street) William Hargraves, owner and master of the schooner *William*, sold anchors, rolls of brimstone, whale lines, dry red ochre and ship bread.

The long streets of the town running north and south were busy with their stores and shops. Among those on Mowat Street were the large business houses of Alexander Leckie and of William Holderness, merchants and shipowners, their stores being between St. John's and St. George's Streets. Near the Cove was the shop of Robert Bruce. James McMaster, a former merchant of Boston, proscribed for importing British goods, had his store near the southern end of Hammond Street south of Prince Street. Well north on Hammond Street were the shops of Samuel Kirk and of William Adams who sold fine Baltimore flour, and somewhere along the street were the stores of Thomas Meston and of Edmund Prior.

With its wharves and stores and warehouses, Dock Street was the busiest in the town. At the southern end of the street near the corner of St. George's, John Lowndes advertised he had for sale 'flour fresh from the mill, oats, bran, and pineboards.' Near his salesroom, with their store facing into Rodney Lane, was the business house of Benjamin Davis, Son, and Company. Former merchants in Massachusetts, banished for their loyalty, they specialized in harpoons, lances and other whaling implements. Like other Shelburne merchants, they had a variety of other goods for sale – fine wines and 'a neat choice of the newest fasion, London made suits of Cloaths... and a collection of well chosen books.' Across the way from Benjamin Davis, on the corner of Dock Street and Rodney Lane, was Joshua Watson's house and store and across Dock Street, facing his store, was his wharf jutting out into the water. His vessels traded in England, in the seaports of New England and in the West Indies and offered his customers mess beef and pork, shipbread and crackers in kegs, and an 'elegant assortment of furniture' – fluted and plain four-post bedsteads, field bedsteads with curtains, elegant prints, framed and glazed, rose blankets and bed quilts, kidderminster and Scotch carpets. Next to Joshua Watson were Richard Townsend and his son Richard, with their stores on their wharf near the foot of St. Patrick's Lane. On the south corner of Dock and Ann were Samuel and Isaac Davenport, Loyalists from Westchester, New York; on the south corner of Maiden Lane were Bartholemew Bower and Robert Sommerville, with their store facing into Maiden Lane. They had a general assortment of ironmongery, carpenter's, joiner's, smith's, and cooper's tolls, with fish hooks, shovels and tongs, groceries, glassware and tobacco.

Further along Dock Street were the merchants Zackdock and William Milby near the north corner of St. John's Street. They continued as merchants in Shelburne long after many of the early shopkeepers had left, with William, as master of his schooner *Dolphin*, scudding along the coast for the goods they sold in their store. Across St. Andrew's Lane from the business house of Thayer and Jarvis was the shop of Graham and McLean with their wharf opposite their store. Theirs was a grocery store with Indian corn, black-eyed peas, bacon, ham, hog's fat and tallow, tar and pitch and West India rum. On the corner of Mason's Lane was the store of the remarkable blind man, George Gracie, merchant and shipowner, a founder of the whaling company, member of the House of Assembly, and vice-president of St. John's Kirk beside which he was buried in 1807 when, on his way to the Assembly in Halifax, the rail of the ship on which he was leaning broke, and he fell into the sea and was drowned. North of George Gracie, Thomas Farrer had his store on his wharf lot at the edge of Mason Lane. Numbers of

EARLY INDUSTRIES, TRADES AND PROFESSIONS

others edged their stores into Dock Street: Peter Bogle and Company, Robert McIntosh and Company, James Ferguson, Ann Taylor and her tiny shop, Hugh Breen, and others.

The short lanes to the waterfront, where the business houses of many of the leading merchants and many small shops were located, were as bustling and crowded as Dock Street. The tiny ladies' store of Elizabeth Harding on St. Patrick's Lane was long remembered for its pretty ribbons and laces. Of the larger business houses, Captain Ebenezer Parker, master of the brigantine *Aurora* and later of the schooner *Success*, had his store on Rodney Lane. In Charlotte Lane were Braine and Reily, William Donaldson and the firm of George and Robert Ross; in Maiden Lane there was William Rose, a Loyalist from North Carolina. William Warden, a perukemaker of Boston, turned merchant and trader and manufacturer of essence of bark, was found on St. Andrew's Lane.

That there were far too many merchants for a small town was soon apparent to the merchants themselves. In a few months many of the leading business houses were closed and partnerships were dissolved. Of those first merchants who invested large sums of money to establish themselves, only four remained until the end of their days: George Ross of the firm George and Robert Ross, who disposed of his property the year before his death in 1816 to Dorcas Thomson; George Gracie, who was here until his death in 1807; James Cox, who clung to his business until the end of his life when his estate was sold by his son to meet his creditors; and Robert Barry. In order to survive as a merchant he expanded his business to Liverpool and, although he no longer lived in Shelburne, he maintained his store and shipping interest long after Shelburne ceased to be a busy seaport.

Tailors, a Calender, Hatters and a Clothier
Numbers of tailors (at least 25 between the years 1783 and 1787) had shops along the streets and lanes of Shelburne. Two were merchant-tailors with their shops on Water Street: Patrick Wall two doors south of St. John's Street near Charlotte Lane and Richard Courtney on the northeast corner of St. George's and Water Streets. Both were natives of Ireland and both had established themselves in Boston as merchant-tailors in the 1760s. In their shops they displayed a wide selection of fabrics: broadcloth in the most fashionable colours, fine white plush, Florentine and black satin, blue strouds, duffle, serge, cotton denim nankeen, India dimity, royal ribs and Dutch cord, long pile shags, moleskin, shalloon, crimson, yellow and white flannel, Scotch plaids; gilt, plated and pinchback buttons; gold and silver lace, buckrams, glazed linen. For children there were morocco and black leather shoes. For men and women they carried Barcelona handkerchiefs,

fancy silk waistcoat patterns, worsted gloves, men's beaver hats and ladies' riding habits made in the newest fashion from London. As tailors, orders would be 'thankfully received and duly executed in the neatest and best manner and upon the lowest terms.' Other tailors also had their shops on Water Street: George Pell, James Duke, Michael McDonald with his journeyman, Dennis Daily, and William McGill who came from Scotland in 1784. In Charlotte Lane were the tailors James Collins and his son James, and John French. In St. Andrew's Lane was Andrew Calder; on Dock Street was David Buchanan; in St. George's Street were Edward Manning and John Dougherty. Among other tailors were Thomas Forsyth on Ann Street, James Howie and John McKenzie on King Street, Samuel Freemantle on Hammond and James McKie on Harriot. On Mowat Street were Michael Murphy, Gavin Veitch and John Miller.

Along with the tailors sewing in their 'best manner' were the hatters William Harper and Peter Colquhon in Ann Street, the clothier, Daniel Connor in Water Street and Peter Ritchie, calender, in St. Andrew's Lane, pressing and rolling paper and cloth until it became smooth and glossy.[10]

Barbers
There were four barbers to serve the early Shelburne settlers: Henry Hodgkinson in St. John's Street, Richard Whetton in St. George's, John McAlpine on Water, and on Mason Lane, John Robertson with his journeyman, Edward Griffiths. John Robertson styled himself a hairdresser:

'John Robertson. Hairdresser. Nigh the Head of Mason Lane, has for sale... Best distilled lavender-water, in large and small bottles, violet, oris and Poland hair powders; hard and soft pomatum of all sorts; tooth powder and brushes; dragon root, razor strops, and dressing combs. N.B. Ladies and Gentlemen dressed, at their own Lodgings, on the shortest notice, and in the newest fashion.'

One of John Robertson's customers was Gideon White who paid him £9.19.6 for two years of hair dressing, for rollers and false hair, for pomatum and for filling his shaving box.[11]

Butchers and Bakers
Only three butchers, Francis Wood, John Harris, and Daniel Jeans were in Shelburne in 1786, perhaps because many families still depended on the King's rations for beef and pork. Bakers fared better. There were 23 of them and their bake shops were in many parts of the town. Nicholas Brown, on the north side of St. John's Street near the water front, baked 'Fresh Bread of the best quality... every morning. Likewise, Brown bread, ship bread

EARLY INDUSTRIES, TRADES AND PROFESSIONS

and butter biscuit.' Nearby in Mason's Lane were Frederick and Sylvester Brown and in St. Patrick's Lane were Sturgis Perry and his partners, Thomas Ketchum and Jacob Hewlet. John Blair had his bakery on Harriot Street near St. John's Market. His assessment of 20 shillings county tax suggests that he had the town's largest bakery. Among other bakers were James White and John Ewing on Hammond Street; Michael Malcome, David McFarlane, and John Fleming, with their bake shops on King Street; David and Bruce Shepherd on Mowat Street. On Digby Street was David Walker, who, in 1807, baked a wedding cake for Gideon White's daughter Joan. There were two bakers among the Blacks: John Seaburn on Hammond Street and Lucas Scipio on Digby Street.

Prices to be charged by the bakers for their loaves of bread were set by the Court of Sessions. For bread of the best fine flour baked in long loaves of two pounds, the price was set at sixpence; bread of good sweet flour of second quality, baked in round loaves of three pounds, was to sell for sixpence; bread of rye flour or rye flour and Indian meal, well baked in round loaves of four pounds, was to be sold for sixpence. Bread was not to be offered for sale in loaves larger than could be sold for one shilling or for less than three halfpence in established proportions. All bread was to be marked with the first two letters of the baker's name. John Blair was fined forty shillings for selling bread that was underweight. A few weeks later, for selling bread baked 'of ships stuff commonly called cornel' and underweight, his bread was ordered forfeited by the Court.[12]

CRAFTSMEN, ARTISANS AND OTHERS
Watchmakers, Copper, Silver and Goldsmiths, Jewellers and Engravers
Numbers of skilled craftsmen were among the Shelburne Loyalists. There were the coppersmiths George Beatie in Water Street and Charles White on St. George's Street, while Michael Withers, silversmith, plied his trade in Digby Street. There were the goldsmiths, Charles Oliver Bruff and Alexander Munro with his workshop on King Street. Among the watchmakers and finishers were Isaac Reed and his journeyman, William Heater on Water Street; George Coldwell, who wanted for cash in 1785 'from one to thirty second hand WATCHES, with good outside Cases'; Dulcina Stoughon on Margaret Lane, Thomas Adams on Ann Street, Michael Weather on Parr Street and Isaac Clemmens, watch finisher and engraver, on St. John's Street, who, when he lived in Boston, rented and worked in Paul Revere's shop. James Smithers, engraver, had his shop on King Street. He engraved the seal for the Shelburne Court of Common Pleas. As might be expected in a new town hewn from the wilderness, there was little work for skilled craftsmen, for goldsmiths and watchmakers, and they soon disappeared

from the town records or turned to other occupations.

The most noted of the workers in metal to come to Shelburne was Charles Oliver Bruff, whose previous work marked him as a master craftsman. During the American Revolution he was a goldsmith and jeweller in New York at the corner of Queen Street and Golden Hill. In Shelburne he advertised himself as a goldsmith and jeweller at the sign of the Tea-pot, Tankard and Cross Swords, corner of Queen and Carleton Streets, near the market, at the head of the Cove. He made and mended 'all sorts of goldsmith's and jeweller's work; repairs clocks and watches, and puts in glasses;... makes surveyor's and mariner's compasses;... keys for locks of all sorts... guns repaired... makes all sorts of mourning rings, with coffin stones; mends stone buckles; and sets miniature pictures.' In Shelburne he found little employment for his talents. He was not even listed as a goldsmith on the assessment roll, his assessment of one shilling county tax and six pence poor tax indicating the struggle that must have been his to maintain himself and his family. In 1793 he removed to Liverpool where Simeon Perkins noted he was 'a man used to different kinds of handy work about Guns... and he says he can work on Watches and any kind of silver work.'

Most successful of the craftsmen was the coppersmith Charles White. In 1785 he opened a shop on the corner of St. George and Mowat Streets near the Cove where he manufactured and sold brass and iron andirons, shovels and tongs, brass shoe buckles, chapes and tongues. He also had for sale a wide variety of metal goods and painter's supplies; rat traps, frying pans, grid and toasting irons; saws, swan shot, bullet and spoon moulds; table, hall and sleigh bells; brass hats and chimney hooks, brass cocks, coffin furniture, candlesticks and snuffers; tea chests and caddys. He had colours ground in oil, Spanish whiting, pumice and rotten stone and stove blacking. For fishermen, there were herring seines, twine, and fishing lines. Among the craftsmen was the bookbinder and candlemaker Andrew Barclay. He had his place of business on Water Street near King Street in his book and stationery store.[13]

Cabinetmakers, Carpenters, Masons
Among the skilled artisans who came to Shelburne were six cabinetmakers. William Black had his place of business on St. John's Street, John Speir was located near the southern end of the town at the corner of Hammond and Duke Streets, and Thomas Hodson, joiner and master cabinetmaker, on Digby Street. The three Goddards, Job, Daniel and Henry, were of the noted cabinetmaking family of Newport, Rhode Island. They established themselves on Water Street. There was little demand for the fine furniture

EARLY INDUSTRIES, TRADES AND PROFESSIONS

they manufactured, and by 1787 they had re-established themselves as carpenters on Fanning Street. Carpenters fared better than cabinetmakers with some 25 to 30 finding employment during the first years of house building. One of the early craftsmen was the master carpenter and designer, Isaac Hildrith, who came to Shelburne in the summer of 1783 from Charleston, South Carolina. He had taken refuge there when he could not continue to live in Norfolk, Virginia, where he had established himself prior to the Revolution as a merchant, house carpenter and surveyor. In Shelburne, he with Aaron White, formed the firm of Messrs. Hildrith and White, carpenters and contractors, and were the designers and builders of Christ Church. Sometime in the early 1790s Isaac Hildrith went to Halifax and was appointed by the Nova Scotia legislature as surveyor of a proposed canal from Dartmouth to the mouth of the Shubenacadie River. In 1800 he was engaged as the architect in charge of the construction of Government House at Halifax, an appointment that marked him as a man of outstanding ability.

Closely connected with the builders of houses were the stonecutters and masons, and the brick layer, John Nichols; the plasterer, John Cole; the painters and glaziers, Moses Pitcher, Joseph Welsh and Thomas Mahon. With many foundations needing cut stone and many chimneys and bakeovens to construct, there was plenty of work for the nine masons and for the stone cutter, John Thomson. That they built solid foundations and sturdy chimneys is evident from the old foundations still supporting numbers of the early Shelburne houses and the granite flues and fireplaces still upright and secure.[14]

Shoemakers and a Saddler
Fifteen workers in leather, shoemakers (or cordwainers as they spoke of themselves) and the saddler, Thomas Nash, on St. John's Street, were among the early artisans. These included Thomas McWaters and his journeyman Henry Hall, and Robert Campbell, on Water Street. Edward Wall and Robert King were located on Hammond Street and Andrew King was on Harriot. Most affluent of the early cordwainers was Frederick Weiser, who was a tanner in New Brunswick, New Jersey, when the war for American independence began. His property was ravaged by both rebel and German mercenaries employed by the British and he lost an estate of £107. In Shelburne he established himself on Rodney Lane and in 1786, as a shoemaker, he was assessed five shillings county tax and two shillings sixpence poor tax, marking him as the most affluent of the early cordwainers.

To learn the trade of a shoemaker, boys were apprenticed to a cordwainer. George Henry Deinstadt was bound by his mother to Joseph Bell 'to learn the Art, Trade and Mystery of a Cordwainer.' For six years, seven months and nine days or until he was 21 years of age, he was to serve his master faithfully 'his Secrets keep, his lawful Commands every where readily obey'; he was to do no damage to his master 'nor see it done by others'; he was neither to waste his 'Master's Goods nor lend them unlawfully to others'; nor 'commit Fornication or Matrimony contract.' At cards, dice, or any other unlawful game 'he was not to play to his Master's damage... with his own Goods, nor the Goods of others, without Licence from his said Master.' He was neither to buy nor sell or 'absent himself Day nor Night from his Master's service, without his leave; nor haunt Alehouses, Taverns, or Play-houses; but in all things behave himself as a faithful Apprentice ought to do.' Joseph Bell, as his master, pledged himself to 'use the utmost of his endeavour to teach or cause to be taught or instructed' his apprentice 'in the Trade and Mystery of a Cordwainer,' to provide 'sufficient Meat, Drink, Clothing, Lodging and Washing, fitting for an apprentice,' and to permit him to attend night school three months each year and pay his schoolmaster and provide paper, pens and ink.[15]

Smiths, Wrights and Others
Of the smiths who lived and worked in early Shelburne there were ten blacksmiths on the assessment roll of 1786. Among them were Alexander and John Currie, John Weir, Richard Penny and David Cameron. There were the tinsmiths Henry King and James Smith on St. John's Street, and the gunsmith Samuel Munn on Water Street. Among the skilled wrights were Jonathan Baxter and Thomas Young, cart and wheelwrights, and the millwrights, Martin Marshall, Robert McQuhae and Robert Drummond. Of other trades and skills the Loyalists and disbanded soldiers and freed Blacks had to offer in the founding of a town, were numbers of labourers, farmers and gardeners. There was one gardening firm, that of Martin and Company, on Ann Street. The two licensed measurers for the town were Nathaniel Munro and John Miller. They were allowed, for measuring coal and cordwood, corn grain and oats, and salt by the hundred bushel, two shilling sixpence for each item. Those 'following the calling of a cartman,' Thomas DesChamp, John McKenzie and William Snider, had their carts strictly regulated as to size by the town and each was licensed and numbered. Among others working in the town were the drover, Edward Burleigh, the huckster, Alexander Stewart and the milkman, John Anderson, who lived opposite the town near the Barracks. There were the weavers, John Brown, a Black, Joseph Maugham, John McQuaid, Alexander McKenzie and the chimney sweep, Edward Elliott; and the two sextons,

EARLY INDUSTRIES, TRADES AND PROFESSIONS

Joseph Black and William Young. Shak Fanman and Ned Taylor were fiddlers; the piper and drummer was Duncan McLean, formerly piper for MacDonald's Highlanders; and John Lahey was the public bellman, who, for a shilling, cried in the streets the arrival of a vessel, houses for sale and horses strayed or stolen.[16]

PROFESSIONS

Among professional men in the new settlement were attorneys, doctors, schoolmasters, surveyors, ministers of the gospel and men who, from their training and experience, were appointed to positions of authority in the community. Among these, in the first years, were the sheriff, James Clark and his deputy, James G. Johnston; justices of the peace and of the inferior Count of Common Pleas; officers of the Sessions; the notary public, William Brantwaite; recorder of deeds, Matthew Hutchins; customs house officials; the commissary, Edward Brinley; surveyors, Christopher Tully, Robert Morris, Robert Gray, John VanNorden, Charles Mason, Benjamin Marston and William Morris.

Attorneys

The first attorneys were Colin Campbell, Martin Wilkins and Richard Combauld. Richard Combauld came to America sometime in the 1770s from London, England. He came to Shelburne with his wife's family, that of Colonel Abraham VanBuskirk's, in the fall of 1783. He established himself in Charlotte Lane and along with his work as an attorney he was a justice of the peace, solicitor of customs for the port of Shelburne, a vestryman of Christ Church and, in 1785, he was the secretary to the Tusket location committee. He remained in Shelburne until the early 1790s. Colin Campbell was long a resident of Shelburne with his office on Water Street, and his clerk was Alexander Cameron. He served the town in many capacities, as member of the House of Assembly from 1793 to 1818, secretary for the County of Shelburne in 1794, president of the Presbyterian church of St. John's Kirk and collector of customs from 1807 to 1823, when he was appointed supervisor of custom officers for the provinces of New Brunswick and Nova Scotia, with his office in St. Andrews, New Brunswick. On his retirement he removed to Weymouth, Digby County, where his son Colin had settled, and where he died in 1835. Martin Wilkins, a son of Isaac Wilkins and a brother of Lewis Morris Wilkins, member of the House of Assembly for Lunenburg County and a judge of the Supreme Court. practiced law in Shelburne for a few years and was in 1787 appointed judge of the Court of Probate of Wills for Shelburne County.

Doctors

A number of doctors came with the Loyalists and disbanded soldiers. These were: Daniel Kendrick, John Perry, John Huggeford, William Burns, Joseph Bond, George Drummond, John Gould, John Hoose, surgeon to the Hessian soldiers, Benjamin Loring and Francis Brinley. Later came Doctor Richard Fletcher from Ireland, with the 6th Regiment. Of these first physicians, Doctor Benjamin Loring, a graduate of Harvard University in 1772, served during the Revolution as surgeon in a regiment in the King's service in South Carolina and later in a military hospital in New York. He was in Shelburne for only a few months before returning to his former home in Boston where he died in 1798. Doctor John Huggeford, captain of a group of Loyalists, came to Shelburne in the *Charming Nancy* in the fall of 1783 and established himself as a surgeon on Harriot Street. He remained in Shelburne as a surgeon until the late 1780s when he returned to New York. Doctor Daniel Kendrick lived in Shelburne until 1790 when he went to Liverpool. Here he founded a system of subscription medical care, providing to each subscriber and his family, for the sum of £3 a year, medical care and medicine, except for midwifery and for smallpox. Doctor Richard Fletcher, who came to Shelburne with the 6th Regiment, married Maria McKinnon, a daughter of Colonel Ranald McKinnon of Argyle and following his retirement from the army, settled in Shelburne. He and his family later removed to Yarmouth.

Four of the first doctors continued to live in the Shelburne area: Doctors Drummond, John Hoose (a strong supporter of the Methodist church), William Burns and John Perry. Doctor Drummond, formerly of Philadelphia where he was a surveyor and teacher, went to New York at the time of the Revolution and was appointed an assistant surgeon to Doctor North. This would seem to be his only training as a doctor. In Shelburne he combined the practice of medicine with the position of surveyor of customs. His remedies were the simple home cures found in the old books of remedies. For a nervous fever for the wife of Captain William Booth, he administered vitriol drops in camomile tea, essence of peppermint with sugar, clysters of camomile and molasses in salt and water, and ordered her arms and feet rubbed with a flesh brush and poultices of mustard and vinegar applied to the soles of her feet. For a stitch in the side he recommended a vigorous rub with rum.

In 1785 Doctors Joseph Bond and Francis Brinley opened a medical store in Water Street with a general assortment of medicine "of the best quality" with approved patent medicines and perfumery. On their shelves were Turlington's balsam, court plasters, Duffy's elixir, essences of lavender, citron and peppermint, oil of rosemary, milk of roses, tooth powder, shav-

EARLY INDUSTRIES, TRADES AND PROFESSIONS

ings of hartshorn, isinglass, liquorice, tamarinds and spices. For two to five guineas could be purchased medicine chests for fishing vessels and for use in small settlements where there were no surgeons.

Illnesses and causes of death as they were diagnosed by the doctors and recorded in early documents were hives, bile and worms and worm fever, fits, sprue, dysentry, smallpox, teeth, measles, consumption and 'a gradual decay' (this for an infant three months old). Dropsy, hectic (consumption) and hectic dropsy were common causes of death. Appople (apoplexy), mortification (gangrene), imposthume (abcess), colic, pleurisy, inflammation of the bowels and childbed fever all took their toll of the early settlers.

Care of the sick who could not provide medical services for themselves devolved upon the Court of Sessions. Doctors were appointed, usually on a yearly basis, with a fixed salary of some £25 with some additional funds for medicine. Smallpox was a scourge dreaded not only as a disease but because it was a 'manifest detriment to trade in the town.' The Court of Sessions forbade all persons afflicted with smallpox from walking on the main streets of the town, and in 1791, and again in 1797, a general innoculation of all adults as well as infants was permitted by the Court, to prevent the spread of the disease.[17]

NEWSPAPERS AND PRINTERS

With the first fleet of Loyalists to arrive in Shelburne came the two printers James and Alexander Robertson. Sons of Alexander Robertson, a printer and a burgess of Edinburgh, Scotland, they came to America prior to the Revolution and in 1769 founded the *New York Chronicle* in New York City. In 1771, on the request of Sir William Johnson, they went to Albany to print and circulate papers to promote the interests of Great Britain. Two years later, in partnership with John Trumbull, they founded the first newspaper in Norwich, Connecticut, the *Norwich Packet*. Finding they must be subservient to the rebels, they disposed of their business and returned to Albany and again published pamphlets and occasional newspapers that inflamed the rebels. James Robertson was forced to hide in a new settlement in the woods. Once the rebels surmised where he was hiding, he fled in the night to Colonel Edmeston's headquarters in Albany and escaped to safety behind the British lines in New York. His pursuers turned on his brother Alexander, who was a cripple and unable to walk, and thrust him and his journeyman into jail. On his release nearly a year later he joined his brother in New York where he had begun to publish the *Royal American Gazette*. Leaving Alexander to publish their newspaper, James went with the army to Philadelphia where he published the *Royal Pennsylvania Gazette*. On the evacuation of Philadelphia by the British he accompanied the army to

Charleston, South Carolina, to print government publications and there established the *Royal South-Carolina Gazette* which he continued to publish until his return to New York in 1782.

Back in New York, James and his brother, now in partnership with Nathaniel Mills and John Hicks, published the *Royal American Gazette* until the end of July 1783. With the end of the war they joined the Port Roseway Associates in the company of Andrew Barclay, a Scot like themselves, who was a bookbinder from Cleish in the lowlands of Scotland. In Shelburne, James Robertson was given land on the public square (on the waterfront on the north side of King Street) to erect a building for 'two perishable cargoes.' Here he and his brother re-established their printing office on King Street, corner of Water Street, and continued the publication of the *Royal American Gazette*. In partnership with William Rigby, James Robertson opened a store in the printing house under the name of Robertson and Rigby. On the death of Alexander Robertson in 1784, James Robertson continued the publication of the *Gazette* under his name.

In the fall of 1784 a second newspaper was established, the *Port Roseway Gazetteer and the Shelburne Advertiser*, printed by James Robertson, Junior, the son of Alexander Robertson, and his two partners, Thomas and James Swords. It was printed on the same press as the *Gazette* and was similar in format. On the invitation of Lieutenant-Governor Fanning to print the laws of Prince Edward Island, James Robertson took his press to Charlottetown in the expectation of being the King's printer under royal authority. Not receiving the appointment, he returned to Scotland and became a bookseller in Edinburgh.

A third newspaper, the *Nova Scotia Packet and General Advertiser*, was published in Shelburne by James Humphreys, the first edition appearing on February 2, 1785. He, as James and Alexander Robertson, had been a victim of the Revolution. As publisher of the *Pennsylvania Ledger*, he was soon known as a supporter of the British and he was obliged to leave Philadelphia. With the British occupation of the city, he returned to Philadelphia and again published the *Ledger*. On the departure of the British troops, he went to New York as a merchant. He came to Shelburne in the summer of 1783 and was alloted a town lot, but it was not until 1785 that he established his printing office in 'Water Street next door below Valentine Nutter's,' which was later moved to the corner of St. George's and Water Streets. The *Nova Scotia Packet* was published until at least 1787 and perhaps much later, as James Humphreys remained in Shelburne until 1797. During his years in Shelburne he was a vestryman of Christ Church, a foreman of the grand jury of the Court of General Sessions, and a member of the House of Assembly for Shelburne County from 1793 to 1796.[18]

12
Use of the Land and Sea

HUNTING

Looking forward to their future needs, the Port Roseway Associates instructed their agents, on their going to Halifax to arrange with the governor for their settlement in the area, to request that the privilege of fishing and hunting 'within the limits of our grants in Rivers and Bays be reserved for the Settlers of Port Roseway.' With the grants to their country lots came the right to all 'Lakes, Ponds, Fishings, Waters and Water Courses' within the boundaries of their allotments, 'together also with Privilege of Hunting, Hawking, and Fowling in and upon the same.'

Moose and bear hunting and the snaring of rabbits became profitable sources of income, with reports of two men on the Jordan snaring 1,100 rabbits in one winter. In the hunting season of 1789 upwards of one hundred moose were killed with most of the meat brought for sale in the Shelburne market, selling for one to two pence per pound. With a number of merchants advertising their goods for sale in exchange for furs, many wild animals fell victim to traps set in their pathways. An early list of wildlife in the woodlands between the Jordan and the Roseway included caribou as well as moose, red fox in plentiful numbers and a few black foxes. There were martins, porcupines, bear and wild cats, minks, brown squirrels and muskrats. Strangely enough, no mention was made of beavers in the early lists of wild animals in the Shelburne area.[1]

AGRICULTURE

Despite the rocky soil and land unfit for the extensive cultivation needed to support a large town, those who came to Port Roseway to farm were soon looking for land to clear, meadows for cattle and pasturage for sheep. Foremost among the farmers was Joshua Pell from Pelham Manor, Westchester County, New York, where he had lost his farm to the rebels. He soon found land for himself and his sons along the southern shore of Lake George, and to the west of their land he surveyed and marked fifteen 20 acre lots for others interested in farming, cutting a road 20 feet wide across the lots which later became part of the road to Annapolis. South of his land, and to the east of the Common, other lots were marked where John Thomson and Isaac Hildrith had their farms. Along the northern boundary of the town, and to the west of the Lake George farm lots, fifteen 50 acre lots were surveyed for farms with Gideon White's at the edge of the town, and to the west of his land, on the west side of the Roseway, was James Dole's farm. Along the south boundary of the town was the farm of David Thomson, the shipbuilder – acres of land he brought into good cultivation. By the summer of 1784 the great block of land set aside as a Common along the east boundary of the town (measuring more than a mile and a half in width and in length) was divided into 177 three acre lots with others of five and six and ten acres. These were allotted by license of occupation to residents of the town for garden lots and as pasture for cattle on condition that the land be improved.

A large acreage for farms on the western shores of the harbour at Churchover was allotted to Joseph Durfee and his son (550 acres); and to Colonel Abraham VanBuskirk (500 acres for a farm he called Woodchurch). Below their land at Gunning Cove, Isaac Wilkins had 500 acres where he built a large house. He named his residence Harmony Hall but his neighbours called it 'Wilkins' Folly' and when he irked them they dubbed it 'Skunk Hall.' On the east side of the Jordan were the well-stocked farms of Sergeants Donald and Gilbert McKay with flocks of sheep, yokes of oxen, cows, horses, hens, geese and pigs. They had acres of land cleared for crops of vegetables and for the growing of barley and rye and for winter hay. On the west side of the Jordan, on Jones Point (McLean's Island) was Jones' Plantation, 150 acres of land granted to Abraham Jones where he had cleared land for farming, meadows for cattle and marshland for salt hay. In the valley of Birchtown Creek, west of the 500 acre farm and mill lots along the banks of the Roseway River, was meadowland 'cleared by nature, ready for use.' Here Charles Mason had his dairy farm with two-and-one-half miles of land on the banks of the creek. Meadows and marshland were eagerly sought by the Loyalists for grazing and for hay as the early settlers of

USE OF THE LAND AND SEA

Round Bay discovered when Loyalists came endeavouring to take their meadowland (and some even their cleared acres) if a reason could be found to dislodge them.

The 50 acre lots of Mason's and of Marston's Divisions, as well as the large lots of land along the rivers, were intended to be cleared and cultivated in accord with the terms of the grants and were later escheated when the land was not improved. By 1787 many of the Loyalists and disbanded soldiers had gone to their farmland and were listed as farmers on the assessment rolls. Land was cleared by labourers for eight and ten dollars an acre. Tons of rocks were lifted and heaped into piles or were built into stone walls that still mark many of the old tree-grown fields. Potato fields were first little more than land where the trees were felled and potatoes were grubbed into the earth in a bed of seaweed. Potatoes grown in kelp and seaweed yielded good crops as Alexander Houston (who cleared land for a farm in Churchover) recorded, 'I did plant 9 bushels of potatoes and I did dig 80 in the whole in the year 1787.' 'Parson Rowland,' William Booth wrote of his friend's farm on the Sandy Point road, found his potatoes grew best in hills, adding that 'he allows the land here to contain some marle and is also of opinion that it is very good for all sorts of light Grain – I never saw finer anywhere than I have seen here.'

Seeds offered for sale by James Cox and Company, for one-and-a-half to three guineas a package, indicate a wide variety of seeds available to farmers, and through Sullivan and Mills a still greater selection could be ordered from John Creighton in Halifax: root and vegetable seeds, herb, grain and grass seeds, and seeds for flower gardens. Crops grown in early Shelburne as noted by observers, were: turnips, carrots, parsnips, onions, cabbage, beets and radishes, peas and beans, potatoes; salad greens, lettuce, parsley and asparagus; cucumbers, pumpkins, squash, musk and watermelons. Wheat, oats, barley, rye and Indian corn were grown, and flax, to be spun into thread. There were small berries and fruit trees: strawberries, gooseberries, raspberries and currants; apples, pears, plums and 'the best of red cherries.'

Farmers had their problems with grubs that destroyed cabbage plants, lettuce and beans, cutting the stalks of the plants. Whole rows of carrots were devastated by an insect smaller than a maggot. Although the soil in places was found to be very good where trouble was taken to cultivate it and gardens produced 'amazingly well,' the land was not rich and required great labour to make it produce crops. William Booth, in 1789, watching the trend away from Shelburne, lamented that the farmers 'who are the men most desirable in every young Country are off or at least very few remaining.'

Of those few who remained and were able to gain a living from their acres was James Hamilton. His land was on the Tusket Road west of the Clyde. He cleared acres of woodland for crops and hayfields and built his gambrel-roofed farm house, which he called Wood Hall, near the Tusket Road and used it as a tavern and inn for wayfarers and those he ferried across the Clyde. Titus Smith, the pioneer naturalist of Nova Scotia, came upon his farm when roaming the woods of the Clyde. 'Mr. Hamilton, notwithstanding the poverty of the soil, has the best crop on his land that I have seen near Shelburne; although he has settled 12 miles from any other whereabouts. But he has the advantage of a Meadow which enables him to keep a large stock of cattle; and his family appears to be uncommonly ingenuous [sic] as well as industrious which enables them to live without the help of others; much better than persons could who could not, like them, do all their own work themselves.'

Farmers with meadowland for cattle fared better than those with only land to till or to clear for pasturage. Most farmers had a few head of cattle, a cow or two, a yoke of oxen and young calves, pigs, sheep and poultry. Householders living in the town used lots on the Common for hay and for grazing to supplement the small plots they had cleared on their town lots. Cattle were imported mainly from Boston in vessels fitted for the accommodation of livestock, as was the schooner *Success*, Captain James, master, that arrived from Boston in three days laden with cattle for Shelburne farmers in the summer of 1785. The importation of cattle from the United States was allowed without hindrance until 1786 when the King-in-Council ordered no goods or commodities grown or manufactured in the United States of America to be imported – except horses, neat cattle, sheep, hogs, poultry, and all other species of livestock and live provisions – which were to be permitted into the country only as long as the governor and council proclaimed it necessary. The governor and his council did not consider it necessary to import livestock or provisions and issued a stern proclamation banning all importations from the United States. It provoked a furor in Shelburne. The Court of Sessions urged the revocation of the proclamation or some other measures taken to enable them to continue to import cattle from the United States. Isaac Wilkins presented their situation to the House of Assembly, declaring there was a scarcity of livestock to be had from the old settled towns. He requested a proclamation by the governor permitting the importation of cattle into the district of Shelburne from the United States. His motion was rejected. But Parr, reconsidering his proclamation, and with the advice of His Majesty's Council, declared permission to import into the province such articles as were needed from the United States 'during such time as their importation seems necessary.' The

USE OF THE LAND AND SEA

Assembly remonstrated. If there was a scarcity of cattle in Shelburne County it arose, they felt, from the lack of roads to the old settlements, and not from a scarcity of cattle in the province. They wanted permission to import livestock into the province confined to the new settlements only.

With the founding of the Court of Sessions, rules and regulations were prepared for the orderly maintenance of farms and livestock, officers were appointed to inspect and to enforce the regulations, and some roads were declared pent roads to confine cattle and prevent their roaming. Alexander Robertson and William Briggs were appointed fence viewers, Charles Oliver Bruff and Thomas Denham were poundkeepers, and John Peck and Jonathan Baxter served as hogreaves. Surveyors and weighers of hay were Charles Church and Alexander Robertson. The regulations restricting swine and other livestock were enforced by the officers. Hogs were not to go at large within the district or in the town of Shelburne unless properly yoked (this was later amended to 'properly yoked and ringed'), the size of the yoke to be determined by the hogreave. Unyoked swine in the streets were impounded; stray goats were forfeited. Hogs roaming the streets became such a nuisance they were prohibited from running westward of Digby Street, and their owners were subject to a fine of forty shillings for each offence – one-third for the prosecutor, the remainder for the poor of the town. With tar or paint, sheep were marked with symbols recorded in the town records. Owners of sheep trespassing into fields lawfully fenced, were fined a shilling for each sheep. Stallions and seed horses were not allowed to run at large in the centre of the town nor were 'breachy' horses unless well and sufficiently yoked. Rams were ordered confined from September 6 to November 15.

Farming and the cultivation of small plots of land for summer vegetables and to fill root cellars provided most households with garden products and with grain to be ground into flour and meal. In 1827, in the township of Shelburne, 3,133 acres of land were under cultivation reaching from the east bank of the Clyde to the west boundary of Queens County. There were ample crops of grain and potatoes, 2,428 horned cattle, nearly 5,000 sheep and 1,754 swine to provide food and clothing for 2,697 persons.[2]

THE FISHERIES

The Port Roseway Associates, anticipating that the fisheries would be an important means of economic security, requested Governor Parr that fishing within the limits of their grants should 'be reserved for the settlers of Port Roseway only.' At the same time, aware of the danger from press gangs, they asked 'that the Landsmen, and Seamen of our Settlement be excempted from Impress forever.'[3]

On their first day of fishing, when five men caught 800 cod, the Associates discovered 'fish never was more plenty nor easeyer come at, than from this place.' They were also soon to learn that to be successful codfishermen required a kind of skill none of them possessed. In their homeland the codfishery had been the business of a few American seaports where proficiency had been developed with years of experience. Without the skill acquired from years of fishing and of curing fish, the first attempt of the Shelburne settlers to prepare cod for export was a failure. With the arrival, in the spring of 1784, of a few fishermen expert in the curing of fish, it was hopefully predicted 'that the exports of Fish from Shelburne and other new places added to the former usual exports from the old ports will be an ample supply for the West Indies this year.'[4]

Although there was an increase in numbers of specially equipped fishing boats engaged in codfishing, from none in 1783 to four the following year and ten in 1785, the catching of cod and the production of dry fish for export failed to produce the quantities and quality required. Two causes impeded the Shelburne fishermen: a lack of suitable vessels, bankers to extend their fishing voyages into weeks and enough able fishermen to catch and properly cure cod for foreign markets. To encourage the codfishery, the Court of Sessions in 1786 was urged to recommend to the Assembly a bounty for every quintal of merchantable codfish made and shipped to Europe out of any of the ports of Nova Scotia. A similar bounty on every quintal of codfish exported to the West Indies was recommended, provided the surveyors judged the fish of sufficient quality for those markets. The bounty would not only stimulate the efforts of the local fishermen but would entice experienced fishermen from abroad to settle in Shelburne. Above all, it might 'serve also to give employment to the many Idlers that are lounging about the Settlement, and prevent them, perhaps, from becoming Burthens to it.'[5]

Four grades of cured codfish were exported from Shelburne. These were: merchantable, which was the highest quality, commanding the highest prices per quintal; madeira, the culls from the quintals of merchantable fish; West India, the poorer grades of madeira, shipped to the West Indies as food for the labourers on the plantations; and dumbfish, which were the darker grades of dryfish. With the hogsheads of dried cod shipped to foreign markets went kegs of cod tongues and cod sounds and barrels of cod oil. In 1787, 10,926 quintals of dry codfish and 131 barrels of oil were exported; in 1788, 13,142 quintals of cod and 149 barrels of oil. In the terms of their grants, the exclusive privilege of fishing in the bays within the bounds of their township was not given the Shelburne settlers. As the years passed and they failed to achieve the success they believed should be theirs, they attributed their failure in part to 'the very liberal indulgencies granted by

USE OF THE LAND AND SEA

the Treaty of Peace with the United States, to their Fishermen in permitting them to catch and even cure their Fish on the Coasts of this Province.' 'Their superior experience in that business,' they pointed out to Lord Grenville, 'precludes us from becoming their Rivals.' If their competitors were encouraged by government to become settlers in the province, with their expert knowledge, and 'with the proximity of the Ports of Nova Scotia to the Fishing Banks,' in a very few years the inhabitants of Nova Scotia would be enabled to 'deprive the Northern States of America of their principal nursery of Seamen by adding them to the King's Colonies.'[6]

The American fishermen annoyed the customs officers in a different way. Under the pretext of fishing, they moved along the shores with the holds of their vessels laden with goods they bartered in the outports for fish and fish oil. They were thus cheating the provincial government of import tax on the goods they traded for fish, and their own government also, since they obtained a bounty on the fish they carried into the United States which they themselves did not catch. On one occasion, hearing that the fishing schooner *Hope* of Boston was at Barrington on a trading voyage, two trusty tidesmen were sent to a neighbouring magistrate for two constables, to seize the vessel and bring her into Shelburne. (Tidesmen, or tidewaiters, were customs officials who boarded ships and watched the landing of goods). On boarding the *Hope*, they were overpowered by the Americans and carried off with threats to throw them overboard or take them to Boston. At last the two tidesmen and one of the constables were set adrift in their boat and they made land 'at risk of their lives.' The fourth was put ashore on an island to reach land in whatever way he could.[7]

As the Shelburne fishermen were striving to establish the codfishery, there was also 'great preparation making nets for salmon, mackerel and Herring fishing.' For the river fisheries, rules and regulations were established by the Court of Sessions for the setting of nets and seines and the use of scoop nets at the falls on the rivers. Abraham Lent, Henry Elvins and Nicholas Ogden were appointed overseers of the river fisheries for 1784, and Daniel Neal and Peter Jenkins were named viewers and gaugers of fish barrels and surveyors of pickled fish. Fishing in the rivers and fishing for mackerel and herring became a profitable enterprise, providing 4,192 casks of pickled fish and 61 casks of smoked salmon for export in 1788.[8]

In a few years fishing ceased to be pursued purposefully. The few merchants who continued to trade in fish in foreign markets went to Newfoundland to complete the loading of their vessels. The failure to provide bountiful catches by those who continued to fish was attributed to indolence on the part of the fishermen and the type of boats they used. Fishing in small, badly fitted craft, totally unsuited to venturing into deep water, the Shelburne fishermen were obliged to hug the shores where the fish were small and it required 140 to make a quintal, whereas 20 of those caught in deep water made the same quantity. Fishing along the shores, a man was hard-pressed to make 20 quintals of fish in a season; in deep water a fisherman could take 60 quintals with ease. In 1805 there was but one fishing boat listed in Shelburne, the schooner *William*, owned and skippered by William Ackerman and manned by a crew of four. It was not until the 1840s that Shelburne fishermen became interested in purposeful fishing and developed a profitable and stable industry.[9]

Whaling
Whaling was considered by those in Shelburne who wished to begin a whaling industry as a simpler business than the codfishery, requiring only 'people dextrous in killing the whale' and not on 'proper dressing and curing as in the codfishery.' With the arrival of a whaler at Shelburne in the spring of 1784 with barrels of whale oil, a whale-fishing company was organized and three vessels (a ship, a brig, and a schooner) were equipped for whaling. Others, as private individuals or as business houses, fitted vessels for whaling. Joshua Watson fitted out a ship, George Gracie, a brig, Messrs. Townsend, a schooner and Messrs. Tench and Taylor and Company, a brig. These vessels were partly equipped in Shelburne and partly elsewhere, the local merchants Benjamin Davis, Son and Company and William Hargraves importing for sale harpoons, lances, heavy whale lines and other implements for whaling.[10]

The Whale Fishing Company, organized mainly by a number of Shelburne merchants in the spring of 1784,[11] by midsummer was ready to purchase vessels for whaling. Instructions for the company's business in England were entrusted to Levi Thayer, one of the directors, on his departure for London. He was to apply to the House of Lane, Son and Frazier and offer them a concern in the company, for which a reserve of £6,000 had been made. They were to negotiate the company's business in England, the shipping of goods and the sale of oil. Should they decline, he was to apply to Gibson Johnson and Company, London merchants, and should they also decline, to any business house he thought proper to conduct their affairs. He was to purchase two or three vessels suitable for the Brazil fishery of about 150 tons or thereabout. One he was to send with freight to Lisbon, there to be loaded with 50 jars of oil for Shelburne. A second was to carry 500 barrels of flour from London to Ireland where she was to be reloaded with a cargo of pork and butter and sent on to Shelburne. The third vessel was to be loaded in London with rigging, cable, anchors and canvas, with three tons of oakum, a ton of brimstone, a ton of chalk, and with such woollens, shoes, 'as

House built for Edward Brindley, Commissary, in the summer of 1783. Later known as the Firth house, it was demolished in the 1920s. It is shown as it appeared in the latter nineteenth century.

you may think proper to purchase for the Company.' Vessels and provisions were to be paid for from the shares in the company deposited in London, or by money advanced by the business house negotiating its affairs. Three vessels were purchased by the company: the 140 ton brig *Tamerlane*, the schooner *Dolphin* and the ship *Gibson*. Other vessels employed were the *Lively* and the *New Hope* to ship oil and other commodities. Gibson Johnson and Company accepted the company's offer of a share in the firm and provided the ship *Gibson*.[12]

In the early summer of 1785 the first of the whalers returned to Shelburne. This was the ship *Minerva*, John Squires, master, from the coast of Brazil, with 123 barrels of spermaceti and oil. Owned by Joshua Watson, the *Minerva* was again ready for sea by the middle of August. With her new master, Captain Solomon Bunker, went the sailing instructions of her owner. He was to proceed to the southward to the most likely place for spermaceti whales and search for them until he had filled her casks with oil. From thence, if he had upwards of 200 barrels of oil, he was to proceed to London and deliver his cargo to the merchant, Philip Sansom; if less, he was to touch at Barbados and deliver his cargo to Messrs. Branch and Cock for conveyance to London. From Barbados he was to sail to New York or Philadelphia with a lading of freight. 'As it is the mutual Interest of every

Person on board, it would be needless for me to press you to exert your utmost endeavours to make the best use of your time.'[13]

Whaling voyages required months at sea, sometimes years, before sufficient oil was taken for the bows of the whalers to be turned homeward bound. In July 1786 two of the Shelburne whalers returned. These were the brig *Good Intent*, Captain Butler, with 180 barrels of spermaceti oil and the brig *Tamerlane*, Captain Bassett, with 260 barrels of oil. In 1787, 313 gallons of sperm and whale oil were exported from Shelburne; in 1788, with the return of the whalers well laden, the export of spermaceti and oil leaped to 14,798 gallons and 4,000 pounds of whale bone. Whale oil was delivered in England not only by the whalers but was shipped in other vessels as well – in the *Lively* and in the *Lord Middleton*, and some 289 gallons of oil was sent to Madeira in the schooner *Sally*. Whale oil which was the product of foreign fishing was subject to a higher duty in Great Britain than oil from whales caught by British crews. The *Lord Middleton* carried casks of oil cured on the coast of South America by the crews of two American whalers and brought into Shelburne for shipment to England. Instructions were immediately sent to the customs officer and the comptroller at Shelburne to henceforth furnish the master of vessels with proper documents 'truly describing the Crew by which the oil imported into your Province was taken, as well as the vessel importing it, so that the oil may be admitted to the proper Duty at the Port of Discharge.'[14]

By 1786 the Whale Fishing Company was in difficulties and a dispute arose over the conduct of Levi Thayer in his discharge of their affairs in London. On the return of the *Tamerlane* in July she was sold at public auction by Gay and Lower at the wharf of Benjamin Davis, Son and Company near the foot of Rodney Lane, with her tackle, whaling stores and whale boats, her four tons of iron hoops, spermaceti, oil and whalebone for £958.15.7½. Her initial cost with outfits had been £2,418.10. By 1789, faced with serious financial losses and the loss of a vessel and, in the five years of operation having shipped only one cargo of oil to England, the Company discontinued its operations.[15]

Whaling in Nova Scotia received a serious blow with the decision of the British government not to extend the privilege of whaling to its colonies, but to confine the industry to Great Britain. With the dissolution of the Whale Fishing Company in 1789 and with the departure from Shelburne of several of the owners of private whaling vessels, whaling ceased to be a Shelburne-based industry.[16]

13
Ships and Shipbuilding

By 1786 shipbuilding, which for many years before the Loyalists came to Nova Scotia was well-established in the province, was a brisk industry in Shelburne. In December of that year the *Nova Scotia Packet* reported that five or six schooners of about 80 tons had been launched 'here and in the neighbourhood, for the merchants of this town, since last spring, besides a number of others of smaller burthens.' Vessels built in Shelburne in 1786 were the 15 ton schooner *Mary and Harriet* designed for the fishing and coasting trade and the schooner *New Hope* of about 80 tons built in Silby's shipyard for William Holderness, a Shelburne merchant. The brig *Clyde* of about 150 tons burden was built for the business house of Messrs. McLean and Bogle and was 'as pretty a vessel as can be built.' She had good accommodation for passengers and in late October she set sail for London in Command of Captain Thomas Pamp with passengers and freight. The brig *Carleton*, built for Hugh Breen, an early Dock Street merchant, was employed carrying freight and the Shelburne mail to Barbadoes and other West Indian islands. The brig *Governor Parr* of 101 tons burden was built by John Silby in his shipyard on Watson's Point for Messrs. Sullivan and Mills. She was described as being 'as handsome a vessel, as well put together as it is possible for workmanship to perform.' She was used by her owners in trading voyages to London and Jamaica with Captain Robert Wirling as her master. Largest of the vessels built in 1786 was the ship *Roseway,* reputed to be about 250 tons burden. She was built for McLean and Bogle by Michael Bousfield in his shipyard on the public square north of King Street, a site used for many years by early Shelburne shipbuilders.[1] As she slipped down the ways in triumph, the year's shipbuilding was completed. 'Be hush'd ye inhabitants of Shelburne,' whispered the *Nova Scotia Packet*, 'nor with your sky-rending acclamations, on these occasions, disturb the quiet tranquillity of the peaceable people of Massachusetts!'[2]

Vessels were also built for Shelburne merchants in 1786 in other than Shelburne shipyards. These were the 80-ton schooner *Acadia*, 'a very handsome well-built vessel,' built at New Edinburgh on the Sissibou River for William Robertson, who sent her on her maiden voyage to Barbados under the command of Captain Major. Another vessel built at New Edinburgh was the schooner *British Queen* of 80 tons for McLean and Bogle, her master Captain MacDonald. In the same year, a vessel of about 80 tons, whose name is unrecorded, built for Thomas Meston, a Shelburne merchant, slid down the ways on November 9, 'as pretty a model and well finished vessel as can be built.'

An impetus to shipbuilding in Nova Scotia in 1786 was a bounty of ten shillings per ton, on all vessels over 40 tons, offered by the General Assembly to encourage the construction of sturdy ships. To admeasure the vessels built in Shelburne County, David Thomson and Joseph Durfee were appointed by Governor Parr to survey and examine all vessels built, and only on their certificates of survey would a bounty be paid. Of the vessels built in Shelburne in 1786 the *Governor Parr*, the ship *Roseway* and the *New Hope* were awarded bounties of £56, £96 and £45.10 respectively. The merchants Thomas Meston, Peter Bogle and Company, and William Robertson also received bounties on their vessels, for the *British Queen*, £35, the schooner *Acadia*, £36 and for Meston's unnamed vessel, £38.10. A similar bounty was offered in 1788 of seven shillings sixpence per ton on vessels of 75 tons and over, to be paid out of the duties of import and excise or out of such aides and supplies granted by law. Two vessels built in Shelburne qualified for the 1788 bounty: the schooner *Plow*, built for William Cunningham and the brigantine *Robert* of 125 tons, built for William Cunningham, Hugh Breen and Thomas Braine who used her in the Mediterranean trade. She sailed to Barcelona in 1789 with passengers, goods and merchandise, with George Douglas, master mariner, in command.[3]

There are a few records of other vessels built in Shelburne during the early years: the *Roseway Yacht*, a remarkable, small, 8-ton schooner, that sailed from Halifax to London in 28 days in the summer of 1786, and the ship *Minerva* built in 1789 for George and Robert Ross, who employed her in voyages to Leghorn and to American seaports and in shipping cattle and

SHIPS AND SHIPBUILDING

provisions to Newfoundland. In the early books of customs house and naval office records are listed numbers of vessels built or owned in Shelburne between the years 1790 and 1800. The first of these was the schooner *Margery* of 48 tons built in 1793 for, and probably by, David Thomson, for himself, Joseph Tooker and David McGill for the New York and Baltimore trade, importing barrels of flour, bread and apples, David Thomson sailing as her master. In 1794 were built the schooners *Juno,* 39 tons, for Peter Guyon and the *Annan,* 41 tons, for George Gracie and Henry Negust. They sailed the New York and Shelburne trade-route laden with flour and corn, tar and turpentine.

The 40 ton schooner *Mary and Elvira* was built in 1795 for Jesse Lear, merchant and carpenter by trade, and for Robert Patterson who sailed in her as her captain. In 1796 three vessels went down the ways: the brig *Tar Kitty* built for William Snyder, the schooner *Mickmack* for the merchants James Cox and Lynde Walter and the schooner *Betsey* for David Wilson and James Dore, all employed in voyages to the New England states for supplies, pitch and tar. The schooner *Dolphin* of 28 tons was built in 1797 for William Milby, master mariner and in partnership with his brother Zackdock, a Shelburne merchant. The schooner *Swallow* of 65 tons and the schooner *Experiment* of 70 tons, were built in 1798. The *Swallow* was built for John and William Roxby, Thomas Bingay, Jr., and others, importers of flour and corn from Philadelphia, and the *Experiment* for George Gracie and Henry Negust for the West India trade, importing bushels of salt, puncheons of rum, bags of cotton and hogsheads of sugar. The brig *Addra,* 84 tons, was built in 1800 for Peter Guyon who named her for his little daughter. Under the command of Captain Murdock McDonald, he used her as a trader in the West Indies, importing rum, coffee and a barrel of candy sugar from Jamaica on her maiden voyage.[4]

Numbers of vessels registered in Shelburne are listed in other records but their places of construction are unrecorded. Among these were the schooners, *Edward* of 57 tons (first registered in Shelburne in May 1787 by Abraham Jones and used to import barrels of bread and flour from New York), and the *Experiment* of 55 tons (owned in 1787 by Stephen Skinner to import and to export fish). In 1788 were registered the schooner *Lucy* of 63 tons, employed by her owner John Sargent in the New York trade in flour and bread and Indian corn, and the schooner *Lorence* of 29 tons, whose owners were George and Robert Ross. Only one new vessel was listed in 1789 – the schooner *Sally* of 43 tons, registered by T. Braine and Company. Other vessels were the schooner *Rebecca,* registered in March 1791 for Thomas McMaster; and in 1792 the schooner *William,* William Carson master and owner, and used by him to import quintals of fish from ports along the coast and boards, shingles and ship's spars from Norfolk, Virginia. Registered in the same year were the schooner *Elsey* of 31 tons, owned by John Hardy, and the ship *Camilla*, of 173 tons, sent by her owners, George and Robert Ross, on long voyages to the West Indies and to American seaports, outward bound laden with spars, masts and hogsheads of dried fish.[5]

The names of a number of vessels which were Shelburne-owned and some of which may have been Shelburne-built appear in the early newspapers of the town and in other documents. Among these were the *Port Roseway Packet;* the brig *Port Roseway,* Captain Wishart, master; the brig *Shelburne,* Captain Penny; the ship *Loyalist* which, under the command of Captain Jesse Hoyl, sailed for Jamaica in December 1788; the schooner *Industry,* commanded by Captain Peter Jenkins in voyages to North Carolina; and the schooner *Sally,* her master Patrick Hare, employed by her owners, George and Robert Ross, in the carrying trade in the West Indies, Madeira and Lisbon. Among other vessels were the schooner *Betsey* owned by William Cunningham and others; the schooner *Experience;* the ship *Governor Wentworth;* and Benjamin Davis' brig *Mary* of 110 tons. Still other vessels were the coasting schooner *Charlotte,* whose owner was James Bruce; the *John and Jane* employed by James Cox in the West Indies trade; the snow *Lively* (the only snow recorded in early Shelburne records), used by Benjamin Davis, Son and Company in a freight and passenger service between London and Shelburne; the brigantine *Friendship;* and the ship *Prince William Henry* owned and commanded by Captain Meader and engaged by the business houses of McLean and Bogle and Thayer and Jarvis as a transport and in the carrying trade from Shelburne to London.[6]

As the years of conflict continued between Great Britain and her adversaries, and French and Spanish vessels fell prey to the King's ships and to Nova Scotian privateers and were condemned in the Court of Admiralty, numbers of prizes were purchased by Shelburne shipowners: the schooner *Sally* purchased by William Synder and John Miller; the *Success* bought by Benjamin Davis; the *Despatch* owned by Robert and Alexander Barry; the *Good Intent* sold to George Gracie; and the schooner *Nelson* purchased by George Gracie, James Cox and others, which converted to a brig, prowled the seas as a privateer sometimes coming into Shelburne with strange cargoes – with serons (hampers) of indigo and cocoa, casks of aniseed water and of mint water.[7]

Shipbuilders

In the early records are listed three shipbuilders and three shipyards. One of the shipbuilders was Michael Bousfield whose shipyard was on the

SHIPS AND SHIPBUILDING

public square on the waterfront north of King Street and to the rear of the King Street market. Associated with him in the building of ships was John Tennon. John Silby's shipyard was on Watson's Point, the finger of land that juts to the right at the southern end of Water Street. He also had a shipyard near Gunning Cove on Fort Point where he was living in 1786. David Thomson, formerly a shipbuilder in Philadelphia, had his shipyard on the shore of his 100 acre lot of land butting the southern boundary of the town, granted to him as a place to build ships. With him worked the master ship carpenter, Neil McDonald. There were numbers of ship carpenters, among them Patrick Murphy, James Dickey, James Muir, Bernard Martin, John Ogden, Samuel Sneden, Elias Marsh, John Ackerman, James Corrin, John Herbert and John Cockery. Among the freed Blacks were a number of competent ship carpenters and able boat builders. One of these was Boston King who was engaged to repair three flat-bottomed boats for the salmon fishery, receiving for his labour one pound for the repair of each boat.

As shipbuilders were busy in the early Shelburne shipyards, others were busy in the shipyards along the shores, in the sheltered bays and inlets, and on the river banks, where, on the Jordan, young Donald McKay, the renowned builder of clipper ships, learned the rudiments of shipbuilding, and where his brother Lauchlan first learned the same principles of sturdy ship construction. Lauchlan later wrote *The Practical Ship-Builder*, used for many years as a textbook in the shipyards of the United States. There are records for only a few of the early vessels built in the vicinity of Shelburne. These included the 14 ton schooners *Mary* and the *Good Intent*, built by William Lyman on his farm lot near Round Bay in 1789; the schooner *Juno* of 37 tons, built at Green Harbour in 1794 by Bradshaw for John Stuart; and the schooner *Ruby* of 35 tons built on the Clyde for the seafaring families of Greenwood and Swaine.[8]

In answer to an inquiry about building vessels in Shelburne, George Ross wrote Messrs. Cunningham and Cleland of Montego Bay in 1788:

'Tho there are several able builders here, there is none in a situation to contract for the delivery of such vessel compliatly fitted with sails, rigging &c... the usual method in such cases being to engage with the builder for the workmanship, Timber and Spars, or for the workmanship only, purchasing the wood of others, but the owner supplying Naval Stores, iron work, oakum, Rigging, &c. The usual price for workmanship only, including that of masts and spars... is from 8 and 8½ dolls per ton. The wood if purchased of others of the dimensions required by the Builder and brought to the yard will cost from 3½ and 4 dolls p ton of wood – 75 tons of wood being about the quantity for a vessel of 100 tons. Acting with economy, and having time to provide the necessary materials – the hull, (of a vessel of 180 tons) with masts, spars &c may be launched for £4.10 p ton being 18 dollars. The iron, naval stores, cordage Sales &c may be procured from the States and tho not admissable by law may be introduced without difficulty or risk. Blacksmiths demand for working up the iron 2½d and 3d p lb. sailmakers charge is 7/6 p bolt of English canvas & 9/ p bolt of Russian made up into sails. The terms required by the builder are ⅓ on raising the stern post, ⅓ on laying the Beams, ⅓ when launched... if furnished with a timely supply of molasses common sugar and some Rum these articles might suffice for the payment of ⅔ of the workmanship and wood.'[9]

Shipbuilding, as George Ross's letter implies, involved the work of many beside ship carpenters. Wheelwrights and ropemakers, blockmakers and sailmakers, blacksmiths, caulkers and riggers, all give of their skill to build a sturdy vessel. In these trades there were capable workmen: wheelwrights, Thomas Young and Jonathan Baxter; blockmakers, Michael Mann and John Atkins; sailmakers, Patrick Byrne, Joseph Ingram, William Summers; staymaker Thomas Hartley; caulker, William Morris; rigger, William Wilmington, and the ropemaker, Benjamin Hart. There were many blacksmiths who shaped on their anvils rudder bands and irons, slings for yards, straps and bolts for bobstays and bowsprits, travellers and bands for booms, dumps and hinges, hasps and nails and spikes. Straps and cranes for the studding sail booms were also the work of the blacksmiths as were the stanchions for the quarterdeck, holdfasts and thimbles, shives for pulleys, mast hoops, plates, gudgeons, screws and rudder irons, withes for masts, catharpins to brace the shrouds, trammel hooks, rudder heads, tillers and anchors.

Early Shelburne vessels, schooners and brigs, were listed as of one deck, without galleries, carvel built, square sterned and square stemmed. Some had a high quarter deck; others had long and low or flush decks. They were rigged with a standing bowsprit with a knee or joist beneath the bowsprit, and had a billethead. Some timber for shipbuilding was brought from the United States and some that was found sound and usable in condemned vessels was used to eke out the supply the local sawmills could provide. When British laws demanded the importation of goods into British colonies in British bottoms, some American shipbuilders brought to Shelburne keels and timber cut and ready to put together. 'She is then to be call'd a British built vessel. This is what they call cheating the D ---l,' one wrote who watched the hull of an American vessel take shape. For those who contracted with a shipbuilder for the workmanship only, there were those whose business it was to provide ship timber, masts and spars and oak knees for sale. Merchants wanting to build vessels advertised in the local papers for ship carpenters, having themselves obtained the timber and ironware

SHIPS AND SHIPBUILDING

for the building. In 1788, with the shipyards busy, Alexander Cocken was appointed to survey and examine vessels for owners wishing to obtain registration papers for their craft.[10]

For many years sailing ships provided the only contact with even nearby seaports and shipbuilding continued a thriving industry. By the early 1790s the shipbuilders John Silby and Michael Bousfield no longer built vessels in Shelburne, but David Thomson and his partner Neil McDonald were still building sturdy ships, and there were ship carpenters and shipwrights building small boats and vessels that slipped down the ways to a waiting harbour. The importance of ships and the sea to early Shelburne and for the township is revealed in the capitation records of 1792 where there are recorded 22 masters of ships, 15 mariners and 6 ship owners. Of the small boats that coasted along the shores fishing and carrying the produce of the land and sea to nearby seaports, there were 18 which were owned mainly by the men who sailed them and who lived along the coast in the settlements edging the open sea.[11]

14
Trade and Commerce

Believing that they had chosen the best situation in the province of Nova Scotia for trade, fishing and farming, the Port Roseway Associates had embarked from New York to found a town designed for trade based on the produce of the land and the sea. Among them were merchants experienced in the methods of trade in foreign ports who already had well-established contacts with trading houses in England and in European seaports, in the West Indies and along the American seaboard. Other Loyalists, seeing in the fine harbour of Port Roseway an excellent situation for a town thriving on trade and commerce, hastened to join the Associates. Still others, merchants and those in other professions, whose names are not recorded, and who were referred to only as 'the English Adventurers,' came to establish themselves in what appeared would be a stable and prosperous town. Among them were serveral persons of considerable wealth who invested their fortunes in the building of stores and warehouses, in the erection of wharves and the building of vessels, and in the construction of large houses as their places of residence.

A greater attraction to these merchant adventurers than Shelburne's fine harbour with its proximity to the fishing banks, was the decision of the British to uphold their laws of trade and navigation, which excluded the Americans as residents of a foreign state, from the carrying trade in the British West Indies. Many who might have tarried in America came to Nova Scotia instead, many to Shelburne. Here they quickly developed, within the framework of the old and well-seasoned British laws, trade in foreign ports and with merchants in distant lands. To complete the cargoes of their vessels for outward bound voyages, they scouted the shores from Liverpool to Halifax and the New England settlements in the sheltered harbours along the coast of Nova Scotia, and established contacts with fish dealers in Newfoundland. Sometimes their vessels were many months at sea, trudging from port to port, trading barrel staves and shingles, boards and ship's knees, furs, dried and pickled fish for molasses, sugar, spices, teas and rum.

The schooner *Betsey*, owned by George and Robert Ross, with William Miller as master, sailed for Kingston and Savannah-La-Mar, Jamaica, in January of 1788 with a cargo of black spruce and birch knees, anchor stocks, barrels of fall herring and mackerel, tierces of cod oil, barrels of choice salmon, hogsheads of codfish and smoked salmon to the value of £435 Jamaica currency. Six months later she was back in Shelburne by way of Philadelphia and was ready for a voyage to Boston for cattle destined for a squadron of the British navy in Newfoundland, for which the Ross brothers held a contract to supply cattle, molasses and ship bread. Plodding back and forth with cattle and provisions between American seaports and Newfoundland, sometimes touching at Shelburne for clearance, the *Betsey* was stranded on Martha's Vineyard in September 1789. Rescued and refitted at a cost to her cargo and hull of £341, she was reloaded with the remains of her cargo of cattle, sheep and hogs, turkeys and fowls, flour, ship and pilot bread, and continued on her way. In December she was in Shelburne laden with the best merchantable fish for the island of Madeira from whence she was to sail with Madeira wine to Teneriffe for a cargo of mules for the Windward Islands. In June 1791 she was shattered in a gale off the American coast. Undaunted once her sturdy frame was repaired, she was again pressed into serving her owners, freighting cattle and hogs and ship bread to Newfoundland.[1]

Other merchants sent their vessels to trade in distant seaports. William Hale in the *Stag* and the sloop *Sally* shipped codfish to the West Indies for hogsheads of the best grade of sugar and for barrels of coffee and rum; sailed to Turks Island for salt; to Halifax for pounds of caraway and coriander, plums and sugar almonds; to London for rope; to American seaports for barrels of good leaf tobacco for wrappers, good pig tail and the best and mildest smoking tobacco and papers. James Cox in the *John and Jane*, Captain James Potter, master, sent herring and train oil (whale oil) to Jamaica for sugar, coffee and rum to barter in a carrying trade between Jamaica and the southern United States. In the schooner *Charlotte*, her owner James Bruce conducted a lucrative carrying trade shipping produce

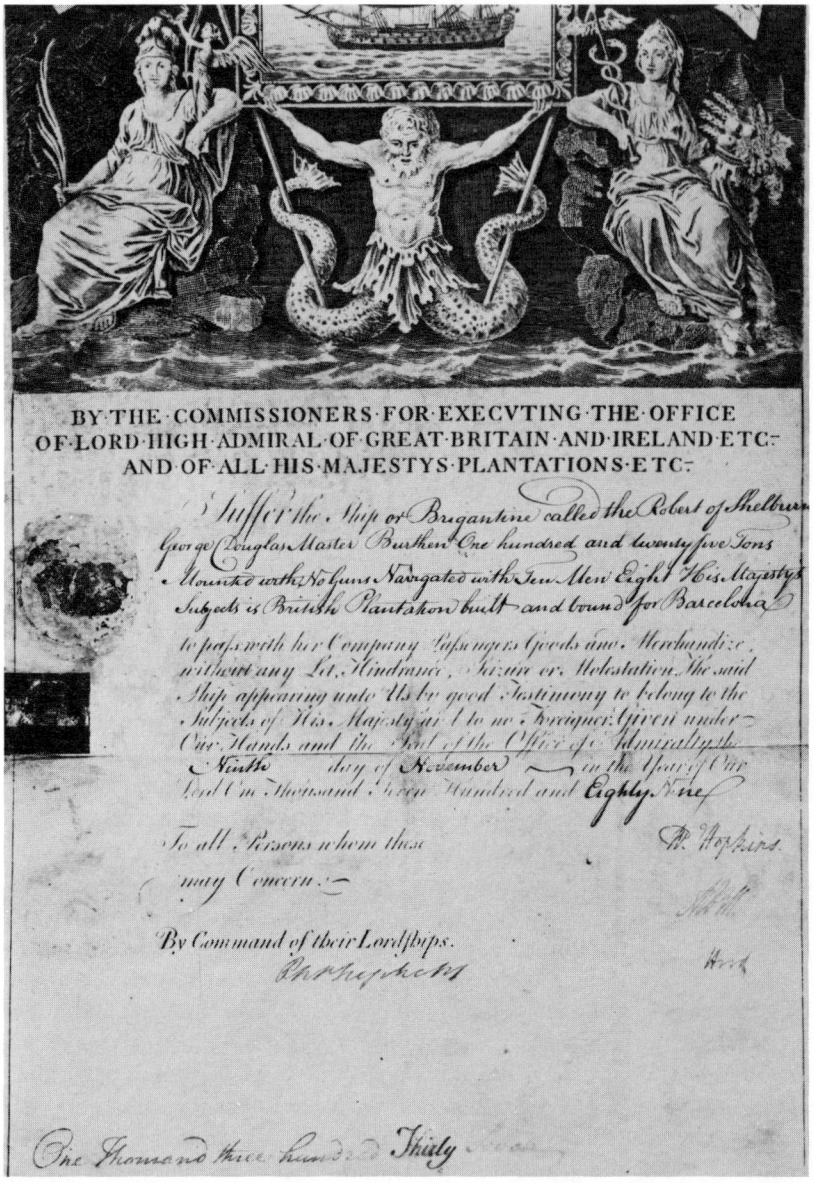

Mediterranean Sea Pass issued by the Commissioners for Executing the Office of Lord High Admiral of Great Britain to Captain Douglas of the brigantine Robert *in 1789. Note that the top edge of the document is scalloped or "indented," so that it would exactly match the second copy, thus guaranteeing its authenticity. (Courtesy Public Archives of Nova Scotia)*

TRADE AND COMMERCE

to Halifax: Irish butter and herring for cotton and ship iron for the shipyards.[2]

To and from London plied ships in trade, the Shelburne merchants shipping fish, lumber and the sugar and molasses they had obtained in trade in the West Indies. In 1785 the brigantine *Friendship*, Paul White, master, sailed for London and Glasgow with freight and passengers. McLean and Bogle were her agents. In June the *Prince William Henry* sailed with squared timber from Jordan River and with passengers and the mail bags. In the *New Hope* came goods from London for McLean and Bogle: tea and black pepper, codhooks, porter in hogsheads and barrels, hair ribbons, kidskin and beaver gloves, umbrellas. In the *Catherine* came hardware, pewter, brass, copper and tinware, cutlery, loaf sugar, hams and cheese and pickled walnuts for Charles Whitworth; in the *Port Roseway Packet* were chaldrons (units of measure) of the best Newcastle coals, split peas in firkins, capers, olives and mushroom ketchup. With the prospect of a continuing brisk trade between London and Shelburne, Henry Hugill, master of the ship *Lord Middleton*, advertised his intention of establishing her as an annual ship for passengers and freight plying between the two ports.[3]

For vessels sailing into the waters of the Mediterranean, passes were issued by His Majesty's customs for the port of Halifax to vessels built in the British plantations manned by His Majesty's subjects, and without mounted guns. On the lists of passes are the names of Shelburne vessels venturing into and near the troubled water of the Mediterranean: the brigantine *Robert*, George Douglas, master, bound for Barcelona; the schooner *Betsey* and the schooner *Experience* for Lisbon; the ship *Governor Wentworth* for the Mediterranean seas; the brig *Mary*, her master, Peter Jenkins, for Spain. Some sailed without passes as did George and Robert Ross' schooner *Sally*, laden with codfish and smoked and pickled herring, Patrick Hare, master, bound for Madeira and from thence to Lisbon, and their ship *Minerva* laden with quintals of fish for Leghorn.[4]

Several of the Shelburne merchants were commission merchants charging one per cent commission providing it was optional to pay for the goods sold in merchantable fish or in bills of exchange. Goods sent to Shelburne on commission considered 'too good a quality for this market,' as bloom raisins, were sent to a vendue master in Halifax. Unsalable items were a dead loss. 'The Gunpowder shipt to me,' one merchant complained, 'is horrid Bad it will scarely take fire, everybody that has had of it complains very much, there was likewise fifty doz. of wood knives shipt for Clasp Knives I have offered them as Presents to the I[n]deans and they have absolutely Laught at them, in short they are not deserving the Name of a Knife.' From the beginning, trade was conducted almost entirely by barter, money to purchase goods being nearly non-existent. As a Shelburne merchant wrote to one of his creditors, 'We could deliver 1000 quintals of codfish with more ease to ourselves than raise £50 in Cash that being an article very scarce here and the Trade of this place solely confined to Barter.' By 1788, for even the few items reserved for cash sales, such as yards of cloth, the merchants were forced to accept fish and to barter spices and tea for pickled herring.[5]

Shelburne merchants were soon aware that Shelburne was 'a very uncertain and trifling market by no means calculated to carry on any scrape of Business without hazard.' They ascribed many reasons for the failure of Shelburne as a prosperous centre for trade and commerce – causes within the town and without that hampered their efforts. Their speculations in the West Indies which depended largely on trade in fish, by 1787 were sharply curtailed by the great quantities of fish exported from Newfoundland to the islands. As disturbing as the overstocking the West Indies with fish by Newfoundland dealers was the action of the British Parliament in regulating trade in the British Islands of the West Indies. Where the Shelburne merchants had believed that only vessels of British registry could trade and only British produce could be imported, the governors of the Island were permitted to grant the privilege of importing lumber and provisions from the neutral islands, a free trade area, in cases of emergency. And in the neutral islands the Americans could unload their cargoes for reshipment to the British West Indies. Turning to the town itself, they pointed out to the Shelburne Court of Sessions that there were too many auctioneers hawking their wares which was prejudicial to the trade of the merchants and shopkeepers. Then, foreign vessels laden with foreign cargoes which were permitted to trade in the port were 'highly pernicious.' Contrary to the British laws of trade and navigation prohibiting Americans from trading in British territory, the governor and council permitted the importation of food from the New England states to relieve the exorbitant prices charged by merchants and farmers for flour and cattle. Since others besides the Shelburne merchants protested American imports, further importation from the United States was forbidden except in British vessels, and cargoes were limited to flour, wheat, rice, corn and rye meal. Additional protest brought action from the King-in-Council. 'No goods or commodities, being the growth or manufacture of the United States,' except livestock and live provisions and lumber, were to be imported, and these only 'by British subjects in British vessels owned and navigated according to law' and they were to be permitted only as long as the governor and council proclaimed it to be necessary.[6]

By the time these arrangements were made, the state of Massachusetts,

TRADE AND COMMERCE

where many of the Shelburne merchants had long-standing ties, had imposed a duty of ten shillings per ton on all British vessels entering any port in the state. Faced with a decreasing population and heavy duties on their imports and exports as well as duties in foreign ports (and fees of £5.5.10 for a square-rigged vessel and £3.11.3 for one of lesser tonnage for entry and clearance at the Shelburne customs house), the local merchants and shipowners were hard-pressed. Their struggle to free themselves from customs-house and naval office fees filled pages of their memorials.[7]

THE CUSTOMS HOUSE AND NAVAL OFFICE

A few days after the arrival of the Port Roseway Associates, Stephen Hall Binney came from Halifax as commissioned collector for the port and district of Port Roseway. He was to collect impost and excise taxes and the duties granted for maintenance of the transient poor imposed on goods imported into the province and sold by adventurers. He, the Associates considered, had been sent to pick their pockets and they were soon 'to windward of him.' Their vessels were transports not subject to fees and they were not adventurers but settlers. He became the victim of pranks, and when he was dropped in the harbour, he returned to Halifax. John Miller, secretary to the Port Roseway Associates, was appointed acting-collector by warrant of defaultion for the collector of His Majesty's Customs at Halifax. Believing that Shelburne soon would be 'a place of National Consequence' and the resort of a great number of vessels, Sir Guy Carleton was requested by the citizens of Shelburne to recommend that John Miller should be appointed the collector of customs for the Port of Shelburne to preserve His Majesty's revenues. In the meantime, in Halifax, Matthew Cahill was appointed collector for the district of Shelburne of the several duties granted to His Majesty by acts of the General Assembly. On his leave of absence, in February 1784, James McEwen was named collector, John Miller deputy collector and John Sargent was appointed gauger and landwaiter for the district of Shelburne. Because of the great inconvenience to vessels having to be taken to Halifax or to Shelburne for clearing and entering, in December the General Assembly asked Parr to have collectors at Halifax and at Shelburne 'appoint vigilant preventive officers to take cognizance of and reports from all vessels putting in from sea or loading at all the outports within their respective Districts.'[8]

Sir Guy Carleton, aware from his years of experience that quit rents and taxation imposed by the British parliament promoted discontent, recommended to Lord North that there should be 'a clear and explicit excemption from all taxation except by their own Legislatures.' His recommendations were echoed in a memorial by the Shelburne Loyalists in the spring of 1784.

They had been 'led to Hope that in consideration of their sufferings... they should be exempt from all Imposts and Duties until circumstances should render the Payment of them equal, just and practicable.' Since their arrival they had been 'disappointed in most of their Expectations.' Few had received any assurance of their lands by grants and they were liable to a heavy impost which, if not suspended, would render them 'wholly incapable of beginning any kind of business whether merchantile or any other and the settlement itself be intirely Ruined.' If the taxes could not be revoked until the town was incorporated and represented in the Legislature, they asked that the money collected should be held by the collector at Shelburne 'for the distinct use and benefit of the town.' As for two other memorials asking for relief from impost duties, Parr assured them he had no power 'to alter or suspend imposing duties of Impost and Excise.'

Undeterred, 'His Majesty's faithful subjects, the Loyalist Merchants, Traders, Farmers, and others settled in the Town and County of Shelburne' pleaded for the relief they needed from taxation to establish their town and its trade and commerce on a firm and lasting foundation. They pointed out to Parr that the proceeds from the impost and excise duties on merchandise, imposed by an act of the Assembly, 'far from being appropriated to purposes of Public Utility to this settlement are to pass to Halifax and either be lost in hands of individuals, or be disposed of by an Assembly in which neither your memorialists are represented nor their fellow Loyalists in the Province.' The act, 'by imposing a duty on Importation without allowing a drawback on exportation,' they regarded as 'most contrary to the true principles of Commerce; and it is in a peculiar manner hurtful to the trade of this Port, which from its favorable situation promises to become a Mart or place of deposit not only for the settlements on the Bay of Fundy; but from the present disinclination of the British merchant both at home and in the West Indies to extend in Credits to the Revolted Colonies; it bids fair to be the Mart for British Commodities for the consumption of the said Colonies. But by the imposition of a Duty not to be drawn back on Exportation the merchant is precluded every hope of such event, and must be compelled to restrain his importations to the actual consumption of the Country.' They asked for an exemption from taxes for the space of ten years, and 'Your Memorialists as on the one hand they mean not to be tributary to the Ancient settlers of the Province so on the other hand they will require from them no pecuniary aid. But contented to rely on His Majesty's paternal care and depending on the efforts of their own industry they will in their county meetings provide such funds as their slender means can afford' for the erection of churches, seminaries for the education of youth, for the building of a jail and other public buildings. Should their request be refused, they

TRADE AND COMMERCE

would present their grievances to their gracious Sovereign. Should they again be denied, 'they pray that they may be permitted free from every impost of the Halifax Assembly to carry off their effects now on hand and such as they may hereafter receive, to such ports of His Majesty's Dominions as they may severally think proper to retire to.' A further memorial in the late fall of 1785 stressed their plea that the monies taken by the impost and excise duties should remain in Shelburne 'for the present' to be 'devoted to the use of this Infant Settlement just Struggling into existence.' Circumstances having forced them 'into this Wilderness' where they were 'as yet unable to supply themselves with the Necessaries of life, and standing in need of almost every Support and assistance... it seems inconsisient and ungenuous to Expect that the small products of Our Trade should be thrown into the Provincial Treasury... when by Employing them for our own particular Advancement and Establishment they must Shortly redound to the General Advantage and Prosperity of the Province and Nation at Large.'[9]

Their requests were partly answered in the establishment of a customs house in Shelburne apart from the customs in Halifax. James Bruce was collector of customs, a position he had held in West Florida in the 1760s, John Allen Martin, who was also from West Florida, was comptroller, Richard Brazil, clerk of the customs house, George Drummond, surveyor and searcher, Richard Combault, solicitor of customs, John Sargent and Thomas O'Brian, tide and landwaiters. In July 1786 the port of Shelburne was ordered to include in its customs district, Digby, St. Mary's Bay, Clare, Yarmouth, Barrington, Shelburne, Green Harbour, Ragged Islands, Sable River and Port Hebert. All other parts of the province were to be under the jurisdiction of Halifax. The Shelburne customs house was at this time on the west side of Mowat Street near the post office and between St. George and William Streets.[10]

About the same time as the customs house was established, naval offices were opened in Shelburne and in the outports nearby, under the naval office in Halifax, with Michael Largin as deputy naval officer. He was succeeded, on his accidental death by drowning in 1790, by Matthew Hutchins.

As vigorously as the Shelburne merchants and shipowners had protested the fees collected by the customs house, they protested the fees of the naval office, 'for, from every coasting vessel, however small, and even from the market craft with hay and vegetables for the use of the town, there is required and rigorously exacted a fee of five shillings at their departure from an out port, and as much on their arrival here.' They wanted the governor to interpose his authority and restrain the collecting of fees that never before had been exacted from coasting vessels, and to grant coasting passes to small vessels as an 'important service to the country.'[11]

As others also protested the naval office and customs house fees, the General Assembly referred their petitions to the governor. They requested him 'to regulate and ascertain the fees of those two offices in such a way as may to yourself appear most expedient and least oppressive' and to publish his regulations 'to prevent in future all mistakes and impositions.' At the same time, they wished him to make such regulations for coasting and market boats as to 'remedy the very heavy and destructive grievance complained of.' Winckworth Tonge, provincial naval officer, defended the fees of the naval office by pointing out that at Shelburne his expenses for rent, stationery and maintaining his deputy for six months exceeded £70 while fees collected amounted to only £20. Two and six was the fee demanded and only on decked vessels of ten tons and over, not on open boats. Unless the masters of small craft reported at the naval office, what contraband goods picked up along the coast and at sea from foreign vessels might they not hide in the holds of their sloops and schooners. 'Upon the whole it seems the Design and Wish of the Petitioners to abolish the naval office (as some have declared) and the reduction of Fees must tend to the same purpose.' The petition rested unresolved and it was not until 1790 that a committee was appointed, with Isaac Wilkins as one of its members, and acceptable fees were established for foreign ships and local coasting vessels. Open boats bringing wood and other produce of the province into port were free of all fees. At the same time fees were set for the officers of the customs house and the naval office.[12]

The exorbitant fees charged for entry and clearance at this time and restrictions on imports encouraged a brisk illicit trade in 'rum, gin, sugars and dry goods.' Even respectable merchants engaged in undercover trade. One merchant wrote in his instructions to the captain of his schooner, returning from Philadelphia, 'You will endeavour to enter this harbour in the Evening and should you have goods not fit to be brought up to the Town you will put them on shore at our store on McNutt's Island taking care to be gone from thence before daylight.' There was considerable slackness in allowing goods to enter the port 'almost without restraint.' With Governor Parr's proclamation prohibiting the importation of molasses from the United States, an American merchant was assured by a Shelburne importer, 'if it can be shipt in any of the Shelburne vessels, we think you may safely venture a few Casks.' Again it was suggested to a firm of Halifax merchants, 'should you determine on trying a cargo of Naval Stores from Bermuda to Halifax – we conceive it might be proper to cause the vessel to touch here putting ashore a few casks and proceeding with a fresh clearance to Halifax; but in suggesting this we do not mean to insinuate that there would be the

TRADE AND COMMERCE

small risk in going directly to Halifax, but from the rapacity of the Custompo [*sic*] and the iniquity of the court of Admiralty an uncommon degree of caution is necessary.' When writing this, George Ross perhaps had in mind the experience of Gregory Springall, when he came to Shelburne as a Loyalist merchant. At the end of the war, having on hand a large quantity of molasses (119 hogsheads or 12,219 gallons), he shipped it in a vessel bound for Halifax, for which 'he was constrained to pay or Subject his property to forfeiture,' £254.11.3.[13]

The pages of the provincial revenue reports show that in the year from March 1786 to March 1787, £906.18.1 was collected in duties at the Shelburne customs house. The following year showed a marked increase to £1,380, falling a year later to £431 as many of the Shelburne merchants departed, whether from the high duties on their imports and exports (which they predicted would oblige them to leave) or from the general crumbling of the town as many hundreds of people departed. In an effort to maintain the port of Shelburne as a place of business it was urged in 1790 that it should be a free port of entry for American vessels. It was thought this would encourage trade and settlers to the town but it was 18 years before Shelburne was named a free port in 1808, along with the ports of Halifax and St. John. By that time (and before 1808) the numbers of vessels owned in Shelburne had shrunk to ten. Of these, seven were schooners and brigs designed for trade in the West Indies and American seaports. Of the seven, four were laid up for lack of employment. It would seem, from the numbers of ships and their cargoes registered at the customs house as inward bound, some slight benefit may have been derived from the admission of vessels free of import duties. But the stimulation to trade and the increase in settlement fell far short of the buoyant hopes of those who first urged that Shelburne should be duty free as it 'would be of great use to the Inhabitants and encourage many to settle here.'[14]

15
The Decline of Shelburne

The decline of Shelburne began almost with its beginning, as many who had expected green fields and pleasant villages such as they had left behind, soon found ways to return to their homeland or to well-established settlements on the shores of Nova Scotia. Many reasons have been given for the rapid decline of the town: its rocky soil, its aristocratic settlers unaccustomed to labour, the animosity of the early settlers, the lack of foresight and wisdom in selecting Port Roseway as a place of refuge. From their own records and from the opinions of those who knew early Shelburne, emerge many reasons for its decline and the departure of the Loyalists.

As the chapters in this book reveal, the Loyalists were disappointed in most of their expectations: in the long delay in grants for their farm land; the hindrances to the development of a stable trade and commerce; the productive but rocky soil; the grinding ice of the winter months; the conflicts with earlier settlers of the province and among the Loyalists themselves; the policies of the provincial administration and the unconcern of the British for the welfare of Loyalists under the terms of the Treaty of Paris. As the records show, one of the foremost reasons for the unhappiness that spread over the town and turned many away was the chaos during the first crucial days when unanimity of purpose and leadership were essential, but there was no one person in authority to maintain order or to direct the founding of the town. The surveyors sent by Parr soon detected the spirit of variance among the Loyalists and between the Associates and their elected captains.

THE DECLINE OF SHELBURNE

Benjamin Marston had noted that they were 'like sheep without a Shepherd,' without men of ability and the experience to found a town, as no one had been appointed by Carleton to direct, and to maintain order. That there were many capable and substantial Loyalists among the first to come to Shelburne is evident from their records. Their lack of a competent leader and the determination on the part of the Port Roseway Associates that town affairs must be settled in public meetings, prevented the clear-cut decisions needed to establish an orderly settlement and give to its citizens the assurance of stability.[1]

As harmful to the future of the community as the lack of firm leadership were the hundreds of Loyalists who, against the wishes of the Associates, pushed their way into the settlement. Many of these were unruly citizens, and disorderly persons crowded the streets. As the records of the Court of Sessions show, there were petty crimes, drunkenness, street brawls; and houses of ill repute sprang up. Dram shops and houses and stores where spiritous liquors were sold became a menace to 'every virtuous Principal in the rising generation.' 'Rum and idle habits,' one wrote of the Loyalists in general, 'are much against them.' Idleness in Shelburne became a cause of concern deplored by the Court of Sessions. Then, the King's Bounty of provisions, so sorely needed by those who were striving hard to establish themselves in a profitable situation, was a bounty for idleness to the shiftless.[2]

The long delay before the farm lots were surveyed and the frustration over grants which prompted the riots of 1784 further increased the dissatisfaction of the Loyalists with Shelburne. Parr, whom they considered 'a Governor without abilities,' himself bewailed the lack of instructions from the home government. With distrust of Parr was mingled distrust of the earlier settlers of the province, in particular, those in Halifax in the House of Assembly, who were 'individuals of principles ever inimical and whose conduct has at time been hostile to His Majesty's interest.' From such men they could look 'for nought but oppression.' At least part of the hostility the Loyalists felt directed toward them by the earlier settlers sprang from their attempts to push the settlers aside, to obtain land where others had laboured, and their assumption that as Loyalists they deserved special consideration. With two contending forces striving for mastery in the province, Governor Parr was pressed between the factions, and his lack of decisive action and hesitation in supporting their demands angered the Loyalists and fostered their discontent.[3]

For the merchants who had expended their capital in building stores and warehouses, wharves and large houses for themselves, the exorbitant duties imposed on all imports and exports spelled disaster. What was to be an even greater disaster sprang from the failure on the part of the Port Roseway Associates to have a careful assessment made of the area's potential to support a viable town before it was chosen as a place of settlement, and their failure to assess their own skills and abilities to profitably develop it. The land, although the soil was productive, was stony and peppered with boulders, and it was soon discovered that extensive cultivation was not possible. The lack of a navigable river to the interior, where there was good timber, prevented the merchants from continuing their trade in lumber in foreign ports when, by 1791, the easily available timber had been cut. After a winter of harbour ice grinding against wooden-hulled vessels, it was evident that the site for the town, located as it was at the head of the harbour, had been poorly chosen. In the summer of 1784 Colonel Morse recommended to Governor Parr that wharves and warehouses could be built on the 241 acres of reserved land at the narrows of the lower harbour where there was no danger from floating ice. The location was not too remote for communication with the town and the problem of the ice would be overcome. The town site was poorly chosen from the point of view of the fishermen also, since they had the long ten mile tack to the harbour's mouth, with still further to sail to good fishing grounds. In the evening they had the same long sail back to port. For the fishermen and those who depended upon fish to maintain their trade in foreign ports, 'the very liberal indulgencies granted by the Treaty of Peace with the United States to their Fishermen' to catch and cure fish along the shores of Nova Scotia, irked and angered those who, in their inexperience in this activity, blamed the American fishermen for their own failures.[4]

There were other disappointments for the Loyalists: the refusal by Governor Parr to incorporate their town; and the decision of Colonel Morse 'that with all the advantages attending the harbour' he did not 'think it an eligible one in a military view.' Nor did he recommend Shelburne as a naval base 'as it would be difficult to defend this harbour against a superior force... the entrance into it at the Narrows' being 'too wide to be secured by batteries.' Among the Loyalists themselves there were animosities that provoked bitterness and resentment and provided a reason for them to seek a happier location. The determination of the Port Roseway Associates that all should share alike in whatever bounties were granted to them soon was shattered when some of their own numbers obtained large grants of land and privileges that hindered others from obtaining property and also rights to the waterfront. To the long delay in laying out the country lots and the frustration that followed the allotment of land 'may be attributed the return of many valuable Settlers... to the American States,' wrote one Loyalist. Among those who were capable of holding government positions there was

THE DECLINE OF SHELBURNE

resentment that half-pay officers and royal refugees who had fled to England during the war, and had been compensated for their losses, monopolized the public offices which were the prerogative of government to bestow. Resentment deepened when it was learned that some obtained their appointments through innuendos that reflected their greed and self-interest. Then there were those, who, although poor, were ambitious parents and returned to America because of the failure on the part of the town to establish charity schools where their children could be educated.[5]

Whatever the reason for the decline of Shelburne and the departure of many hundreds of Loyalists, once confidence had been lost in it as a town, many years of slow growth were required before it regained a measure of its former promise.

THE DISPERSAL

As to where the Loyalists and disbanded soldiers went when they left Shelburne, there are records for only a few hundred. Estimates of the numbers who left, made at the time of the rapid decline of the town, indicate that the greatest number returned to the United States. It was natural that they should return where they knew friends were awaiting them, and where there were opportunities that were lacking in a new settlement at the edge of a wilderness, on a rocky shore and ice-bound in the winter.

As hundreds left, the Court of Sessions took steps to prevent anyone leaving the province without a pass signed by John Miller and a receipt for taxes paid, from the collector of taxes. Of those who left, records show that a few went to London on the *Lord Middleton* and in the *Perseverance;* some went to the West Indies, to Barbados, New Providence, Jamaica and other West Indian islands in the *Charming Nancy,* the schooner *Polly,* in the *Roseway* and in the *Charming Betsey.* One went to Cape Breton in the *Two Friends;* others travelled to Quebec in the *Lady.* Those who returned to the United States did so on available vessels that came into port. Many went to New York in the *Sally* and in the *Edward,* in the *John and Jane,* the *Catherine* and the *Lord Middleton.* Others reached Portsmouth in the *Charlotte* and the *Roseway;* some went to Boston in the *Success;* still others left for Penobscot in the *Governor Parr.*[6]

There are a few records regarding Loyalists and disbanded soldiers who departed in groups to found new settlements or to take up land in other locations. Among the first of the groups to relocate themselves were a number of Hessian soldiers and their wives and children who took up land in Argyle in the summer of 1784. In this group were 49 men and 23 women and children whose passage to Argyle and supplies were provided by the Board of Agents for the location of settlers.[7]

Not far from the Hessian soldiers were those who went to Tusket in the summers of 1784 and 1785. Many of these were of Dutch ancestry, descendants of the early Dutch families in America. They, as many others, were anxious to find good land and a good location in Nova Scotia. Among the Tusket grantees were two families, those of Dennis Van Tyle and Jacob Tooker, who came to Shelburne in November 1783 in Van Tyle's schooner *Cherry Bounce,* Captain John Gilchrist, master. They anchored in Robertson's Cove south of the town and built a log house on the shore. In the spring when the snow melted, revealing a land of rocks, they decided to go elsewhere, setting sail with 13 others for Yarmouth. Finding the land settled, they came back along the shores to Tusket where they found a site to their liking. Returning for their families, they arrived in Tusket on May 11, 1784. An association for the Tusket location was organized with Lieutenant-Colonel Abraham Van Buskirk and Captains Thomas Leonard and Nathaniel Richard agents for the associates, Richard Combauld, secretary, and Valentine Nutter, keeper of the subscribers' roll. By June 27 Thomas Leonard submitted returns for 86 families who had requested 200 acres each on the branches of the Tusket River, a total of 17,200 acres of land. In November, William Morris and Thomas Leonard surveyed the land and on January 16, 1785, 86 families requested warrants of survey for their lots of land of 200 acres each. A few weeks later the Associates met in Mrs. Lowrie's Tavern in Ann Street. They arranged for the escheat of certain lands that interfered with their proposed location, each Associate to share in the cost involved and each to receive land in proportion to his subscription. On a proposed road from Shelburne to Tusket River each subscriber was to receive 50 acres of land abutting and bounding the road for every 20 shillings subscribed or for work on the road at the rate of two shillings six pence per day per labourer. The fact that many subscribed for land in the Tusket location indicates that it was a favoured place for Shelburne Loyalists to go.[8]

Other groups of Loyalists and disbanded soldiers went to Prince Edward Island in response to a proclamation by Governor Patterson posted along the streets of Shelburne, offering land on the Island on the same terms as grants in Nova Scotia and in Quebec. By midsummer of 1784 four groups of Loyalists and disbanded soldiers were ready to sail for Prince Edward Island. In the first group to leave, which arrived on the Island on July 26 and settled in Bedeque, were several Loyalists, a number of men from the 17th Light Dragoons, and one soldier from the 37th Regiment: in all, 27 men, 10 women and 22 children. Later, on September 13, arrived 26 men, also with women and children; on September 19, came 55 settlers and on September 25, 12. Others went to the Island in 1785 and later. Among these

THE DECLINE OF SHELBURNE

were James Robertson, with his printing press, and Captain Robert Gray, mariner and master of the schooner *Lorence* until she was sold by her owners, George and Robert Ross.[9]

Numbers of both Loyalists and disbanded soldiers who left Shelburne remained in Nova Scotia, pushing along the shores to the villages settled by New Englanders – westward to Barrington and to Yarmouth; eastward to Liverpool. Some went to Chester and Lunenburg and Halifax; others were attracted to farm land in the Annapolis Valley. Still others went to New Brunswick.

Early writers portrayed the unhappy town at this time, with its disheartened settlers, its vacant houses, its empty streets, the stumps of trees still left in the ground. By 1787 there were 360 deserted houses. Two years later, two-thirds of the town was uninhabited. By 1791 it was considered that the decline of the town had reached its peak, leaving behind in its wake the few who had entrenched themselves in the town's economy. Long lists of absentee estates for the town and district of Shelburne were prepared. Those buildings with taxes unpaid were advertised for sale, and, when unsold, were ordered to be demolished by the firemen. Some stood in desolation for years with cattle and hogs roaming 'through parlours and wine cellars.' Strangers who stood beside the ruins 30 and 40 years later wrote of its grass-grown streets, its broken cellar holes, its wharves falling into the water, and marvelled that these ruins existed within a few years of their first erection – tragic proof that towns are not built without careful forethought and resolution.[10]

16
Epilogue

SOME WHO CAME AFTER 1783

As many hundreds of the Loyalists and disbanded soldiers left Shelburne for places better suited to their needs, others began to filter into the area to take up the land that they had vacated or to obtain grants of land still unassigned to settlers. These were neither Loyalists nor disbanded soldiers since they came mostly from across the sea – some from Scotland and some from Ireland, others from Wales. A few were from New England and some from other parts of Nova Scotia. Many came by chance, the wind and sea decreeing their destination. For most, there are few records as to when and from whence they came; for others, their coming is recorded only in family memories. From the few records that exist, from which these notes have been written, emerges a picture of a people who, in most cases, were resourceful and eager to accept the challenges of a new land and to acquire for themselves a sturdy independence founded on hard labour.

Among the first who came to Shelburne in this period were William and David McGill. They came from Scotland in 1784. William was a native of Straiton, Ayrshire; David, a native of Sutherlandshire. William, who was known in his church in Scotland as a young man who behaved 'soberly and honestly,' established himself as a tailor. He was later a shopkeeper and had a tavern. David McGill was a blacksmith with an interest in vessels and was part owner of the schooner *Margery*. They founded families who became substantial citizens as merchants, shipbuilders and shipowners, farmers and millowners.

EPILOGUE

Among the early settlers from Scotland was John MacKenzie, master weaver of fine linen from Inverness. Treachery brought him and his family to the shores of Shelburne County. Having lost three of their children in a diphtheria epidemic, John and Nancy MacKenzie, with their two remaining children, decided to go with a number of other families to Baltimore, Maryland. The first land sighted was the coast of Nova Scotia and when off the shores of Woods Harbour the captain anchored to replenish their drinking water. The passengers were told they could go ashore and when the puncheons were filled with water, boats would be sent for them. To their dismay no boats were sent and the ship sailed without them. Friendly French and Indians helped them to find their way to nearby villages. John MacKenzie with his family came toward Shelburne and found land at Green Harbour where he became a weaver and farmer. There is a tradition that with them came two other families, their surnames recorded as Firth and Fraser.

Lauchlan and Elizabeth McPherson came from Scotland in 1787. When they sailed from their homeland they intended to settle in Pictou. Stormy seas drove their ship to the south shore of Nova Scotia, where they made port at East Jordan. For a time they lived near Shelburne on land still known as "Lauchey's" and where, according to tradition, they planted the seeds of Scotch broom. Later they bought land at East Jordan where they farmed and fished and raised a family of twelve children. Two of their sons, John and Lauchlan, became able shipbuilders in East Jordan. Their daughter Ann, the wife of Hugh McKay, was the mother of the remarkable shipbuilding family of McKays, their son Donald being the builder of the great clipper ships, *Great Republic* and *Flying Cloud*.

In 1803 several families came from Scotland on the *Nelly Morrison*. Bound for an American seaport, she came into Shelburne harbour and fifteen families decided to remain as settlers in Nova Scotia. Their names are unrecorded except for William and Catherine McKay who were from Durness, Sutherlandshire. They found land to their liking on Hart's Point where William McKay established himself as a farmer, fisherman and mariner. Two of his brothers later came to Shelburne: Robert and his wife Janet in 1816, and James in about 1823. Robert McKay chose land on the west side of the Roseway River, a hill above two lakes now known as the McKay Lakes. Here he cleared land for a farm he called 'Kinlock' and cut and split staves for casks and puncheons. He built a sawmill on the falls of the Roseway a mile below his farm. When James McKay came from Scotland he was given land at Kinlock where he built a house on the site now occupied by one built later (about 1866) by Robert McKay's son, James.

Another Scot to settle in the Shelburne area in 1816 was Donald McKay, who became known as 'Barracks' McKay, from his living in a house on the barracks grounds, where, in 1819, he was granted a license of occupation to 200 acres of land fronting on Barracks Cove. He and his wife Ann and their first three children came from the village of Strathbeg in the parish of Durness, Sutherlandshire. Another Donald McKay from Strathbeg, who came about 1804, settled on the Clyde as a farmer and lumberman. His wife Catherine died on the voyage, three days from Shelburne, and was buried at sea. He later married Elizabeth Hamilton of Wood Hall on Clyde River, a daughter of James and Anna Hamilton. A Scot who may have come at the same time as Donald and Robert McKay in 1816 was David McKay, a native of Thurso, Caithness. He bought farm land on the west side of the Jordan River below the falls. He married Janet McPherson, a daughter of Lauchlan and Elizabeth McPherson. It is remembered that he spoke Gaelic by choice and English with a strong Scottish burr.

Among the early settlers from Scotland was Murdock McDonald who, it is believed, came about 1794 when he married Ann McKenzie of Little Harbour. He was a master mariner, captain of the brigantine *Addra* in 1800 and later was the sailing master of the privateer *Nelson*. Another Scottish settler in Little Harbour was Donald McDonald, a native of the Island of Lewis. Among other Scottish families was that of John and Elizabeth Martin. They came from Glasgow in the early 1790s. Others who came later were Alexander Bethune, and John and Ann Bethune from Sutherlandshire; John and George and Alexander Morrison who were also from Sutherlandshire; Margaret Neil Rae from Fifeshire; George Clarke from Montrose; Robert McIntosh, a native of Ross-shire, and Archibald McKenna who was a native of Galloway. Another Scot was Alexander Walker, a stonecutter who lived on one of the small islands in Shelburne Harbour still known as Sandy's Island. The Rev. Matthew Dripps, a native of Kilmarnock, came in 1803 as minister to the Shelburne Presbyterians. Shortly after his arrival, St. John's Kirk was built on the hill granted to the Church of Scotland in 1784. He was buried near the foundations of his church in 1828.

From Ireland came William Kean and John Quinlan. William Kean came, it is believed, sometime in the 1820s and married Sophia Ryer settling at Jordan Bay as a farmer and fisherman. John Quinlan first settled with his family in Pubnico where, in 1811, he was given 300 acres of land on Pubnico Harbour and 200 acres at Abuptic. He later came to Shelburne and settled on Long Island (200 acre lot no. 20) on the Roseway River overlooking Lake Deception. Here he cleared land for a farm, cultivated his meadow land for hay and cattle, and planted an orchard of apple trees from

EPILOGUE

The home of Samuel Marshall, potter and brickmaker, built 1783-1784. In more recent years it was the home of the Hon. Robert Irwin, Lieutenant-Governor of Nova Scotia from 1938 to 1940. (Photograph by Nancy Hart)

saplings he brought from Ireland. At least one settler was from the New England States – James Cox, a carpenter, who came to repair a Marblehead fishing schooner stranded at Ragged Islands. He settled in Shelburne and established himself as a carpenter, shipbuilder, and farmer, in 1802 marrying Elizabeth (Rowland) Hemeon. Their descendants became merchants, shipbuilders and shipowners. In deeds, census rolls and other records are the names of others who came to the area in the late 1700s and in the early 1800s, many of them from other parts of Nova Scotia. Among these are the names Ringer, DeMolitor, Harlow, Acker, Eisenhauer, Wolfe, Rudolf, Wentzel, Hupman, Seaboyer, Backman, Pentz, West.

THE FRENCH FROM ST. PIERRE AND MIQUELON

Some who came have left no record that any among them remained nor are there records of where they went when they left Shelburne. These were the French from St. Pierre and Miquelon. As the French Revolution continued the islands of St. Pierre and Miquelon were considered a menace to the British and were seized in May 1793 by an expedition sent from Halifax. Of the 450 persons evacuated from the islands in the spring of 1794, twenty-five to thirty families were sent to Shelburne. Governor Wentworth had chosen

Liverpool and the fishing villages of Port Mouton and Port Medway for their settlement and the Liverpool brig *Princess Amelia* was sent to bring them to Nova Scotia. On their arrival in Nova Scotia, the French wished to settle together as a community, and were sent on to Shelburne, followed a few days later by Governor Wentworth to arrange for their settlement. As 'sober, industrious, quiet and orderly' citizens and fishermen 'more skillful and industrious than the British Fishermen,' Governor Wentworth had great expectations that they would 'introduce a better mode of curing fish which will enhance its value and credit in all foreign markets.' Where Wentworth set aside land for the French within the district of Shelburne is uncertain. Only once are they mentioned in the town records. At a Court of Special Sessions held in October 1794, persons who had wounded one and molested others of 'the French people in this district' were arraigned in Court.[1]

THE WELSH SETTLERS

The story of the Welsh settlers, as remembered by their descendants, is of people seeking a better life in a new land. In Wales they were tenant farmers. Taxes were high. Even to have panes of glass in their windows they paid an extra tax. Some Welsh settlers had gone to Philadelphia and others decided to follow. In the spring of 1818 they set sail from Carmarthen in the brig *Fanny*. When well away from the land the captain bent their course to the northward. Unheeding the protests of those who knew better, he persisted on course until they sighted the shores of Greenland. Swinging to the southward they eventually made the port of Halifax.

We learn from surviving documents that they arrived in Halifax on the brig *Fanny*, Captain Pearson, master, on May 16, 1818, forty-two days from Carmarthen, with 112 persons aboard. Stricken with smallpox, they were held in quarantine in the Naval Hospital on Melville Island. With the sailing of the *Fanny* they were left in Nova Scotia. Fortunately for them, Governor Dalhousie was searching for suitable settlers for the vast unsettled lands in the province. On the staff of the Naval Hospital was a native of Shelburne whose name was recorded only as D. Rowland. He knew of uninhabited land near Shelburne. On the request of the Hon. Michael Wallace he offered his suggestions for the settlement of the Welsh. He proposed that they should be sent to Shelburne free from all expense to themselves. On their arrival they were to state the amounts of money they had brought with them to a committee appointed in Shelburne to superintend their settlement. Those not requiring relief would have a small proportion of land allotted to them above those in want of aid. They would be given food: rye, barley, Indian meal and oatmeal, pork and beef; and tools of

EPILOGUE

husbandry: axes, hoes, Irish shovels, common spades, tomahawks, and lines and hooks for fishing. If given permission, they could try to raise potatoes near the barracks for the indigent among them. Wallace recommended the Rev. Thomas B. Rowland be one of the committee of management and from among the Welsh he suggested that John Richards, Morgan Jeffreys, and John Davies 'be plac'd as the supreme of the new village.'[2]

The governor was impressed with Rowland's suggestions. He immediately arranged for the settlement of the Welsh and for their passage to Shelburne. In a note to Michael Wallace he offered his shallop to take the emigrants to the *Dee* and the *Wye*. 'The admiral has just been with me to say that the *Dee* and *Wye* will go to sea tomorrow and take the settlers from Wales if ready. I wish therefore that they be assembled at 10 o'clock at the Kings, or the Market Wharf, as you like, and my shallop shall take them off.' They were to be divided equally between the two vessels and were to carry their provisions with them. They were to be put down at Shelburne where they were to settle further arrangements with Mr. Campbell and the barracks master, for whom Richards had letters and an order for land from the surveyor general.[3]

With many of the Welsh still suffering from smallpox, they were unable to sail on the *Dee* and the *Wye*, and it was not until June 15 that they were mustered on board the schooner *Two Brothers*, Captain Jonathan Fowler, master, and were outward bound for Shelburne. With John Richards, Morgan Jefferys and John Davies as their managers, they were enrolled in family groups and as groups of individuals – 63 in all. On the list were:

John Richards, 40
Margaret Richards, 40
David Richards, 21
Elizabeth Richards, 19
Martha Richards, 17
John Richards, 15
Susannah Richards, 12
William Richards, 10
Henry Richards, 8
Rachel Richards, 6
Benjamin Richards, 3

Morgan Jefferys, 35
Ellenor Jefferys, 30
Morgan Jefferys, 10
Mary Jefferys, 8
Evan Jefferys, 6

Sarah Jefferys, 4
Ann Jefferys, 2

John Davies, 32
Anne Davies, 42
Phebe Davies, 7

William Davies, 50
Margaret Davies, 45
David Davies, 20
Mary Davies, 18
Ann Davies, 14
John Davies, 9
Margaret Davies, 20

John Owens, 34
Catharine Owens, 32
Anna Owens, 9

Ann Owens, 8
Sarah Owens, 6
Mary Owens, 2

David Thomas, 30
Nancy Thomas, 29
Ann Thomas, 11
Margaret Thomas, 9
John Thomas, 8
William Thomas, 6
Rachel Thomas, 2

Thomas James, 36
Rachel James, 32
Jonah James, 8
Sarah James, 6

John Thomas, 30
Esther Thomas, 28

Mary Thomas, 5
Margaret Thomas, 3

Evan Evans, 40
Maria Evans, 38
Rachel Evans, 14
David Evans, 10
John Evans, 12
Owen Evans, 4

William Davies, 22, Carpenter
Walter Thomas, 18, Labourer
Joshua Davies, 21, Blacksmith
David Powell, 21, Tailor
John Davies, Labourer
William Thomas
Sarah Thomas
Mary Thomas[4]

On the list were eighteen marked unable to sail on the *Two Brothers*. These were William and Margaret Davies and their five children; David, Elizabeth and Martha Richards; William Thomas, William Davies, carpenter, Joshua Davies, David Powell, John Davies, labourer; William, Sarah, and Mary Thomas. Others who came later in the summer of 1818 were William Morgan, carpenter, 20 years of age, and Llewellin Evans, farmer, 22 years old, Thomas Bulgin, David Jenkins, Jonathan Jones, Thomas Jones and Walter Thomas.[5]

With the Welsh went instructions to the four men in Shelburne (Gideon White, Jacob Van Buskirk, Colin Campbell and the Rev. Thomas Rowland) who had been appointed to assist them in their settlement. They were to have the use of the barracks for their temporary accommodation until land was laid out for them, and were permitted to use and plant 'for this season' the ground attached to the barracks. There were orders from the surveyor-general to his deputy-surveyor to locate the Welsh as nearly together as possible. The governor favoured their location on one end of Long Island, leaving the other end for the Indians and a licence of occupation to Bower for 50 to 100 acres contiguous to the house he had built. Along with the Welsh settlers were sent 'a few implements of Husbandry and a small quantity of provisions to prevent their being in distress on their landing, and until they can look out for themselves, but no further aid is to be expected from Government.'[6]

The provisions and tools ordered by the Earl of Dalhousie, on the advice

EPILOGUE

of His Majesty's Council, provided the new settlers with 100 bushels of potatoes, 6 bags of bread, 20 bags of oatmeal, 5 barrels of Indian meal, barrels of beef and pork, 176 pounds of cheese and 10 bags of salt. To clear their land and to build houses there were picks, felling and broad axes, field hoes, shovels, spades and carpenter's adzes. For the provisions and tools, empty barrels for potatoes, the truckage of provisions, tools, and the baggage of the Welsh from Melville Island to the *Two Brothers*, to John Richards for three days attendance collecting the settlers and stores, the government paid £116.3.7. To Jonathan Fowler for freight to Shelburne of passengers, baggage, and provisions was paid a further £23.5 for a total of £139.8.7.[7]

On their arrival in Shelburne, Richards, Jeffreys and Davies, as the managers for the Welsh, were taken to the barracks by the Shelburne committee appointed to assist them in their settlement. Deserted since the last soldier marched from Shelburne, the barracks were too wretched to live in and the land, overgrown with trees and bushes, was unfit for cultivation. Somewhere in the town accommodation was found for the Welsh. In August, when land was still not ready for them, they accepted an unused lot on the west side of the Roseway River opposite Navy Island until a location was surveyed and laid out for their settlement. Here they cleared small plots, built huts for the winter, and Richards planted seeds of rye and wheat. By October they were ready to move to the land offered them. It was then they realized that they had no licence of occupation confirming their right to the property. Although long idle, it had been granted to others and they could be pushed from their clearings. They appealed to the governor to give them 'under the hand of your Excellency' a document 'to guard and protect' us 'from all interuptions.'[8]

As they could neither live in the barracks nor plant potatoes in the barracks's grounds to eke out their provisions as the governor had anticipated, when they went to their winter huts their provisions were gone. Only John Richards could write understandable English. He appealed to Colin Campbell and others of the Shelburne committee: 'I beg to acquaint you our present distressed situation. Owing in one respect that we could not get our land in time to set potatoes but we have been here upwards of two months idling about the town till all our provisions was gone. Now we have been built our Huts and being oblig'd to buy all provisions which is very dear, owing particularly that we have no money to pay for it and indeed I am afraid that we could not get any more upon credit as we have had a deal of trouble to get some last week. The winter is coming on and we intend to move to the woods this week, but how to go without provisions with such large families.' He had himself managed to sow one bushel of rye and a little wheat. He had cleared enough land to sow three more bushels but had no

KING'S BOUNTY

money to buy seeds. He asked for provisions and seeds 'against the spring.'[9]

To emphasize the distressing needs of the Welsh settlers, Richards was sent to Halifax to ask for assistance. The Welsh had proved that they were sober, industrious and orderly in their behaviour as the governor had believed they were. If there had been land to till there would be no need for them to ask for assistance. The decision that they were to receive no further aid from government was rescinded. Colin Campbell was instructed to purchase 100 bushels of potatoes. From Halifax were sent two barrels of pork and Richards and his associates were granted £20 worth of provisions to be purchased in Shelburne. Thus, for the sum of £190.16.11 valuable settlers were enabled to establish themselves in the Shelburne area as competent farmers, woodsmen, and as skilled artisans.[10]

Land for Their Settlement

Shortly after their arrival, eager to see the land favoured for their settlement by the Earl of Dalhousie, the Welsh went with Robert Thomson, the surveyor-general's deputy-surveyor, up the Roseway River to Long Island. In his trim, leather-bound notebook, Robert Thomson recorded their day in the forest-covered land.

'Thursday 25 June 1818

Agreeable to instructions from the Hon. Charles Morris Surveyor General and on order from the magistrates of Shelburne I went with the Welch Emigrants to Long Island in Roseway River to survey the same and Employed John Swineburgh as a Pilot. At 12 o'clock noon rested at Welch Hill on said Island. 7 miles N by W from the south point of the Island in Company with the following.

	John Richards
	Morgan Jefferies
Welchmen	John Davis
	David Thomas
	John Thomas
	Evan Evans
	John Owen
	William Davies
	Walter Thomas
	John Swineburgh Pilot
	& myself Robt Thomson Deputy Surveyor.

Went round by the head of the Lake at the Upper or north end of the island. good land with a fine growth of maple, birch, oak and hemlock with some small ash.'[11]

The Welsh were pleased with Long Island. With the proposal that each

EPILOGUE

should have 200 acres of land to accommodate his large family, it was agreed that they should go with Robert Thomson to lay out the island in lots of 200 acres. They set out to do this on July 27. On reaching the island they found that the Indians on its upper end where the soil and timber were superior, had marked as their own 1,200 to 1,500 acres extending southward some four miles from the northern tip of the island. Although after sixteen years of living on the land, they had cleared and cultivated not more than three acres. The Welsh, afraid of Indians, refused to dispute their claim.[12]

On a rough pencil sketch of Long Island made in August 1818 is marked the land claimed by the Indians. This included all of the island north of a line which ran east and west approximately, near the southern tip of Lake Deception then known as Grand Lake. At the southern end of the island were the white inhabitants who were 'immical to the Welsh Emigrants settling there as it would in a great measure deprive them of many advantages which they have enjoyed viz. Hay and Timber for more than thirty years past.' Directly south of the Indians were four miles of hills which extended to the land which was occupied by Adam Bower, who had 'as much as 100 acres chiefly meadow but not wooded – the immediate space' having 'been burnt over in some places adjacent to the river.'[13]

Fearing the Indians and the hostility of the white settlers, the Welsh looked for another location where they could make a peaceful settlement. On the west side of the Roseway was land liable to escheat – lots four, five, and six, of 500 acres each. They would be glad to have this land, they assured the Shelburne committee, 'until other things be settled and we will take the remainder of our portion on Long Island.'[14]

Forwarding their request for land on the west side of the Roseway to the Hon. Michael Wallace and James Fraser, the committee explained the difficulties confronting the settlers. The Indians' intimidation of the Welsh had arisen 'from the bad advice of evil disposed persons.' They had sent for the principal man among the Indians 'but owing (we conceive) to the same Influence he has declined to come near us.' Three miles above Long Island on the east side of the river was a tract of land where 'the Indians would be content to remove, but they expect some renumeration [sic] for their improvements.' If the Indians remained on the island, the Welsh would not go there for they 'entertain the most horrid Ideas of the savage Dispositions of the Indians.' It would be desirable to remove the Indians to the land above Long Island, and with the Welsh on the island it 'would in a few years be in a very forward State of cultivation.' In the meantime, Richards and his associates wished for lots of land on the west side of the river. The governor was incensed. On the back of their letter he scribbled. 'I would have Mr.

Campbell to intimate to the Indians and white people who [are] on Long Island, that if they are not cautious in their conduct I will most assuredly remove every one of them from off those reserved lands' for 'it is my intention to place settlers on Long Island. In the mean while the Welsh may place themselves on the lots named.'[15] The governor was determined that at least part of their farm land should be on Long Island and Robert Thomson was sent up the river to survey and mark the lots. By late October, with the assistance of deputy-surveyor, Donald McKay, he had completed the survey of the island and had marked six farm lots of 200 acres each. These were for John Richards, lot no. 1, David Richards, no. 2, David Thomas, no. 3, Evan Evans, no. 4, John Owens, no. 5, John Thomas, no. 6. Five others of the Welsh settlers were to have 200 acres of land admeasured and laid out for each of them. These were Thomas Bulgin, David Jenkins, Jonathan Jones, Thomas Jones and David Powell. Two hundred acres on the south of the island were to be laid out for Adam Bower including his improvements. The lots were to be confirmed by grant 'to those who shall settle and cultivate their respective lots within the term of one year from this date 7th November 1818.' About this time the Rev. Thomas Rowland had a happy meeting with Joseph Loxy, chief of the Micmacs on Long Island. He was determined to hold the land occupied by the tribe, but was well-disposed and friendly toward the Welshmen. No longer afraid, 'the Welsh families are quite reconciled to settle near the Indians, who we have no doubt, will prove good neighbours.' The Indians were absent from the island when Robert Thomson marked the land for the Welsh. To set off their land on the northern end of the island from the Welsh settlers, he blazed a line across the island forty chains north of the Welsh. To the northeast of the Indians' land he reserved a meadow as a common for the use of the proprietors of the island.[16]

With the Indians no longer hostile, in early May 1819 John Richards and his associates began to work on their land. At the same time a number of the Welsh families, including John Richards, went up the bank of the Roseway to the lots of land, nos. 4, 5 and 6, promised them by the governor. Many settlers were clamouring for land, and the Earl of Dalhousie, in the spring of 1819, ordered an investigation of the areas adjacent to and bordering the rivers Jordan, Roseway, and Clyde which had been granted to individuals and were for the most part derelict and without cultivation. He ordered that unused acres be re-granted to the Welsh and other emigrants. To investigate the vast acreage of idle land, Donald McKay of Jordan Falls, formerly a non-commissioned officer in the 76th Regiment or McDonald's Highlanders, was engaged to view the tracts under process of escheat, to report their state under oath, and to furnish the necessary evidence required by

EPILOGUE

law on the day of trial.[17]

By the early fall of 1819 those who had gone up the west bank of the Roseway had spread north along the river from well below Courtney's Lake to and above the southern borders of Birchtown Lake (Welshtown Lake), a distance of three to four miles, and were waiting for the land to be escheated (reclaimed by the province). John Richards prepared for the governor a sketch of the lots they were interested to have for their settlement. They consisted of the nine 500 acre lots which included the lots no. 4, 5 and 6 which had been granted to a number of Loyalists for mill lots and farm land, and five 200-acre lots in Cameron's location contiguous to the nine 500 acre lots. With his sketch of Cambria Settlement (as the Welsh first called it) and his statement 'we want a great many more' lots, John Richards listed the Welsh already on plots of land and those waiting for allotments. On the list he gave their occupations in the Old Country:

John Richards, Farmer	Henry Thomas, Tanner and Glover
David Thomas, Carpenter	David Davies, Farmer
Evan Evans, Farmer	John Richards, Clothier and Fuller
John Thomas, Labourer	William Richards, Weaver
John Owens, Carpenter	David Rogers, Blacksmith
David Jenkins, Millwright, Carpenter and Wheelwright	Enos Owen, Carpenter
	John Richards, Jr., Farmer
Thomas Jones, Painter and Glazier	Samma Richards, Farmer
David Powell, Tailor	Henry Harris, Farmer
William Hitchens, Farmer	Samma Harris, Farmer
John Jones, Farmer	John Thomas, Carpenter
Hugh Jones, Farmer	John Thomas, Farmer
Thomas Jones, Mason	John Davies, Farmer
James Jones, Farmer	Samuel Davies, Farmer
Lewis Lewis, Shoemaker	John Evans, Farmer
Evan Owens, Cooper	Including children 104 in number
John Harris, Farmer	

Eleven of the settlers had cleared garden plots and had built houses. They were: Henry Thomas on lot no. 3; Evan Evans and David Thomas on lot no. 4; John Richards on lot no. 5; John Thomas and John Owen on lot no. 6; David Jenkins on lot no. 7; Thomas Jones on lot no. 8 near the northern end of Courtney's Lake; David Powell, John Harris and David Davies on lot no. 9. To the north of the 500 acre lots, on lot no. 2, Cameron's location, was David Horton's house. The houses stood, except Thomas Jones' and the house of David Horton, to the west of the road they had cut from Shelburne with the £90 the Earl of Dalhousie had requested the House of Assembly to allow them for a road to their settlement.[18]

With his sketch of Cambria Settlement, John Richards presented a memorial to the Earl of Dalhousie. It was a plea for assistance to push their road through Cambria Settlement on toward Annapolis. He had been up the Roseway River for upwards of 32 miles and the farther he had gone the better the land. If a road were opened there would soon be a strong farming settlement along the river, and 'in a short time Shelburne merchants would not be under the necessity of sending their dollars to buy Flour, &c to the United States.'[19]

On his return to Cambria Settlement John Richards discovered two of the Welsh families had left the community. It was soon rumoured that they all intended to leave 'had they money for the purpose,' and the governor's request for funds for their road was dismissed by the Assembly. Undismayed, in December the Welsh prepared a memorial to the newly arrived governor, Sir James Kempt. Among so many people, all were not perfect. If some had left 'that will never discourage any of us who work on the land, for by farming we mean to live.' But without a road it could not be expected that their settlement could thrive. They begged him to address the honourable representatives for money for their road, and to assist them to obtain the grants to their land which had been promised to them by the Earl of Dalhousie. The governor, impressed with their petition, recommended it to the Assembly. 'In the meantime,' he wrote, 'assure the petitioners that I shall give them all the assistance in my power.'[20]

By 1822 there were a number of changes in Cambria Settlement, by then known as New Cambria. Following the presentation by John Richards of his sketch of Cambria Settlement to the Earl of Dalhousie in 1819, the governor issued a warrant of survey to Charles Morris to admeasure and lay out lots of land lying and being on the Roseway and Birchtown Rivers to John Richards, 500 acres; David Davis, John Harris, Henry Thomas, David Thomas and David Jenkins, each 200 acres. On August 9, 1823, with the land surveyed and laid off into lots and substantial improvements made, Charles Morris requested the lieutenant-governor to issue the necessary warrants to have the properties confirmed to them by grants according to the intention of the government.[21] By 1822 there were others marked as settlers on John Richards' new map of New Cambria. These were: John Richards, Jr., William Richards, John Jenkins, David Harris, John Davies, and David Harris. Of the 1819 settlers, three were no longer living in New Cambria: Evan Evans, John Thomas and John Owens. The land where Thomas Jones, stone mason, had settled in 1819 had been claimed by Colin Campbell as the original grantee. In 1822 he was settled on land south of his first settlement and was next to David Jenkins. Thomas Jones, painter and

EPILOGUE

glazier, found land to his liking on the Roseway River south of Indian Creek. On March 11, 1822, he petitioned the lieutenant-governor for 200 acres on the east side of the Roseway River where he settled and gave his name to the lake near his homestead.[22]

In addition to their acreage in New Cambria, John Richards and David Thomas, to make up their full allotment, had lots on the east side of Birchtown River. The low land, some 34 acres lying where the brooks meet that flow from Birchtown and Western Birchtown Lakes (which they wished to have for its meadows) was divided among John Richards, David Jenkins, John Harris, David Thomas, David Davies and Henry Thomas. In 1825, 400 acres of land on Little Birchtown Lake (Gold Lake) were ordered to be surveyed for David Davies and John Harris, land described by John Richards as 'covered with good hardwood few Scatering Pine and Spruce back,' which they wanted for a sawmill they were erecting on Birchtown Creek. The first of the Welsh settlers to go up the road cut through the wilderness above New Cambria was David Horton. In 1827 he asked for a grant of 200 acres on Hemlock Creek. Later, in the late 1830s, Michael Davies and David Davies, sons of David and Mary Davies, whose sturdy house stood for many years in Welshtown, as New Cambria came to be called, cleared land in Upper Clyde and built houses in the fields they took from the wilderness.[23]

As the Welsh and a number of Scottish settlers spread along the banks of the rivers and creeks, farmland was opened to the plough and good timber was cut – pine and oak and hemlock – and floated down the streams on the spring freshets to the waiting mills. To these settlers the land was a challenge. They met it with the same fortitude that the early founders of Shelburne County, the Scots-Irish and the New Englanders, had shown when in the 1760s they established lasting communities and achieved economic stability through fishing and shipbuilding and by trade in local and distant seaports. The Loyalists who had tilled only the fertile land and the open fields their ancestors had cleared, or who had toiled in cities, were disappointed by the tree-covered, rocky land rather than inspired to carve personal independence from a forbidding environment. Despite the limitations of the soil, some of the Loyalists and disbanded soldiers did accept the challenge of the land. They settled along the lower courses of the rivers and along the shores and soon became self-sufficient citizens in their new homeland.

In the town itself, as many hundreds left for locations better suited to their way of living, or returned to their former homes, others took their places. Some were Scots, others were from New England and still others from the early New England settlements of Nova Scotia. As a result, the town slowly gained the stability it lacked when many dissatisfied people roamed its streets.

In the same way as the early settlers had established their economic independence, so those who were left, along with the more recent arrivals, developed trade and commerce, shipbuilding and the fisheries, and rebuilt Shelburne on a sure foundation.

Notes

1 PROLOGUE TO 1783

1. Silas Rand, *Micmac Place-Names in the Maritime Provinces and Gaspe Peninsula*. Ottawa, Geographic Board of Canada, 1919, p. 75; Silas Rand, *A First Reading Book in the Micmac Language*, Halifax, N.S., Nova Scotia Printing Co., 1875, p. 81; Marion Robertson, *Red Earth*, Halifax, N.S., Nova Scotia Museum, 1969, Introduction and note p. 84. The more recent interpretation of the Micmac name for Shelburne Harbour by old Mali, a Micmac Indian in her seventies in the 1950s.
2. Rand, *First Reading Book*, pp. 86, 90, 99. *Cobscooch* from local Micmac translation.
3. Public Archives of Nova Scotia (PANS), RG 1, Vol. 228.
4. Samuel de Champlain, *The Works of Samuel de Champlain*, Toronto, The Champlain Society, 1922-36, Vol. 1, p. 239.
5. Sable Bay (Bay de Sable), Barrington Bay.
6. Probably Green Island.
7. Lobster Bay. Champlain called it Baye Currante because of its strong tidal currents.
8. The Seal Islands, named Isles aux Loups Marins by Champlain, due to the number of seals found there.
9. The Mud Islands: Noddy, Mud, Round and Flat. Champlain called them Isles aux Margos for the gannets, from the French *le margot*, perhaps a corruption of the Micmac name for the gannet, *tadagoo*.
10. Nicolas Denys, on his roughly sketched map of 1672, has Port Rasoir located where Shelburne Harbour should be, with the land masses roughly indicating the shape of the harbour. Nicolas Denys, *Description and Natural History of the Coasts of North America (Acadia)*, Toronto, The Champlain Society, 1908.
11. It would seem that placing Port Jolly west of Rivière des Sables, instead of east, may have been an error of the mapmaker. Villebon, in his survey of Acadia in 1699, makes the same mistake, as does an English cartographer as late as 1755.
12. Public Archives of Canada (PAC) Report, 1905, Vol. 2, Appendix A, Part 3, p. 6.
13. Denys, *Description and Natural History*, footnote p. 342. W.F. Ganong writes the title 'Sieur de Rivedon.'
14. Round Bay River. Port Rochelois on the Carte de l'Acadie, 1703, marked the body of water lying between Port Roseway and Cape Negro.
15. William Inglis Morse, *Acadiensia Nova (1598-1779)*, London, Quaritch, 1935. Vol. 1, pp. 145, 149, 151, 155, 189. Census of Acadia by de Gargas, 1687-1688.
16. PANS, RG 1, Vol. 2, Doc. 48. Memoires sur l'Acadie et la Nouvelle Angleterre, Census 1693.
17. Joseph Robineau de Villebon, 'Last Journal send to Court Pontchartrain'; 'Memoir on the Settlements and Harbors from Minas at the Head of the Bay of Fundy to Cape Breton,' in J.G. Webster, *Acadia at the End of the Seventeenth Century*, Saint John, N.B., New Brunswick Museum, 1934, pp. 124, 134, 135.
18. Denys, *Description and Natural History*, p. 342.
19. Denys does not give a date for the establishment of Rivedon's fishery. His failure in the fisheries perhaps turned his attention to the land and he may have been the 'Sieur de Rivedu,' aged 58, listed as a farmer at Cape Negro in the census of 1671. Old apple trees near the Haul Over at Cape Negro were long known by the New England settlers and their descendants as 'the French apple trees.'
20. Villebon, 'Memoir on the Coast Fisheries of Acadia and the Method of Conducting

Them,' in Webster, *Acadia at the End of the Seventeenth Century*, p. 138. An excellent description of French fishing and curing of fish is found in Denys' *Description and Natural History*.
21 Villebon in Webster, *Acadia*, p. 139.
22 *Ibid.*, p. 128, 129.
23 *Ibid.*, p. 139.
24 *Ibid.*, p. 126.
25 Beamish Murdoch, *A History of Nova Scotia or Acadie*, Halifax, N.S., James Barnes, 1865-67, Vol. 1, p. 280.
26 *Ibid.*, p. 302.
27 *Ibid.*, p. 176.
28 Kermit K. Kingsbury, 'Hereabout and Thereabout,' *Worcester Sunday Telegram*. Undated clipping.
29 Mount Allison University Library, Bell Collection Cartes de l'Acadie, 1702, 1703, 1744; Joseph Bernard, marquis de Chabert de Cogolin, *Voyage Fair par Ordre du Roi en 1750 et 1751, dans l'Amérique*, Paris, Imprimerie Royale, 1753. De Cogolin marked two new place names on his chart south of Pointe de Bacareau: Baton (Bantam Rock) and Brezil (Brazil Rock), suggestive of a long lost tale of sailors in search of the mythical isle of Brazil with its treasure and fine brazilwood.
30 Thomas B. Akins, ed., *Selections from the Public Documents of the Province of Nova Scotia*, Halifax, N.S., Charles Annand, 1868, p. 49.
31 *Ibid.*, p. 57.
32 PAC, Adm. Lib. American, Vol. 2, Map No. 18. A Draught of Port Wager on the Sea Coast of Accadia in the Province of Nova Scotia, Survey'd in Anno 1734 by Capt. Thos. Durell. Was 'Port Wager' Captain Durell's rendering of 'Port Razoir'? Other words would seem to be a slip of the pen, or Captain Durell's poor spelling.
33 Akins, ed. *Public Documents of Nova Scotia*, p. 300. Orders and Instructions to Major Prebble by Governor Lawrence, Halifax, April 9, 1756, p. 300.
34 Captain John Knox, *An Historical Journal of the Campaigns in North America for the Years 1757, 1758, 1759 and 1760*, Edited by A.G. Doughty. Toronto, The Champlain Society, 1914, pp. 271, 277.
35 *Ibid.*, November 15, 1958, p. 275.
36 PANS, RG 1, Vol. 211, pp. 27-28. Minutes of His Majesty's Council, October 12, 1758.
37 Murdoch, *History of Nova Scotia*, Vol. 2, p. 359. Thomas Hancock to Governor Lawrence.
38 PANS, RG 1, Vol. 211, pp. 35-38. Minutes of Council, January 11, 1759.
39 *Ibid.*, pp. 133, 134. Minutes of Council, November 3, 1760.
40 It would seem that McNutt's rank was that of captain, but he became known as Colonel McNutt and was so referred to in a number of contemporary local documents.
41 W.O. Raymond, 'Colonel Alexander McNutt and the Pre-Loyalist Settlements of Nova Scotia.' In *Royal Society of Canada. Transactions*, Section II, 1912, pp. 201-215.
42 Akins, ed. *Public Document of Nova Scotia*, p. 473. General Amherst to Governor Lawrence, New York, April 17, 1760.
43 PANS, Akins Collection, Vol. 221, Doc. 5. Minutes of Commissioners for Trade and Plantations, Whitehall, February 27, 1761.
44 PANS, RG 1, Vol. 221, Doc. 6. Memorial of Alexander McNutt to the Lords of Trade and Plantations, March 16, 1762.

NOTES

45 Colonial Office (CO), Series 217, Vol. 18, pp. 305-316. Minutes of meeting of the Lords of the Committee of Council for Plantations, April29, 1762.
46 PANS, RG 1, Vol. 211, pp. 410-412. Minutes of Council, April 30, 1765. If the surveyor pinpointed correctly the site intended by McNutt for 'Jerusalem,' it was to be at the southern tip of Hart's Point. (PANS, N.S. General, 1766)
47 The small river that flows into Green Harbour.
48 PANS, RG 1, Vol. 374, Land Book 1760-66, p. 85. Halifax, October 3, 1765.
49 PANS, Crown Land Grants, Books 7 (old) 26; 7 (old) 122; 7:21, granted October 13 and 30, 1765.
50 PANS, Crown Land Grants, Book 6, p. 414, Halifax, October 15, 1765.
51 PANS, RG 1, Vol. 211, Minutes of Council, Halifax, April 30, 1765; Ian F. Mackinnon, Settlements and Churches in Nova Scotia, 1749-1776, Montreal, Walker Press Ltd., n.d.
52 Simeon Perkins, *The Diary of Simeon Perkins*, Toronto, The Champlain Society, 1948-1967. Vol. 1, October 23, 1766; PANS, RG 1, Vol. 221, Doc. 69, Isaac Deschamp, "Sketch of the Province of Nova Scotia."
53 PANS, Crown Land Grants, Petition of Agnes McNutt to Governor Parr, May 20, 1789; Shelburne Court House Records (SCHR), Map of land granted to the early settlers of Port Roseway, 1785.
54 Wellesley College Library, Wellesley, Mass., McNutt Genealogical notes, Rand Manuscripts; Perkins, *Diary*, Vol. 1; SCHR, Deed 3:534; Tax List, 1790.
55 SCHR, Location lists; SCHR, Deeds, 6:437, 6:538; Shelburne Court of Sessions Records, 1788, 1797; Map, 1785, *loc. cit.*
56 PANS, Supreme Court Records, 1768-1774, Doc. 11, pp. 1, 2, 3, November 12, 1768. For the £201.10s.8d. he owed, for want of goods, chattles, land and tenements, he was cast into jail in Halifax. In the opinion of the appraisers, John and William Giffin, and Henry Bush, the land of Jerusalem, wooded and cleared, was sufficient 'to satisfy the Execution.' Sometime prior to May, 1774, Jerusalem became the property of Benjamin Gerrish and was offered for sale at public auction at the home of John Rider in Halifax; *Nova Scotia Gazette*, May 17, 1774.
57 PANS, Crown Land Grants, Book 17 (old) 45; PANS, Supreme Court Records, 1768-1774, November 12, 1768; PANS, RG 1, Vol. 211, Minutes of Council, Halifax, April 30, 1765; Edmund D. Poole, *Annals of Yarmouth and Barrington (Nova Scotia) in the Revolutionary War*, Yarmouth, N.S., J. Murray Lawson, 1899, pp. 45, 46; Lexington, Virginia, Court House Records, Book of Deeds, A 1778-88, p. 135; Lexington, Virginia, Court House Records, Appraisal, estate of Alexander McNutt, Will Book 3, pp. 493-497.
58 Map, 1785, *loc. cit.*; Poole, *Annals*, p. 39; SCHR, Deeds, 5:89; 5:391.
59 Manchester, Massachusetts. Vital Statistics. She was the daughter of John and Sarah (Pearse) Tuck and the widow of Joseph Belcher.
60 PANS, MG 1, Vol. 957, Account Book, 1776-1778, White Collection, Doc. 1515.
61 Perkins, *Diary*, Vol. 1, September 8, 1779, June 21 and September 30, 1781; PANS, Crown Land Grants Book 17 (old) 71.
62 PANS, Crown Land Grants, Book 17 (old) 71; Crown Land Index Sheet, Map no. 19; Map, 1785, *loc. cit.*
63 *Alfred Alder Doane, The Doane Family and Their Descendants*, Salem, Mass., The Salem Press Co., 1902, pp. 69, 105; District of Shelburne, Assessment roll, 1786; SCHR, Deeds; Privately owned (P), Surveyors' papers, 1785; Perkins, *Diary*, Vol. 1, May 19, 1776, September 24, 1778, September 8, 1779, June 21, 1781; Map, 1785, *loc. cit.*

64 Edwin Crowell, *A History of Barrington Township and Vicinity, Shelburne County, Nova Scotia, 1604-1870*, Yarmouth, N.S., n.p., 1923, pp. 461, 462; SCHR, Deeds, 6:256, 5:263; PANS, Annual Report, 1936, 'List of ships entering port of Halifax, 1778-1781'; Poole, *Annals*, pp. 50, 104.

65 The exact location for many of the early settlers is difficult to determine. The term 'Port Roseway' was used to indicate the land bordering the shores of Port Roseway Harbour and along the shores westward to at least Round Bay. Point Carleton, in early Loyalist documents, was used to indicate roughly the area extending from a little below Birchtown to and including Round Bay. The brook was Roseway River and the area was known as Roseway River. As a more particular nomenclature developed, the area north of Point Carleton (Fort Point) became Churchover and Gunning Cove; south of the point became known as Carleton Village, the 'village of the old settlers,' and Roseway River became Roseway.

66 Crowell, *Barrington Township*, p. 479; District of Shelburne, Assessment roll, 1786; SCHR, Deeds, 4:316; 4:390; Map, 1785, *loc. cit.*

67 Poole, *Annals*, pp. 11, 104; Perkins, *Diary*, Vol. 2, August 19, 1781; District of Shelburne, Assessment roll, 1790; Ambrose Church Map of Shelburne County, 1882; Map. 1785, *loc. cit.*

68 F.E. Crowell, 'New Englanders in Nova Scotia,' *Yarmouth Telegram*, February 28, March 6, 1928; SCHR, Deeds, 2:383, 3:256, 6:448; Dalhousie University Archives (DUA), Naval Office Records, Port of Shelburne, 1801, 1815; (P) Account Book, Blacksmiths W. and G. McGill.

69 F.E. Crowell, op. cit., September 13, 1929; Poole, *Annals*, p. 8b; Naval Office Records, *op. cit.*, 1815, 1822; PANS, Annual Report, 1937, Appendix C, Ships entering port of Halifax, pp. 39, 41, 43, 45; SCHR, Deeds, 6:244, 6:257.

70 Perkins, *Diary*, Vol. 1, November 25, 1779, October 10, 1780, March 19 and June 21, 1781; SCHR, Deeds, 5:485, 7:244, 8:82; SCHR, Probate papers, A 229; PANS, Crown Land Grants, Book 17 (old) 71.

71 District of Shelburne, Assessment roll, 1786, PANS, MG 1, Vol. 957, Account Book, White Collection, Doc. 1515.

72 SCHR, Location lists; District of Shelburne, Assessment roll, 1786; Crown Land Index Sheet, Map No. 19.

73 Compiled from the first location lists of settlers, census returns (1787), assessment rolls (1786, 1787), Perkins *Diary* and early maps. There were, no doubt, many other early settlers whose names were lost through failure to list them as "old settlers" in the early records.

74 Perkins, *Diary*, Vol. 1, October 15, 1766; July 30, 1767.

75 Poole, *Annals*, pp. 49, 50; Perkins, *Diary*, several citations; PANS, MG 1, Vol. 957, Account Book, White Collection, Doc. 1515.

76 Poole, *Annals*, p. 45; District of Shelburne, Assessment roll, 1786; SCHR, Probate Records, A 182, appraisement of the estate of Ira Pride. Captain Pride died of smallpox at his home on February 2, 1828. He had taken a cargo to Halifax and was warned while there to be vaccinated. He refused, trusting to tobacco and camphor, according to a newspaper account at the time.

77 J. Robinson and T. Rispin, *A Journey Through Nova Scotia*, York, Etherington, 1774, pp. 48, 49.

78 Perkins, *Diary*, Vol. 1, August 22, September 5, 1779, December 5, 1781; Henry Alline, *The Life and Journal of the Rev. Henry Alline*, Boston, Gilbert and Deane, 1806.

79 PANS, RG 1, Vol. 212, Minutes of Council, June 16 and 20, 1775, p. 253; Order in

NOTES

Council, May 6, 1775.
80 Beamish Murdoch, *A History of Nova Scotia or Acadie*, Halifax, James Barnes, 1865-67, Vol. 2, pp. 558, 559.
81 Perkins, *Diary*, several citations; Poole, *Annals*, pp. 47, 104.
82 This is the only known instance where the early settlers of the Ragged Islands-Port-L'Hebert-Sable River area called their land the township of Hebron. Loyalist records refer to the area as Port Hebere.
83 Perkins, *Diary*, Vol. 2, December 19, 1781, June 21, 1782, June 17, 1783; PAC, MG 9, B 9-14, Vol. 1, Minute Book of the Port Roseway Associates, p. 64.

2 THE PORT ROSEWAY ASSOCIATES

1 Carleton Papers (CP), New York, May, 1782. David Mathews, mayor of New York, on behalf of the Inhabitants to Sir Guy Carleton.
2 Christopher Ward, *The War of the Revolution*, New York, Macmillan, 1952, Vol. 2, p. 895; CP, Whitehall, March 2, 1782, to Carleton; *Ibid.*, Letters Patent appointing Carleton and Digby commissioners of peace, March 21, 1782.
3 CP, Carleton and Digby to General Washington, New York, May 1782 (letter published in newspapers, August 2, 1782).
4 *Ibid.*, Address of the Associated Loyalists to Sir Guy Carleton, May 30, 1782.
5 *Ibid.*, Loyal Inhabitants and Refugees within the British lines at New York to Carleton and Digby, New York, August 10, 1782.
6 *Ibid.*, Carleton to General Campbell, New York, May 30, 1782.
7 *Ibid.*, Carleton to Hammond, New York, August 25, 1782.
8 PANS, RG 1, Vol. 45, Doc. 116.
9 PANS, RG 1, Vol. 136, p. 307.
10 PAC, MG 14, B 11, 1, (14), Minute Book, Port Roseway Associates, 1782-3, p. 25.
11 *Ibid.*, pp. 9, 26, 30, 72, 85, 86.
12 *Ibid.*, p. 27.
13 *Ibid.*, pp. 26, 29-31.
14 *Ibid.*, pp. 34-36.
15 *Ibid.*, pp. 37-40.
16 *Ibid.*, pp. 46, 47.
17 *Ibid.*, pp. 56-58.
18 PANS, RG 1, Vol. 369, Doc. 150.
19 PAC, Minute Book, pp. 59-66.
20 *Ibid.*, p. 71.
21 *Ibid.*, pp. 78-80.
22 *Ibid.*, p. 73.
23 *Ibid.*, pp. 72, 73, 87.
24 *Ibid.*, pp. 3-22, 83, 86, 88, 90, 92, 98.
25 *Ibid.*, pp. 81, 86, 88, 89, 91.
26 *Ibid.*, pp. 93, 94.
27 Murdoch, *History of Nova Scotia*, Vol. 3, p. 13; PAC, Minute Book, p. 96; University of New Brunswick (UNB), Winslow Papers, Benjamin Marston's Diary, Manuscript Document; PANS, RG 1, Vol. 170, Doc. 339, Orderly Book, October 31, 1768-1792; Crown Land Records, Halifax, Shelburne Portfolio, No. 5.
28 CP, Instructions to Lieutenant Lawson, New York, April 19, 1783.

29 PAC, Minute Book, pp. 88, 89, 92, 97; PANS, RG 1, Vol. 223, Doc. 3, List of Lieutenants.
30 PAC, Minute Book, pp. 98, 100.
31 *Ibid.*, p. 99
32 *Ibid.*, pp. 95, 96.
33 CP, Memorial, Officers commanding His Majesty's Provincial Regiments to Sir Guy Carleton, New York, March 14, 1783.
34 CP, Commanding Officers of Provincial Corps to Sir Guy Carleton, New York, March 15, 1783.
35 CP, Carleton to T. Townshend, New York, March 15, 1783.
36 Murdoch, *History of Nova Scotia*, Vol. 3, pp. 12, 15; CP, Lord North to Carleton, Whitehall, August 8, 1783.
37 For the settlement of the Blacks see Chapter 4.
38 CP, Orders from Headquarters, New York, April 15, 1783; *Ibid.*, Carleton to General Washington, New York, May 12, 1783; PANS, RG 1, Vol. 369, Dorchester papers, Doc. 194.
39 CP, Morgan to W. Elliott, New York, March 1783.
40 PAC, Minute Book, April 1783, pp. 91, 101-102. Port Roseway Associates to Sir Guy Carleton, New York, March 23, 1783.
41 CP, Carleton to Thomas Townshend, New York, April 12, 1783.
42 CP, Carleton to Parr, New York, April 26, 1783; *Ibid.*, Parr to Carleton, Halifax, May 7, 1783; *Ibid.*, Carleton to Washington, New York, May 12, 1783.
43 UNB, Winslow Papers, Vol. 22, Benjamin Marston's Diary, May 5, 1783; Murdoch, *History of Nova Scotia*, Vol. 3, p. 16; *Boston Gazette*, April 14, 1783.

3 ARRIVAL AND EARLY DAYS IN SHELBURNE

1 UNB, Marston's Diary, May 4, 5, 1783; PANS, Manuscript File, Shelburne (Founding), William Morris's Notes on the Settlement of Shelburne, May 4, 5, 1783.
2 Marston's Diary, May 5, 1783; CP, Returns of Loyalists gone to Port Roseway, undated; PAC, Minute Book, Port Roseway Associates, p. 97; PAC, MG 9, B 9-14, Vol. 1, Muster of Freed Blacks of Birchtown, 1784.
3 Morris, Notes, May 3, 4, 6, 1783.
4 Marston's Diary and Morris's Notes, May 7, 8, 1783.
5 Marston, May 9, 1783; Morris, May 9, 15, 1783; PAC, Minute Book, Port Roseway Associates, p. 96; Crown Land Grants Office, Halifax, Shelburne Portfolio, Map No. 5; *Ibid.*, No. 56; PANS, early map of Shelburne; PANS RG 20, Series C, Vol. 93, Docs. 5, 89.
6 Morris, May 14, 16, 1783; Marston, May 13, 16, 1783; *The Remembrancer*, London, 1874, Part 1, p. 376, Shelburne magistrates to William Affleck, October 9, 1783.
7 Morris and Marston, May 21, 1783; PAC, Minute Book, pp. 46, 71.
8 Marston, May 22, 24, 1783; Morris, May 21, 22, 24, 25, 26, 29, 30, 1783.
9 Morris, May 7, 16, June 20, 1783; Marston, May 24, June 8, 9, 1783; PANS, MG 1, No. 948, White Collection, Doc. 308.
10 CP, Returns of numbers gone to Port Roseway (undated); *Ibid.*, List of captains commissioned by Carleton, spring and summer, 1783; New Brunswick Historical Society *Collections*, Vol. 8, pp. 248, 249.
11 CP, Commissary Generals Returns.
12 Murdoch, *History of Nova Scotia*, Vol. 3, p. 9; PAC, CO, Nova Scotia MG 11, 1783, Parr

NOTES

to Nepean, Halifax, January 22, 1783, Paterson to Townshend, Halifax, January 23, 1783.
13 He is identified only as Colonel Hambleton by Pynchon and as Lieutenant-Colonel Hamilton by Carleton.
14 PAC, Minute Book, p. 66, Pynchon to Port Roseway Associates, Halifax, January 23, 1783; CP, Draft of letter ordering provisions, New York, March 4, 1783; *Ibid.*, F. MacKenzie to Brook Watson, New York, March 4, 1783.
15 Marston and Morris, several citations, June-October, 1783; PANS, RG 1, Vol. 170, Orderly Book, October 31, 1768-1792, p. 340. Early maps and charts of Shelburne and environs.
16 Marston and Morris, from their notes, June, July and August, 1783.
17 *Boston Gazette*, July 28, 1783; SCHR, Book of Memorials; Marston, August 8, 9, 1783.
18 Morris, June 4, 25, 1783; Marston, June 4, 26, 1783; PANS, MG 1, Vol. 948, White Collection, Doc. 210.
19 PANS, MG 1, Vol. 948, White Collection, Doc. 210, James Courtney to A. Cunningham, Port Roseway, July 1, 1783; PAC, Report, 1921, Appendix E., p. 361.
20 It has long been a tradition that the place appointed for Parr's reception was the house later known as the Firth House, believed to have been built by Andrew Barclay, and that he stood on the steps of the house when he named the town. According to the records, the house stood on water lot number 5, block A, South Division, drawn by Edward Brinley, the Commissary, a few days before Governor Parr's arrival. On November 12, 1783, Benjamin Marston, who lived in the house before its completion, wrote, 'Can tarry no longer at Brinley's; his house is so thronged with carpenters, work benches, &c, that I have no lodging room.' In 1802 Edward Brinley sold lot 5 with house and buildings to Michael Gordon, a trader and tavern keeper (SCHR, Book of Deeds, 5:353). In 1813 the property was purchased at a sheriff's sale by James Barclay. Another tradition about the house is that it was lived in by Lord Stanley, who, at the time he was supposed to be living in Shelburne, was the Secretary of State and writing letters in London. This would seem to be a confusion with the name Stanhope. Stanhope was a captain of His Majesty's ship *Mercury* and lived, while in Shelburne, in the house built by Brinley. (PANS, microfilm copy of manuscript history of Shelburne County, 1871, by Thomas Robertson, in King's College Library.)
21 Murdoch, *History of Nova Scotia*, Vol. 3, p. 18; UNB, Winslow Papers, p. 98, Edward Winslow to W. Chipman, July 7, 1783; Marston, July 20-22, 1783; PANS, RG 1, Vol. 169, Commission Book, p. 44.
22 CP, Parr to Carleton, Shelburne, July 25, 1783; PAC, Report, 1921, Appendix E, p. 362, Parr to Lord Shelburne, Shelburne, July 25, 1783.
23 PANS, MG 1, Vol. 948, White Collection, Doc. 264; PAC, Report, 1894, Parr to Nepean, Halifax, May 25, 1784; UNB, Winslow Papers, p. 142, S. Winslow to B. Marston, Halifax, October 18, 1783; Marston, May 22, 1783.
24 PAC, Report, 1894, Whitehall, July 1, 1783, to the Lord President of the King's Council *Ibid.*, North to Parr, July 24, 1783.
25 Marston, July 30, August 1, 1783; PAC, Report, 1894, Parr to Nepean, Halifax, April 11, 1784; *Ibid.*, Parr to Lord Sydney, Halifax, April 16, 1784.
26 CP, Parr to Carleton, Halifax, May 7, 1783; Murdoch, *History of Nova Scotia*, Vol. 3, p. 17; PAC, Report, 1894, Parr to Lord North, April 10, 1783 and October 21, 1783; PAC, MG 11, Colonial Office, Nova Scotia (CONS), 1783-1784, Account of Charles Morris.

KING'S BOUNTY

27 Marston, August 7, 10, 28, 29, 1783.
28 CP, Map of Shelburne, 1783, No. 10423.
29 CP, James Dole to Carleton, New York, September 19, 1783.
30 CP, Carleton to Elias Boudinot, August 17, 1783.
31 Murdoch, *History of Nova Scotia,* Vol. 3, p. 15; PANS, MG 1, Vol. 948, White Collection, Doc. 193; Wilbur Henry Siebert, *Loyalists of East Florida, 1774-1785,* Vol. 1, Deland, Florida State Historical Society, 1929, p. 134; UNB, Winslow Papers, p. 87, Sarah Winslow to Benjamin Marston, Halifax, April 10, 1783.
32 Siebert, *Loyalists of East Florida,* p. 210.
33 PAC, Report, 1921, Appendix E, pp. 362, 363, Parr to Lord Shelburne, Halifax, July 9 and October 25, 1783.
34 CP, Brook Watson to Major MacKenzie, New York, August 19, 1783; *Boston Gazette,* October 6, 1783; CP, North to Carleton, Whitehall, August 8, 1783.
35 CP, Returns of Loyalists going to Port Roseway and Returns of Commissions by Carleton; PAC, Provincial Records (Nova Scotia), MG 9, B 6.
36 *Manual of the Corporation of the City of New York, 1870,* cited by W.O. Raymond, 'The Founding of Shelburne,' New Brunswick Historical Society *Collections,* Vol. 8, 1908, pp. 251-252.
37 Marston, several notations, months of August, September and October, 1783.
38 CP, Memorials to Carleton and recommendations for grants of land in September, October, November, 1783; J.R. Campbell, *History of Yarmouth,* St. John, J. and A. McMillan, 1876, p. 87.
39 Allotted to: Block A: John McKinney, James Neal, Gideon Boyce, Daniel White, William Hargil, John Mason, George Whetton, Timothy Cain, Isaac Redman and Edward Johnson. Block B: John Dunn, John Aimes, Alexander Murray, James Robert and Robert Watts.
40 Lancelot Killigrove, Henry Killigrove, James Neal, Gideon Boyce, William Hargil, John Aimes and James Roberts.
41 PANS, RG 1, Vol. 223, Doc. 6, Admiral Digby to Parr, New York, July 4, 1783; PANS, RG 1, Vol. 394, Marston to C. Morris, Shelburne, September 20, 1783; Marston, October 2, 20, 1783; (P) Early Maps; County location lists; S. Hollingsworth, *Present State of Nova Scotia,* 2d ed., Edinburgh, Printed for W. Creech, 1787.
42 CP, Officers commanding Provincial Regiments to Carleton, New York, March 14, 1783; *Ibid.,* Carleton to Fox, New York, August 22, 1783.
43 CP, Officers of Provincial Troops to Carleton, New York, August 19, 1783.
44 CP, Carleton to Parr, August 22, 1783.
45 PAC, Colonial Office 5, Vol. 3, Returns Commissary General's Office; PAC, MG 9, B 6, Provincial Records (Nova Scotia - Shelburne).
46 Murdoch, *History of Nova Scotia,* Vol. 3, p. 12, Parr to Townshend, Halifax, February, 1783; CP, Lord North to Parr, Whitehall, May 5, 1783; Lord North to Officers commanding forces in Halifax, Whitehall, May 1783; Carleton to Fox, New York, August 22, 1783 and September 29, 1783.
47 CP, Carleton to Lord North, New York, October 6, 1783; *Ibid.,* Instructions signed by Adjutant General DeLancy, New York, September 9, 1783; *Ibid.,* Returns British Regiments going to Nova Scotia, New York, September 26, 1783; Returns of vessels transporting Loyalists and soldiers, New Brunswick Historical Society *Collections,* Vol. 8, 1908, Supplementary Appendix.
48 Marston's Diary and location lists and grants.
49 UNB, Winslow Papers, p. 238, E. Winslow to C. McEvers, Halifax, October 4, 1784;

NOTES

PANS, Land Papers, Memorial, G. Thomas and 14 others to Parr, Shelburne, April 6, 1784; Muster of Freed Blacks; Location lists; Thomas Raddall, 'Tarleton's Legion,' Nova Scotia Historical Society *Collections, Vol. 28, pp. 1-50.*

50 Seibert, *Loyalists of East Florida;* J. Leitch Wright, Jr. *Florida in the American Revolution,* Gainesville, University of Florida, 1975; CP, Brook Watson to Carleton, Commissary General's Office, New York, June 10, 1783; PANS, RG 1, Vol. 223, Doc. 110, Nova Scotia Government to William Campbell, Halifax, February 19, 1785; PAC, CO 217/14, B 1035, pp. 415, 423, Parr to Campbell, Halifax, May 3, 1785, J. York to Campbell, Halifax, May 4, 1785, Campbell to Lord Sydney, Halifax, May 4, 1785; *Port Roseway Gazetteer,* May 26, 1785, *Royal American Gazette,* August 1, 1785.

51 CP, Returns, Loyalists &c, gone to Nova Scotia, Commissary General's Office, New York, October 12, 1783; PAC, CO, Vol. 3; PAC, MG 23, B 1, Vol. 3, Returns, Commissary General's Office; PAC, MG 9, B 9-14, Vol. 1, Victualler's list; PAC, MG 9, B 6, Territorial Records, Nova Scotia, Muster of 1784.

52 PAC, Minute Book, Port Roseway Associates, p. 94; UNB, Winslow Papers, p. 108, Carleton to General Fox, New York, July 18, 1783.

53 CP, Brook Watson to Carleton, New York, June 10, 1783.

54 Crown Land Grants Office, Halifax, N.S., Map of Shelburne, No. 3; Acadia University Library, 208673 #6, William Booth, 'Rough Notes and Memorandums, 1789'; CP, Brook Watson to Major MacKenzie, New York, July 22, 1783; CP, Report, contracts for flour, November 22, 1783; PAC, CO, B 1035, Returns, Colonel Campbell, Halifax, December 25, 1783; PAC, MG 9, B 9-14, Col. 1, p. 208, Victualler's returns, January 8, 1784.

55 PAC, CO 217/14, B 1035, Ration returns, Campbell, December 25, 1783; *Ibid.,* General returns, muster masters, 1784, 1785; *Ibid.,* Campbell to London, December 18, 1783; *Ibid.,* Proclamation, Halifax, March 31, 1784; PAC, Report, 1894, Sydney to Campbell, Whitehall, June 7, 1784.

56 PAC, CO 217/14, B 1035, Campbell to Whitehall, Halifax, February 28, 1784; PAC, Report, 1921, Appendix E, p. 364, Parr to Lord Shelburne, Halifax, March 22, 1784; *Royal American Gazette,* January 31, 1785; (P) Letter Book, Joshua Watson to Hale, New York, October 10, 1785; PAC, MS Group 14, B 11, Series 1-14D, Memorial, Shelburne merchants to Parr (undated); PAC, CONS, MG 11, 1783, Alexander Leckie to B. Watson, Shelburne, May 1785; PAC, Report, 1894, Shelburne magistrates to Parr, Shelburne, September 8, 1785; *Nova Scotia Packet,* August 17, 1786.

4 THE FREED BLACKS

1 National Library, Ottawa, Ont. Proclamation by Sir Henry Clinton, Phillipsburg, Pa., June 30, 1779, *The Royal Gazette,* July 31, 1779, microfiche; CP, Carleton to Washington, New York, May 12, 1783; PAC, MG 9, B 9-14, Vol. 1, Muster of Freed Blacks of Birchtown, 1784.

2 Proclamation, *op. cit.*

3 Boston, King, 'Memoirs,' *The Methodist Magazine,* April, 1798; SCHR, Shelburne General Sessions, July 1791; Thomas Jones, *History of New York During the Revolutionary War,* New York, N.Y. Historical Society, 1879. Vol. 2, p. 256.

4 Boston King, 'Memoirs.'

5 CP, Petition of the Inhabitants of Norfolk and Princess Ann Counties to Carleton, April 28, 1783; *Ibid.,* Carleton to Washington, New York, May 12, 1783.

6 CP, Lord North to Carleton, Whitehall, August 8, 1783.

7 *Ibid.*, Headquarters, New York, April 15, 1783, signed by O. DeLancey, Adjutant-General.
8 PAC, Muster of Freed Blacks of Birchtown, 1784; PANS, MG 1, Vol. 948, White Collection, Doc. 196.
9 PANS, RG 1, Vol. 423, Extracts from the Dorchester papers relating to the blacks.
10 PAC, CP, No. 1, MG 23, B 1, Vol. 12.
11 PAC, Muster of Freed Blacks, 1784; *The Independent Chronicle and the Universal Advertiser*, Boston, May 8, 1783. See lists of ships and the Loyalist Companies that included blacks, Appendix A, p. 202.
12 PAC, Muster of Freed Blacks, 1784.
13 PAC, Report, 1921, Appendix E, p. 3; PANS, RG 1, Vol. 136, p. 320, Bulkeley to J. Pynchon, Halifax, August 15, 1783; *Ibid.*, p. 321, Bulkeley to Pynchon, Halifax, August 19, 1783. Although only one black, Joseph Restine, is known to have received a grant of land in the town, the Black Quarter referred to by Governor Parr may have been the block of land on Harriot Street (Letter L, North Division) in which Restine was given his town lot.
14 Marston, August 27, 28, 1783; PANS, RG 1, Vol. 423.
15 Acadia University Library, 208673 # 6, Manuscript Document, Capt. William Booth, 'Rough Notes and Memorandum, March 14, 1789'; PAC, Muster of Freed Blacks, 1784; PANS, RG 1, Vol. 169, 1781 to 1792, p. 103, Commission appointing Stephen Bluck, Lieutenant Colonel.
16 Marston, August 30, September 1, 1783; Boston Kin, *op. cit.*
17 PAC, Map Division, H 3/240 [1783] Shelburne; Crown Land Grants Office, Halifax, Shelburne Portfolio, Maps 25, 37, 38; (P) Map of early Shelburne area; PAC, Map 240, Shelburne, 1785; Marston, September 7, 19, 1785.
18 PAC, Muster of Freed Blacks, 1784.
19 *Ibid.*
20 CP, Lt. Colonel Morse to Brigadier General Fox, Halifax, August 23, 1783; PAC, Report, 1884, 'Report on Nova Scotia by Col. Robert Morse, R.E., 1784'; SCHR, Court of General Sessions, September 2, 1784.
21 Marston, July 26, 27, 1784.
22 William Dyott, *Dyott's Diary*, Reginald W. Jeffery, ed. London, Constable, 1907, Vol. 1, p. 57.
23 Boston King, 'Memoirs.'
24 Aul, Booth, 'Rough Notes', March 14, 1789; Boston King, *op. cit.*
25 SCHR, Special Sessions, July, 1788; PAC, MG 9, B 6 (1), Memorial, Overseers of the Poor, Shelburne, February 3, 1789.
26 SCHR, General Sessions, April 12, 1802, April 10, 1786.
27 SCHR, General Sessions, November 1, 1791; Special Sessions, August 21, 1788, April 21, 1800.
28 PANS, RG 1, Vol. 136, Letter Book, 1760-1784, Secretary's office to Shelburne magistrates, Halifax, August 19, 1783; Shelburne Court Records, 1786; SCHR, General Sessions, April 6, 1784; SCHR, Special Sessions, September 8, 1785.
29 PAC, Muster of Freed Blacks, 1784; Perkins, *Diary*, December 20, 1783; PANS, MG 4, Doc. 141. T.W. Smith, 'History of Shelburne County,' manuscript.
30 PAC, Muster of Freed Blacks, 1784, p. 195, 196; *Port Roseway Gazetteer*, August 11, 1785; Aul, Booth, 'Rough Notes,' June 2, 3, 1789.
31 SCHR, General Sessions, November 2, 1791; PAC, MG 9, B 9-14, Will, Thomas Robinson; Nova Scotia Historical Society *Collections*, Vol. 10, p. 62.

NOTES

32 CP, Memorial, David Hurd to Carleton (undated); SCHR, General Sessions, July 5, 1791; (P) Letter Book, George and Robert Ross, June 3, 1789; *Nova Scotia Packet*, November 6, 1786.
33 SCHR, General Sessions, April 5, July 7, 8, 11, 19, November 4, 1791.
34 SCHR, Special Sessions, August 25, 1785; General Sessions, April 12, 1786.
35 SCHR, Special Sessions, May 12, 19, 1785; Special Sessions, May 31, August 9, 1786; Special Sessions, June 17, 1789; Special Sessions, July 8, 1795.
36 SCHR, Special Sessions, August 25, 1785; Special Sessions, September 6, 1786.
37 SCHR, General Sessions, November 3, 6, 1784; April 14, 1789; Quarter Sessions, August 19, 1820; Special Sessions, June 16, August 11, September 29, 1785.
38 SCHR, Special Sessions, February 24, August 4, 1785, May 31, June 4, 1786, January 31, 1787.
39 'An Account of the Life of David George as Given by Himself,' J. Rippon, *Baptist Annual Register, 1793-1802*, Vol. 1, pp. 473-483.
40 Boston King, *op. cit.;* PANS, Vertical File, Anthony Kirk-Greene, 'David George; the Nova Scotian Experience,' p. 117; (P) Document relative to the Rev. John Morrant; T.W. Smith, *History of the Methodist Church of Eastern British America*, Halifax, N.S., Methodist Book Room, 1877-90, p. 144.
41 New Brunswick Historical Society *Collections*, Vol. 8, p. 284, 289.
42 Minutes of the Associates of the Late Doctor Bray and letters in the files of the Associates under dates from February 3, 1785 to November 17, 1813, used with the courteous consent of the Associates of the Late Doctor Bray; PANS, Bulletin, Vol. 1, No. 1, p. 34, Report, Schools, Shelburne District, 1824. Thomas Bray, a son of Thomas and Mary Bray, was born in Marton, England, near the Welsh border hills, in 1658. He studied at Oxford and at other universities and was ordained a clergyman in 1682. In 1690 he was appointed rector of Sheldon where he began the writing of his *Catechitical Lectures* which brought him renown as a scholar. He was appointed by the Bishop of London as his commissary in Maryland where he became aware of the unhappy plight of the Blacks. He devoted many years to the welfare and education of the poor and distressed, to the improvement of prisons, the reformation of prostitutes, to the founding of parochial and lending libraries in England and in the colonies, and to the establishment of schools for the education of the poor and for religious instruction of Blacks in America. He was the founder of the Society for the Propagation of the Gospel and the Society for Promoting Christian Knowledge. In 1723 he was bequeathed £900 by Abel Tassin, Sieur D'Allone, for the instruction of the Blacks in the British Plantations. To administer the trust he founded the Bray Associates, known after his death as the Associates of the Late Doctor Bray. (H.P. Thompson, *Thomas Bray*, London, SPCK, 1954)
43 PAC, Colonial Correspondence of New Brunswick (CCNB), Vol. 3, Memorial, Thomas Peters, enclosed in dispatch No. 15, Dundas to Carleton, August 6, 1791.
44 PAC, CO, 217/63, Dundas to Parr, Whitehall, August 3, 1791.
45 PANS, Publication No. 11, Charles Bruce Fergusson, *Clarkson's Mission to America, 1791-1792*, pp. 34, 35.
46 *Ibid.*, p. 40. Stephen Bluck to Lawrence Hartshorne, Birchtown, October 10, 1791.
47 *Ibid.*, pp. 42, 51, 53, 61.
48 *Ibid.*, pp. 35, 53, 54.
49 *Ibid.*, p. 56.
50 *Ibid.*, pp. 56, 57.
51 *Ibid.*, p. 60.

KING'S BOUNTY

52 *Ibid.*, pp. 65, 66, 71; *Royal Gazette,* November 22, 1791.
53 Fergusson, *Clarkson's Mission to America,* pp. 101, 102, 104, 107.
54 *Ibid.*, pp. 102, 125, 149; PAC, CONS, Vol. 21, p. 448.
55 PAC, MG 11, CO 217, Nova Scotia A, Vol. 116. The return of the Blacks going to Sierra Leone as listed by Stephen Skinner included: 84 farmers, 19 carpenters, 5 masons, 12 sawyers, 2 blacksmiths, 3 coopers, 1 pilot, 1 sailor, 3 caulkers, 1 baker, 1 barber, 12 labourers, 1 shoemaker, 1 blockmaker, 1 tailor, 1 saddler, 1 weaver, 5 preachers, three of whom were listed only under the occupation in which they earned their living. In the group were 58 soldiers, a corporal and a captain, evidently members of Colonel Bluck's militia, and three who had served in the corps of Black Pioneers. Some had axes, hoes, saws, spades and boxes of tools to take to their new farms in Sierra Leone; a few had muskets. Some families had a bed and a blanket, a table and a chest or two; some women had spinning wheels. Some dogs went with their masters due to the kindly affection Clarkson felt for the bond between a master and his dog. David George's dog went with him and with Stephen Trickley were a dog and a puppy.
56 Anthony Kirk-Greene, *David George,* pp. 112-115.
57 PANS, CO 217/63, Dundas to Bulkeley, Whitehall, January 15, 1792.
58 PAC, Colonial Correspondence of Nova Scotia (CCNS), Vol. 21, p. 430, Stephen Skinner to Dundas, Halifax (no date); PANS, MG 1, Vol. 950, Doc. 560.
59 PAC, MG 11, CO 217, Nova Scotia A, Vol. 116, p. 293. Bluck to Governor Parr, Birchtown, November 1, 1791.
60 PAC, CONS, Vol. 21, p. 286. Governor Wentworth to the King, Halifax, September 12, 1792.
61 SCHR, Quarter Sessions, April 12, 1802.

5 THE MILITARY

1 CP, Instructions to Lieutenant Lawson, New York, April 19, 1783.
2 *Ibid.*, Carleton to General Washington, New York, May 12, 1783; *Ibid.*, Carleton to General Paterson, New York, April 26, 1783.
3 CP, Carleton to officers of His Majesty, New York, August 1, 1783; UNB, Winslow Papers, p. 108, Carleton to Brigadier General Fox, New York, July 18, 1783; New Brunswick Historical Society *Collections,* Vol. 8, p. 245, E. Winslow to B. Marston, Halifax, May 30, 1784; PANS, Manuscript File, Shelburne (Founding), W. Morris, surveyor's notes.
4 PAC, H 3/240, Chart, Port Roseway Harbour, 1784; PAC, H 3/240, Map, Shelburne, 1785; Crown Grants Office, Halifax, Index Sheets 18, 19; Crown Land Records, Shelburne Portfolio, No. 1.
5 PAC, Report, 1884, Col. Robert Morse, 'Report, 1784.'
6 PANS, Report, 1934, p. 50. Booth, 'Journal on a Tour with General Campbell, 1785.'
7 PANS, RG 20, Series C, Vol. 93, No. 43, Plan of Point Carleton, 1786, by Robert Morris.
8 UNB, Winslow Papers, p. 122, General Fox to Carleton, Halifax, August 15, 1783; Locations, Marston's Division; PAC, Report, 1884, Col. Robert Morse, 'Report, 1784'; Crown Land Grants Office, Halifax, Shelburne Portfolio, Map of barracks, No. 3; PANS, Report, 1934, p. 49; AUL, Booth, 'Rough Notes,' November 26, 1789; PAC, CO 217/41, B 1035, General Campbell, Halifax, June 15, 17, 1784.

NOTES

9 Dyott, *Diary*, p. 56; PAC, CO 217/41, Campbell to Sydney, Halifax, September 28, 1786; PANS, Report, 1934, p. 49; AUL, Booth, 'Rough Notes,' April 23, 1789.
10 PAC, Report, 1894, General Campbell to Lord Sydney, Halifax, July 11, 1786; Dyott, *Diary*, Vol. 1, pp. 56, 57.
11 *Nova Scotia Packet*, November 9, 1786; *Royal American Gazette*, June 2, June 13, 1785; SCHR, Court of Special Sessions, September 20, 1786, July 19, 1790.
12 SCHR, Special Sessions, July 28, 1785; General Sessions, May 6, 1788, April 16, 1789; AUL, Booth, 'Rough Notes,' January 23, July 3, October 7, 18, 1789; *Nova Scotia Magazine*, 1791; Tombstone, Christ Church burial ground, Shelburne, N.S.
13 AUL, Booth, 'Rough Notes,' June 22, 1789; General Sessions, July 8, 1791.
14 CP, Carleton to T. Townshend, New York, March 15, 1783; Shelburne Magistrates to W. Affleck, Shelburne, October 9, 1783, *The Remembrancer*, Vol. 1, p. 376; UNB, Winslow Papers, p. 150, Sarah Winslow to B. Marston, Halifax, November 29, 1783.
15 PANS, RG 1, Vol. 223, Doc. 174, Naval Reserves; PANS, RG 1, Vol. 49, Commissioners of the Navy, Halifax, October 8, 1784.
16 PAC, Report, 1884, Col. Robert Morse, 'Report, 1784.'
17 PANS, MG 1, Vol. 949, Doc. 405; *Ibid.*, Vol. 950, Docs. 576, 578; PANS, RG 1, Vol. 49, Wentworth to Commissioner of the Navy, Halifax, October 8, 1784; Dyott, *Diary*, p. 56; PAC, CCNS, Vol. 18, p. 239, Vol. 19, p. 230 and Vol. 20, p. 281; SCHR, Address, Shelburne Magistrates and Citizens to Sir Richard Hughes, Shelburne, October 4, 1791.
18 PAC, Minute Book, pp. 88, 89; PANS, RG 1, Vol. 171, Military Commissions, 1787-1793; SCHR, Court of Quarter Sessions, September 2, 1784; *Nova Scotia Packet*, September 28, 1786; PANS, MG 1, Vol. 959, Doc. 1555; Henry Edward Napier, *Journal*, Salem, Mass., Peabody Museum, 1939, p. 50.

6 BUILDING THE TOWN

1 PANS, MG 1, Vol. 948, White Collection, Doc. 210, J. Courtney to A. Cunningham, Port Roseway, July 1783; New Brunswick Historical Society *Collections*, Vol. 8, p. 254, Parr to Shelburne, Halifax, December 16, 1783; *Ibid.*, p. 268, Marston to I. Mauduit, September, 1784.
2 Campbell, *History of Yarmouth*, Letter, Mrs. Van Tyle, p. 87; PAC, Report, 1884, Col. Robert Morse, 'Report, 1784'; Fergusson, *Clarkson's Mission*, p. 50; Rippon, *Baptist Annual Register*, Vol. 1, pp. 473-483.
3 Perkins, *Diary*, Vol. 2, May 28, 1783; New Brunswick Historical Society *Collections*, Vol. 8, p. 270, Marston to I. Mauduit, September, 1784; PANS, RG 1, Vol. 49, pp. 1-3, Wentworth to Portland, Halifax, October 21, 1783.
4 CP, Lord North to Parr, Whitehall, May 5, 1783; PAC, Report, 1894, Parr to North, Halifax, November 20, 1783; PAC, CCNS, Vol. 20, p. 346, Alexander Leckie to an unknown recipient, Threadneedle Street, London, March 16, 1790; AUL, Booth, 'Rough Notes,' March 3, 1789; (P) Alexander Houston, Notebook; PANS, MG 1, Vol. 948, Doc. 308; *Royal American Gazette*, January 24, 1785.

7 DISTRIBUTION OF THE LAND

1 PAC, Report, 1921, Appendix E, p. 361, Parr to Lord Shelburne, Halifax, January 24, 1784.
2 PANS, Shelburne Box of Documents, Letter written by Marston, Shelburne, January

2, 1784; PANS, RG 1, Vol. 223, Docs. 41, 42, Marston to Parr, May 4, 17, 1784; (P) Alexander Houston, Notebook.
3. SCHR, Shelburne Magistrates to Parr, May 3, 1784; *Ibid.*, Alpin and Clarke to Shelburne Magistrates, May 13, 1784.
4. PAC, Report, 1921, Appendix E, pp. 363, 365, Parr to Lord Shelburne, Halifax, October 25, 1783, March 22, 1784; SCHR, Memorial, B. Davis to Shelburne Magistrates, Shelburne, July 23, 1784.
5. PANS, Shelburne Box, Letter by Marston, January 2, 1784; Marston's Diary, May 18, 1784; (P) Houston, Notes; PANS, MG 1, Vol. 939, Doc. 50, Wentworth Papers, Pynchon to Wentworth, Shelburne, May 19, 1784.
6. Murdoch, *History of Nova Scotia*, Vol. 3, p. 32; PAC, CO 217/41, B 1035; SCHR, Memorial, B. Davis, Shelburne, July 23, 1784.
7. Perkins, *Diary*, July 29, August 2, 1784; Marston, July 26, 1784; SCHR, Court of Quarter Sessions, April 6, August 5, 1784.
8. PAC, Report, 1921, Appendix E. p. 368, Parr to Lord Shelburne, Halifax, August 13, 1784; Marion Gilroy, *Loyalists and Land Settlement in Nova Scotia*, PANS, Publication No. 4, pp. 146-153.
9. SCHR, J. Alpin and J. Clarke to Shelburne Magistrates (undated); PANS, RG 1, Vol. 170, Orderly Book, October 31, 1768 to 1792, pp. 369-378.
10. PANS, CO 217/35, pp. 32-114, Instructions.
11. PANS, MG 1, Vol. 948, White Collection, Doc. 308.
12. *Ibid.;* PANS, RG 1, Vol. 136, pp. 342-343, Parr to Sir Charles Douglas, Halifax, August 31, September 2, 1784; CP 217/41 B 1035, Campbell, Military Dispatch, August 26, 1785; Marston, August 31, 1784, PAC, General Sessions, November 5, 1784.
13. PAC, Report, 1921, Appendix E, p. 364, Parr to Lord Shelburne, Halifax, January 24, 1784; PAC, Report, 1894, Parr to Sydney and Parr to Nepean, Halifax, May 12, 1784.
14. (P) Locations returns; SCHR, Location lists; Map, Murray location; Crown Land Grants Office, Halifax, Index sheets, Nos. 18, 19; PAC, MG 9, B6, Territorial Records; *Royal American Gazette*, January 24, April 4, 1785.
15. *Port Roseway Gazetteer*, January 24, June 9, 1785; Gilroy, *Loyalists and Land Settlement;* SCHR, Court of General Sessions, April 7, 1784.
16. *Port Roseway Gazetteer*, March 31, 1785; PAC, Shelburne Papers, Parr to Lord Shelburne, Halifax, September 28, 1785.

8 THE COURTS OF SESSIONS AND THE COURTS OF JUSTICE

1. PAC, Minute Book, pp. 39, 40, 89.
2. Observations by Marston and Morris.
3. SCHR, Oath of Allegiance, July 22, 1783; PANS, RG 1, Vol. 169, p. 44; RG 1, Vol. 136, pp. 320-321, Provincial Secretary to J. McEwen and J. Pynchon, Halifax, August 19, 1783; *Ibid.*, Parr to Shelburne Magistrates, Halifax, October 3, 1783.
4. Perkins, *Diary*, Vol. 2, September 15, 1783; PANS, RG 5, Vol. 6, Statutes 1780-1785; C. Bruce Fergusson, *Local Government in Nova Scotia*, PANS, Bulletin No. 17.
5. PANS, RG 1, Vol. 169, pp. 59, 60, 61, 66; SCHR, Oath of Allegiance; PAC, Nova Scotia Local Records, HG 9, B 9-14, Shelburne, N.S.; SCHR, Court of General Sessions, March 30, April 3, 6, 1784.

NOTES

6 SCHR, Court of General Quarter Sessions, *op. cit.;* Court of Special Sessions.
7 SCHR, Special Sessions, February 6, March 12, 15, 1786; PAC, Shelburne, N.S. Records, Court of General Sessions, Hg 9, B 9-14, March 29, April 10, 11, 1786.
8 PANS, RG 5, Series S, Vol. 6, Act of the House of Assembly, Statutes of Nova Scotia, 1780-1785; SCHR, Oath of Allegiance.
9 PANS, Letter Book, 1760-1784, No. 136, p. 343; *Nova Scotia Packet*, November 9, 1786.
10 CP, Dole to Carleton, New York, September, 1783; PANS, RG 1, Vol. 136, Bulkeley to Shelburne Magistrates, Halifax, August 19, 1783; SCHR, General Sessions, April 6, 7, September 2, November 8, 1784, October 15, 1787; Special Sessions, May 19, September 30, 1785.
11 SCHR, Special Sessions, March 10, 11, May 14, August 4, 1785, July 23, 1789, September 23, 1796, March 18, April 1, 1800, March 25, 1802.
12 SCHR, General Sessions, April 4, October 26, December 10, 1784, April 12, September 22, 1785, March 31, April 1, 1786, November 24, 1789; PANS, Map Division, Early Map of Shelburne.
13 SCHR, Special Sessions, January 8, September 6, 1766; General Sessions, March 1788, July 1799.
14 Perkins, *Diary*, Vol. 2, November 7, 19, 1784; PANS, Letter Book, Vol. 137, Bulkeley to Justice Brenton, Halifax, October 11, 1784; Murdoch, *History of Nova Scotia*, Vol. 3, p. 37; Christ Church, Shelburne, N.S. Burial Records, November 19, 1784.
15 SCHR, Special Sessions, March 22, 31, June 14, 21, July 12, 1786.
16 SCHR, Special Sessions, June 14, 1786; General Sessions, November 2, 1786, April 2, 1788; *Nova Scotia Packet*, September 21, 1786, January 4, 1787.
17 SCHR, General Sessions, March 27, 28, 1787, April 22, 1788; PANS, MG 1, Vol. 950, Doc. 553; PANS, RG 1, Vol. 169, p. 206.
18 SCHR, General Sessions, March 17, November 7, 1785, April 3, 1787, October 29, November 1, 1788; Special Sessions, May 12, June 9, July 7, 1785, January 5, 1791; Quarter Sessions, October 11, 1819.
19 SCHR, General Sessions, March 29, 1785, April 13, August 23, November 2, 7, 1786, April 6, 1787, November 3, 1795, March 9, 1798; Special Sessions, August 11, 1785.
20 SCHR, General Sessions, April 5, 15, 1785, March 15, 1786; Special Sessions, February 24, 1785, May 31, June 14, July 6, 1786.
21 PANS, RG 1, Vol. 136, p. 324, Parr to Shelburne Magistrates, Halifax, October 3, 1783; SCHR, General Quarter Sessions, April 7, November 22, 1784, April 12, 1785; Crown Land Grants Office, Halifax, Map of King Street Market; (P) Alexander Houston, Notes; PANS, RG 1, Vol. 223, Doc. 43, James Robertson to Parr, Halifax, November 29, 1784.
22 SCHR, Quarter Sessions, April 12, 1785; Special Sessions, April 28, May 12, 1785.
23 PANS, RG 20, Vol. 20, Memorial, Shelburne Magistrates, February 22, 1 87; PANS, Grant, March 29, 1787.
24 SCHR, Special Sessions, September 15, November 17, 1787; General Sessions, March 14, 1797, March 18, 1800.
25 Marston, September 18, 26, 1783; *Nova Scotia Packet*, January 24, 1785.
26 SCHR, General Quarter Sessions, April 6, 7, 1784, April 12, 1802; Special Sessions, April 19, 1788; *Royal American Gazette, February 21, 1785*.
27 SCHR, General Quarter Sessions, April 10, 1786, January 28, 1794; Special Sessions, July 16, 1789, December 1, 1791.
28 SCHR, Special Sessions, June 7, 8, 1790, February 7, 1791.
29 AUL, Booth, 'Rough Notes,' March 7, 11, 1789.

30 SCHR, Special Sessions, July 2, 1788; General Sessions, April 12, 1802; District of Shelburne, Assessment roll, 1807; PAC, MG 9, B 9-14, Overseers to Shelburne Magistrates, Shelburne, February 3, 1789.
31 SCHR, General Quarter Sessions, April 7, 1784, April 15, June 9, 1785, April 14, 1787, July 9, 1790; Special Sessions, February 3, 1785.
32 SCHR, Quarter Sessions, April 22, September 8, 1785, April 10, 1786; (P) Account Book, William and George McGill.
33 (P) Rules and Regulations of the Friendly Fire Club.
34 SCHR, General Sessions, April 12, 1785, April 10, 1786, May 19, July 9, 19, November 13, 1790, November 2, 1791, April 12, 1802; Special Sessions, June 28, 1796; PANS, House of Assembly Papers, March 17, 19, 1796; AUL, Booth, 'Rough Notes,' November 5, 1789.
35 Perkins, *Diary*, Vol. 3, June 28, 1792; PANS, Report, 1946, Munro, 'Description and History,' p. 40; Murdoch, *History of Nova Scotia*, Vol. 3, p. 101; PANS, MG 1, Vol. 950, Doc. 560; SCHR, General Sessions, July 10, 1792, April 22, 1794.
36 SCHR, General Sessions, April 6, 1784.
37 PAC, Minute Book, pp. 60, 61, 62, Pynchon to Associates, January 23, 1783; PANS, RG 1, Vol. 394, pp. 1-3, Charles Morris to B. Watson, Halifax, January 27, 1783.
38 Marston, July 30, September 8, 12, December 8, 1783; CP, Map, 178.
39 UNB, Winslow Papers, p. 152, S. Winslow to Marston, Halifax, November 29, 1783; *Ibid.*, p. 85, E. Winslow to Marston, May 30, 1783; PAC, Report, 1884, Campbell to Parr, Halifax, June 8, 1784; *Ibid.*, Parr to Campbell, Halifax, June 15, 1784; PAC, Report, 1884, Col. Robert Morse, 'Report, 1784.'
40 SCHR, Special Sessions, February 24, March 10, 1785.
41 *Nova Scotia Gazette*, July 5, 1785; SCHR, Special Sessions, July 14, September 27, 1785, April 10, 1786, August 6, 1787.
42 PAC, CCNS, Vol. 16, p. 288, Shelburne Magistrates to Parr, Shelburne, September 8, 1785; *Nova Scotia Gazette*, October 25, 1785.
43 A.F. Church, Map of Shelburne County, 1882.
44 *Royal american Gazette*, January 24, 1785; (P), Lottery ticket, Pell's Road; *Port Roseway Gazetteer*, May 12, 1785.
45 *Nova Scotia Packet*, July 20, 1786; PANS, Nova Scotia. House of Assembly. Journals, December 26, 1785, House of Assembly Papers, December 8, 1787; Crown Land Grants Office, Halifax.
46 *Nova Scotia Packet*, October 26, 1786; A.T. Smith, 'Transportation and Communication in Nova Scotia, 1749-1815.' M.A. thesis, Dalhousie University, 1936.
47 SCHR, Special Sessions, October 6, 1790, May 29, 1799; Quarter Sessions, March 11, 1801; *Nova Scotia Packet*, December 7, 1786.
48 Map, 1814 (Cabotia); (P) J. Snow to R.R. Thomson, March 3, 1848.
49 Perkins, *Diary*, Vol. 2, February 21, 1784, May 6, 1786; PANS, House of Assembly Records, 1787; SCHR, Special Sessions, October 17, 1784; Quarter Sessions, July 8, November 4, 1800, March 11, 1801.
50 Murdoch, *History of Nova Scotia*, Vol. 3, p. 52; PANS, Report, 1946, Munro, p. 39-41.
51 *Port Roseway Gazetteer*, March 31, April 18, 1785.
52 *Nova Scotia Packet*, July 13, 1786; PANS, House of Assembly Records, 1787; G.S. Brown, *History of Yarmouth*, p. 327.
53 SCHR, Special Session, June 8, September 1, 1790, June 16, 1795; PANS, Report, 1946, Munro, p. 47.

NOTES

54 SCHR, Quarter Sessions, April 14, 1795, April 12, 1799, March 18, 1800, March 25, 1802.
55 SCHR, General Sessions, March 29, October 31, 1786.
56 SCHR, Special Sessions January 17, 1787, June 3, 1794; Quarter Sessions, March 25, 1802.
57 SCHR, Special Sessions, October 6, 1785; November 6, 1788, October 4, 1796; *Nova Scotia Packet,* July 20, 1786; PANS, Report, 1937, p. 29, 'Tour from Windsor to Cape Negro, 1822,' *The Acadian Recorder,* March 8, 1823.
58 SCHR, Special Sessions, January 3, June 3, 1785, July 20, September 6, 1786, May 2, 1788; Quarter Sessions, April 15, 1785; General Sessions, March 29, November 6, 1788.
59 SCHR, Special Sessions, March 10, 1785, May 19, 1790; General Sessions, March 29, 1786; Quarter Sessions, November 10, 1801.
60 SCHR, Special Sessions, September 29, 1785, April 1, 1786, May 9, June 6, 1787; General Sessions, May 1, 1787.
61 SCHR, General Sessions, November 16, 1790, March 12, 1791.
62 SCHR, General Sessions, September 15, 1784, April 22, 1785, April 6, 10, 1786, March 11, 1801; Special Sessions, July 19, 1787. Dyott, *Diary,* October 28, 1788; Henry Edward Napier, *Journal,* Salem, Mass., Peabody Museum, 1939, p. 50.
63 SCHR General Sessions, April 7, 1784, October 31, 1786, April 16, 1789, April 16, 1790; Special Sessions, September 20, 1786, June 3, 1789, June 16, 1795, September 27, 1798; Quarter Sessions, March 25, 1801, August 24, 1802; *Nova Scotia Packet,* January 18, 1787.
64 SCHR, Quarter Sessions, March 11, 1801; PANS, House of Assembly Records, March 24, 1818.
65 SCHR, General Sessions, July 5, August 12, 1784, April 11, 15, 1785.
66 SCHR, General Sessions, July 5, August 12, 1784, April 11, 12, 1785, April 7, 1786.
67 SCHR, General Sessions, November 6, 1788, April 14, 1795.
68 SCHR, Court of Quarter Sessions, April 7, 1784; SCHR, Memorial to Parr, May 4, 1784; *Ibid.,* Shelburne Agents to Magistrates, Halifax, May 15, 1784; PANS, RG 5, Series S, Vol. 6, Statutes, 1780-1785; PAC, MG 14, B 11, Series 1-14 D, Memorial to Parr (undated) signed by Ross, Campbell, Robertson; PANS, RG 1, Vol. 137, pp. 7-8, Bulkeley to Magistrates, Halifax, February 18, 1785; Murdoch, *History of Nova Scotia,* Vol. 3, pp. 30, 34, 37, 46.
69 PANS, Journals of the House of Assembly, December 19, 1785, March 1, 1790, March 20, 1793, February 20, 1800, November 18, 1806, February 6, 1812, November 12, 1820; Murdoch, *History of Nova Scotia,* Vol. 3, pp. 170, 186.

9 CHURCHES, SCHOOLS AND SOCIAL LIFE

1 Charles Stayner, 'Sandemanian Loyalists,' Nova Scotia Historical Society Collections, Vol. 29, pp. 62-123; *Port Roseway Gazetteer,* August 17, 1786, *Nova Scotia Packet,* September 26, 1786; PANS, Land Grants; PANS, Society for the Propagation of the Gospel (SPG), Letter 288 (microfilm); Perkins, *Diary,* March 27, 1784.
2 Rippon, *Annual Register,* Vol. 1, pp. 473-483; David Benedict, *A General History of the Baptist Denomination in America,* New York, Colby, 1848, pp. 51, 59, 295; SCHR, Court of General Sessions, November 3, 1795; Acadia University Library, A 286 M OM O$_3$2D, J.A. Durkee, 'Baptist Church of Ragged Islands, 1782-1882' manuscript; (P) T.W. Smith, manuscript notes.

3 Marion Robertson, 'History, Trinity United Church, Shelburne' (Methodists), manuscript.
4 Marion Robertson, 'History, Trinity United Church Shelburne' (Presbyterians): SCHR, General Sessions, July 2, 1788; PANS, Journal, House of Assembly, April 25, 1785, 1787; PANS, Report, 1946, James Munro, 'Description and History of the Southern and Western Townships of Nova Scotia, 1795'; (P) Alexander Houston, Manuscript notebook; PANS, MG 1, Vol. 952, Doc. 803; PANS, MG 1, Vol. 742, Doc. 14, Rev. George Patterson, 'Pioneers of Presbyterianism.'
5 PAC, Minute Book, February 1, 8, 1783; Ontario. Bureau of Archives. Second Report, 1904, Claim No. 10, p. 557; James H. Stark, *The Loyalists of Massachusetts*, Boston, J.H. Stark, 1910, p. 338, 342; PANS, MS Docs., RG 1, Vol. 433, Doc. 5; PANS, SPG Records (microfilm), Reel 73, Letters 276, 277, 279, 297, 298, 299, 303, 306, 311, 312; *Ibid.*, Reel 19, Letters 57, 60, 61; *Port Roseway Gazetteer*, February 1785; PANS, MG 1, Vol. 479, Bishop Charles Inglis, Memoirs, 1775-1814; SCHR, Deeds, land purchased by Parish of St. Patrick and St. George and by Christ Church, October 1, 10, 1788.
6 SCHR, General Quarter Sessions, April 7, 1784, January 14, March 19, 1793, April 1, 1800; Society for Promoting Christian Knowledge, London, Minutes, Associates of the Late Dr. Bray, Vol. 3, p. 286; PANS, Bulletin, Vol. 1, A Documentary Study of Early Educational Policy, pp. 34, 35; Murdoch, *History of Nova Scotia*, Vol. 3, p. 306; PANS, RG 14, Vol. 58, Shelburne County School Papers, 1811-1846; PANS, SPG Records (microfilm), Letter 288, Report, Rev. T.B. Rowland, Shelburne, February 3, 1819; *Royal American Gazette*, June 27, 1785; PANS, MG 1, Vol. 479, Bishop Charles Inglis, Memoirs, 1775-1814; PANS, MG 1, Vol. 951, White Collection, Docs. 778, 780; (P) Deed, Robert Barry, Schoolmaster, to William Taylor, June 16, 1785; AUL Booth, 'Rough Notes,' March 23, 1789.
7 PAC, MG 9, B 9-14, Vol. 1, pp. 212-217, Fraser, 'A Sketch of Shelburian Manners, anno 1787;' Marston, June 4, 9, 26, 1783, January 19, 1784; PANS, Report, 1946, Munro, 'Description and History,' p. 43; (P) T.W. Smith, manuscript notes; PAC, Report, 1921, No. 30, Appendix E., p. 363, Parr to Lord Shelburne, Shelburne, July 25, 1783; AUL, Booth, 'Rough Notes,' February 2, 1789; *Nova Scotia Packet*, December 27, 1786; *Port Roseway Gazetteer*, June 9, 1785; SCHR, General Sessions, April 7, 1784; Grand Lodge Library, Freemason's Hall, London. Personal communication; Grand Masonic Lodge of Nova Scotia, Halifax. Personal communication.

10 TAVERNS AND INNS, POSTMASTER AND POST OFFICES, PORT ROSEWAY LIGHTHOUSE

1 *Nova Scotia Packet*, July 13, 1786; *Port Roseway Gazetteer*, May 12, August 31, 1785; SCHR, Special Sessions, July 7, 14, 28, September 1, 15, 19, 1785; General Sessions, November 8, 1784, April 6, 1786, March 18, 1800; Quarter Sessions, March 25, 1802. The word 'bate' as used in the Court of Sessions records was probably the word 'bait' defined by the *Oxford English Dictionary* as feed for horses or a slight repast for travellers upon a journey.
2 PANS, *Nova Scotia Gazette and Weekly Chronicle*, November 25, 1783; *Port Roseway Gazetteer*, July 21, 1785; *Nova Scotia Packet*, September 7, 1786; Crown Land Grants Office, Halifax, Grant, Town Lots, St. John's Division, Letter 1; *General Orders for the Government of Officers in the Plantations (1764-1805)*, London, H.M.S.O., 1805, pp. xlix, lxxxviii; (P) Post Office Memorandum Book; C.M. Jephcott and others, *Postal*

NOTES

History of Nova Scotia and New Brunswick 1754-1867, Toronto, Sessions Publications, 1964.
3 PAC, Report, 1884, Col. Robert Morse, 'Report, 1784.'
4 John Thomson died in 1788 before the completion of the lighthouse. Cut into his tombstone in St. John's kirkyard is the same insignia as that cut into the keystone of he lighthouse – two circles, the inner circle enclosing a triangle and with check marks flecked into the stone between the two circles.
5 PAC, H 3/240, Chart, Port Roseway Harbour, 1784; SCHR, General Sessions, April 10, 1786; PANS, Nova Scotia. House of Assembly. Journals, July 8, 1786, March 27, 1793; PANS, William Hale, Letter Book, 1788-1791 (microfilm); SCHR, Special Sessions, June 9, 1790; PANS, RG 7, Vol. 43, Alexander H. Cocken to Joseph Howe, June 1, 1860.
6 *Nova Scotia Packet*, January 18, 1787; PANS, House of Assembly Papers, December 8, 1787; PANS, Lighthouse Papers, Vol. 1.
7 AUL, Booth, 'Rough Notes', November 24, 1789; SCHR, General Sessions, April 19, 1790; PANS, Nova Scotia. House of Assembly. Statutes, 1787, Cap. 3; PANS, RG 31, Treasury Papers, Lighthouse Duties; PANS, RG 1, Vol. 169, p. 176, March 27, 1788; PANS, RG 7, Vol. 43, Alexander H. Cocken to Joseph Howe, Shelburne, June 1, 1860; PANS, Lighthouse Papers, Vol. 1.
8 Murdoch, *History of Nova Scotia*, Vol. 3, p. 103; PANS, Report, 1946, p. 46, Munro, 'Description and History.'
9 PANS, RG 7, Vol. 43, Alexander H. Cocken to Joseph Howe, Shelburne, June 1, 1860.

11 EARLY INDUSTRIES, TRADES AND PROFESSIONS

1 District of Shelburne, Assessment rolls, 1786, 1787; SCHR, Special Sessions, August 15, 1787; SCHR, Deeds relative to J. Bell's Land; PANS, Crown Land Grants; *Royal American Gazette*, April 11, 1785.
2 PAC, Minute Book, p. 78; Marston and Morris, May 17, 1783; PANS, RG 1, Vol. 49, pp. 1-3, Wentworth to Lord Commissioners of the Treasury, Halifax, October 21, 1783.
3 PANS, RG 1, Vol. 394, Morris to Marston, Halifax, August 26, 1783; PANS, Shelburne Documents, Marston to Parr, January 2, 1784; PANS, Crown Grants, S. Shakespeare et al, April 12, 1784; *Ibid.*, Watson and Company, February 24, 1785; PANS, RG 1, Vol. 394, C. Morris to Marston, July 16, 1784.
4 New Brunswick Historical Society *Collections*, Vol. 8, p. 269, Marston to I. Mauduit, September 1784; PAC, CONS, A 107, MG 11, A. Leckie to B. Watson, Shelburne, May 9, 1785; (P) Deed, J. Courtney to A. Williams, January 25, 1790; PANS, Crown Land Grants, relative to Pell's land; Grants to Hall and Hannah.
5 SCHR, General Sessions, April 16, 1787; District of Shelburne, Assessment roll, 1786; PANS, RG 31, Bounties on Mills, 1787; SCHR, Deed, Vol. 3, p. 52; PANS, RG 1, Vol. 443, Capitation Tax, 1792.
6 PAC, Report, 1921, Appendix E., p. 367, Parr to Lord Shelburne, Halifax, June 16, 1784; Charles Bruce Fergusson, 'Eighteenth Century Halifax,' Canadian Historical Association Report, 1949, p. 36; *Royal American Gazette*, June 20, 1785; Murdoch, *History of Nova Scotia*, Vol. 3, p. 78; SCHR, General Sessions, April 6, 1784, April 10, 1786.
7 PAC, CONS, Vol. 21, p. 33, Shelburne to Grenville, Shelburne, June 28, 1792.
8 SCHR, Deeds, Vol. 4, pp. 44, 483; (P) Document (1826) relating to grist stones;

KING'S BOUNTY

PANS, MG 1, Vol. 483c, Alexander Houston, Notebook; Uniacke, *Statutes of Nova Scotia*, pp. 162, 252.
9. PANS, MG 1, Vol. 949, White Collection, Doc. 500; SCHR, Court of Sessions, August 12, 1792.
10. District of Shelburne, Assessment rolls; *Port Roseway Gazetteer*, June 9, 1785.
11. District of Shelburne, Assessment rolls; *Port Roseway Gazetteer*, January 27, 1785; PANS, Mg 1, Vol. 949, White Collection, Doc. 482.
12. *Nova Scotia Packet*, July 6, 1786; District of Shelburne, Assessment rolls, 1786-1787; PANS, MG 1, Vol. 952, Doc. 870; SCHR, Special Sessions, June 25, 1786.
13. District of Shelburne, Assessment rolls; *Port Roseway Gazetteer*, August 11, 1785; *Royal American Gazette*, January 24, 1785; *New York Gazette*, January 12, 1778; SCHR, Special Sessions, January 31, 1787; Perkins, *Diary*, Vol. 2, January 24, 1785.
14. District of Shelburne, Assessment rolls; M. Robertson, 'Isaac Hildrith,' *The Coast Guard*, Shelburne, July 8, 1965.
15. District of Shelburne, Assessment rolls; Ontario Bureau of Archives, Second Report, Loyalist Claims, Toronto, 1905, Claim of F. Weiser, No. 507; (P) Indenture, Apprenticeship of G.H. Deinstadt to J. Bell, 1807.
16. District of Shelburne, Assessment rolls, 1786, 1787; SCHR, Quarter Sessions, April 22, 1785; General Sessions, April 10, 1786, April 1, 1790.
17. PANS, RG 1, Vol. 169, Commissions, 1781-1792; Stark, *The Loyalists of Massachusetts*; Perkins, *Diary*, Vol. 3, October 7, 1790; AUL, Booth, 'Rough Notes'; *Royal American Gazette*, January 24, 1785; SCHR, Court of Sessions; District of Shelburne, Assessment rolls, 1786-1787.
18. London Record Office, Colonial Correspondence for Prince Edward Island, Vol. 9, p. 389, Claim, James and Alexander Robertson; Robertson family notes, Miss Eleanor Berry Kemnay, Scotland; Douglas C. McMurtrie, *The Royalist Printers at Shelburne, Nova Scotia*, n.p., Privately printed, 1933; PANS, RG 1, Vol. 23, Doc. 43, Memorial, J. Robertson to Parr, Halifax, November 29, 1784.

12 USE OF THE LAND AND SEA

1. PAC, Minute Book, p. 38; PANS, Report, 1946, Munro, 'Description and History'; AUL, Booth, 'Rough Notes,' March 26, 1789.
2. PANS, *Shelburne Documents, Marston to Parr, January 2, 1784;* PANS, *Grants and location lists; AUL, Booth, 'Rough Notes,' March 14, May 12, June 21, 1789; Nova Scotia Packet*, July 6, 20, 27, 1786; *Royal American Gazette*, August, 1, 1785; *Port Roseway Gazetteer*, May 9, 1785; PANS, RG 1, Vol. 483c, Alexander Houston, Notebook; PANS, Report, 1946, Munro, 'Description and History,' p. 44; (P) Drawing of Wood Hall, Account Book; PANS, RG 1, Vol. 380, Titus Smith, Diary, 1768-1850; Murdoch, *History of Nova Scotia*, Vol. 3, p. 50; SCHR, Court of General Quarter Sessions, April 6, 1784, April 10, 1786, May 7, 1788; Census Returns, 1827.
3. PAC, Minute Book, pp. 38, 39.
4. Marston, May 13, 1783; PANS, MG 1, Vol. 948, White Collection, Doc. 210, J. Courtney to A. Cunningham, Port Roseway, July 1, 1783; New Brunswick Historical Society Collections, Vol. 8, p. 269, Marston to I. Mauduit, September 1784; UNB, Winslow Papers, P. 190, E. Winslow to W. Chipman, Halifax, April 26, 1784.
5. PAC, CONS 1785, A 107, MG 11, Alex Leckie, to B. Watson, Shelburne, May 9, 1785; SCHR, General Sessions, April 10, 1786.
6. Murdoch, *History of Nova Scotia*, Vol. 3, p. 25, Treaty of Peace, Article 3; *Ibid.*, p. 78;

NOTES

PAC, CCNS, Vol. 21, p. 33-40, Petition, Shelburne Merchants and Citizens to Lord Grenville, Shelburne, June 16, 1791.
7 DUA, Campbell Papers, MS 4-1, Letter Book, Shelburne Customs House, 1796-1822.
8 SCHR, General Sessions, April 7, 1784, Aprl 10, 1786; PAC, CCNS, A 107, MG 11, A. Leckie to B. Watson, Shelburne, May 9, 1785; Murdoch, *History of Nova Scotia*, Vol. 3, p. 78.
9 PANS, Report, 1937, 'Tour from Windsor to Cape Negro, 1822,' p.28; PANS, RG 7, Vol. 43, A. Cocken to J. Howe, Shelburne, June 1, 1860.
10 New Brunswick Historical Society Collections, Vol. 8, p. 269, Marston to I. Mauduit, September, 1784; PAC, CONS, A 107, MG 11, A. Leckie to B. Watson, May 9, 1785; *Royal American Gazette*, December 2, 1784; *Nova Scotia Packet*, July 6, 1786.
11 The shareholders were: Thayer and Jarvis, £2,000, Ebenezer Parker, Philip Marchinton, Charles Whitworth, each £1,000, Joseph and Robert Burton, £1,000, William Holderness, £250, Greggs Farish, £100, Gibson Johnson and Company, £1,000. Benjamin Davis was also a member of the Company.
12 *Nova Scotia Packet*, July 20, 1786, Instructions, Whale Fishing Company; PANS, MG 1, Vol. 949, White Collection, Doc. 496, Statement, Whale Fishing Company.
13 *Royal American Gazette*, June 20, 1785; (P) Letter Book, J. Watson, Joshua Watson to Capt. Bunker, Shelburne, August 15, 1785.
14 *Nova Scotia Packet*, July 20, 1786; Murdoch, *History of Nova Scotia*, Vol. 3, p. 78; PANS, MG 1, Vol. 949, White Collection, Document 496; *General Orders for the Government of Officers in the Plantations*, London, His Majesty's Stationery Office, 1805, p. xxxvii.
15 *Nova Scotia Packet*, July 27, 1786; PANS, MG 1, Vol. 949, White Collection, Doc. 496, Statement, Whale Fishing Company.
16 PANS, CCNS, *Vol. 17, p. 16, Sydney to Parr, Whitehall, April 20, 1786.*

13 SHIPS, SHIPBUILDING AND SHIPBUILDERS

1 The launching of the *Roseway* was reported in the American newspaper, *The Daily Advertiser*, January 18, 1787, with the erroneous statement that she was 'the first *ship* that had been launched in this Province since its first settlement.' From the amount of the bounty (£96) paid on the *Roseway*, she was a vessel of about 192 tons burden. Her tonnage was registered as 181. (Charles A. Armour and Thomas Lackey, *Sailing Ships of the Maritimes*, Toronto, McGraw-Hill Ryerson, 1975, P. 14.
2 *Nova Scotia Packet*, July 13, September 21, 28, October 19, December 7, 14, 1786; (P) Letter Book, p. 216, G. Ross to Captain Wirling, Shelburne, May 25, 1789; AUL, Booth, 'Rough Notes,' January 21, 23, 1789.
3 *Nova Scotia Packet*, October 5, November 16, December 7, 1786, January 4, 178; Murdoch, *History of Nova Scotia*, Vol. 3, p. 45; PANS, RG 31, Bounty Certificates, 1787-1791; PANS, Mediterranean Passes, 1767-1789, No. 1337; *Nova Scotia Packet*, November 9, 1786.
4 Nova Scotia Packet, September 21, 1786; (P) Letter Book, G. and R. Ross; DUA, Naval Office Records, Campbell Papers, MS 4-1.
5 DUA, PRO, Home Office Papers, HO 76, 1, 2 (1790-96) microfilm.
6 *Port Roseway Gazetteer*, December 2, 1784, July 21, August 11, 1785; *Royal American Gazette*, December 2, 1784, June 20, 1785; PANS, Lighthouse Duties, December, 16, 1788 – March 16, 1789; (P) Letter Book, G. and R. Ross.

KING'S BOUNTY

7 PANS, Mediterranean Passes, 1767-1792; DUA, Naval Office Records, Campbell Papers, MS 4-1.
8 District of Shelburne, Assessment rolls, 1786-1787; Boston King, *op. cit.*; SCHR, Deed, Vol. 3, p. 429; Perkins, Vol. 3, *Diary*, October 23, November 22, December 4, 1794.
9 (P) Letter Book, G. Ross to Messrs. Cunningham and Cleland, Shelburne, May 31, 1788.
10 District of Shelburne, Assessment rolls, 1786-1787; (P) Blacksmith McGill's Account Book, Shelburne, N.S., PANS, Ship's Registry Papers (microfilm); *Port Roseway Gazetteer*, May 12, 1785; PANS, RG 1, Vol. 169, Commission Book, 1781-1792, p. 157.
11 PANS, RG 1, Vol. 443, Captitation Tax, 1792.

14 TRADE AND COMMERCE

1 (P) Letter Book, G. and R. Ross.
2 *Ibid.*; PANS, Letter Book, William Hale, microfilm.
3 *Port Roseway Gazetteer*, December 2, 1784, May 11, 26, June 20, 27, August 11, 1785; *Nova Scotia Packet*, June 27, 1786.
4 PANS, Mediterranean Passes; (P) Letter Book, G. and R. Ross.
5 *Ibid.*; PANS, MG 1, Vol. 949, White Collection, Doc. 341.
6 (P) Letter Book, Joshua Watson, J. Watson to W. Hale, New York, September 30, 1785; (P) Letter Book, G. and R. Ross; SCHR, General Sessions, April 7, 1784, April 12, 1785; Murdoch, *History of Nova Scotia*, Vol. 3, pp. 35, 41, 45, 49.
7 *Royal American Gazette*, June 27, 1785; PAC, MG 14, B 11, Series 1-14D, Memorial, Ross et al to Governor Parr.
8 PANS, RG 1, Vol. 169, Commission Book, 1781-1792; Marston, May 17, 20, June 3, 1783; Morris, June 8, July 3, 1783; CP, Inhabitants of Shelburne to Carleton, September 6, 1783; PANS, House of Assembly. Journals, 1784, p. 39.
9 CP, Carleton to Lord North, New York, June 15, 1783; SCHR, Memorial, Inhabitants of Shelburne to Parr, May 3, 1784; PANS, Letter Book, RG 1, Vol. 137, Parr to Shelburne Magistrates, Halifax, February 18, 1785; PAC, MG 14, B11, Series 1-14D, Memorial, R. Ross et al; PANS, House of Assembly Papers, RG 5. Series A, Vol. 1A, 1775-1785, No. 12, Memorial, I. Wilkins et al, Shelburne, November 2, 1785.
10 District of Shelburne, Assessment Rolls, 1786-1787; Murdoch, *History of Nova Scotia*, Vol. 3, p. 54; *Nova Scotia Packet*, September 7, 1786.
11 SCHR, General Sessions, April 10, 1786; *Nova Scotia Packet*, July 13, 1786.
12 PANS, RG 5, Series A, Vol. 2, 1786, Tonge to Parr and His Majesty's Council; PANS, RG 1, Vol. 298, Docs. 101, 126, Province of Nova Scotia Legislative Council Papers.
13 PAC, Memorial, R. Ross et al, *op. cit.*; (P) Letter Book, G. and R. Ross; PANS, RG 5, Series A, Vol. 3, Petition, G. Springall to Parr, Shelburne, June 9, 1786.
14 PANS, Nova Scotia. House of Assembly. Journals. Revenue Reports, 1787; PANS, RG 1, Vol. 223, Doc. 158; PAC, CCNS, Vol. 20, p. 346, A. Leckie, Threadneedle Street, March 26, 1790.

15 THE DECLINE OF SHELBURNE

1 Marston and Morris.
2 CP, Dole to Carleton, New York, September 19, 1783; UNB, Winslow Papers, p. 337, Col. Thomas Dundas to Earl Cornwallis, St. John, December 28, 1786; SCHR,

NOTES

General Sessions, April 10, 1786.
3 UNB, Winslow Papers, p. 205, E. Winslow to W. Chipman, Halifax, May 12, 1784; PAC, MG 14, B 11, 1-14, Memorial, R. Ross et al to Parr, Shelburne, undated; (P) Charles Mason, Surveyor's Notes.
4 PAC, R. Ross et al, *op. cit.;* PAC, Report, 1884, Col. Robert Morse, "Report, 1784"; PAC, CONS, A 116, Petition, Shelburne merchants, et al to Honourable Lord Grenville, Shelburne, June 16, 1791.
5 PAC, Report, 1884, Morse, *op. cit;* PAC, Minute Book, p. 71; PAC, CCNS, Vol. 21, S. Skinner to the Honourable Henry Dundas, undated; PAC, MG 9, B 9-14, Vol. 1, "A Sketch of Shelburnian Manners, anno 1787"; SCHR, General Sessions, Memorial to Bishop Inglis, January 12, 1793.
6 SCHR, General Sessions, April 11, 1786; PANS, MG 1, Vol. 949, White Collection, Doc. 464.
7 PAC, MG 9, B 6, MUSTER OF îç-, Territorial Records (Shelburne); PANS, RG 1, Vol. 223, Doc. 102.
8 Campbell, *History of Yarmouth,* p. 87; PANS, Crown Land Grants; *Port Roseway Gazetteer,* March 31, 1785.
9 W.H. Siebert and Florence E. Gilliam, 'The Loyalists of Prince Edward Island,' Royal Society of Canada Transactions, Section II, 1910, pp. 110-111.
10 Dyott, *Diary,* p. 56; SCHR, General Sessions, April 12, 1802; (P) Absentee Estate Papers; PANS, Report, 1937, Traveller, *Acadian Recorder,* March 8, 1823.

16 EPILOGUE

1 MOURDOCH, *History of Nova Scotia,* Vol. 3, p. 112; PAC, Report, 1894, p. 505; PANS, RG 1, Vol. 51, p. 227, Wentworth to the Duke of Portland, Halifax, December 21, 1794; *Ibid.,* p. 108, Wentworth to Dundas, Halifax, May 19, 1794; *Ibid.,* p. 100-102, Wentworth to John Thomas, Halifax, May 22, 1794; Perkins, *Diary,* Vol. 3, May 25, July 22, 24, August 7, 13, 1794; SCHR, Court of Special Sessions, October 28, 1794.
2 PANS, RG 1, Vol. 228, Doc. 97, D. Rowland to M. Wallace, Naval Hospital, Halifax, June 8, 1818.
3 *Ibid.,* No. 98, The Earl of Dalhousie to Michael Wallace, Halifax, June 1818.
4 PANS, RG 20, Series C, Vol. 93, Muster Roll of Welsh Emigrants to sail on the *Two Brothers.* Ages have been added from a second list of Welsh settlers bound for Shelburne (PANS, RG 1, Vol. 228, Doc. 110).
5 *Ibid.,* and Crown Land Grants, Petition No. 335.
6 PANS, RG 1, Vol. 228, Doc. 99, M. Wallace and J. Fraser to Shelburne Committee, Halifax, June 15, 1818.
7 *Ibid.,* Doc. 100.
8 PANS, RG 20, Series C, Vol. 93, Thomas Bulgin and John Richards to the Earl of Dalhousie, undated.
9 PANS, RG 1, Vol. 228, Doc. 107, J. Richards to C. Campbell, Shelburne, October 28, 1818.
10 *Ibid.,* Docs. 100 and 109.
11 (P) Robert Thomson's surveyors' notebook.
12 PANS, RG 1, Vol. 228, Doc. 102, Shelburne Committee to M. Wallace and J. Fraser, Shelburne, July 28, 1818.
13 *Ibid.,* Doc. 104, Sketch of Long Island with notations.

14 *Ibid.*, Doc. 105, Welsh Settlers to Shelburne Committee, August 8, 1818.
15 *Ibid.*, Doc. 103, Shelburne Committee to M. Wallace and J. Fraser, Shelburne, August 12, 1818.
16 PANS, RG 20, Series C, Vol. 93, R. Thomson to C. Morris, Shelburne, October 27, 1818; PANS, Crown Land Grants, Petitions No. 355; PANS, Vol. 228, Doc. 108, Rev. T. Rowland to Wallace and Fraser, Shelburne, October 28, 1818.
17 PANS, RG 20, Series C, Vol. 93, R. Thomson to C. Morris, Shelburne, May 8, 1819; PANS, RG 1, Vol. 458, Docs. 10, 11, Account of D. McKay for surveying land, Halifax, December 10, 1819.
18 PANS, Map of Cambria Settlement, October 7, 1819, by John Richards; PANS, RG 20, Series C, Vol. 93, John Richards to the Earl of Dalhousie, October 1819.
19 *Ibid.*
20 *Ibid.*, Petition of J. Richards and others, December 14, 1820.
21 *Ibid.*, Surveyor General, request for warrants for grants, August 9, 1823.
22 *Ibid.*, Plan of New Cambria, 1822; *Ibid.*, Thomas Jones to Lieutenant-Governor James Kempt, Shelburne, March 11, 1822.
23 *Ibid.*, Plan of New Cambira, 1822; PANS, Crown Land Grants, Plan of land for D. Davis and J. Harris, March 21, 1825; PANS, Crown Land Grants, David Horton, 1827, Michael Davis, 1842.

Appendix

GRANTEES

This list of grantees and those recommended to receive grants of the King's Bounty of land was compiled from the surveyors' lists, from the recommendations of the Board of Agents appointed by Governor Parr in August 1784 to assign the land according to His Majesty's instructions, from records of land grants in the Public Archives of Nova Scotia and in the Crown Grants (Land Registry) Office, Halifax, and from the grants issued under the Great Seal of the province, signed by Governor Parr and the provincial secretary.

Not all whose names are on this list received grants to their allotments, for many had left before the grants were issued and their land was given to others; nor were all on the lists Loyalists or disbanded soldiers, a few others finding ways of presentation to the Board or to a surveyor for an allotment of land. No attempt has been made to indicate the vagaries of the eighteenth century spelling of surnames as they occurred on the surveyors' lists and in the records of the Board of Agents. That many names are spelt differently today will immediately be evident to those searching for an ancestor.

An asterisk (*) marks members of the Port Roseway Association.

Ackerman, Elizabeth	Ackerman, Richard	Ackerson, John
Ackerman, John	Ackerson, Abraham	Ackerson, Thomas
Ackerman, John W.	Ackerson, Edward	*Ackland, Philip
Ackerman, Peter	Ackerson, Jacob	Acres, Thomas

KING'S BOUNTY

Adams, Francis
Adams, Thomas
Adams, William
Addington, Andrew
Aiken, Andrew
Aiken, George
Aiken, Thomas
Aiken, William
Aikman, John
Airs, John
Akerman, John
Alcock, Nathaniel
Alder, James
Alexander, Archibald
Alexander, James
Alexander, Peter
Alexander, Thomas
*Allen, James
*Allen, Jeremiah
Allen, John
Allen, Lawrence
Allen, Peter
Allen, Thomas
Allen, William
*Allsworth, Samuel
Alstine, Joseph
Alstine, Richard
Amen, Christopher
Amies, John
Amis, William
Anderson, Andrew
Anderson, Archibald
*Anderson, John
*Anderson, Peter
Anderson, Walter
*Anderson, William
Andes, Conrad
Andes, George
Andrews, John
Andrews, Richard
Angus, Hercules
Annely, Thomas
Anns, Thomas
Anthony, John
Antonio, John
Apple, Christopher
Appleby, James
Appleby, Robert
Archibald, Edward

Armiger, James
Armour, William
Armstrong, Thomas
Arnant, James
*Arrant, Stephen
Arthur, Joseph
Arthur, Peter
Ashby, John
*Ashley, James
*Ashley, Joseph
*Ashley, William
Ashton, John
Astwick, Thomas
Aswell, John
Aswell, Jonathan
Atkins, John
Atkinson, John
Auchmuty, James
Auchmuty, Robert
Auld, William
Avery, Francis
Avery, Richard
Aymar, John

Babcock, David
Bagnell, Samuel
Bailey, John
Bailey, Thomas
Bain, David
Bain, Peter
Baker, Andrew
Ball, Peter
Ball, William
Bankett, Daniel
Banks, Sarah
Banta, Simon
*Banta, Weart
Bantley, Felix
Barber, Robert
*Barclay, Andrew
Barnard, John
Barnard, Samuel
Barnes, John
Barnes, Peter
Barnett, James
Barnett, Samuel
Barnett, William
Baron, James
Barr, James

*Barr, John
Barren, James
Barrett, Joseph
Barrett, Lawrence
Barrett, Michael
Barringate, Daniel
Barron, James
Barron, John
Barrow, Thomas
Barry, Alexander
*Barry, Robert
Bartlett, Edward
Bartlett, Thomas
Bartram, Alexander
Barwell, John
*Batt, Thomas
Battersby, John
*Baxter, Jonathan
*Baxter, Samuel
Bayrne, Matthew
Beamorld, John
Bean, John
Beasley, William
Beattie, David
*Beattie, George
Beaumont, John
Beckworth, Elisha
Bedford, John
Beek, Amos
Beker, Christopher
Bell, John
Bell, Joseph
Bell, Richard
Bell, Robert
Belvidere, George
Bender, Frederick
Bennet, William
Bennison, George
Benson, Seth
Benson, William
Bentley, Felix
Bergh, Adam
Bergh, Christian
Bering, Jonathan
Berry, David
Berry, Daniel
Berry, Francis
*Berry, Robert
Berry, Samuel

APPENDIX

Bethel, William
Biggum, Andrew
*Billington, John
Billington, William
Bingay, Thomas
Binney, James
Binney, Stephen
Birch, Joseph
Birge, John
Birge, Joseph
Birkly, David
Birkly, William
Birmingham, James
Birmingham, Richard
Birn, Matthew
Birrick, John
Bishop, John
*Black, Joseph
Black, Martin
Black, Thomas
*Black, William
Blackburn, Hugh
Blackie, James
Blackmore, Joseph
*Blackwell, John
Blades, Henry
Blair, David
Blair, John
Blanchard, Lewis
Blauvelt, Theunis
Blewer, Jacob
Blewer, John
Blewer, Peter
Blight, Richard
Blockbirge, John
Boardman, John
Bode, Charles
Boelhman, Andreas
Bogart, Abraham
Bogart, Jacobus
Bogart, John
Bogetlein, Andreas
Boggs, Jane
Boggs, Robert
*Bolton, Henry
Bond, Joseph
Boole, Francis
Boorham, Justin
Bouflerie, Jacob

Bough, James
*Boulby, Edward
Bousfield, Michael
Bowen, Charles
Bower, Adam
Bower, Bartholomew
Bower, Charles
Bower, Philip
Bowie, Nichol
Bowman, George
Bowman, Robert
Boyce, Alexander
Boyce, Gideon
Boyce, Jacob
Boyd, James
Boyd, John
Boyd, Richard
Boyd, William
Boydell, Joseph
Boye, Nicholas
Boyland, John
Bracker, John
*Bradburne, Alexander
Bradley, Martin
Brady, Joseph
Brady, Mary
Braine, Samuel
Brookelby, William
Brookman, Ruth
Broome, James
Broome, John
*Broome, William
Brothers, Alice
Brough, James
Broughton, John
Brown, Andrew
Brown, Charles, Sr.
Brown, Charles, Jr.
Brown, David
Brown, Duncan
Brown, James
*Brown, John, Sr.
*Brown, John, Jr.
Brown, Joseph
Brown, Michael
*Brown, Nicholas
Brown, Richard
Brown, Robert
Brown, Thomas

*Brown, Samuel
Brown, William
Browning, John
Bruce, Andrew
Bruce, James
Bruce, John
Bruce, Peter
Bruce, Robert
Brudenel, Edward
*Bruff, Charles O.
Bryan, Hugh
Bryan, John
Bryans, William
Burke, Michael
Burke, Thomas
*Burke, William
Burling, Samuel
Burn, Benedict
Burn, Hugh
Burn, John
Burne, Mathew
*Burnham, John
Burns, William
Burnside, Thomas
Burrage, George
Burrows, John
Burton, Daniel
Burton, Joseph Hugh
Burton, Peter
Burton, Robert
*Burton, William
Bush, Henry
Bushton, William
Butler, John
Butler, Mathew
*Butler, Samuel
Butler, William
Butterworth, Samuel
Buys, Jacob
Byars, Jacob
Byars, John
Bydder, Joseph
Bydell, Joseph
Byrne, Aime
Byrne, Benedict
Byrne, Christopher
Byrne, Matthew
Byrne, Patrick
Braine, Thomas

Branding, Charles
*Branthwaite, William
Brannon, Daniel
*Brazil, Richard
Breen, Hugh
Brewer, Jacob
Brewer, Joseph
Brewer, Ross
Bridgford, Robert
Briggs, Joseph
Briggs, William
Bright, Moses
Bright, Richard
Brinley, Edward
Brinley, Thomas
Brisely, Timothy
Brisely, Thomas
Brook, Francis
Brooks, Daniel
Bryce, James
Bryne, Christopher
Buchan, Robert
Buchanan, David
Buchanan, Donald
Buchanan, George
Buchanan, Robert
Buck, Richard
Budd, John
Bulfinch, Richard
Bullock, Robert
Bulkley, Richard
Burett, Nicholaus
Burford, Robert
Burk, Aaron
Burk, Walter
Burke, Isaac
Burke, James

Caddel, James
Cadenham, John
Caine, David
*Calder, Andrew
*Caldwell, William
Callahan, David
Callahan, William
Callow, Robert
Callow, Thomas
Cameron, Alexander, Sr.
Cameron, Alexander, Jr.

Cameron, Allan
Cameron, Angus
Cameron, Daniel
Cameron, Donald
Cameron, Duncan
*Cameron, Evan
Cameron, John
Cameron, Kenneth
Cameron, Murdock
*Cameron, William
Cames, John
*Campbell, Alexander
*Campbell, Archibald
Campbell, Cole
Campbell, Colin
Campbell, Daniel
*Campbell, Dugald
Campbell, Farquhar
*Campbell, George, Sr.
*Campbell, George, Jr.
Campbell, Hugh
Campbell, James
Campbell, Jean
*Campbell, John
Campbell, Oliver
Campbell, Robert
Campbell, Roderick
Campbell, Samuel
Campbell, Thomas
Campbell, William, Sr.
Campbell, William, Jr.
Capel, Andrew
Capel, Chilion
*Capewell, John
Carberry, William
Cardiff, Charles
*Carland, Patrick
Carleton, Christopher
Carleton, Thomas
Carman, Jonathan
*Carmichael, William
Carnes, George
Carnes, John
Carney, Barney
Carney, Patrick
Carpenter, George
Carpenter, John
Carr, John
Carr, Joseph

*Carrol, Daniel
Carrol, Dennis
Carrol, Lawrence
Carrol, William
Carson, John
*Carson, William, Sr.
*Carson, William, Jr.
Carter, Charles
Carter, Francis
Carton, Daniel
Carver, John
Casely, Richard
Casey, John
Casey, Thomas
*Castle, William
Caswell, John
Caswell, Philip
Catherwood, David
Cavan, Edward
Cavins, David
Chadwick, James
Chadwick, Thomas
Chambers, John
Chambers, Richard
Chandler, Rufus
Chase, John
*Cheese, John
Cheeters, Joseph
*Chetwynd, Thomas
Chick, Thomas
Chisholm, Andrew
*Chisholm, George
Christian, Eric
Christie, Alexander
Christie, John
Christy, Charles
Christy, Mathew
*Church, Charles
Clandon, John
Clanson, Nathan
Clapp, Margaret
Clapper, Henry
*Clark, Archibald
Clark, Charles
Clark, James
Clark, John
Clark, William
Clarke, Hugh, Sr.
Clarke, Hugh, Jr.

APPENDIX

Clarke, Robert
*Clawson, John
Cleaton, John
Cleghorn, Robert
Clelan, John
Climpson, William
Clipping, James
*Clisby, John
Close, Henry
Clowden, John, G.
Clum, John
Cobb, John
*Cock, James
*Cocken, Alexander
Cocklin, Timothy
Cockran, Abraham
Cockran, John
Cockran, Michael
Cockwood, Amos
Coffay, Thomas
Coffey, Michael
Coleworthy, William
Collard, John
Collins, James, Sr.
Collins, James, Jr.
Collins, Thomas
Collow, Thomas
Colquhon, Pater
Colthrop, Isaac
Combauld, Richard
Compton, Thomas
Condon, William
Conkey, Israel
Conlin, Henry
Connell, James
Connell, John
*Connell, Robert
Connoly, James
Connoly, Peter
Connor, Charles
Connor, Daniel
Connor, Derby
Connor, Hugh
Connor, Jeremiah
Connor, John
Connor, Mary
Cook, Alexander
Cook, George
*Cook, John

Cook, Michael
Cook, Obediah
Cook, William
Cooling, George
Cooling, Michael
Cooper, James
*Cooper, John
Cooper, William
Copeland, William
Corbet, Peter
Corbet, William
Corckray, John
Corcoran, Mathew
Cormick, Alexander
Cormick, James
Cornthwait, Thomas
Cornwall, Melancton
Cornway, James
Corrin, James
Cotman, Christopher
Couch, Henry
Coughtery, Richard
Coulby, John
*Courtney, James
*Courtney, Richard
*Courtney, Thomas
Covell, Robert
*Cowan, Alexander
Cowan, George
Cowdry, Joseph
*Cowling, John
Cox, James
Cox, Jonathan
Cox, John
Coyle, Patrick
Craig, Andrew
Craig, John
Craiger, Martin
Craighton, John
Crane, Timothy
Crawford, James
*Crawford, Margaret
Crawford, Peter
Crawford, Robert
Cray, William
Crocheron, Jane
Crocker, Mary
Crofton, Charles
Croneen, Mathew

Crooks, Charity
Crow, Jonathan
Crow, Peter
Crow, William
Crowley, Jeremiah
*Cruikshank, William
Crump, William
Cruse, George
*Cullum, Arthur
Cummins, James
Cummins, William
Cummian, Michael
Cunningham, Archibald
Cunningham, Charles
Cunningham, Cornelius
Cunningham, John
Cunningham, Paul
Cunningham, William
Curran, John
*Curran, Thomas
Currier, Martin
*Curry, Alexander
*Curry, John
Curry, Samuel
Cutt, Donald
Cutt, John
Cutter, George
Cutter, Thomas
Cuzzena, John

Daily, Dennis
Daily, James
Daily, John
Dall, Robert
Dalton, Thomas
Darling, George
Darling, John
Davenport, Isaac
*Davenport, Samuel
*Davidson, John
Davila, Christian
Davis, Benjamin, Sr.
Davis, Benjamin, Jr.
Davis, George
Davis, Isaac
Davis, James
*Davis, John
Davis, Thomas
Davison, Ethal

KING'S BOUNTY

Davison, John
Davison, Robert
Davy, Benjamin
Dawkins, William
Day, Joseph
Day, Peter
Days, Francis
Dean, James
Dean, John
Dean, Nicholas
Deane, William
Decker, Benjamin
Decker, Isaac
Decker, Jeremiah
Deffendorf, George
Deffendorf, Jacob
Deisner, Christian
Deitell, Johann
Delahide, James
*Delaney, Daniel
Demelt, Isaac
Demilind, Ludowic
*Dempsay, Roger
*Denham, Thomas
Dennin, John
Denny, Charles
Denny, Dennie
Denny, Vincan
Derkinderen, James
DesChamp, Thomas
DeRivier, John
Deveraux, William
Dewer, Alexander
Dick, James
Dick, John
Dickens, John
Dickey, James
Dickey, Walter
Dickey, William
Dickinson, John
*Dickinson, Nathaniel
Dickinson, Roger
Diggles, Richard
Dingley, Thomas
Dindales, Hunhodo
Doale, Francis
Dogherty, Anthony
*Dogherty, Hugh
Dogherty, John

*Dole, James
Dombofskay, Johann
Donaldson, James
Donaldson, Samuel
Donaldson, Thomas
Donaldson, William
Donelly, Arthur
Dongan, Thomas
Donovan, Daniel
Doris, John
Dorland, James
*Dorney, Luke
Dorney, Jappie
Dorwood, Alexander
Doughty, Timothy
Doughty, William
Douglas, Alexander
Douglas, George
Douglas, James
Douglas, William
*Dove, Alexander
Dow, Henry
Dow, William
Dowd, Charles
Dower, Alexander
Dowers, Joseph
Dowie, George
Dowling, William
Downey, Henry
Downey, Mathew
Doyle, Francis
Doyle, Hugh
Drake, Joseph
Draper, Joseph
Draper, Daniel
Drescol, James
Drew, Richard
Drogarty, Anthony
Drum, Philip
Drummond, Robert
Drury, John
Dryer, John
Duckett, Christopher
Duddy, John
Duffee, William
Duggan, John
Dunahou, Gilbert
Dunbar, George
Dunbar, Robert

Dunbarnget, John
*Duncan, George
Duncan, Henry
Duncan, Hugh
Duncan, James
*Duncan, Thomas
*Dundas, George
Dunlop, Alexander
Dunlop, Francis
Dunn, Gideon
Dunn, James, Sr.
Dunn, James, Jr.
Dunn, Walter
Dunscomb, Daniel
Dunshee, John
Dunsire, David
Dunsley, Andrew
Durant, Christopher
*Durfee, Joseph
*Durfee, Robert
Dwight, Sereno, E.

Eaking, George
Eagle, Hugh
Eagleson, Charles
Earle, Peter
Early, John
Early, Thomas
Eary, William
Eastman, Andrew
Easton, Anthony
*Easton, Robert
Eaton, George
Eckland, Henry
Edgenton, Andrew
*Edmonds, John
Edmondson, Robert
Edwards, Alexander
Edwards, John
Edwards, Joseph
Edwards, Samuel
Edwards, William
Edweter, Joseph
Egan, Thomas
Elliot, William
Ellis, Caven
*Ellis, James
Ellis, Thomas
Ellison, Abraham

APPENDIX

Ellison, Elizabeth
Ellison, Jane
Ellison, Mary
Ellison, Sarah
*Elvins, Henry
English, Job
*English, Joseph
Ensie, William
*Enslow, Isaac
Erskine, Caleb
Ensor, George
Etherington, John
Etter, Franklin
Etter, John
Evans, James
Evans, John
Evans, Margaret
Evat, John
Every, Richard
Ewing, John

Fair, John
Fair, Margery
Fairclow, George
*Fairley, Alexander
Falconer, Thomas
Fanning, Edward
Farish, George
Farish, Greggs
Farnes, John
Farnes, Joshua
Farrar, Benjamin
Farrar, Lancelot
Farrar, Thomas
Farren, James
Farrens, John
Farrier, George
Farris, John
Farthing, John
Fash, George
Faygan, Lawrence
Faygan, William
Fenner, Lawrence
Ferguson, Donald
Ferguson, Duncan
*Ferguson, James
*Ferguson, John
Ferguson, Patrick
Ferguson, Thomas

Fernandes, Alexander
Fernandes, Mary & Son
Fin, Michael
*Finley, Jonathan
Finncane, Andrew
Fischer, Frantz
Fisher, Daniel
Fisher, George
Fisher, Peter
Fisher, Philip
Fitzgerald, Daniel
Fitzgerald, Thomas
Fitzimons, Henry
*Fitzpatrick, John
Fitzroy, Michael
Flack, Robert
Flewlings, Thomas
Flinn, Osborne
Flood, John
Floute, John
Fogarty, Edmond
Fogarty, John
Fogo, David
Foles, Younger
Forbes, Alexander
Forbes, Donald
Forbes, Duncan
Forbes, William
Ford, John
Foreman, William
Forgay, James
Forrester, John
Forster, Coynel
Forsyth, Thomas
Forth, Moses
Foshouse, Henry
Fosset, William
*Foster, William
Fountaine, Peter
Fowden, John
*Fox, Robert
Foy, Sarah
Frank, Johann
*Fraser, Alexander
*Fraser, Daniel
Fraser, Elizabeth
Fraser, Francis
*Fraser, Rev. Hugh
*Fraser, Hugh

*Fraser, Simon
Fraser, Thomas
Frazier, Alexander
Frazier, Daniel
*Frazier, James
Frazier, John
Frazier, widow
Freeman, William
Freity, Abraham
Freity, Catherine
Freity, John
Freity, Peter
French, Adolphus
French, George
French, James
French, John
French, Robert
Friedmiller, John
Friend, John
*Full, Thomas
Fullerton, Alexander
Fullerton, Samuel
Fullum, Michael
Fulton, Samuel
Furnass, Joseph

Galbreath, Joseph
Galguey, Thomas
Gallahan, William
Galloway, William
*Gamage, James
*Gammil, Mathew
Garbot, George
Gardler, Samuel
Gardiner, Benoni
Gardiner, Nathaniel
*Gardner, John
Gardonier, Jacob
Garell, John
Garland, Alexander
Garlick, Adam
Garnet, John
Garret, James
Garrey, Robert
Gates, James
Gatherer, Alexander
*Gautier, James
Gavel, John
Gay, Alexander

KING'S BOUNTY

Gay, James
Gearing, Patrick
Geary, Robert
Geddes, Charles
Gedney, Betsy
Gedney, Joshua
Geisner, Isaac
Geisner, John
Gernon, James
Gerow, Reynard
Gibson, Andrew
Gibson, Thomas
*Gibson, William
Gidney, Mary
Gilbert, Francis
Gilbert, Sarah
Gilchrist, William
Gildert, Mary
Gildert, Robert
Gill, Robert
Gilleese, Charles
Gillet, widow
Gillis, Roger
Gillison, Alexander
Gilroy, James
Ginworth, William
Given, John
Glass, John
*Glann, William
Glysop, John
Goddard, Daniel
Goddard, Elias
*Goddard, Henry
*Goddard, Job
*Goddard, John
Goddard, Lemuel, Sr.
Goddard, Lemuel, Jr.
Goff, James
Goldberger, Mathew
Golding, James
Goodick, Alexander
Goodick, Andrew
Goodwin, William
*Gordon, Alexander
Gordon, John
Gordon, Michael
Goring, Patrick
Gorman, Edmund
*Goswell, George

Govan, John
Gow, Robert
Gowans, Alexander
Graff, John
Graham, Edward
Graham, James
*Graham, John
*Graham, William
*Grandine, Daniel
Grandine, Samuel
Grant, Alexander
Grant, Daniel
*Grant, Gregory
Grant, James
Grant, John
Grant, Lewis
*Grant, Peter, Sr.
*Grant, Peter, Jr.
*Grasman, Caspar
Gratt, Michael
Graves, John
Graves, Thomas
Gray, George
*Gray, Isaac
Gray, James
*Gray, Peter
Gray, Reuben
Gray, Robert, Sr.
Gray, Robert, Jr.
Gray, William
Grayson, James
Greedy, George
*Green, Edward
Green, Thomas
Greer, Charles
Gregg, John
Gregg, William
Gregory, George
Gregory, John
Grey, Andrew
*Griffin, James
Griffin, John
Griffiths, Edward
Griffiths, Thomas
*Grosvenor, Benjamin
Grovestine, Garret
Gruber, Caspar
Grutzmacher, Johann
*Guest, Henry

Guinniet, William
Guyon, Peter
Gyssop, Jeremiah

Hadden, Jeremiah
Hagard, Stephen
Halbert, Titus
*Hale, William
Hall, Archibald
Hall, Henry
Hall, James
Hall, Richard, Sr.
Hall, Richard, Jr.
Hall, Samuel
Hall, Thomas
Hamiam, Ichongary
Hamiam, Nicholas
Hamilton, Alexander
Hamilton, Charles
Hamilton, Hugh
Hamilton, James
Hamilton, John, Sr.
Hamilton, John, Jr.
Hammond, Timothy
Hancock, Robert
Hand, Elizabeth
Handley, Patrick
Hannah, Edward
Hannah, Jean
*Hannah, Nathaniel
Hannegar, John
Hanney, Ephraim
*Hanney, Edward
Hanney, Nathaniel
Hanover, William
Harcourt, George
Harding, Elizabeth
Harding, George
*Harding, Jasper
Harding, Richard
Harding, Robert
Hardy, George
*Hardy, Joseph
Hardy, William
Hare, Thomas
Hargill, William
Hargin, Samuel
Hargraves, George
*Hargraves, William

APPENDIX

*Harper, William
Harrick, Thomas
*Harris, Daniel
Harris, Sarah
Harrison, Benjamin
Harrison, James
Harrison, Richard
*Harrison, Samuel
Hart, Anthony
Hart, Benjamin
*Hart, Charles
Harter, John
*Hartley, Thomas
Hartshaugh, George
Hartshorne, Lawrence
Hartshorne, Richard
Hartze, Jacob
Harvard, William
Harvey, John
Harvey, William
Harveyson, John
Hatch, William
Hatten, Robert
Haulenbeck, Isaac
Havily, widow
Hawkins, Thomas
Hay, John
Hay, Hugh
Hayden, Joseph
Hayden, Nathan
Hayden, Stephen
Haygan, Baret
Haygan, Samuel
Hayes, Jacob
Hayes, James
Hayes, Thomas
Hayley, James
Hayman, Adam
Haynes, John
Haynes, Mary
Haynes, Robert
Hays, Andrew
Hays, John
Hays, William
Hazzard, Stephen
Heath, Joseph
Heart, Joseph
Heffron, Richard
Hely, Timothy

Helley, James
Helyar, Samuel
Hembray, John
Hemion, Adam
Hemion, Henry
Hemmings, Robert
Hemmington, Edward
Hemson, Henry
Henderson, Alexander
Henderson, John
Henley, Patrick
Henley, Robert
Henreitz, Johann
Henry, John
Henryham, John
Hentz, Johann
Herbert, John
Herbert, Samuel
Herring, Abraham
Hetfield, Jacob
Hetfield, James
Hetfield, Job
Hetfield, Nathaniel
Hervey, St. John
Hervey, William
Hervison, William
Hewet, Andrew
Hewlings, Thomas
Hewstone, James
Hiat, Joseph
Hickey, Jeremiah
Hickey, Patrick
Hickman, David
Hicks, John
Hicks, Paul
Higgins, John
Higgins, William
Higgs, Richard
Highes, William
Hildrith, Isaac
Hill, Charles
Hill, Hugh
Hill, James
*Hill, Joshua
Hill, Nazareth
Hill, Robert
*Hill, William
Hilliard, Christopher
Hind, David

Hinselwood, Alexander
Hipworth, Joseph
*Hislop, John
Hoarow, Hugh
Hoary, Hugh
Hodgins, Robert
Hodgins, William
*Hodgkinson, Henry
Hodgkinson, Thomas
*Hodgson, Thomas
Hogarth, Andrew
Hogg, Alexander
Hokes, John
*Holden, James
Holden, William
*Holderness, William
Holland, George
Holland, Humprey
Holland, James
Hollingsby, Richard
Hollyday, William
Holmes, Joseph
Holmes, John
Holmes, William
Holstead, John
Holstead, William
Hoose, John
Horn, William
Horton, James
Horton, Jonathan
Horton, Richard
Hossiter, Herman
*Houston, Alexander
Houston, James
*Houston, Robert
*Houston, Thomas
Howard, Thomas
Howlings, Thomas
Howarth, James
Howe, John
Hoys, John
Hoyster, Herman
Hubbs, Zephaniah
Hubert, Adam
Hudson, Thomas
Huggeford, John
Hughes, Charles
Hughes, James
Hughes, John

KING'S BOUNTY

Hughes, Robert	James, David	Kaness, John
Hughes, Thomas	James, Francis	Keans, George
*Hughes, William	James, William	Keans, John
Hugby, James	Jamieson, Andrew	Kearny, Mary
Hulburt, David	Jamieson, Samuel	Kearny, Patrick
Hulburt, Titus	Jappie, Paul	Keeley, John
Huld, Michael	Jaram, Francis	Keenon, James
Hulick, Jacob	Jardine, John	Kees, Anne
Hull, Sylvester	Jarvis, Richard	Keesling, George
Hull, William	Jeans, Daniel	Keiler, John
Humphreys, James	*Jeans, Jenkinson	Kellum, Peter
*Hunt, Enoch	Jeans, Samuel	Kelly, Barney
Hunt, Gilbert	Jefferson, John	Kelly, Bartholomew
Hunt, Thomas	Jefferson, Joseph	Kelly, Hugh
Hunter, Duncan	Jeffrey, David	Kelly, James
Hunter, Francis	Jeffrey, John	Kelly, John
Hunter, George	Jenkins, David	Kelly, Michael
Hunter, Samuel	Jenkins, Peter	Kelly, Philip
Hurd, David	Jenkins, Richard	Kelly, Thomas
Hurry, Mary	Jenner, James	Kelly, William
Hutchins, Matthew	Jenner, Thomas	Kemble, Richard
Hutton, Robert	Jeram, Thomas	Kendal, William
Hyde, William	Jessop, Jeremiah	Kendrick, Daniel
	Jessop, John	Kenell, Robert
Ingham, Elizabeth	Johnson, George	Kennedy, Alexander
Ingham, Isaac	Johnson, Harman	Kennedy, Charles
Ingleson, Charles	Johnson, Joseph	*Kennedy, Dennis
Inglis, James	Johnson, John	Kennedy, Hugh
Inglis, William	Johnson, Lycas	Kennedy, John
Ingraham, Henry	Johnson, Patience	Kennedy, Michael
Inness, Stephen	Johnson, Robert	*Kenney, John
Inness, Robert	Johnson, Thomas	Kepling, Kiffin
Irvine, Daniel	*Johnston, John	Kert, John
Irvine, Serjeant	*Johnston, William	Kidd, George
Irwin, James	Johnstone, George	Kidder, William
Irwin, John	Johnstone, James	Killigrove, Henry
Irwin, William	Jolliffe, Richard	Killigrove, John
Isaac, William	Jolly, Joseph	Kilmerton, Miles
	*Jolly, Richard	Kilpatrick, James
Jack, James	Jones, Abraham, Sr.	King, Andrew
Jack, Robert	Jones, Abraham, Jr.	King, Eleanor
Jacklin, John	Jones, Benjamin	King, Henry
Jackson, Basil	Jones, James	King, Jacob
Jackson, Benjamin	Jones, Jedediah	King, John
Jackson, John	Jones, John	King, Patrick
Jackson, Samuel	Jones, Thomas	King, Robert
*Jackson, William	Jones, William	Kingsland, Cornelius
*Jackways, John	Jordan, Jeremiah	Kingsland, James
Jacobson, John	Joyce, Mathew	*Kingston, John

APPENDIX

Kinley, John
Kirk, John
Kirk, Samuel
Kitfield, Nathaniel
*Knapp, David
Knight, Samuel
Knopforadel, Johann
Knowland, Christopher
Knowland, James
Knowland, Richard
*Knox, Henry, Edward
Koesbar, Johann
Kysack, Michael

Lacey, James
Lacey, Richard
Laffan, Robert
Lafferty, Daniel
Lahey, John
Lamb, Richard
Lamb, William
Lambton, William
*Lamey, Michael
Lanaghan, Thomas
Lancefield, Attained
Lander, Mary
Lang, James
Langdon, John
Langrell, Charles
Langton, James
Laquaine, Francis
Largin, Michael
Larozay, William
Lathan, John
Laurens, Peter
Laughton, Hugh
Laurence, John
Laurence, Nicholas
*Laurence, Thomas
Lavender, Robert
Lavender, William
*Lawler, Dennis
Lawson, Douglas
Lawson, James
Lawthorp, Isaac
Layborn, Robert
Layton, John
Leader, Henry
Lear, Christopher

*Lear, Jesse
Leary, Michael
Leckie, Alexander, Sr.
Leckie, Alexander, Jr.
Leckie, James
Leckie, John
Leferew, Margaret
Legg, Andrew
Legget, John
Lehler, Johann
*Leighton, John
Lemmon, Joseph
Lenahan, Francis
Lennen, Andrew
Lenox, David
*Lenox, Peter
Lenox, Robert
Lent, Abraham
Lent, James
Lenzi, Philip
Leonard, James
Leonard, Jeremiah
Leonard, John
Leonard, Thomas, Sr.
Leonard, Thomas, Jr.
Leonard, William
*Leslie, James
Levi, John Lavan
Lewis, David
Lewis, Erasmus
Lewis, John
Leyburn, Robert
Light, William
Lighton, John
Limiken, Zebedec
Limmerman, Leonhard
Lindsay, James
Lindsay, Margaret
Lindsay, Michael
Lindsay, Ninian
Lippincut, Jacob
Lippincut, James
Lisle, John
Lissett, Maurice
Lister, James
Lithwit, James
Little, James
*Little, Peabody
Littlejohn, Thomas

*Littlewood, James
Lloyd, Thomas
Lockner, Gregorins
*Lodge, James
Logan, Patrick
Logie, John
Long, James
Lonsdale, John
Lord, Stephen
Lording, Charles
Lording, Edward
Lorier, Joost
Loring, Benjamin
Lorton, Lewis
Lothrip, Isaac
Lott, Levi
Loughran, Hugh
Loughran, James
Lowe, Charles
*Lowe, George
Lowe, John
*Lowndes, John
Lowney, John
Lowrey, Mary
Lowrey, Thomas
Lowrey, William
Lowrie, Robert
Lowrie, William
Luke, George
Lumley, Thomas
Lurton, Lewis
Luther, Henry
Luther, John
Lyle, Gavin
Lyle, John
Lyman, Oliver
Lymas, Thomas
*Lynch, Peter
*Lyon, Charles
Lyon, William

Mabey, Isaac
Macafee, Joseph
Mackie, John
Macklin, Henry
Madden, Michael
Mahan, Thomas
Mahane, Henry
*Mahane, Timothy

Mahany, Jeremiah
Mahany, John
Mailing, Barnet
Malcolm, Mary
Malcolm, John
*Malcome, Michael
Maldon, Charles
Malone, Anthony
Manderson, Archibald
Mann, James
Mann, John
*Mann, Samuel
Manning, Edward
Mannon, Edward
Mansfield, Isaac
Marchea, William
Marglar, Valentine
Marks, Conrad
Marling, Barnet
Marquis, William
Marsh, Elias
Marsh, John
Marsh, Joseph
Marsh, Thomas
Marshall, Alexander
Marshall, James
Marshall, John
Marshall, Richard
Marshall, Robert
Marshall, Samuel
Marsland, William
Marston, Benjamin
Martin, Archibald
Martin, Daniel
Martin, John
Martin, Robert
Martin, Thomas
Martin, William
Mason, Charles
Mason, George
Mason, John
Mason, Samuel
Massey, John
Mather, Andrew
Mathews, William
Mathieson, Alexander
Mathieson, Donald
Mathieson, John
Matthews, Daniel

Maugham, Joseph
Maxwell, Daniel
*Maxwell, David
May, Johann
May, William
Maybee, Cornelius
Maybee, Isaac
Maysey, John
Maysey, Thomas
Meeks, Joseph
*Mellow, David, Sr.
*Mellow, David, Jr.
Melville, William
Menzie, Alexander
*Menzie, John
Meredith, Matthew
Merrit, Robert
Mersey, Thomas
*Merston, Thomas
Messenis, Peter
Meter, Frederick
Meyer, George
*Meyers, John
Meyers, Thomas
Michaeler, Daniel
Michaeler, Peter
Michloe, Charles
Middleton, James
Middleton, Thomas
Midworth, Broomley
Milby, William
Milby, Zackdock
Miles, Francis
Miles, Thomas
Millar, John
Miller, Alexander
Miller, Andrew
Miller, Ann
Miller, Charles
Miller, Ezekiel
Miller, Frederick
Miller, George
Miller, Godfrey
Miller, Hugh
Miller, Isaac
*Miller, James
*Miller, John
Miller, Mathew
Miller, Richard

Miller, Robert
Miller, Thomas
Miller, William
Mills, Francis
Mills, Nathaniel
Milner, John
Milson, Edward
Minns, William
Minshull, John
Mismore, Ann
Mitchell, Alexander
Mitchell, Colin
Mitchell, Joseph
Mitchell, John
Mitchell, Thomas
Mitchell, William
*Moffat, James
*Moffat, Robert
Molloy, Michael
Molloy, Thomas
Molineux, William
*Moody, William
Mooney, Patrick
Mooney, William
Moor, George
Moor, Jonathan
*Moor, Robert
Moor, William
*Moore, James
Moore, Jasper
Moore, John
Moors, John
Moorfield, Richard
Moran, Thomas
More, Hampton
Morehead, John
Morewise, John
*Morgan, Caleb
Morgan, Willoughby
Morris, Alexander
Morris, Charles, Sr.
Morris, Charles, Jr.
Morris, Nathaniel
Morris, Noah
Morris, Robert
Morris, William
Morrison, Charles
Morrison, Edward
Morrison, George

APPENDIX

Morrison, John
Morrison, Peter
Morrison, Robert
Morrison, Samuel
Morrison, William
Morse, Ebenezer
Morse, Edward
Morton, Amos
Mortuney, Joseph
Mosely, Benjamin
*Mosely, George
Mosher, Elisha
Mosman, William
Moss, Ebenezer
Mott, Jasper
Mounsey, Thomas
Mountain, Richard
Mucham, Samuel
Mugford, Robert
*Muir, James
Muir, William
Muler, Matthew
Mulhall, Richard
Mullan, James
Mullen, Barney
Mullen, John
Mulligan, Peter
Mullin, Arthur
Munday, James
Munns, Alexander
Munns, Benjamin
Munns, James
Munro, Alexander
Munro, Benjamin
Munro, Bennet
*Munro, Daniel
Munro, John
*Munro, Nathaniel
Munro, William
*Murchy, William
Murphy, Arthur
Murphy, Francis
Murphy, James
Murphy, John
Murphy, Michael
Murphy, Patrick
Murphy, Thomas
*Murray, Alexander
Murray, Andrew

Murray, Archibald
Murray, Daniel
Murray, George
Murray, John, Sr.
Murray, John, Jr.
*Murray, William
Murreils, William
Murrow, John
*Musgrove, Bartholomew
Musgrove, William
*Myers, Frederick
*Myers, Jeremiah
Myers, Thomas
Myner, Philip
McAdam, James
McAlpine, Daniel
*McAlpine, Donald
McApline, Dougald
*McAlpine, John
*McAlpine, John
McAndrew, Alexander
McArthur, Archibald
McArthur, Colin
McArthur, John
McAulay, John
McAusland, Alexander
McBain, Donald
McBride, Thomas
McCaffey, John
McCallum, Colin
McCan, John
McCandry, Alexander
McCartin, James
McCarty, Dennis
McCarty, Florence
McCarty, James
McCarty, John
McCarty, Mary
McCarty, Timothy
McCarty, William
McClellan, John
McConisky, Neil
McConnachy, Peter
McConnel, John
McConnel, William
McCord, John
McCormick, Daniel
McCormick, John
McCormick, Nathaniel

McCowan, James
McCoy, Angus
McCracken, John
McCrary, John
McCrea, George
*McCrea, William
McCrugal, Neil
*McCrummin, Donald
*McCullock, Robert
McCullom, John
McDenough, Patrick
McDermot, John
McDonald, Alexander, Sr.
McDonald, Alexander, Jr.
McDonald, Angus
McDonald, Archibald
McDonald, Charles
McDonald, Christiana
*McDonald, Donald
McDonald, James
McDonald, John
McDonald, Michael
*McDonald, Neil
McDonald, Norman
*McDonald, Robert
McDonald, Roderick
*McDonald, Ronald
McDonald, Rory
*McDonald, Soirle
McDonald, William
McDonnaugh, Patrick
McDonnel, Michael
McDougal, Alexander
McDougal, Archibald
McDougal, Daniel
McDougal, Duncan
McDougal, Roderick
McDowal, Elenezer
McEcheron, Angus
*McEwen, James
*McEwen, John
*McEwen, William
McEwing, Michael
McFail, John
McFarlane, Archibald
McFarlane, Duncan
McFarlane, Peter
McGoughey, Robert
McGennis, Donald

McGeorge, John
*McGhee, John
McGilveray, Donald
McGilveray, John
McGinnis, Angus
McGonegall, John
McGossaghill, John
McGow, John
McGowan, John
McGragh, Ann
McGragh, James
McGregor, Alexander
McGregor, Charles
McGregor, Donald
McGregor, John
McGregor, Robert
McHenry, Neil
McIlroy, Hugh
McInnis, Donald
McIntire, Duncan
*McIntire, John
McIntyre, Angus
*McIntyre, Donald
McIntyre, Neil
McIntyre, Peter
McIntyre, Raymond
*McIntyre, Ronald
McIntosh, Alexander
McIntosh, Duncan
McIntosh, Finlay
McIntosh, John
McInulty, Jenkin
McIsaac, Neil
McIver, Donald
*McKay, Alexander
McKay, Donald
McKay, Gilbert
McKay, John
McKay, Neil
McKay, Robert
McKay, Thomas
McKay, William
McKegan, William
McKenney, Gilbert
McKenney, John
McKenney, Murdock
McKenyon, Duncan
*McKenzie, Alexander
McKenzie, Daniel

McKenzie, David
McKenzie, Donald
McKenzie, Francis
McKenzie, James
McKenzie, John
McKenzie, Kenneth
McKenzie, Mary
McKenzie, Murdock
McKenzie, Norman
McKenzie, Roderick
McKenzie, Valentine
*McKenzie, William
MacKenzie, John, Sr.
MacKenzie, John, Jr.
*McKerlie, John
McKerry, Francis
McKibbin, Henry
McKibbin, William
McKie, George
McKie, James
*McKie, John
McKillip, John
*McKinley, Colin
McKinley, John
McKinney, James
McKinney, John
McKinney, Joshua
McKinny, Elizabeth
McKinny, Gilbert
McKinny, John & Son
McKinny, Robert
McKinnon, Charles
McKinnon, Laughlan
McLachlan, Charles
McLachlan, William
McLaughlan, Archibald
McLaughlan, Charles
McLaughlan, Fardy
McLaughlin, Alexander
McLaughlin, Ferdinand
McLarlin, Alexander
McLaw, Charles
McLay, John
*McLean, Alexander
McLean, Allan
McLean, Donald
McLean, Duncan
McLean, Farquhar
McLean, James

McLean, John
McLean, Lachlan
McLean, Ludowick
McLean, Neil
McLean, Timothy
McLellan, Henry
McLellan, John
McLeod, Alexander
McClellan, John
McLeod, Angus
McLeod, Barbara
McLeod, David
*McLeod, Donald
*McLeod, John
McLeod, Murdock
McLeod, Robert
*McLeod, William
*McLinden, John
McManus, Thomas
McMaster, Daniel
*McMaster, James
McMaster, John
McMaster, Thomas
McMillan, Eleanor
*McMillan, Hugh
McMillan, John
McMullan, Duncan
McMullen, Alexander
McMurray, John
McNab, Alexander
McNab, James
McNabb, Donald
McNabb, William
McNamara, John
McNaughton, Duncan
McNeil, Charles
McNeil, Daniel
McNeil, Hannah
McNeil, James
*McNeil, John
McNeil, William
McNevin, Duncan
McNicol, Donald
McNicol, John
McPherson, Donald
McPherson, Evan
McPherson, John
*McPhiel, John
McQuaid, John

APPENDIX

McQuhae, Robert
McQuillon, Rowley
McRarry, John
McRoberts, James
McSperling, Isaac
McSparrow, Isaac
McTire, Alexander
McTire, John
McVane, Donald
McVicar, Donald
McVicker, John
McWaters, John
*McWaters, Thomas
McWilliam, Archibald

Nailer, Charles
Nairn, David
Napier, Robert
Neal, Daniel
Neal, James
Neale, Michael
Needham, Sebastian
Neil, Sebastian
Neilson, Robert
*Nelson, Anthony
Nelson, James
Nelson, Robert
Nelson, William
*Nesbit, Archibald
Newbury, Edward
Newman, Thomas
Newport, Sampson
Newton, Thomas
Nichole, Edward
Nicholl, William
Nichols, Duncan
Nichols, James
*Nichols, John
Nicholson, Caleb
Nicholson, Donald
Nicholson, Malcolm
*Nicholson, Neil
*Nicholson, Peter
Nixon, Thomas
Noe, Lewis
Norman, Joseph
Nostrand, John
*Nowland, Richard
Nugent, Arthur

Nunn, Samuel
*Nutter, Valentine

Oakes, Thomas
Oakes, William
Oakley, Arthur
O'Brian, Edward
O'Brian, John
O'Brian, Thomas
Odell, John
Ogden, Isaac
Ogden, John
Ogden, Nicholas
O'Hyrne, Morgan
O'Kelly, Michael
Olandson, John
Olinberg, Philip
Oliver, Charles
Oliver, Joseph
Omand, John
O'Neal, Barnaby
*O'Neal, John, Sr.
*O'Neal, John, Jr.
Oram, James
Orchard, Benjamin
Orcut, Joseph
Orr, John
Orr, widow
Otis, James
Owens, Thomas
*Owens, William
Oxford, Peter
Oxley, William

*Pack, John
Pagan, William
Paget, George
Paisley, John
*Palmer, Alpheus
*Palmer, Benjamin
Palmer, Jonathan
*Palmer, Lewis
Pannell, Obediah
Panton, George
Parbert, George
Parent, Thomas, Sr.
Parent, Thomas, Jr.
Parish, William
Park, John

Parker, Ebenezer
*Parker, Joshua
*Parker, Peter
Parkerhide, William
Parkinson, Martin
Parmeter, Lewis
Parr, William
Parsons, William
*Pashley, George
Pashley, William
Paterson, David
Paterson, George
Paterson, James
Paterson, Robert
Patient, John
*Patton, George
Patton, Ivis
Patton, John
Peachy, John
Peachy, Richard
Pearsol, Abraham
Pearson, Benjamin
Pearson, Jonathan
Peat, David
Peck, John
*Peck, William
Pederick, John
Peirce, Pitt
Peirce, Robert
*Pell, George
*Pell, Jonathan
*Pell, Joseph
*Pell, Joshua, Sr.
*Pell, Joshua, Jr.
*Pell, Samuel
Pendergrass, Matthew
Pendergrass, Thomas
*Penny, Richard
Penny, Samuel
Perbert, George
Perkins, Richard
Perrow, Richard
Perry, Jacob
Perry, John
*Perry, Samuel, Sr.
*Perry, Samuel, Jr.
*Perry, Silas
Perry, Spencer
Perry, Stephen

KING'S BOUNTY

Perry, Sturgis
*Perry, Thomas
Petit, John
Petit, John Samuel
Petit, Mary
Petrie, Newman
*Phillips, David
*Phillips, John
Phillips, Martha
Phillips, Mary
Phillips, Mathew
Phillips, Patrick
Phillips, Thomas
Philstead, John
Pike, Benjamin
Pike, Thomas
Pillar, John
Pimlo, Thomas
*Pitcher, Moses
Ploughman, Jacob
Ploughman, John
Ploughman, Peter
Plummer, Ezra
Pomroy, Richard
Pope, George
Porter, Andrew
Post, Isaac
Potter, David
*Potter, James
Potter, John
Potter, Thomas
*Potts, Christopher
Potts, John
Potts, Stephen
Potts, Thomas
Powell, David
Powell, Francis
Powell, Henry
Powell, John
Powell, Nathaniel
Powell, William
Powers, James
*Powers, Thomas
Pownal, Charles
Prentice, Archibald
Price, George
Price, James
Price, John
Price, Joseph

Price, Richard
Prichard, James
Prim, John
Prince, Reynold
Prior, Edmund
*Prior, James
Proctor, Isaac
Proctor, Thomas
Propert, William
*Prout, Timothy
Prow, John
Prynn, John
Purdy, John
Purney, Thomas
Pyberte, Francis
Pynchon, John
*Pynchon, Joseph
Pynchmate, Henry

Quin, Francis
Quin, Hugh

Raines, Robert
Rains, David
Ramsey, James
*Rand, Nathaniel
Randall, Amos
Randall, John
Randall, Robert
Randall, Thomas
*Randall, William
Randolph, Sarah
Ranky, Frederick
Rankin, Duncan
*Rankin, William
Rapalie, Cornelius
Rapalie, George
Rapp, John
Raton, David
Rawlings, Thomas
Ray, James
Raymond, George
Rayne, James
Read, William
Readon, Daniel
Reath, Archibald
*Reath, James
Reath, Kenneth
Redhead, William

Redman, Michael
Reed, Henderson
Reed, William
Rees, James
Rees, Thomas
Reeves, John
*Reid, Alexander
*Reid, Colin
Reid, George
Reid, Hugh
Reider, Michael
Reilly, Terence
Reily, Dennis
*Reily, Patrick
Reily, Paul
Rene, John
Renkie, Frederick
Ressler, Frederick
Ressler, Jacob
Revell, Richard
Rex, George
Reynolds, James
Reynolds, Nathaniel
Rhinelander, Frederick
Rhinelander, William
Rhode, Charles
Rice, James
Rice, Joseph
Rich, James
Rich, widow
Richard, Nicholas
Richards, Edward
Richards, John
Richards, Nathaniel
Richardson, John
Richardson, Thomas
Richmond, William
Rickets, John
Rickets, Joseph
Rider, Michael
Rider, Stephen
Rider, Thomas
Rigby, James
*Rigby, William
Riley, Patrick
Rine, George
Ringley, Elizabeth
Rioch, Alexander
Ritchie, John

300

APPENDIX

Ritson, John
Roach, Kenneth
Robb, John
Roberts, Henry
Roberts, James
Roberts, John
Roberts, Owen
Roberts, Thomas
*Robertson, Alexander
*Robertson, Alexander
*Robertson, James
Robertson, John
Robertson, John
Robertson, Neil
Robertson, William
Robins, William
*Robinson, Anthony
Robinson, John
*Robinson, Peter
Robinson, Robert
*Robinson, William
Rodman, Walter
Rogers, Barney
Rogers, Peter
Rogers, William
Rohl, Andrew
Roof, John
Roome, William
Root, John
Rose, Alexander
Rose, Benjamin
*Rose, James
Rose, John
Rose, Jonathan
*Rose, William
Ross, Alexander
*Ross, Andrew
Ross, Donald
Ross, Friend
Ross, Henry
Ross, James
Ross, John
Ross, Malcolm
*Ross, William
Rothwell, Thomas
Rourke, Daniel
Rowan, John
Rowat, Thomas
Rowe, Mathew

Rowe, Peter
*Rowlands, Thomas
Rowlands, William
Rowlett, John
Roxby, William
Roy, Charles
Russell, James
Russell, John
Rutherford, James
Ruton, David
*Ryan, Cornelius
Ryan, James
Ryan, Peter
Rymer, Andrew
Rymer, Hubert

Sampson, Robert
Sandford, Richard
Sargent, John
Savage, Abraham
Savage, Joseph
Saville, John
Sayer, Samuel
Schneider, George
Schneider, Samuel
Schneider, William, Sr.
Schneider, William, Jr.
Schooly, Michael
Schooly, Robert
Schweitzer, Frantz
*Scott, George
Scott, John
Seal, George
Seaman, Henry
Seaman, John
Sears, Samuel
Sellers, Archibald
Selkirg, Alexander
Selkirg, James
Semple, Thomas
Senter, Caleb
Senter, Philip
Servant, Abraham
Shackleton, Mark
Shaine, Donald
Shakespear, David
*Shakespear, Stephen
Shanahan, John
Shane, John

Shanley, William
Shank, Henry
Sharp, John
Sharpe, Alexander
Sharpe, Peter
Shaughnesy, John
Shaw, Donald
Shaw, John
*Shaw, Thomas
Sheekleton, Martin
Shellman, John
Shene, Donald
Sherry, Francis
Shipman, William
Shockney, John
Shoemaker, Joseph
Short, James
Shortoe, Samuel
Shoul, John
Shultz, Conrad
Silby, John
Simmons, Joseph
Simpson, James
Sinclair, Henry
*Sinclair, John
*Singleton, George
Sinsaber, Jacob
Sinsaber, William
Siverly, John
Skeddan, John
Slater, James
Slater, Joshua
Sline, James
Sline, John
Smallwood, William
*Smart, John
Smart, Thomas
Smith, Archibald
Smith, Aymar
*Smith, Benjamin
*Smith, Caleb
Smith, Daniel
Smith, David
*Smith, Emphraim
Smith, Eric
Smith, Hannah
Smith, Jacob
Smith, James
Smith, Job

301

KING'S BOUNTY

Smith, John
Smith, Michael
Smith, Peter
Smith, Thomas
*Smith, Whitford
Smith, William
*Smither, James
Somers, Paul
Sommerville, Robert
Sorrels, William
*Sparewater, Peter
*Sparling, Peter
*Speed, Paul
Speering, Henry
Speke, John
Spekeman, John
*Spencer, John
Spicer, Francis
Spiers, Agnes
Spiers, Francis
Spiers, Hugh
Spiers, John
Spiers, Robert
Spike, Daniel
Spillard, Timothy
*Spinks, James
Springall, Gregory
Sproat, David
Sproul, Andrew
Squires, William
*Stacy, Mathew
Stafford, John
Stalker, John
Standford, Richard
Stanhope, Henry
Stanley, William
*Stanton, John
*Stanton, Latham
Stanton, Mary
*Start, Moses
Stayer, Daniel
St. Clair, Henry
St. Clair, John
Stearman, Alexander
Stedrode, Jaspar
Steel, Adam
Steel, Andrew
Steel, Patrick
Steiger, Cornelius

Steinback, Thomas
Stephani, Gothelt
Stephens, Alexander
Stephens, William
Stephenson, John
Stevens, Abraham
Stevens, Alexander
Stevens, John
Stevenson, James
Stevenson, John
Stewart, Abraham
Stewart, Alexander
Stewart, Duncan
Stewart, John
Stiles, William
Stobart, Mathew
Stokes, James
Stokes, John
Stone, William
Stonehouse, Widget
Storey, John
Storey, William
Storell, Henry
Stout, David
*Stout, Delina
Strahan, James
Strahan, John
*Stremboock, Thomas
Strickland, John
Strong, Laurence
Strhum, Jacob
Strummy, Frederick
Stuart, Elizabeth
Stuart, George
*Stuart, John
Stuart, Mary
Stuart, Neil
Stuart, Robert
Stuart, William
Stubbords, Matthew
*Styman, Jacob
Styman, John
Such, widow
Such, William
Sullivan, Batholomew
Sullivan, Florence
Sullivan, Patrick
Summers, William
Sunderland, John

Sutherland, Adam
Sutherland, Daniel
Sutherland, John
Sutherland, Peter
Sutherland, Samuel
*Sutherland, William
Suthert, John
Sutliff, William
Swazey, John
Swift, Edward
Swinsburg, Christian
Swords, James
Swords, Thomas

Tail, John
Talbut, John
Tankard, Mathew
Tanley, John
Tanley, Thomas
Tannery, Michael
Taunton, George
*Taylor, Ann
Taylor, Charles
Taylor, David
Taylor, James
*Taylor, John
Taylor, Margaret
Taylor, Peter
Taylor, William
Teal, John
Telfair, Charles
Telford, Samuel
Temple, John
Templeton, Oliver
Tenbroeck, Henry
*Tench, John
Tennor, Thomas
Terrill, John
Terrill, William
Thomas, Edmund
Thomas, Edward
Thomas, George
Thomas, Jonathan
*Thomas, Nathaniel
*Thomas, Richard
Thomas, William
Thompkins, Abraham
Thompson, Alexander
Thompson, Archibald

APPENDIX

Thompson, Ezekial
*Thompson, James
Thompson, Richard
Thompson, William
*Thomson, David, Sr.
*Thomson, David, Jr.
Thomson, George
*Thomson, John
*Thomson, Robert
Thorne, Anthony
Thornhill, Peter
Thynne, James
Timpson, Benjamin
Tochar, John
Togay, John
*Tolbut, John
Toles, Younger
Tomlinson, Richard
Tonge, Mercy
Tonge, William
Tooker, Jacob
Torgay, James
Torrance, Hugh
Torvine, James
Tottie, William
Townsend, Benjamin
Townsend, Jacob
Townsend, John
Townsend, Richard, Sr.
Townsend, Richard, Jr.
Townsend, Thomas
Townsend, Timothy
Towzie, Francis
Tracy, John
Trapp, John
*Tribe, William
Trighler, Mary
Triglith, Edward
Truston, Robert
Tuckeness, John
Tullock, Peter
Tullock, Robert
Tully, Christopher
Tully, Thomas
Tunnercliffe, Joseph
Tuns, John
Turnbull, John
*Turnbull, Robert
*Turnbull, Thomas

Turnbull, Walter
*Turner, John
Turner, Joseph
Turner, Silas
*Turrel, John
Tyler, Margaret
Tyson, Cornelius

Underwood, Benjamin
*Ure, John
Urquhart, John

Vassey, John
*Vassey, Joseph
Veitch, Gavin
Vent, Joshua
Vernon, Nathaniel
Vincent, William
Vinckler, Joseph
Voght, Christopher
Van Blarckon, Peter
Van Blarckon, Ryah
Van Buskirk, Abraham
Van Buskirk, Andrew
Van Buskirk, Jacob
Van Buskirk, John
Van Buskirk, Lawrence
Van Buskirk, William
Vanderhoern, Minard
Van Emburge, Adonijah
Van Emburgh, Gilbert
Van Emburgh, James
Van Emburgh, John
Van Horne, Cornelius
Van Irestein, John
Van Loe, John
Van Norden, Cornelius
Van Norden, Gabriel
Van Norden, John
Van Norden, Stephen
Vanright, John
Van Ripeh, Cornelius
Van Tuyle, Dennis
Van Vaert, Ann
Van Vaert, John
Van Voorst, Arron
Van Vousin, David

*Wade, John

Wadhem, Thomas
Wainwright, John
Walker, Alexander
Walker, David
Walker, Hugh
*Walker, John
*Walker, Richard
Walker, William
Wall, Edward
*Wall, George
Wall, Patrick
Wallace, Mathew
Wallace, William
Walsh, James
*Walsh, Joseph
Walson, Daniel
Walter, William
Walters, James
Waltham, Thomas
*Ward, Edmund
*Ward, Ira
Ward, Patrick
Ward, Thomas
Ward, William
Wardell, Ann
Wardell, John
Warden, George
Warden, William
Wardlaw, John
Warner, John
Waterman, Margaret
Waters, John
Watson, Alexander
Watson, Catherine
Watson, Daniel
Watson, David
*Watson, George
Watson, James
*Watson, John
Watson, Joshua
Watson, Robert
Watson, William
Watt, William
Watts, Charles
Watts, George
Watts, Hugh
Waugh, James
Weaver, Michael
Webber, Oliver

Weber, Michael
Webster, Henry
*Webster, John
Webster, Thomas
Weir, Archibald
*Weir, Thomas
Weiser, Frederick
Weiser, Jacob
Weisner, Leonard
Wells, Benjamin
Wells, Dudley
*Wells, George
Welsh, Isabella
Welsh, James
Welsh, John
Welsh, Joseph
Welsh, Thomas
West, Benjamin
Western, Joseph
Westervelt, Garret
Westfall, Frederick
Westland, Thomas
Westwood, Samuel
Wetherall, Nathaniel
*Wetton, Richard
White, Aaron
White, Alexander
*White, Amos
White, Briton
White, Cabel
*White, Charles
*White, David
*White, Duncan
White, Eleanor
*White, Gideon
*White, James
White, John
*White, Richard
White, Robert
Whitehouse, William
Whitham, John
*Whiting, Thomas
Whitman, John
Whitmore, Rachel
Whitmore, Richard
Whittal, David
Whitten, Richard
Whitworth, Charles
Whunn, James

Wier, William
Wilkie, John
Wilkins, Isaac
Wilkins, Martin
*Wilkins, Robert
Wilkinson, John
Wilkinson, William
Willett, John
Williams, Arthur
*Williams, Daniel
Williams, Drummer
Williams, Jacob
*Williams, John, Sr.
*Williams, John, Jr.
Williams, Oliver
*Williams, Richard
*Williams, Samuel
Williams, William
Williamson, George
*Williamson, Richard
Williamson, Tunis
Williamson, William
Will, Lawrence
Wills, Samuel
Wilson, Andrew
*Wilson, David
*Wilson, James
*Wilson, John
Wilson, Michael
Wilson, Thomas
*Wilson, William
Wilton, Richard
Winants, John
Winckler, Joseph
Winn, Francis
Wise, John
Wise, Joshua
Witham, John
Withers, Michael
Witherspoon, William
Wittendale, Alexander
*Wood, Benjamin
Wood, Francis
Wood, Joseph
Wood, Richard
Wood, Robert
Wood, Thomas
Woodman, William
Wooley, Edward

Worth, Benjamin
Worth, James
Worth, Thomas
Worthley, John
Wren, Mary
*Wright, Daniel
Wright, David
Wright, James
Wright, Thomas

Yanks, Crine
Yates, James
Yates, John
Yelvin, Henry
Yeoman, Ezekiel
Young, Alexander
Young, David
Young, Edward
Young, James
Young, Peter
Young, Robert
Young, William
*Yule, James
Yule, Peter

APPENDIX

Black Grantees to Land in Shelburne Township Bordering Beaver Dam Lake

Aarons, Jacob
Aitkins, Andrew
Anderson, Isaac
Aysh, William

Bachus, Thomas
Baley, Charles
Baley, George
Bennet, Joseph
Berges, Jefry
Bowler, Arthur
Bracey, Jonas
Broughton, Benjamin
Brown, John
Brown, John
Brown, Patty
Brown, Simon
Bush, Isaac
Bush, Richard

Campbell, Ezekiel
Channel, Scipio
Cheese, William
Christian, Sally
Church, Limuch
Colethurst, Rachel
Conner, Philis
Cook, Henry
Cooper, John
Cox, Edward
Cox, Ned
Cromwell, Peggy

Davis, Thomas
Davis, William
Dickson, Absolum
Dickson, Samuel
Dixon, Charles

Earl, Hannah
Elliot, Edward
Evans, Thomas

Farmer, Jupiter
Ford, Charles
Ford, Demps
Francis, Peter

Freeman, Thomas
Frost, Benjamin

Garnett, Bristol
George, Elizabeth
Gibbons, John
Glasgow, Jonathan
Godfry, Ely
Gray, Harry
Gwin, Harry

Halstead, James
Harden, Peter
Harris, Betsy
Harrison, Francis
Hazel, Abraham
Hector, James
Henry, Elizabeth
Howard, Ansel

Jackson, John
Jackson, Judith
Jeffry, Godfry
Johnson, Diana
Johnson, George
Johnson, James
Johnson, Levin
Johnson, Peter
Johnson, Prince
Johnson, Thomas
Johnson, Tobias
Johnson, Tobias
Jones, Francis
Jones, John
Jones, Shadrick
Jordan, Luke
Joy, John

Kelly, Moses

Langley, Jane
Lawrence, Philip
Lawrence, Richard
Lawson, Edward
Lawson, Jacob
Lawson, Joseph
Lawson, Solmon

Lawton, Richard
Low, Cesar

Marrant, John
McKay, John
Miller, Doublin
Miller, Richard
Mills, Renty
Mills, Thomas
Moore, Lewis
Moore, Sanuel
Morris, Robert
Moses, Hoalstead
Moses, Murray
Moseman, Susannah

Newcomb, James

O'Neal, William

Pandarvis, Lewis
Parelay, Daniel
Patrick, Thomas
Paul, John
Perkins, Cato
Perry, Prince
Peters, Stephen
Pharo, Peter
Phripp, Daniel
Pool, Benjamin
Prentice, John
Prior, John
Propyt, Richard

Raimant, Dover
Ramsey, Elinor
Raven, Joseph
Ray, James
Reid, James
Rich, Christopher
Richard, Sloan
Right, Caithness
Rippon, Austin
Rivers, Rachel
Roach, Richard
Robinson, Niel
Robinson, Prince

305

KING'S BOUNTY

Robinson, William	Sullivan, Demps	Waring, John
Russel, Hannah	Taskew, Nathan	Washington, Harry
	Taylor, John	White, Elizabeth
Salsberry, John	Thomas, Amos	White, Samuel
Salsberry, Peter	Thomas, John	Whitten, Samuel
Sanders, David	Thompson, Charles	Wicks, Peter
Sanders, Thomas	Thompson, James	Wilkins, Toney
Sawyer, Berry	Thompson, James	Wilkinson, Charles
Seaburne, John	Toney, Jane	Wilkinson, Moses
Shatter, Isaac	Trowel, Joseph	Williams, Billy
Sheppard, Benjamin	Truin, Henry	Williams, Cesar
Sheppard, Thomas	Trust, Anthony	Willis, Herbert
Shields, Thomas	Turner, Nathaniel	Wills, William
Smith, Luke	Turner, Robert	Willson, Luke
Smith, Sandy		Willoughby, Edward
Smith, William	Upham, John	Wise, George
Snowball, Nathaniel		
Spurr, Cyres	Venters, London	York, Charlotte
Stewart, James		York, Samuel
StJago, John	Waiscoat, Joseph	Young, James

Stephen Bluck, lot no. 4, Thomas Lawrence, lot no. 1, each 200 acres at the rear of Captain Durfee's land on the west side of Shelburne Harbour.

Grants to Black pilots:
Joseph Restine, Town lot, block L, no. 5, North Division, Shelburne Water lot, block A, no. 104, North Division, Shelburne McNutt's Island, lot no. 27, 50 acres.

James Jackson, London Jackson, Richard Leach, James Robertson each 12½ acres of 50 acre lot no. 23, McNutt's Island.

References

REFERENCES CONSULTED

Among the documents given to me or which were loaned and copied for use in this history were deeds, copies of the assessment rolls for 1786 and 1787, excerpts from the General Sessions, 1786-1791, Special Sessions for the County of Shelburne, 1786-1801, Special Sessions for the Town of Shelburne, 1784-1786, tombstone records, letter books, account books, naval records of vessels entering the port of Shelburne, 1796-1822, diaries and notebooks, and a photocopy of the Minute Book of the Port Roseway Associates. Some of these documents have been placed, since I copied them, in libraries and archives, notably the Booth Diaries ('Rough Notes and Memorandums') in the Acadia University Library (AUL), the Naval Office records in the Dalhousie University Archives (DUA), and the photocopy of the Minute Book of the Port Roseway Associates in the Public Archives of Nova Scotia. Privately owned documents have been listed in the reference notes with the designation (P).

In the Shelburne Court House (SCHR) I copied such records as memorials, excerpts from the Court of Session Records, deeds, wills and probate records and lists of grantees. The Public Archives of Canada (PAC), Ottawa; the Public Archives of Nova Scotia (PANS), Halifax; Dalhousie University Archives (DUA), Halifax; Acadia University Library (AUL), Wolfville, N.S.; the National Library (NL), Ottawa; Court House Records, Lexington, Virginia; the University of New Brunswick Library (UNB), Fredericton, N.B.; and the Library, Colonial Williamsburg, Williamsburg, Virginia, have yielded many documents from which excerpts were taken and many hundreds of pages photocopied. The following includes the chief of these documents.

DOCUMENTS

Public Archives of Nova Scotia, Halifax, N.S.
In the series RG 1, documents from the following volumes: 2, 23, 31, 45, 49, 51, 136, 137, 169, 170, 211, 212, 221, 223, 228, 28, 369, 374, 394, 423, 443, 458; RG 5, Series A, Vol. 1A, 2, 3; RG 7, Vol. 43; RG 14, Vol. 58; RG 20, Vol. 20, Series C, Vol. 93; RG 31, Treasury Papers, Lighthouse Duties, Bounty Certificates.
From MG 1, Vols. 947-962, White Collection of documents

KING'S BOUNTY

MG 1, Vol. 479, Memoir 1775-1814, Bishop Charles Inglis
MG 1, Vol. 742, No. 14, Pioneers of Presbyterianism, Rev. G. Patterson
MG 4, Vol. 141, "History of Shelburne County," T. W. Smith

Colonial Office Papers (CO), 217/18, 217/63, 217/35

Other records and manuscripts:
  Census, 1693
  Supreme Court Records, 1768-1773
  Surveyor's notes, Founding of Shelburne, 1783, William Morris
  Crown Grant Records and Petitions for Land
  History of Trinity Church by Marion Robertson (manuscript)
  Mediterranean Passes, 1767-1789
  Ship's Registry Papers (microfilm)
  Manuscript File (Shelburne)
  Revenue Reports, Nova Scotia House of Assembly Papers
  Statutes of Nova Scotia, 1787, cap. 3
  Letter of the Society for the Propagation of the Gospel (microfilm)
  Dorchester Papers

Public Archives of Canada, Ottawa, Ont.
Minute Book, Port Roseway Associates, MG 9, B 9-14, Vol. 1, which includes under the same number the Muster Book of the Freed Black Settlement of Birchtown, 1784, Memorial of the Overseers of the Poor to Shelburne Magistrates, February 3, 1789, and "A Sketch of Shelburnian Manners, 1787."
Carleton Papers (CP) or British Headquarters Papers
Colonial Office (Nova Scotia) Papers (CONS), documents from Vols. 17, 18, 19, 20, 21
Colonial Office (Nova Scotia) Papers, A 116, Memorial, Shelburne Merchants, 1791
Colonial Correspondence, Prince Edward Island, Vol. 9, Document 389

Memorials, Returns, Wills, Dispatches:
  Memorial, Shelburne Merchants (c. 1785), MG 14, B 11, Series 1-14D
  Memorial, Church of Scotland (Shelburne), MG 21 BM add 19071, folio 220
  Return of Negroes going to Africa, MG 11, CO 217, Nova Scotia A, Vol. 116
  Early Wills of Shelburne, Nova Scotia Local Records, MG 9, B 9-14
  Provincial, Local and Territorial Records, Nova Scotia, MG 9, B 6
  Military Dispatches (microfilm), Public Record Office, London, CO 217/41, B 1035

REFERENCES

General Sessions of the Court of Shelburne, 1786; Extracts of General Sessions of the Court of Shelburne, 1787-1860; Extracts of General Quarter Sessions, 1784-1785; Extracts of Special Sessions, 1784-1800, Nova Scotia Local Records, Shelburne, MG 9, P 9-14

Shelburne Court House Records, Shelburne, N.S.
Court of Session Records
Court of Probate Records
Register of Deeds and other documents pertaining to the history of early Shelburne

Mount Allison University Library, Sackville, N.B.
Winthrop Bell Collection

University of New Brunswick Library, Fredericton, N.B.
Winslow Papers, Marston's Diary (manuscript), Vol. 22

Dalhousie University Archives, Killam Library, Dalhousie University, Halifax, N.S.
Naval Office Records, Port of Shelburne, Ships Entering Port 1796-1827 (microfilm)
Campbell Papers, MS 4-1
Home Office Papers, Public Record Office, London, HO 76 and 2 (1790-1797) (microfilm)

Acadia University Library, Wolfville, N.S.
Captain William Booth, 'Rough Notes and Memorandums, 1789,' 208673 #6
J.A. Durkee, Baptish Church of Ragged Island, 1782-1882, (manuscript), A 286, M OM $O_3$2D

National Library, Ottawa, Ont.
General Clinton's Proclamation, Rivington's Royal Gazette, July 31, 1779 (microfiche)

Court House, Lexington, Virginia
Deeds and Appraisal of the estate of Alexander McNutt

Library, Colonial Williamsburg, Virginia
British Headquarters Papers or Carleton Papers

KING'S BOUNTY

Library, Wellesley College, Wellesley, Massachusetts
Rand manuscript
Notes on McNutt family

Society for Promoting Christian Knowledge, London
Letters and Minutes of the Society, relative to the Bray Schools in Birchtown and Shelburne

MAPS AND CHARTS

Nova Scotia Department of Lands and Forests, Land Registry and Research (Crown Grants Office), Halifax, N.S.
Shelburne Portfolio: maps and plans, Nos. 3, 5, 7, 16, 25, 37, 38, 50, 51, 56, 61
Plans of warehouse lots (Cove), B. Marston, January 2 and April 18, 1784
Plan of Murray Location copied from original by R.E. Dickie, 1945
Plan of North End of Shelburne, August 30, 1785
Compiled Plan of the Town of Shelburne, V-153A
Index Sheets Nos. 17, 18, 19, 25
Plan of Shelburne Common

Public Archives of Nova Scotia, Halifax, N.S.
Plan of Shelburne Township with engineer's reserves, RG 20, Series C, Vol. 93, Document 89
Plan of Point Carleton, RG 20, Series C, Vol. 93, Document 43
Plan of land grant to Alexander McNutt and Associates, N.S. Gen. 1766.
Maps of 1500s:
    Jean Rotz, c. 1535 (completed 1542)
    Diego Homen, 1558
    Lozaro Luis, 1563
Maps of 1600s:
    Samuel de Champlain, 1607
    Nicolas Denys, 1672
    Jean Baptiste Louis Franquelin, 1686
Maps of 1700s:
    Carte de l'Acadie, 1703
    Carte de l'Acadie, 1744
    A new map of Nova Scotia and Cape Britain [sic], 1755
    Chart, 1755, ordered by Charles Lawrence
    Map ordered by Edward Cornwallis, 1759
    Barrington Township, 1761

REFERENCES

Maps of 1800s:
  "Cabotia," made by His Majesty's Officers and Surveyors, 1814
  A.F. Church map, Shelburne County, 1882

Public Archives of Canada, Ottawa, Ont.
Carte de l'Acadie, J.B.L. Franquelin, 1702
Port Wager, by Captain Thomas Durell, 1734 (H3/240)
South West Coast of the Peninsula of Nova Scotia, surveyed by Captain Des Barres, 1776
Chart, Port Roseway Harbour, 1784 (H3/240)
Shelburne [1783] (H3/240)
Roseway or Shelburne Harbour with engineer's reserves, 1785 (240)
Shelburne or Port Roseway Harbour, by Thomas Backhouse, 1798 (VI/240)

Shelburne Court House Records
Plan of land for old settlers of Port Roseway, 1785

Other Maps
South-West Coast of Acadia, 1751, in Joseph Bernard, marquis de Chabert de Cogolin, *VGOYAGE Fair par Ordre du Roi en 1750 et 1751, dans l'Amérique,* Paris, Imprimerie Royale, 1753.

NEWSPAPERS, JOURNALS

Baptist Annual Register, 4v. by J. Rippon. London, 1793-1802, Vol. 1, pp. 473-483, Acadia University Library, xerox.
Port Roseway Gazetteer, Royal American Gazette, Nova Scotia Packet, Public Archives of Nova Scotia (PANS), M 54, Vol. 142
Nova Scotia Magazine, 1971, PANS
Nova Scotia Gazette, PANS
Yarmouth Telegram, PANS
The Remembrancer, "Events for the Year 1784," London, 1874, Part 1, Public Archives of Canada (PAC)

REPORTS, BULLETINS, TRANSACTIONS, COLLECTIONS

New Brunswick Historical Society.
  Collections, Vol. 8. W.O. Raymond, "The Founding of Shelburne."

Public Archives of Nova Scotia
   Report, 1933. William Booth, "Journal of a Tour with Genl. Campbell in July and August 1785"
   Report, 1937. "Tour from Windsor to Cape Negro"
   Report, 1946. James Munro, "Description and History of the Southern and Western Townships of Nova Scotia, 1795"
   Bulletin, Vol. 1, No. 1, *A Documentary Study of Early Educational Policy in Nova Scotia*.
   Bulletin, Vol. 1, No. 17, *Local Government in Nova Scotia* by C. Bruce Fergusson
   Nova Scotia Historical Society. *Collections*, Vol. 28, Thomas H. Raddall, 'Tarleton's Legion'
   Collections, Vol. 29, Charles Stayner, "Sandemanian Loyalists" Ontario. Bureau of Archives. Second Report, 1905, 2 v. 'Loyalist Claims' Royal Society of Canada. *Transactions*, 1910, Sect. II, Series 3, Vol. 4, W.H. Siebert and F.E. Gilliam, "The Loyalists in Prince Edward Island"
   Transactions, 1912, W.O. Raymond, "Colonel Alexander McNutt and the Pre-Loyalist Settlements of Nova Scotia"

Public Archives of Canada
   Report, 1884. 'Report of Col. Robert Morse, R.E., 1784.'
   Report, 1894. 'Calendar of Papers Relating to Nova Scotia, 1603-1801.'
   Report, 1905, Vol. 2, Appendix A, Part 3. Laurent Molin, Census, 1671.

BOOKS

Akins, Thomas B., *Selections from the Public Documents of the Province of Nova Scotia*, Halifax, N.S., Charles Annand, 1869.

Alline, Henry. *The Life and Journal of the Rev. Henry Alline,* Boston, Gilbert and Dean, 1806.

Benedict, David, *A General History of the Baptist Denomination in America*, New York, Colby, 1848.

Bernard, Joseph, marquis de Chabert de Cogolin, *Voyage Fait par Ordre du Roi en 1750 et 1751, dan l'Amérique*, Paris, Imprimerie Royale, 1753.

Brown, George S., *Yarmouth, Nova Scotia*, Boston, Rand Avery Company, 1888.

Campbell, J.R. *History of the County of Yarmouth, N.S.*, Saint John, N.B., J. & A. McMillan, 1876.

Champlain, Samuel de, *The Works of Samuel de Champlain*, Toronto, The Champlain Society, 1922-36.

REFERENCES

Crowell, Edwin, *A History of Barrington Township and Vicinity, Shelburne County, Nova Scotia, 1604-1870,* Yarmouth, N.S., n.p., 1923.

Denys, Nicolas, *Description and Natural History of the Coasts of North America. (Acadia),* Toronto, The Champlain Society, 1908.

Doane, Alfred Alder, *The Doane Family and Their Descendants,* Salem, Mass., Salem Press, 1902.

Dyott, William, *Dyott's Diary.* Reginald W. Jeffery, ed., London, Constable, 1907.

Fergusson, Charles Bruce, *Clarkson's Mission to America, 1791-1792,* Public Archives of Nova Scotia, Publication No. 11, 1971.

General Orders for the Government of Officers in the Plantations (1764-1805), London, Printed by H. Teape for H.M.S.O., 1805.

Hollingsworth, S. *Present State of Nova Scotia,* 2d ed., Edinburgh, Printed for W. Creech, 1787.

Jephcott, C.M., V.G. Green and J.H. Young, *Postal History of Nova Scotia and New Brunswick, 1754-1867,* Toronto, Sessions Publications, 1964.

Jones, Thomas, *History of New York During the Revolutionary War,* Edward F. DeLancey, ed., New York, N.Y. Historical Society, 1879.

Jost, A.C., *Guysborough Sketches and Essays,* Kentville, N.S., Kentville Publishing Co., 1950.

Kirk-Green, Anthony, 'David George: the Nova Scotia Experience.' The Sierra Leone Studies, 1960. PANS vertical file.

Knox, John, *An Historical Journal of the Campaigns in North America for the Years 1757, 1758, 1759 and 1760.* Edited by A.G. Doughty, Toronto, The Champlain Society, 1914.

MacKinnon, Ian F., *Settlements and Churches in Nova Scotia, 1749-1776,* Montreal, Walker Press, nd.

Morse, William Inglis, ed. *Acadiensia Nova,* 2v., London, Quaritch, 1935.

Murdoch, Beamish, *A History of Nova Scotia or Acadie,* 3v., Halifax, N.S., James Barnes, 1865-1867.

Napier, Henry Edward, *Journal of Henry Edward Napier, Lieutenant in HMS Nymphe.* Walter Muir Whitehead, ed., Salem, Mass., Peabody Museum, 1939.

Nova Scotia. House of Assembly. Journals, 1784-1789.

Nova Scotia. Laws, Statutes, etc. *The Statutes at Large Passed in the Several General Assemblies Held in His Majesty's Province of Nova Scotia,* ed. by Richard John Uniacke. Halifax, N.S., John Howe and Son, 1805.

Perkins, Simeon, *The Diary of Simeon Perkins,* 4v., Toronto, The Champlain Society, 1948-1967.

Poole, Edmund Duval, *Annals of Yarmouth and Barrington, Nova Scotia in the Revolutionary War,* Yarmouth, N.S., Yarmouth Herald, 1899.

Rand, Silas T., *A First Reading Book in the Micmac Language*, Halifax, N.S., Nova Scotia Printing Co., 1875.
Micmac Place-Names in the Maritime Provinces and Gaspe Peninsula, Ottawa, Geographic Board of Canada, 1919.
Raymond, W.O., ed., *Winslow Papers, 1776-1826*, Saint John, N.B., New Brunswick Historical Society, 1901.
Robinson, John and T. Rispin, *A Journey Through Nova Scotia*, York, C. Etherington, 1774.
Siebert, Wilbur Henry, *Loyalists in East Florida, 1774-1785*, DeLand, Florida State Historical Society, 1929.
Smith, T.W., *History of the Methodist Church in Eastern British America*, 2v., Halifax, N.S., Methodist Book Room, 1877-90.
Stark, James H., *The Loyalists of Massachusetts*, Boston, J.H. Stark, 1910.
Ward, Christopher, *The War of the Revolution*, 2v., New York, Macmillan, 1952.
Webster, J.G., *Acadia at the End of the Seventeenth Century*, Saint John, N.B., New Brunswick Museum, 1934.
Wright, James Leitch, Jr., *Florida in the American Revolution*, Gainesville, University of Florida, 1975.

INDEX

A

Acker, 249
Ackerman, John, 71, 228
Ackerman, William, 220
Ackland, Philip, 168
Ackland's Landing, 166
Adams, Thomas, 205
Adams, William, 164, 201
Adamson, John, 57
Affleck, Capt. William, 55, 113
Aimes, John, 72
Alline, Rev. Henry, 25
Alpin, Joseph, 125, 129, 170
Anderson, David, 97
Anderson, John, 208
Anderson, Samuel, 79, 96
Andes, Peter, 190
Annapolis, 62, 104, 113, 136, 160-161
Annapolis, road to, 158-161
Annapolis (Rell's) Road, 159-163
Annapolis Royal, 79, 159
Anna's River, 8
Apel Creek, 9
Appleby, John, 193
Appleby, Robert, 71, 141, 155
Argyle, 79, 95, 142, 143, 148
Argyle Road, see Tusket Road

Argyle Township, 136
Armstrong, William, 85
Arnold, Benjamin, 22, 26, 27, 135, 166
Artisans, 206-207
Ash, William, 98, 105
Ashton, Philip, 7
Aspect Lake, 160
Assessors, 141
Atkins, John, 228
Atkinson, John, 60
Atkinson, Thomas, 76
Attorneys, 209
Atwood, Jesse, 22
Auchumty, James, 108
Aymar, John, 71

B

Bacalhaos, 3
Backman, 249
Bain, Alexander, 163
Bald Mountain, 160
Ball, Lieut. Nicholas, 112
Ball, Thomas, 97
Bakers, 204-205
Banta, Weart, 43
Barbers, 204

Barclay, Andrew, 33, 41, 43, 135, 162, 200, 206, 212
Barclay, Major, 95
Barr, John, 43
Barracks; abandoned, 112-113; constructed, 110; ferry, 168; Inspected by Prince William Henry, 111; mentioned, 248, 252, 253
Barrack's Cove, 248
Barrington, 62, 142, 164, 170, 174
Barry, A. and R., 200, 226
Barry, Alexander, 200, 226
Barry, Robert, 167, 173, 174, 182, 200, 203, 226
Basque, 1, 2
Battery Point, 115
Baxter, Jonathan, 141, 208, 217, 228
Bay Chaleur, 91
Beattie, George, 40, 141, 151, 205
Beaver Dam Lake, 91
Belchar, Elizabeth, 18
Bell, Joseph, 71, 76, 155
Bell, Joseph, 194, 208
Bell and Company, 194
Bellman, 209
Benjamin Davis, Son, and Co., 202, 220, 222, 226
Benning, Gilbert, 22, 134
Bernard, Benjamin, 143
Berry, Ebenezer, 21, 22, 24
Berry's Point, 165, 178
Bertrand, Catrine P., 5
Bertrand, Claude, 5
Bethune, Alexander, 248
Bethune, Ann, 248
Bethune, John, 248
Beusablom, 3
Bingay, Thomas, Jr., 225
Binney, Stephen Hall, 235
Birch, Brig-General, 47, 84, 86, 87
Birch Point, 164
Birchtown, 47, 77, 79, 83-106, 129, 141, 144, 154, 163, 181
Birchtown Bay, 8, 110
Birchtown Creek, 135
Birchtown Lake, 257
Black, David, 198
Black, Joseph, 209
Black, William, 40, 193, 206

Black, Rev. William, 173
Black's Brook, 160, 194
Blacks; Black Pioneers, 84, 86, 89; Freed Blacks, 47, 51, 70, 77, 79, 83-106; Ships and Companies Blacks came in, 86-88, 108; to Sierra Leone, 99-106
Black Strap Cove, 8
Blacksmiths, 208, 228
Blackwell, John, 40
Blair, John, 205
Blanchard, Lewis, 71
Blewer, John, 61
Blewer, Peter, 61, 135
Blockmakers, 228
Bluck, Col. Stephen, 87, 89, 99, 101, 105, 141, 144, 159
Blue Island, 136, 193
Board of Agents; appointed, 129; mentioned, 122; Parr supports, 137; work of, 129, 134-137
Bond, Dr. Joseph, 210
Boole, Francis, 135
Booth, Capt. William, 94, 110, 112, 118, 154, 210, 215
Boudinot, Elias, 68
Bounty of Provisions, 80-82
Bousfield, Michael, 223, 226, 229
Bower, Adam, 61, 112, 187, 201, 255
Bower, Charles, 61
Bower, Philip, 61
Bowers, Bartholomew, 155, 202
Bowman, George, 141
Bowood, 62
Boyce, Gideon, 73
Boyd, James, 174
Boyd, John, 174
Bragh, Elisha, 146
Braine, Thomas, 152
Braine and Reilly, 203
Brandon, Mrs., 187
Brantwaite, William, 209
Bray, Dr. Thomas, (Associates of), 99, 181
Brazel, Richard, 43, 99, 181, 237
Breen, Hugh, 71, 203
Brewer, Joseph, 129, 140, 201
Brewers, 193
Breynton, Rev., Dr., 99
Brickmakers and bricklayers, 193, 207

INDEX

Bridges, 167
Bridges, Capt. Robert George, 88
Bright, Mr., 193
Briggs, William, 141
Brinley, Edward, 80, 210
Brinley, Dr. Francis, 210
Broad Bay, 9
Brown, Elizabeth, Jr. 150
Brown, Frederick, 205
Brown, John, 208
Brown, Rev. Joseph, 172
Brown(e), Nicholas, 40, 43, 204
Brown, Patty, 97
Brown, Roswell, 99
Brown, Sylvester, 205
Bruce, Andrew, 148
Bruce, James, 79, 188, 226, 231, 237
Bruce, Robert, 76, 141, 201
Bruff, Charles Oliver, 33, 141, 206, 217
Buchanan, David, 204
Budnet, George, 57
Building the town, 117-122
Bulgin, Thomas, 252, 256
Bulkeley, Richard, 32, 34, 35, 68, 105
Bunker, Capt. Solomon, 221
Burial Grounds, 62
Burleigh, Edward, 208
Burling, Samuel, 72, 125, 131, 134, 144
Burns, Dr. William, 104, 210
Burnside, Thomas, 190
Burnt Head, 109
Burton, Rev. John, 172
Burton, Joseph, 60, 201
Burton, William, 33
Bush, Henry, 22
Bush, Lemuel, 21
Butchers, 204
Byrne, Patrick, 228

C

Cabinetmakers, 206-207
Cahill, Mathew, 143, 152, 235
Cain, Timothy, 268
Calder, Andrew, 204
Caldwell, Elizabeth (Widow), 16, 18
Caldwell, John, 16, 18
Caldwell, Richard, 14

Caldwell, William, 14, 15
Calender, 204
Cambria Settlement, 257, 258
Cameron, Alexander, 209
Cameron, Daniel, 135
Cameron, David, 208
Cameron, Duncan, 57
Campbell, Archibald, 43, 194
Campbell, Brig-Gen., 31, 78, 80, 81, 110, 111, 127, 158, 159
Campbell, Colin, 166, 170, 176, 209, 251, 252, 253, 254, 258
Campbell, George, 187
Campbell, Robert, 207
Campbell, Col. Samuel, 61, 143, 201
Campbell, William, 78, 79
Campbell's Point, 194
Candlemakers, 206
Cannon, Arcada, 94
C. de S. Jaque, 2
C. Neigre, 4, 7
C. du Cap de Sable, 4
Cap de Sable, 5, 7
Cape Negro, 3, 22, 67, 73, 88, 164, 187, 195
Cape Negro Harbour, 124, 164
Cape Negro Island, 20
Cape Negro River, 14, 136, 163
Cape Negro Shores, 22, 136
Cape Roseway, 8, 190
Cape Sable, 3
Cape Sable Island, 20
Carleton, Sir Guy, 30-138, *passim*, 235, 241
Carleton Village, 19, 21, 24
Carman, Jonathan, 150
Carpenters, 206-207, 228
Carson, William, 225
Cartmen, 208
Cartwrights, 208
Castle, William, 33, 43, 194, 195
Caulkers, 228
Cavan, Edward, 133
de Cogolin, Chabert, 7
Chads, Capt., 85
Chamber of Commerce, 155
Champlain, Samuel de, explores coast, 3-4
Chandler, Dr., 177

317

Charles Point, 9
Charleston, 90, 95, 98
Cheever, Rev. Israel, 25
Chester, Gov., 78
Chimney sweep, 208
Chisholm, George, 33
Christian, Capt., 87
Christy, John, 78
Church, Charles, 141, 217
Churches and Religions,
    171-180; Anglican (Church of
    England), 98, 177-180; Baptist, 97-98,
    172-173; Calvinist, 172; Calvinist
    Methodist (Countess of Huntington
    Connexion), 98; Christ Church, 112,
    180, 181; Congregational, 172;
    Descendants of Huguenots, 171-172;
    Lutheran, 314; Presbyterian, 174-176;
    Sandemanians, 171; St. John's Kirk,
    176, 202; Society of Friends
    (Quakers), 171; Wesleyan Methodist,
    98, 173-174
Churchill, Josiah, 22, 134
Churchover, 62, 125, 135
Clark, James, 125, 209
Clark, John, 57
Clarke, George, 248
Clarkson, Lieut. John, 100-104, *passim*
Clarkson, Thomas, 100
Clemmens, Isaac, 205
Clerk, Robert, 92
Clinton, Sir Henry, 29, 47, 83
Clippen, Margaret, 92
Clisby, John, 43
Clothier, 204
Clyde River, 14, 62, 91, 136, 157, 163,
    164, 167, 216, 227, 248
Coattam, Thomas, 181, 182
Cobscooch, 2
Cockawhite, 136
Cocken, Capt. Alexander, 40, 41, 141,
    190, 191, 229
Cockery, John, 227
Coffeehouses, see Taverns
Coffin, Hannah, 92
Coffin, John, 143
Colby, John, 22, 26
Coldwell, George, 205
Cole, John, 207

Collins, James, Sr., 152, 204
Collins, James, Jr., 204
Colquhon, Peter, 204
Colville, James, 16, 18, 19
Combauld, Richard, 143, 209, 237
Commissionary, appointed for
    Shelburne, 80
Commissary Island, 80, 113, 144
Common, for farm lots, 62, 136, 214, 216
Connor, Daniel, 204
Connor, Jeremiah, 182
Constables, 141, 219
Cook, Francis, 143
Cooke, John, 43
Cooling, Michael, 145
Cooper, John, 155
Coopers, 194
Coppersmiths, 205, 206
Cordwainers, 208
Cornwallis, Lord, 29
Corrin, James, 227
Cotman, Christopher, 22, 135
Council for Plantations, 13
Courtney, James, 33, 43, 63, 166, 195,
    197
Courtney, Richard, 33, 43, 201, 203
Courtney, Thomas, Jr., 79
Courtney, Thomas, Sr., 33, 34, 128
Courtney's Lake, 257
Courts, mentioned, 92, 93, 95, 96, 216,
    219, 241, 243, 250
Courts of Justice, established; Inferior
    Court of Common Pleas, 143; Court
    of Oyer and Terminer, 144, 149-150
Courts of Sessions; administrative
    responsibilities, 152-170; established,
    138-143; judicial responsibilities,
    146-152; officers of courts appointed,
    139-144
Cove market, 151-152
Cowling, John, 181, 182
Cox, James, 249
Cox, James, 57, 93, 95, 96, 170, 195, 201,
    203, 225, 226, 231
Crab Rocks, 9
Craig, John, 22, 141, 172
Cranberry Lake, 160
Crane's Point, 20
Crawley, Jeremiah, 187

INDEX

Crawley, John, 143
Creighton, John, 215
Crowell, Ansel, 19, 20
Crowell, Archelaus, 19, 20, 26
Crowell (Crowe), Joshua, 22
Crowell, Moses, 19, 20
Cullers of fish, 141
Cullers and inspectors, hoops and barrels, 141, 219
Cummin, James, 195
Cunningham, Archibald, 140, 170, 188, 189
Cunningham, William, 199, 224, 226
Currie, Alexander, 208
Currie, John, 208
Customs House, Naval Office, and Officers, 114, 235-239
Cutt, Donald, 78
Cutt, John, 78

D

Daily, Dennis, 204
Dalhousie, Earl of, 250, 254, 256, 258
"Dancing beggars", 183
Davenport, Isaac, 202
Davenport, Samuel, 155, 161, 162, 202
Davidson (Davison), John, 33, 40, 140, 148
Davies, Ann, 251
Davies, Anne, 251
Davies, David, 251, 257, 259
Davies, David, Jr., 259
Davies, John, 251, 253, 254, 257
Davies, John, 252
Davies, John, Jr., 251, 258
Davies, Joshua, 252
Davies, Margaret, 251, 252
Davies, Margaret, 251
Davies, Mary, 251, 259
Davies, Michael, 259
Davies, Phebe, 251
Davies, William, 251, 252
Davies, William, Jr., 252
Davis, Benjamin, 129, 140, 142, 143, 144, 148, 152, 155, 171, 226
Dean, Capt. Nicholas, 124, 134
Debtor's room and dungeon, 145

Decline of Shelburne and disposal of settlers, 240-245
Deinstadt, George Henry, 208
DeLancey, Adj.-Gen. Oliver, 47, 57
DeMings, Anthony, 18, 19, 26
DeMings, Mrs. Anthony, 25
DeMolitor, 249
Denham, Thomas, 141, 217
Deschamp, Isaac, 16
DesChamp, Thomas, 208
Dexter, Jesse, 19, 20, 21, 26
Dexter, Jesse, Jr., 21
Dexter, Elisha, 21
Dexter's Brook, 21
Dickey, James, 227
Dickinson, Nathaniel, 40
Dickson (Dixon), Robert, 22
Digby, Admiral, 30, 34, 40, 41, 49
Distribution of the land, 123-137
Divisions, Marston's, 125, 215; Mason's, 125, 135, 215; of town, 53, 61; of township, 61-62, 125-126
Doane, Asa, 19
Doane, Eleazer, 19
Doane, Nathan, 19, 169
Doane, Samuel O., 26
Dole, Capt. James, 33, 34, 35, 43, 57, 68, 141, 166, 168, 188, 194, 195, 214
Donaldson, James, 188
Donaldson, Pompey, 96
Donaldson, Samuel, 152
Donaldson, William, 203
Donnough, Patrick, 140
Dore, James, 225
Doris (Dores), John, 61
Dorney, Luke, 40
Doty, Thomas, 19, 20
Dougherty, John, 204
Douglas, Sir Charles, 114
Douglas, George, 136, 224, 233
Dowers, Joseph, 71, 76
Dripps, Rev. Matthew, 175, 176, 181, 248
drover, 208
drummers and pipers, 209
Drummond, Dr. George, 210, 237
Drummond, Robert, 195, 208
Duke, James, 204
Duncan, James, 174

Duncan, Thomas, 43
Dundass, George, 43
Dunlop, Alexander, 141, 158
Dunmore, Lord, 94, 95, 179
Durell, Thomas, 8, 108
Durfee, Joseph, 32, 33, 34, 41, 43, 65, 135, 139, 140, 143, 164, 190, 214, 224
Durkee, Thomas, 143
Dyott, William, 111

E

Eagle, Hugh, 135, 168
Eagle's Road, 164
Earle, Peter, 141
East Jordan, 134, 165
East Ragged Islands, 22
Edmeston, Col., 211
Edwards, Major, 111, 112
Edwards, Samuel, 73
Edwards, Simeon 21-24
Eisenhauer, 249
Elliott, Edward, 87, 155, 208
Elliott, W., 48
Ellison, Abraham, 141, 155
Elphinston, Capt., 65
Elvins, Henry, 43, 141, 219
Engravers, 205
d'Entremont, Phillippe, 5
Enslows Point, 164
Evans, Evan, 252, 254, 256, 257, 258
Evans, David, 252
Evans, John, 252, 257
Evans, Llewellin, 252
Evans, Maria, 252
Evans, Owen, 252
Evans, Rachel, 252
Ewing, John, 145, 205

F

False Passage, 8, 9, 17, 136
Fanman, Shak, 209
Fanning, John, 79
Fanning, Lieut.-Gov., 212
Farrer, Thomas, 168, 202
Farish, Greggs, 150, 163, 200

Farish's Road, see Tusket Road
Farming, 6, 208, 214-217
Fees; for ferries, 168-169; for measures, 208; for town crier, 209
Fence viewers, 19, 141, 217
Ferguson, Henry, 17
Ferguson, James, 203
Fernandes, Alexander, 188
Ferries, 168-169
fiddlers, 209
filemaker, 193
Fire Engine, 155
Fires, 157, 197
Fire Protection: Firemen (Firewards) appointed, 141, 155; regulations and prices for sweeping chimneys, 141, 155
Firth, 247
Fisheries, 5-6, 8, 64, 217-220
Fleming, John, 205
Fletcher, Dr. Richard, 210
Fogarty, Edmond, 182
Forsyth, Thomas, 204
Fort Elliot, 115-116
Fort Point, 23, 64, 109, 227
Fowler, Capt. Jonathan, 251, 253
Fox, Brig-Gen., 75, 80, 89, 108
Fox Point, 8
Fox, Robert, 140
Fraction, Capt. George, 88
Franquelin, J.B.L., 4
Fraser, Hugh, 33, 201
Fraser, Rev. Hugh, 174, 175
Frazer, Alexander, 43, 146
Frazer, Alexander, Jr., 43
Frazer, James, 33
Freemantle, Samuel, 204
Freitz, Abraham, 61
Freitz, John, 61
French explorers and mapmakers, 2-4
French from St. Pierre and Miquelon, 249-250
French settlers, 4-10
French, James, 204
French, John, 204
Fretz, Catherine, 201
Frost, Joshua, 143
Frude, Peter, 22

INDEX

G

Gamage, James, 33, 43, 144, 148, 161
Gammel, Robert, 92
gardeners, 208
Garretson, Freeborn, 173-174
gaugers, 141, 235
Gautier, James, 40, 140, 143
Gay, Alexander, 141
Gay and Lowe, 200, 222
General Assembly, 238
George, David, 97, 98, 104, 172
George and Greggs Farish, 200
George and Robert Ross, 203
Georgia, 90, 135
Gibbon, Abraham, 171
Giffin, Widow, 22
Gilbert (Gildart), Frances, 78
Gilchrist, Capt. John, 244
Gilfillan, Ann, 16, 17, 19
Gilfillan, Capt., 85
Gill, Capt. Robert, 60
Goddard, Daniel, 206
Goddard, Henry, 206
Goddard, Job, 206
Goddard, Lemuel, 141, 179
Godfrey, Enoch, 22, 135
Gold Lake, 259
Goldsbury (Goldburg), Mathews, 71
goldsmith, 206
Golfe de Petis, 3
Gordon, John, 198
Gordon, Michael, 140, 168
Gould, Dr. John, 210
Gould, Thomas, 96
Government Point, 8, 109
Governor and Council, 37, 217, 234
Gow, Robert, 73
Gracie, George, 170, 176, 202, 203, 220, 225, 226
Graham, John, 152
Graham and McLean, 202
Grandin(e), Daniel, 43, 93
Grand Lake, 255
Gray, Jesse, 79, 95, 96
Gray, Robert, 129, 134, 143, 190, 209
Gray, Capt. Robert, 191, 245
Gray Island, 136
Great Bay, 166

Greer, John, 97
Green Harbour, 7, 22, 124, 134, 165, 227, 247
Green Island, 22, 136
Green River, 14
Greenwood, William, 18, 22
Grenville, Lord, 197, 219
Grenville, William, 100
Griffiths, Edward, 204
grist mills, 195-197
Grist mills, 195, 197
Grosvenor, Benjamin, 40, 43
Guest, Henry, 155, 181
Gunning Cove, 9, 19, 21, 62, 73, 124, 136, 163, 227
gunsmith, 208
Guyon, Peter, 225

H

Hale, William, 43, 136, 152, 190, 191, 193, 200, 231
Halifax, 55, 79, 128
Hall, Henry, 207
Hall, Richard, 159, 179, 193, 195, 200
Hambleton, Col., 37, 60
Hamilton, Anna, 248
Hamilton, Elizabeth, 248
Hamilton, James, 71, 163, 168, 216, 248
Hamilton, John, 89
Hammond, Sir Andrew Snape, 32, 34, 68
Handsled Lake, 160
Handy, Rufus, 40
Hannah, Nathaniel, 195
Harbour Point, 8
Harding, Elizabeth, 203
Harding, George, 33, 135, 141, 186, 197
Harding, Jasper, 33, 136
Harding, Richard, 33
Harding, Robert, 33
Hardy, John, 152, 226
Hardy, Joseph, 22
Hare, Capt. Patrick, 108, 233
Hargill, William, 73
Hargraves, William, 201, 220
Harlow, 249
Harmony Hall, 214
Harper's Lake, 135

Harris, David, 258
Harris, Henry, 257
Harris, John, 257, 258, 259
Harris, John, 92, 204
Harris, Samma, 257
Hart, Benjamin, 193, 228
Hart, Charles, 43, 193
Hartley, Thomas, 40, 43, 228
Hart's Point, 8, 67, 110, 112, 114, 135, 193, 247
Hartshorne, Lawrence, 100, 101
Harvey, William, 129, 141, 174
hatters, 204
Hawkes River, 9
Hayden Lake, 16
Hayden, Capt. Nehemiah, 71, 72
Hayden, Thomas, 22, 24, 134
Hayes, Hugh, 140, 187
Heater, William, 205
Hefferman, Christian, 182
Hefferman, John, 40
'Hemeon, Elizabeth (Rowland), 249
Hemlock Creek, 259
Henderson, Anthony, 15
Henderson, Jean, 79
Henderson, John, 95
Henderson, Samuel, 14, 15
Herbert, John, 94
Herbert, Sarah, 94
Herbert, Thomas, 94
Herring Falls, 61, 135
Hessian soldiers, 76, 70, 243
Hewet, Andrew, 79
Hewit, Hercules, Jr., 22
Hewit, Hercules, Sr., 22
Hewit, John, Sr., 22, 24
Hewit, John, Jr., 22
Hewlet, Jacob, 205
Hicks, John, 212
Hildreth, Isaac, 134, 135, 179, 207, 214
Hill, Joshua, 33, 150
Hill, William, 33, 34, 95, 140, 155
His Majesty's Council, 216, 234
His Majesty's Council of Nova Scotia, 8, 9, 13, 17
Hitchens, William, 257
Hobbard, Matthew, 150
Hodgkinson, Henry, 204
Hodgson, Michael, 57

Hogg's Island, 20
hogreaves, 141, 217
Holderness, William, 201, 223
Holmes, Deborah, 172
Holmes, William, 172
Homer, John, 143
Hoose, Dr. John, 148, 174, 210
Hopkins, John, 22
Horton, David, 257, 259
House of Assembly, 212, 217, 241, 257, 258; members of, 169-170
House of Correction, 146-147
Houston, Alexander, 181, 197, 215
Howe, Gen., 47
Howe, John, 171
Howe, Sir William, 177
Howie, James, 204
Hoyl, Capt. Jesse, 191, 226
huckster, 208
Hudson, Thomas, 43
Huggeford, Dr. John, 71, 76, 210
Hughes, John, 94
Hughes, Mary, 112
Hughes, Owen, 40
Hughes, Sir Richard, 114
Humphreys, James, 157, 170, 201, 212
Hurd, David, 95
Huskins, Joseph, 22
Hutchins, Capt., 87, 88
Hutchins, Matthew, 209, 237
Huskins, Job, 22

I

Indian Creek, 259
Indian Leap, 8
Inglis, Bishop Charles, 177, 180, 181
Ingomar, 22
Ingram, Joseph, 99
Ingram, Joseph, 228
Irish at Port Roseway, 5
I. aux Cannes, 4, 7
I. aux Herons, 7
I. aux Loups Marins, 4
I. du Bon Portage, 7
I. Moillée, 7
Isle of Cormorants, 3
Isle of Tousquet, 5

INDEX

J

Jack, Light Horse, 97
Jackson, James, 73
Jackson, Landon, 73
jail, 146-147
James Cox and Company, 201, 215
James, Jonah, 252
James, Rachel, 252
James, Sarah, 252
James, Thomas, 252
Jeans, Daniel, 204
Jefferys, Ann, 251
Jefferys, Ellenor, 251
Jefferys, Evan, 251
Jefferys, Mary, 251
Jefferys, Morgan, 251, 253, 254
Jefferys, Morgan, Jr., 251
Jefferys, Sarah, 251
Jenkins, David, 252, 256, 257, 258
Jenkins, John, 258
Jenkins, Capt. Peter, 141, 194, 219, 226, 233
Jenkins, Richard, 71, 134, 194
Jenner, Thomas, 140
Jerusalem, township of, 14
Jessop, Daniel, 141
Jessop, William, 174
jeweller, 206
Johnson, Col., 111
Johnson, Edward, 268
Johnson, Levin, 88
Johnson, Mary, 146
Johnson, Tobias, 91, 154
Johnson, William, 40
Johnson, William, Jr., 40
Johnson, Sir William, 211
Johnston, James G., 209
Johnston, John, 168, 187
Johnston, Josiah, 148
Jolly, George, 93
Jones, Abraham, 71, 214, 225
Jones, Francis, 87, 88
Jones, Henry, 93, 95
Jones, Hugh, 257
Jones, Jacob, 22, 26
Jones, James, 257
Jones, John, 136
Jones, John (from Wales), 257

Jones, Jonathan, 252, 256
Jones, Sarah, 149
Jones, Thomas, 252, 256, 257, 258
Jones, Thomas (Mason), 257
Jones Harbour, 19, 22, 135, 136
Jones Point, 126, 165, 214
Jordan, 162
Jordan Bay, 21, 125, 134, 248
Jordan, East, 134, 195, 247
Jordan Ferry, 168
Jordan Roads, 164-166
Justices of the Peace, 64-65, 139, 142

K

Kannisay, Cato, 85
Kean, William, 248
Keaquick, John, 57
Keeling, Charles, 201
Keeling, John, 155
Kempt, Sir James, 258
Kendrick, Dr. Daniel, 93, 210
Kennedy, Dennis, 43
Kennedy, Hugh, 88
Kennedy, John, 148
Kespoogwit, 1, 2
Ketchum, Thomas, 205
Killigrove, Henry, 73
Killigrove, Lancelot, 268
King, Andrew, 207
King, Boston, 84, 87, 91, 97, 98, 105, 227
King, Henry, 208
King, Isaac, 22, 24, 143
King, Robert, 207
King, William, 99
King in Council, 216, 234
King Street Market, 151-152
King's broad arrow, 113
King's Forest, 114, 165
King's Pilots, 72-73, 135
King's slip, 113
King's wharf, 113
Kings Wood, 67
Kinlock, 247
Kirby, Benjamin, 19, 20
Kirby's Cove, 20
Kirby's Creek, 20
Kirk, Samuel, 71, 76, 141, 150, 161, 201
Knox, Henry Edward, 43, 65

L

La beaubai, 3
Lahey, John, 166, 209
Lake Courtney, 195
Lake Deception, 160, 248, 255
Lake George, 135, 160, 195, 214
Lake John, 134, 165
Lake Rodney, 135, 165
Lalloue, Amand, 4
Lalloue, Amand, Sieur de Rivedu, 4
Lalloue, Ammant, 4
Lalloue, Ellisabet, 4
Lalloue, Ellisabet N., 4
Lalloue, Janne, 4
landwaiter, 235
Largin, Michael, 78, 129, 191, 237
Latham, John, 22
"Lauchey's", 247
Lawrence, Gov., 9, 10
Lawrence, Thomas, 194
Lawrence, York, 87, 88
Lawson, Lieut. William, 42, 55, 61, 66, 107, 108, 110
Leach, Richard, 73
Lear, Jesse, 43, 93, 181, 225
Leary, W., 182
Leckie, Alexander, 81, 122, 129, 141, 143, 169, 170, 195
Leckie, James, 141
Leeds, Hysem, 96
Lent, Abraham, 141, 158, 219
Lenzi, Philip, 146
Leonard, Capt. Thomas, 71, 76, 136, 244
Les jardines, 3
Levi, Levin, 160
Lewis, John, 22
Lewis, Lewis, 257
Lewis Head, 23
Lighthouse, Cape Roseway, 189-192
Limerick, 98.
Lisitt, Patrick, 79
Little Harbour, 22, 135, 248
Littlewood, James, 141
Liverpool, 20, 21, 23, 98, 161, 167
Liverpool Road, 161-162
Liverpool Township, 29
Lobster Shoal, 8
Locke, Jacob, 21, 22
Locke, Jonathan, Jr., 22, 134
Locke, Jonathan, Sr., 22, 134, 172
Locke, Mrs. Jonathan, Sr., 172
Locke, Mary, 172
Lockeport, 22
Lodge, James, 40
London, 89, 100
London, Thomas, 93
Londonderry, Ireland, 15
Londonderry, Nova Scotia, 15, 17
Long, George, 61
Long Island, 114, 124, 248, 252, 254-256
Loon's Point, 8
Lords of Trade and Plantations, 10-14
Loring, Dr. Benjamin, 71, 210
Low, Ned, 7
Lowe, George, 43
Lownds, John, 40, 43, 129, 159, 194, 202
Lowrie, Mrs., 162, 187, 244
Loxy, Joseph, 256
Loyal, Anthony, 93
Loyal, Hagar, 93
Loyalists; from Carolina, 60-61; from Florida, 78-79; from Marblehead, 55; from Port Mouton, 77
Lunsford, Isaac, 174
Lyman, Oliver, 62, 67, 88, 124, 158
Lyman, William, 227
Lynch, Peter, 33, 34, 43, 129, 140, 166, 194
Lynch and Kelley, 200
Lyon, Rev. James, 15

M

McAfee Lake, 160
McAlpine, John, 43
McAlpine, John (Barber), 204
McCrimmon (McCrummon), Lt. Donald, 78, 168
McCullum, John, 193
McDermott, Patrick, 187
McDonald, Alexander, 168
McDonald, Donald, 248
McDonald, Michael, 204
McDonald, Capt. Murdock, 225, 248
McDonald, Neil, 227, 229
McDonald, Soirle (Savil), 19

INDEX

McEwen, James, 64, 129, 139, 140, 143, 174, 235
McEwen, John, 43
McFarlane, David, 205
McGill, David, 225, 246
McGill, George, 155
McGill, William, 155, 204, 246
McGill's Point, 194
McGrath, James, 168
McIntosh, Robert, 248
McKay, Ann (McPherson), 247
McKay, Catherine, 248
McKay, David, 248
McKay, Donald, 247, 248
McKay, Donald "Barracks", 113, 248
McKay, Donald (from Scotland), 227, 248
McKay, Sgt. Donald, 214, 256
McKay, Sgt. Gilbert, 214
McKay, Hugh, 247
McKay, James, 247
McKay, James (from Scotland), 247
McKay, Janet, 247
McKay, Lanchlan, 227
McKay, Robert, 247, 248
McKay, William, 247
McKay Lakes, 247
McKenna, Archibald, 248
McKenzie, Alexander, 208
McKenzie, Ann, 248
McKenzie, John (cartman), 208
McKenzie, John (tailor), 204
MacKenzie, John (weaver), 247
MacKenzie, Major, 70
MacKenzie, Nancy, 247
McKenzie, Roderick, 189
McKie, James, 204
McKinnon, Maria, 210
McLean and Boyle, 199, 223, 224, 226
McLean, Duncan, 209
McLean's Island, 126, 214
McLean's Point, 165
McLeod, Donald, 19
McLeod, John, 61
McMaster, James, 33, 201
McMaster, Thomas, 225
McMillan, Duncan, 22
McNeil, Charles, 129, 141, 143, 169, 170
McNutt, Agnes, 16, 17, 19, 24

McNutt, Alexander, 10-18, 23, 24, 62, 135
McNutt, Arthur, 16, 17, 19
McNutt, Benjamin, 16, 17
McNutt, Bernard, 16, 17
McNutt, Francis, 16
McNutt, John, 16, 17
McNutt, Joseph, 14, 15, 16
McNutt, Martin, 16, 24
McNutt Island Road, 166
McNutt's Island, 8, 17, 67, 109, 136, 166, 190
McPhail, John, 195
McPhail, Thomas, 201
McPherson, Donald, 78
McPherson, Elizabeth, 247, 248
McPherson, Janet, 248
McPherson, John, 247
McPherson, Lauchlan, 247, 248
McPherson, Lanchlan, 247
McQuaid, John, 153, 208
McQuhae, Robert, 161, 195, 208
McWaters, Thomas, 207
Mactier, Mackie and Company, 200
Mahon, Thomas, 207
Major, Captain, 224
Malcome, Michael, 205
Mallow, David Henry, 155
Mann, James, 174
Mann, John, 141, 173, 174
Mann, Michael, 228
Mann, Capt. Samuel, 93
Manning, Edward, 204
Mansfield, Isaac, 171
Maple Point, 8
Marketplace, 151-152
Clerks of the market, 141
Marks, Conrad, 61
Mark's Brook, 160
Marrant, Rev. John, 98
Marsh, Elias, 227
Marshall, Martin, 195, 208
Marshall, Samuel, 136, 193
Marston, Benjamin, 42-241, *passim*
Martin, Bernard, 227
Martin, Capt., 22
Martin, Elizabeth, 248
Martin, John, 162, 248
Martin, John Allen, 79, 237

Mascarene, Paul, 8
Mason, Charles, 52, 61, 67, 88, 209, 214
Mason, John, 268
Masonic Lodges, 185
masons, 207
Mathews, Daniel, 22, 135
Mathews, John, 22, 134
Maugham, Joseph, 208
Maugham, William, 95
Meader, Capt., 196, 226
Measures of coal, grain, salt, 141, 208
Medical store, 210-211
Megumaagee, 1
Merchants and shopkeepers, 198-203
Meston, Thomas, 202, 224
Michaeler, Daniel, 61
Michaeler, Peter, 61
Micmac, 1-3
Migler, Daniel, 79
Milby, Sarah, 92
Milby, William, 92, 141, 202, 225
Milby, Zackdock, 202, 225
Military, 107-113
Military reserves, 108-110
milkman, 208
Mill Companies, 194-195
Mill owners, 194-195, 197-198
Mill wrights, 195, 208
Miller, Capt, 96
Miller, James, 33, 57
Miller, John, 33, 51, 129, 141, 146, 155, 194, 195, 204, 208, 226, 235, 243
Miller, William, 231
Mills, Joseph, 22
Mills, Nathaniel, 212
Minshull, John, 71, 76, 141, 200
Mistaken Point, 8
Mitchell, James, 148
Moffatt, James, 40, 43, 135, 146, 155
Molin, Laurent, 4
Molleson, Col., 77, 88
Monts, Sieur de, 3
Moore, Joseph, 171
Morgan, William, 252
Morvan's Road, 164
Morris, Charles, 38, 42, 67, 158, 254, 258
Morris, Robert, 134, 209
Morris, William, 42, 52, 53, 55, 56, 61, 63, 67, 68, 78, 108, 124, 209, 244

Morrison, Alexander, 248
Morrison, George, 248
Morrison, John, 248
Morse, Col. Robert, 42, 67, 79, 89, 107, 111, 114, 159, 189, 242
Morvan's Road, 164
Moses, William, 201
Mowat, Capt., 65, 114
Mullneaux, William, 73, 164, 187
Munro, Alexander, 205
Munro, Rev. James, 162, 163, 175, 192
Munro, Nathaniel, 33, 141, 197, 208
Murphy, Michael, 204
Murphy, Patrick, 227
Murray, Alexander, 34, 43, 65, 134, 139, 182
Murray, Alexander (pilot), 268
Murray, Britain, 97, 147, 148
Murray, James, 148
Murray, Capt. Scott, 88
Murray, William, 40

N

Nairn, David, 193
Napier, Lieut., 116
Nash, Thomas, 207
Naval Office, see Customs House
Navy, 113-115; naval reserves, 113, 114; large reserves resented, 127; naval base not favoured, 114, 243
Navy Island, 113, 253
Neal, James, 73
Neale, Daniel, 141, 219
Negust, Henry, 225
Neilson, Sarah, 92
Nepean, Evan, 60, 66, 133
Nesbitt, Archibald, 43
Neseamk, 2
New Englanders, land offered, 10; settlers, 18-28
Newburgport, 20
New Cambria, 258
New Jerusalem, 62
New Providence, 94, 95
newspapers and printers, 211-212
Nichols, John, 207
Nicholson, Robert, 87, 88

INDEX

Nickerson, Eldad, 20
Nickerson, Jesse, 19, 20
Nigger Road, see Tusket Road
North, Lord, 30, 66, 67, 70, 85, 121, 122, 169, 235
North East Bluff, 110
North East Harbour, 22, 164
North West Harbour, 22, 87
Notary public, 209
Nouranjean, Francis, 5
Nouranjean, Marie P., 5
Nunn, Samuel, 208
Nutter, Valentine, 71, 76, 129, 140, 141, 143, 155, 163, 167, 194, 200, 244

O

O'Brian, Thomas, 141, 237
Ogden's Brook, 195
Ogden, John, 227
Ogden, Nicholas, 129, 141, 142, 143, 144, 148, 152, 195, 219
Oldsworth, Samuel, 140
Oliver, Joseph, 194
Oohigunsuk, 2
Osborne Harbour, 134
Overseers; of public buildings, 141; of river fisheries, 141, 219
Owens, Ann, 252
Owens, Anna, 251
Owens, Catherine, 251
Owens, Evan, 257
Owens, Enos, 257
Owens, John, 251, 254, 256, 257, 258
Owens, Mary, 252
Owens, Sarah, 252

P

Paget, George, 182
painters and glaziers, 207
Palmer, Alpheus (Alphea), 93, 161
Palmer, Gideon, 71
Pamp, Capt. Thomas, 223
Panton, Rev. George, 98, 177-179
Papoose Brook, 8
Parker, Alexander, 40

Parker, Capt. Ebenezer, 129, 141, 143, 155, 203
Parker, Peter, 40, 141
Parr, Gov. John, 34-242, *passim*
Parr Town, 137
Pashley, George, 40, 43, 88, 146
Parsons, William, 160
Paton, George, 155, 168
Paton, John, 155
Patterson, Gov., 187, 244
Patterson, Mrs., 187
Patterson, Capt. Robert, 225
Patton, George, 43
Pearson, Capt., 250
Peck, John, 141, 217
Pell, George, 204
Pell, Jonathan, 162
Pell, Joshua, 33, 34, 71, 76, 127, 129, 135, 141, 143, 158, 159, 161, 194, 195, 214
Pell's Mill Brook, 195
Pell's Road, 87, 113, 127, 136, 160-161, 214
Pendergrass, Matthew, 194
Pendergrass, Thomas, 141, 158, 194
Penny, Capt., 226
Penny, Richard, 208
Pentz, 249
Perkins, Cato, 98, 105
Perkins, Simeon, 16, 19, 27, 61, 93, 128, 161, 172, 206
Perry, Dr. John, 210
Perry. Samuel, 34
Perry, Silas, 19
Perry, Sturgis, 205
Perth, Cesar, 87, 88
Peter Bogle and Company, 203, 224
Peters, Thomas, 100, 106
Philipps, Gov., 8
Phillips, Patrick, 135
Pierce, Thomas, 22
Pijeboogawek, 2
Pilot Town, 72
Pinkstone, Fleming, 34
Pirates, 6-7
Pitcairn, Major, 67
Pitcher, Moses, 57, 207
Pitt, Rt. Hon. William, 175
Plan for town; approved, 42; changed by

surveyors, 53
plasterers, 207
Point Carleton, 64, 108, 109, 110, 112, 113, 115, 137, 184
Pointe Blanche, 4
Pointe de Baccare, 4
pomatum maker, 193
Pompey Point, 110
Poole, Samuel Sheldon, 143
Poor; care of, 153-154; children of, 153; houses rented, 153; overseers, 92, 154; rations, 153-154
Population of early Shelburne, 79
Porpus Point, 8
Port a ours, 4
Port a Bear, 7
Port Habere, 14
Port Jolly (Joli), 135, 162
Port La Bear, 162
Port l'Herbert, 7, 14, 22, 135, 142, 166
Port Mouton, 3, 14, 66, 78, 157
Port Mutton, (see also Port Mouton), 14
Port Mutton Great River, 161
Port Rasoir (Rasair, Razoir), 5, 7
Port Rochelois, 4, 5
Port Roseway, 8, 14, 64, 158, 159; origin of name, 4
Port Roseway Associates, founded, 32-33; mentioned, 52, 56, 63, 65, 67, 68, 70, 115, 123, 127, 139, 144, 177, 212, 217, 241, 242; work, preparing to leave New York, 32-50
Port Roseway Harbour, 21, 47
Port Roseway Island, 8, 17
Port La Tour, 6
Port Wager, 8
Port Saxon, 22
Porterfield, William, 22
Portland, Duke of, 120
Portuguese, 1, 2
Postell, Mary, 95
Post office and post masters, 188-189
Potter, Capt. James, 40, 43, 231
Potts, Capt., 71
Poulet, Guillaume, 4
poundkeepers, 141, 217
Powell, David, 252, 256, 257
Powers, Thomas, 140
Prices; set for bread, 205; for meals, 187;

for sweeping chimneys, 155
Pride, Ira, 22, 23
Pride, William, 22
Primus, Marion, 93
Prince Edward Island, Loyalists to, 244
Prince William Henry, 111, 114
printers, 211-212
Privateers, 115, 226
Proff, Simon, 148
Prout, Timothy, 43
Provision Island, 113, 144
Pryor, James, 136
Pyncheon, Joseph, 33, 34, 35, 37, 39, 43, 44, 52, 60, 65, 127, 139, 140, 159, 171

Q

Quinlan, John, 248

R

Rae, Margaret Neil, 248
Ragged Islands, 14, 22, 24, 25, 26, 98, 134, 165, 172, 197, 249
Ragged Island Bay, 166
Ragged Island Harbour, 165
Rapalie, George, 141, 158
Reath, James, 148
Read, Capt. James, 88
Recorder of deeds, 209
Redick, Cloe, 153
Redman, Isaac, 268
Reed, Isaac, 205
Regiments; Provincial, (see also Hessian soldiers), 44-47, 73-75, 79; British, 75-77, 79
Reserves; of land, 67-68, 73, 108-109, 113, 114, 131-132; resentment over, 127-128
Restine, Joseph, 73
Reth, Archibald, 148
R. de Jardins, 3
R. de Montanas, 3
Rice, Joseph, 145
Richards, Benjamin, 451
Richards, David, 251, 252, 256, 257
Richards, Elizabeth, 251, 252

INDEX

Richards, Henry, 451
Richards, John, 251-259, *passim*
Richards, John, Jr., 251, 257, 258
Richards, Margaret, 451
Richards, Martha, 251, 252
Richards, Capt. Nathaniel, 136, 244
Richards, Rachel, 451
Richards, Samma, 257
Richards, Susannah, 451
Richards, William, 251, 257
Richards, William, 258
Richard's Road, see Tusket Road
Richmond, William, 171
Rider, John, 22
Rigby, William, 212
Ringer, 249
Riots, 127-128
Rippon, Dr., 172
Ritchie, Peter, 204
Rivedon, 5
Riviere de Pomoncoup (Pubnico), 6
Riviere du rocheloy, 4
roads, 158-167
Robert, James, 268
Robert McIntosh and Company, 203
Roberts, Abigail, 112
Roberts, John, 193
Robertson, Alexander (farmer), 34, 40, 43, 129, 141, 217
Robertson, Alexander (printer), 135, 199, 212
Robertson, James, 64, 65, 135, 149, 151, 155, 159, 160, 199, 212, 245
Robertson, James, Jr., 212
Robertson, John (barber), 204
Robertson, John, 135, 139, 140, 151
Robertson, Neil, 135
Robertson, William, 201, 224
Robertson and Rigby, 198, 212
Robertson's Cove, 72, 244
Robins, William, 78
Robinson and Rispin, report, 24
Robinson, James, 73
Robinson, Peter, 40, 43, 94
Robinson, Thomas, 94
Robinson, Thomas, Jr., 94
Rogers, Betsey, 93
Rogers, David, 257
Rogers, Robert, 182

Rolleson, George, 79
Rose, William, 203
Roseneath, 17, 109
Roseway Island, 67
Roseway Lake, 160
Roseway River, 8, 113, 124, 131, 135, 159, 160, 164, 166, 167, 168, 195, 197, 214, 247, 254, 255
Rose, George, 79, 95, 203, 224, 225, 226, 227-228, 231, 233, 238-239, 245
Ross, Margaret, 176
Ross, Robert, 79, 95, 203, 224, 225, 226, 231, 233, 245
Roubalet's Tavern, 33
Round Bay, 17, 20, 21, 136, 163, 164, 168
Round Lake, 160
Rowland, D., 250
Rowland, Rev. John Hamilton, 179, 180
Rowland, Rev. Thomas, 181, 182, 215, 251, 252, 256
Rowland, William, 73
Roxby, John, 225
Roxby, William, 225
Royal Artillery, 108
Royal Engineers, 86, 89, 107
Rude, Jacob, 22
Rudolf, 249
Ryer, Sophia, 248

S

Sable River, 22, 62, 135, 162, 165, 166, 167, 195
saddler, 207
Sagamore Reach, 2, 8
Sagamore River, 2, 8
sailmakers, 228
Saint John, 79, 80
St. John River, 137
Sandeman, Robert, 171
Sandy Point, 67, 109, 115, 125, 165, 193, 215
Sandy Point, Lower, 109, 197
Sandy's Island, 248
Sansom, Philip, 221
Sargent, John, (Barrington), 143, 170, 225

Sargent, John, 235, 237
Sargent, William Browne, 170
Sargent, Winthrop, 170
saw mills and saw pits, 39, 120, 194-196
Savage, Capt. Abraham, 71, 160
Scarborough Point, 9, 108
schools, 99, 153, 180-182
school masters, 99, 181-182
school mistresses, 182
Scipio, Lucas, 205
Scoodiac Lake, 160
Scotch broom, 247
Scots-Irish settlers, 10-18
Scott, John B., 140, 143
Seaboyer, 249
Seaburn, John, 205
sealers of leather, 141
Selkrig, Mr., 145
Sesiktaweak, 2
Settlers after 1783; from Ireland, 246, 248; from New England, 249; from Scotland, 246-249; from Wales, 246, 250-260
sextons, 208
Shakespeare, David, 194
Shakespear(e), Stephen, 43, 93, 194, 195, 201
Shannon and Doyle, 147
Sharp, Granville, 100
Shave, John, 79
Shave, Richard, 79
Shelburne, Earl of, 62, 64, 65, 70, 86, 117, 123, 126, 128, 133, 176, 183
Shelburne, named by Parr, 64; name resented, 65-66
Shelburne Harbour, 125, 168, 191
Shelburne Road, see Tusket Road
Shepherd, Bruce, 205
Shepherd, David, 205
Shepherd, Thomas, 97
Sherriffs, 140, 209
Shipbuilding, 223-229; Ship artisans, 228; Shipbuilders, 226-229
Ship carpenters, 227
Ship owners, 223-226
Ship rigger, 228
ship staymaker, 228; shipyards, 223, 224, 227
Ships, see Vessels

ships registered in Shelburne, 225
Shipman, William, 142
Shipton, Francis, 125
shoemakers, 208
Sierra Leone, 100-106, *passim*
Sierra Leone Co., 100
Silby, John, 145, 223, 227, 229
Silby, William, 155
Silvery Lake, 160
Simpson, John, 203
Skinner, Stephen, 16, 77, 101, 103, 105, 170, 190, 200, 225
Skunk Hall, 214
Smallpox, inoculation for, 211
Smallwood, Brayn, 21
Smart, Thomas, 193
Smith, Archelaus, 26, 143
Smith, Benjamin, 171
Smith, Catherine, 154
Smith, Elisha, 22
Smith, Emphraim, 128
Smith, James, 208
Smith, Joseph, 22
Smith, Mary, 187
Smith, Theodore, 22
Smith, Titus, 216
Smithers, James, 205
Sneden, Samuel, 227
Snyder (Snider), William, 208, 225, 226
Snow, Mary, 20
Snow, Joshua, Jr., 21
Snow, Joshua, Sr., 19, 20, 24
Snow, Joshua, 3rd, 21
Snowball, Nathaniel, 87, 88
snuffmill, 198
soapmaker, 193
social life, 182-185
Sogumkeagun, 1
Sommerville, Robert, 141, 202
Sparling, Peter, 88
Speirs, Capt. John, 135, 206
Spencer, Capt. John, 78
Spinney, John, 22
Springhall, Gregory, 141, 143, 200
Squaw Brook, 8
Squires, John, 221
Stanhope, Capt. Henry Edwin, 112, 113, 147
Stanhope's Hill, 97, 149, 166

INDEX

Steele, Patrick, 151, 186
Stevenson, John, 193
Stewart, Alexander, 208
Stewart, Peter, 40
Stewart, Rebecca, 16
Stocket, Richard, 174
Stokes Brook, 197
stonecutters, 207
Stonehouse, Mary, 149
Stoughon, Dulcina, 205
Strhum, Jacob, 61
street lamps, 167
Strueve, John Charles, 182
Stuart, John, 40, 43
Stuart, John (Green Harbour), 227
Sullivan, Bartholomew, 71
Sullivan and Mills, 198, 215, 223
Summers, William, 228
Summerville, Robert, 93
surveyors; of hay, 141, 217; of highways, 141; of land, 42, 52, 66-67, 133-134; of lumber, 141; of pickled fish, 141, 219
Sutherland, William, 17, 19, 40
Swaine, Chapman, 22
Swaine, Ephraim, 22
Swaine, John, 22
Swansburg's Brook, 162
Swineburgh, John, 254
Sydney, Lord, 66, 111, 133

T

tailors, 203-204
Tallant, Margaret, 150
tanners, 194
taverns, inns and coffeehouses, 186-188; mentioned, 94, 103, 136, 161, 162, 183, 184, 185, 186, 188, 193
tax collectors, 141
Taylor, Ann, 172, 203
Taylor, Ned, 209
Taylor, Peter, 187
Taylor, William, 172, 173
T. Braine and Company, 225
Tea Chest, 8, 109
Tench, John, 40, 41, 143, 149
Tench and Taylor, Andrew Bruce and Company, 201
Tennon, John, 227
Thatcher, Abel, 43
Thayer and Jarvis, 202, 226
Thomas, Ann, 252
Thomas, David, 252, 254, 256, 257, 258, 259
Thomas, Esther, 252
Thomas, George, 134, 135, 142
Thomas, Henry, 257, 258, 259
Thomas, John, 254, 257, 258
Thomas, John, 256
Thomas, John (carpenter), 257
Thomas, John (farmer), 257
Thomas, Margaret, 252
Thomas, Mary, 252
Thomas, Nancy, 252
Thomas, Nathaniel Rae, 33, 71, 160
Thomas, Rachel, 252
Thomas, Sarah, 252
Thomas, Walter, 252, 254
Thomas, William, 252
Thomson, David, 62, 114, 129, 140, 143, 174, 190, 214, 224, 225, 227, 229
Thomson, Dorcas, 203
Thomson, John, 190, 207, 214
Thomson, Robert, 254, 256
Thomson, Robert Ross, 189
tidewaiters, 219
Tinkham, Joseph, 140, 144, 147
tinsmiths, 208
Tom's Hole, 9
Tonge, Winckworth, 238
Tonyn, Gov., 78
Tooker, Jacob, 244
Tooker, Joseph, 225
Townsend, Richard, 141, 195, 197, 202
Townsend, Richard, Jr., 202
Townshend, Thomas, 46, 49
Trade and Commerce, 430-439
trade in timber, 195-197
Trap Lake, 160
Trost, Benjamin, 94
Trumbull, John, 211
Tully, Christopher, 67, 72, 77, 88, 209
Tully, Thomas, 92, 149
Turnbull, Robert, 93
Turnbull, Thomas, 40, 43
Turpin, Michael, 22

Turpin's Cove, 134
Tusket, 62, 244
Tusket Associates, 162, 244; location, 162; road, 136, 162-163, 168, 216, 244
Tusket River, 162, 244

V

Van Buskirk, Lieut. Col., Abraham, 72, 75, 129, 136, 139, 143, 162, 209, 214, 244
Van Buskirk, Capt. Jacob, 115, 170, 252
Vance, Arthur, 14, 15
Vance, Arthur, Jr., 15
Van Norden, John, 71, 134, 135, 209
Van Tile, Peter, 92
Van Tyle, Dennis, 244
Veitch, Gavin, 204
Vernon, Capt. Nathaniel, 78
Vernon, Lieut. Nathaniel, 78
Vessels:
Brigantines, *Addra*, 225, 248; *Aurora*, 203; *Carleton*, 223; *Clyde*, 223; *Fanny*, 250; *Friendship*, 226, 233; *Good Intent*, 222, 226; *Governor Parr*, 223, 224, 243; *Greyhound*, 94; *Lovely Lass*, 57; *Mary*, 226, 233; *Port Roseway*, 226; *Robert*, 224, 233; *Tamerlane*, 222; *Tar Kitty*, 225; *Tyger*, 57
Schooners, *Acadia*, 224; *Acadian*, 23; *Betsey*, 20, 26; *Betsey*, 226, 231, 233; *Betsey and Sally*, 57; *British Queen*, 224; *Camilla*, 226; *Charlotte*, 191, 226; *Christian*, 23; *Dashen*, 21; *Deborah*, 103; *Dolphin*, 202, 221, 225; *Edward*, 225, 243; *Elizabeth*, 20; *Elsey*, 226; *Endeavour*, 21; *Experience*, 233; *Experiment*, 225, 226; *Good Intent*, 227; *Hope*, 219; *Industry*, 226; *Juno*, 225; *Lorence*, 225; *Lucy*, 225; *Mary*, 227; *Margery*, 225, 246; *Mary and Elvira*, 225; *Mary and Harriet*, 223; *Mickmack*, 225; *Nelson* (privateer), 226, 248; *New Hope*, 223, 224, 233; *Plato*, 21; *Plow*, 224; *Polly*, 57, 243; *Rebecca*, 225; *Roseway Yacht*, 224; *Ruby*, 227; *Sally*, 222, 225, 226, 243; *Sally*, 226, 233; *Success*, 203, 216; *Swallow*, 225;

William, 201, 220, 225; Ships, *Friendship*, 71, 76; *Gibson*, 221; *Loyalist*, 191, 226; *H.M.S. Mercury*, 112, 113, 127, 133; *Minerva*, 221, 224, 233; *Roseway*, 223, 224, 243; *Governor Wentworth*, 226, 233; *William*, 71
Sloops, *Fanny*, 57; *Industry*, 57; *Sally*, 231; *Weazel*, 115
Snows, *Despatch*, 142; *Lively*, 226
Others, *Andromeda*, 111; *Annan*, 225; *Apollo*, 57; *H.M.S. Assistance*, 114; *Brisk*, 111; *Castor*, 76; *Catherine*, 233, 243; *Charming Betsey*, 243; *Charming Nancy*, 57, 76, 210, 243; *Charming Polly*, 57, 201; *Charming Sally*, 97; *Cherry Bounce*, 72, 244; *Clinton*, 76; *Congress*, 76; *Despatch*, 226; *Diana*, 60; *Dolphin*, 18; *Duc de Chartres*, 55, 113; *Elizabeth*, 57; *Esther*, 60; *Garland*, 34; *G.D. Russia*, 76; *H.M.S. Hermione*, 114; *Hero*, 57; *Hiram Rixby*, 189; *Hopewell*, 15; *John and Jane*, 226, 231, 243; *Kingston*, 60, 71; *L'Abondance*, 76; *Lady*, 243; *La Sophie*, 64, 65, 114; *Lively*, 222; *London Frigate*, 57; *Lord Middleton*, 222, 233, 243; *Mary Ann*, 111; *Mercury*, 20; *Nancy*, 71, 76; *Nelly Morrison*, 247; *H.M.S. Nymphe*, 116; *Port Roseway Packet*, 226, 233; *Prince William Henry*, 196, 226, 233; *Princess Amelia*, 250; *Prosperous Armilla*, 76; *Salley*, 18; *Spartan*, 16; *Spring*, 79; *Stag*, 231; *Success*, 226, 243; *Thisbe*, 111; *Three Sisters*, 57; *Two Brothers*, 21; *Two Brothers*, 251, 252, 253; *Two Friends*, 243; *Wye*, 251
De Villebon, Governor, 5, 6, 7

W

Wainwright Lake, 160
Walker, Alexander, 248
Walker, David, 176, 197, 205
Walker, Hugh, 146
Walker, John, 195, 197
Walker, John, 40
Wall, Edward, 207
Wall, Patrick, 71, 129, 141, 160

INDEX

Wall, Richard, 197
Wallace, Hon. Michael, 104, 250, 251, 255
Walter, Lynde, 225
Walter, Rev. William, 177-180
Ward, Edmond, 34, 71, 76
Wardell, John, 57
Warden, George, 193
Warden, William, 193, 203
Wardens of the Port, 141
Warren, Joseph, 96
Washington, Gen., 47, 49, 84, 85
Watson, Brook, 40, 41, 70, 80, 81
Watson, David, 168
Watson, John, 40, 41
Watson, Joshua, 129, 140, 195, 202, 220, 221
Watson's Point, 115, 223, 227
Watts, Capt. Hugh, 57
Watts, Robert, 268
Weather, Michael, 205
weavers, 208
Weir, John, 208
Weiser, Frederick, 207
Weiser, Jacob, 189
Welch, Hill, 254
Welsh, Joseph, 207
Welshtown, 194
Welshtown Lake, see Birchtown Lake
Wentworth, Gov. John, 106, 113, 114, 120, 127, 131, 191, 249, 250
Wentworth, Lady, 191
Wentzel, 249
Wesley, John, 98
West, 249
Western Head, 22, 134
Westley, James, 147
Westley, Phyllis, 149
Wetton, Richard, 43
whaling and whaling companies, 220-222
Wheaton, Joseph, 93
Whelton, George, 268
wheelwrights, 208, 228
Whetton, Richard, 204
Whipple, David, 157
White, Arron, 179, 207
White, Charles, 129, 152, 173, 205, 206
White, Daniel, 268

White, Gideon, 19, 23, 26, 40, 77, 105, 143, 149, 150, 170, 176, 197, 204, 214, 252
White, James, 205
White, Paul, 233
White, Richard, 43
White, William, 162
Whiting, Thomas, 112, 155, 186
Whitworth, Charles, 201, 233
Whyte, Col., 113
Wickfall, Jacob, 93
Wickham, Lieut., 104
Wiggins, Alicia, 148
Wiley, Samuel, 93
Wilkins, Isaac, 73, 77, 99, 129, 137, 142, 143, 144, 148, 152, 164, 169, 170, 190, 209, 216
Wilkins, Lewis Morris, 209
Wilkins, Martin, 209
Wilkins, Robert, 40, 57
Wilkin's Folly, 214
Wilkinson, Moses, 98, 105
Willard, Col. Abjab, 47
Williams, Amos, 195, 197
Williams, Cryus, 93
Williams, John, 40
Willock Point, 8
Wilmington, William, 228
Wilson, David, 225
Wilson, Joseph, 15
Wilson, Obediah, 20
Windsor, John, 96, 147
Winslow, Edward, 158
Winslow, Sarah, 66, 158
Wirling, Capt. Robert, 223
Wishart, Capt., 226
With, Capt. Jacob, 88
Wolfe, 249
Wood, Benjamin, 43
Wood, David, 19, 20, 21
Wood, Elisha, 21
Wood, Francis, 187, 204
Wood, Samuel, 21
Wood, Rev. Samuel, 21
Wood Hall, 216, 248
Woods Harbour, 136, 247
Woodside Pond, 198
Wright, Capt., 158
Wright, Daniel, 71

Wright, Gilbert, 22
Wright, James, 79
Wright's Road, 135, 158, 198

Y

Yarmouth, 142, 143, 163, 244
Young, James, 91, 154
Young, Thomas, 208, 228
Young, William, 93, 209